AUGUSTUS TO CONSTANTINE

AUGUSTUS TO CONSTANTINE

THE EMERGENCE OF CHRISTIANITY IN THE ROMAN WORLD

Robert M. Grant

BARNES
&NOBLE
BOOKS
NEW YORK

This edition published by Barnes & Noble, Inc., by arrangement with
Harper San Francisco, a division of HarperCollins Publishers Inc.

1996 Barnes & Noble Books

ISBN 0-76070-138-5

Printed and bound in the United States of America

M 9 8 7 6 5 4 3 2

FG

CONTENTS

PART THREE

CHRISTIANITY IN THE THIRD CENTURY

PART FOUR

THE TRIUMPH OF THE CHRISTIAN MOVEMENT

PART FIVE

THE CONTINUITY OF THE CHRISTIAN MOVEMENT

ABBREVIATIONS

ATR—*Anglican Theological Review*

CAH—*Cambridge Ancient History* (ed. S. A. Cook *et al.*)

Chrest.—See Grundzüge

CIJ—*Corpus Inscriptionum Judaicarum* (ed. J. B. Frey)

CIL—*Corpus Inscriptionum Latinarum* (ed. T. Mommsen *et al.*)

CPJ—*Corpus Papyrorum Judaicarum* (ed. V. A. Tcherikower and A. Fuks)

CSEL—*Corpus Scriptorum Ecclesiasticorum Latinorum*

DCB—*Dictionary of Christian Biography* (ed. W. Smith and H. Wace)

DTC—*Dictionnaire de théologie catholique* (ed. A. Vacant and E. Mangenot)

Grundzüge—*Grundzüge und Chrestomathie der Papyruskunde* (ed. L. Mitteis and U. Wilcken)

H. E.—*Historia Ecclesiastica*
HTR—*Harvard Theological Review*
IG—*Inscriptiones Graecae* (ed. A. Kirchhoff *et al.*)
IGR—*Inscriptiones Graecae ad Res Romanas pertinentes* (ed. R. Cagnat *et al.*)
ILCV—*Inscriptiones Latinae Christianae Veteres* (ed. E. Diehl)
ILS—*Inscriptiones Latinae Selectae* (ed. H. Dessau)
ILT—*Inscriptions Latines de la Tunisie* (ed. A. Merlin)
JBL—*Journal of Biblical Literature*
JEH—*Journal of Ecclesiastical History*
JJS—*Journal of Jewish Studies*
JRS—*Journal of Roman Studies*
JTS—*Journal of Theological Studies*
KP—*Der Kleine Pauly* (ed. K. Ziegler and W. Sontheimer)
MAMA—*Monumenta Asiae Minoris Antiqua* (ed. W. M. Calder *et al.*)
M. P.—*Martyrs of Palestine* (Eusebius)
OGIS—*Orientis Graeci Inscriptiones Selectae* (ed. W. Dittenberger)
P. E.—*Praeparatio Evangelica* (Eusebius)
PG—*Patrologia Graeca* (ed. J. P. Migne)
PL—*Patrologia Latina* (ed. J. P. Migne)
RAC—*Reallexikon für Antike und Christentum* (ed. T. Klauser *et al.*)
RE—*Real-Encyclopädie der classischen Altertumswissenschaft* (ed. A. Pauly, G. Wissowa *et al.*)
RGG³—*Die Religion in Geschichte und Gegenwart* (ed. 3, ed. K. Galling *et al.*)
RHE—*Revue d'histoire ecclésiastique*
SEHRE²—*Social and Economic History of the Roman Empire* (ed. 2, M. Rostovtzeff)
SHA—*Scriptores historiae Augustae*
SIG³—*Sylloge Inscriptionum Graecarum* (ed. 3, ed. W. Dittenberger)
SVF—*Stoicorum veterum fragmenta* (ed. H. von Arnim)
TAPS—*Transactions of the American Philosophical Society*
TU—*Texte und Untersuchungen* (ed. O. Gebhardt, A. Harnack *et al.*)
TZ—*Theologische Zeitschrift*
VC—*Vigiliae Christianae*
V. C.—*Vita Constantini* (Eusebius)
ZKG—*Zeitschrift für Kirchengeschichte*
ZNW—*Zeitschrift für die neutestamentliche Wissenschaft*

PREFACE

The Christian movement came to the attention of Roman provincial authorities in Palestine on the eastern frontier about the year 30 of what is now known as the Christian era, or in about the 783rd year from the foundation of Rome. A generation later, it was known, and unfavorably regarded, in the city of Rome itself. After another fifty years Roman governors made reports to the emperors about their difficulties with the Christians and with enforcing the laws which they understood as proscribing Christianity. At intermittent points of crisis in the life of the empire during the second and third centuries, harsh measures of repression were undertaken against the Christians, and during the decade after 303 a violent assault upon them was made in the eastern half of the empire, where their numbers were greatest. The emperor Constantine, victorious in a struggle for supreme power, gave them his support, however, and when he became a Christian himself they were soon recognized as the leading religious group in the empire. Under his successors, in spite of a brief reaction under Julian (361–363), the Christian community became the official church of the empire. Though the empire was threatened in the east and overrun by barbarian tribes in the north and west, the church retained its official position and survived the collapse of the western empire, sending out missions which finally converted the barbarians. At the end of the sixth century Pope Gregory the Great was as influential as his imperial predecessor had been.

The movement had begun as a sect within Palestinian Judaism, following its leader, Jesus of Nazareth, in expecting the imminent action of God: God would establish his own reign through the ministry of Jesus and his disciples. After a period of tribulations all worldly political and social structures would vanish, and Jesus and his disciples would preside over a society motivated by love and justice. Jesus, however, was crucified by Pontius Pilate, Roman prefect of Judaea, at the instigation of civil and religious authorities in Palestine, and the movement nearly collapsed. The disciples were soon convinced that though he had been put to death God had raised him up again, and that the Spirit of God was present with their group and with individuals in it. In spite of official hostility they went out to proclaim that Jesus was alive again and that the reign of God still lay in the immediate future. The most important among their converts was a Pharisaic Jew named Saul (Paul), who was inspired by a vision of the risen Jesus to attach himself to the community and, after a considerable interval, to begin propagating the Christian message in Asia Minor and Greece.

There was considerable tension between Paul and the older disciples in Palestine. In their view the mission was essentially Jewish; that is to say that it was addressed primarily to Jews and to those gentiles who were willing to observe the Jewish law. In Paul's view the gospel of the risen Lord transcended all distinctions of nationality; in Christ there was neither Jew nor Greek. Even though a council at Jerusalem agreed to lay only minimal requirements upon gentile converts, Paul insisted that these requirements were peripheral, not essential. Though many Christians observed them until the end of the second century, they gradually lost their importance. Paul's insistence upon the universal nature of Christianity became dominant. It meant that Christianity gradually separated itself from orthodox Judaism during the first and second centuries.

The peculiar status of Judaism within the Roman empire had been recognized in a series of treaties which exempted Jews from civic obligations in conflict with their exclusive form of monotheism and their revealed law. As Christianity came to be distinct from Judaism it no longer enjoyed the privileges provided by these treaties. Its adherents were suspected of various crimes alleged to flourish among devotees of non-Roman religions. At the same time, the Christian rejection of ordinary actions, such as sacrifice, characteristic of Greek and Roman religion, and the Christian denunciation of all gods but their own rendered them suspect in the eyes of the authorities.

Even though investigation suggested that the crimes were nonexistent, the Christians' intolerance of other groups and their refusal to conform to Roman custom involved them in frequent conflicts with hostile crowds and with Roman magistrates.

Within the Christian communities of the second century two different but equally extreme minority positions were assumed. On the one hand, there were those, especially in Asia Minor, who under the influence of apocalyptic prophecy insisted upon an intensified expectation of the imminent end of society and the descent of the "heavenly Jerusalem" in Phrygia. On the other, there were those who turned their backs on the world and took the gospel to refer to the awakening of a divine spark in man which was to escape from the world through the planetary spheres above and come to the otherwise unknown Father whom Jesus had proclaimed.

Both these positions were rejected by the majority of Christian leaders, who recognized the reality of the world and its social structures and looked for their gradual conversion to Christianity before the coming of the end. These leaders were loyal to the Roman government and were able to find much of value in what they regarded as the best of Graeco-Roman culture. Intimations of their basic attitude were to be found in Paul's comments on the validity of "the existing powers" (Romans 13) and in the address at Athens ascribed to him in Acts 17. They had also learned much from the Hellenistic Judaism represented by Philo and Josephus, as well as from the fate of those Palestinian Jews who rebelled against Rome in the first and second centuries. As early as 150 a Roman apologist found the cross typified in the standards of the Roman legions, and a generation later several bishops in Asia Minor explicitly asserted the compatibility of Christianity with the Roman state.

From the late second century onward, Christian leaders often complained of the injustice of the Roman state toward the church and criticized the excessive "worldliness" of those Christians who erased the lines between the church and non-Christian society. At the same time, in spite of official church objections, Christian theologians continued a vigorous effort to interpret Christianity in terms derived from the leading philosophies of the day. The church was sharply divided in consequence of losses during the brief but severe persecutions under Decius (250) and Valerian (257), but the policy of readmitting those who lapsed permitted survival even under the harsh repression of Galerius (305–311). In spite of various vicissitudes and individual deviations from the general pattern, it is clear that during the third century Christians were making ready for the time when the church would be recognized by the state and there would be an empire at least nominally Christian.

The fourth century saw the recognition of Christianity as the state religion of the empire. It was a time of consolidation and expansion, and paganism, now deprived of state support, suffered a drastic decline which Julian was unable to check. The circumstances of the church had completely changed. Formerly persecuted, Christians now took steps to apply against paganism the proscriptions once enforced against themselves. At the same time, the efforts of the church's leaders to enforce moral standards and to promote uniformity in theological expression resulted in the flowering of Christian literature in east and west alike. Meanwhile the empire itself, so recently won by the church and with such difficulty, was cracking under the strain of barbarian pressure, especially in the west. Rome itself was captured in 410.

This book examines the history of early Christianity as it arose in Roman-controlled Judaea soon after the foundation of the Roman empire, spread throughout the Roman world in spite of intermittent but explicit opposition from the state, and finally won the allegiance and the support of the first Christian emperor. It attempts to coordinate Christian and Roman history and seeks to explain the course of Christian events in relation to what was going on in the empire. It begins with the death of the first Roman emperor in A.D. 14 and ends with the death of the first Christian emperor in 337. Both deaths mark the ends of revolutionary movements, first the one which R. Syme called "the Roman revolution," second what S. J. Case entitled "the social triumph of the ancient church." The intervening three centuries saw the rise, transformation, and victory of a movement which began as a sect within Judaism and finally became the religion of the Roman emperor. The process will be treated primarily in relation to institutions and events. The analogous transformations within Christian theology will receive less attention, not because they were unimportant but because the history of doctrine deserves, and has often received, separate discussion.

There are, of course, other important ways of viewing the early Christian movement. One cannot neglect the approach made by historians of Greek and Roman religion (for example, in the great study entitled *Conversion* by my teacher A. D. Nock) or that of E. R. Dodds, who includes insights derived from modern psychology in his *Pagan and Christian in an Age of Anxiety*. Christians appear among the "enemies of the Roman order" considered by R. MacMullen. For the relations between philosophy and Christian thought a model is provided by H. Chadwick in his *Early Christianity and the Classical Tradition*. My concerns are not precisely identical with theirs; I view this book not as supplanting or transcending their works but as supplementing them specifically in regard to the social and political history of the early church in the Roman world.

My primary concern is to set the Christian movement in its Graeco-Roman context and try to assess how much the direction of its development owed to its environment or environments. At times, no doubt, I have let my interest in the Roman world carry my account too far from the Christian story. Few early Christians were concerned with the government budgets or military dispositions discussed in the first chapter, but they provide important aspects of the background. They suggest that while we do not possess the kinds of statistics that modern students of social history would find invaluable in dealing with Christianity, such statistics did exist in some areas of ancient life. There are few points, however, at which we find what may be called Christian statistics, and where they occur they are hard to assess.

The difficulties encountered in dealing even with what we have can be indicated by one example. There is a list of Christians martyred in Gaul about 177; though our copies are late it seems to be reliable. It contains the names of twenty-five men and twenty-three women. But as Hirschfeld long ago pointed out, it is likely that in many instances the list gives both the *nomen* and the *cognomen* of the martyrs. On his view the number of martyrs would be reduced to nineteen men and eighteen women, thirty-seven in all.[1] Again, in his treatise *Contra Celsum* (3, 8) Origen says that "a few, whose number could be easily enumerated, have died occasionally for the sake of the Christian religion." It is by no means clear, however, what he meant by "a few" or whether he actually knew how many martyrs there had been.

To a considerable extent, therefore, we are confined to the study of general trends or tendencies or to the rather detailed examination of a number of specific instances. In this book emphasis is laid on the specific instances, on the ground that for the historian such instances may prove to be more illuminating than the generalizations that might be built up out of them. This is not to say that the generalizations will be completely lacking. History is not just one thing after another. But the kinds of evidence upon which large-scale social theories can be built are not available.

Another problem arises out of the nature of the evidence we do possess. In spite of our concern for papyri and inscriptions, most of the evidence is both literary and highly selective. This fact means that it is doubly selective. The literary character of most of it means that we are dealing with the works of the more highly educated Christians, not with "average" or "medium" examples. In some measure the ideas of the others can be recovered by reading between the lines of what the literate theologians wrote. We are always in danger, however, of ascribing undue importance to the literary evidence. The second kind of selectivity is due to the concerns of those who transmitted the documents we possess. During the fourth and fifth centuries an effort seems to have been made to rewrite much of early Christian history. The original letters of Ignatius were supplanted by a collection of forged and interpolated epistles. The *Didache* was replaced by the *Apostolic Constitutions*. One must wonder to what extent documents which came to be viewed as heretical or outmoded were allowed to perish. Both kinds of selectivity suggest that within, and on the edges of, the early Christian communities there was considerably more diversity than the evidence now indicates.

[1] O. Hirschfeld in *Sitzungsberichte der preussischen Akademie der Wissenschaften zu Berlin* (1895), 381-409; cf. H. Quentin in *Analecta Bollandiana* 39 (1921), 113-38.

Among the modern studies I have found especially helpful are the *Economic Survey of Ancient Rome,* edited by Tenney Frank, and Rostovtzeff's social and economic histories of the Hellenistic world and the Roman empire. I must certainly also mention W. H. C. Frend's important studies of *The Donatist Church* and *Martyrdom and Persecution in the Early Church,* though I incline to share the reservations expressed by A. H. M. Jones in asking the question, "Were ancient heresies national or social movements in disguise?"[2] And of course Jones' own book on *The Later Roman Empire* has proved invaluable, not least for its emphasis on the sources.

[2] *JTS* 10 (1959), 280-97; reprinted in *Facet Books, Historical Studies,* 1 (Philadelphia, 1966).

PART ONE-THE RISE OF CHRISTIANITY IN THE ROMAN WORLD

CHAPTER I
THE ROMAN EMPIRE

I-THE DEATH OF AUGUSTUS

The emperor Caesar Augustus died at Nola, north of Mount Vesuvius, on August 19 in the fourteenth year of the Christian era. He was nearly seventy-six years old. During his lifetime and under his guidance the Roman state had been transformed from a republic into a monarchy. In the year of his birth the Roman general Pompey had taken the supposedly impregnable fortress of Jerusalem; by the year 14 it belonged to a province governed by a Roman prefect whose capital was named Caesarea.

More than a year earlier Augustus had taken pains to make a will disposing of his estate, since he was the richest man in the empire, and had deposited it with the Vestal virgins along with three other documents. These four books were now read in the senate. His will began with the sentence, "Since a cruel fate has deprived me of my sons Gaius and Lucius, Tiberius Caesar is to be heir to two-thirds of my estate"—an estate amounting to approximately 150 million sesterces.[1] Tiberius, by no means the emperor's first choice, had be-

[1] Suetonius, *Aug.* 101.

come co-regent only in the year 13, when the senate had voted him an un-limited *imperium proconsulare* and thus had made him heir to the throne.[2] The first of the other documents gave instructions for the emperor's funeral; the second provided an account of his achievements, to be engraved on bronze tablets and set up before his Mausoleum; the third summarized the military and financial situation of the empire and warned against expanding the empire beyond its present limits.[3]

The bronze tablets have perished, but three copies from Asia Minor—Ancyra, Apollonia, and Antioch—have survived, thus providing a public record of Augustus' own view of his career.[4] Syme points out that "it would be imprudent to use the document as a sure guide for history, petulant and pointless to complain of omission and misrepresentation." He reminds us, however, that the emperor's adversaries and victims are not named and his allies are barely mentioned, while nothing is said of the *imperium proconsulare* used to control the provinces and the armies, or of the real nature of the tribunician power.[5]

Augustus' story began when he was nineteen years old and undertook to restore liberty to the republic, punishing those who had killed his father (by adoption) Julius Caesar. He undertook wars throughout the world and was always ultimately victorious. He provided for the food supplies and other needs of the Roman people and practically rebuilt the city of Rome. The senate, the equestrian order, and the whole Roman people continually offered him honors and powers, most of which he rejected. His army and navy won countless new provinces, as well as alliances with peoples not subjugated.[6] Embassies came to him even from the kings of India. At the very end of the story he speaks of the title Augustus itself, of his valor, clemency, justice, and piety, and of the title *pater patriae*. A summary, provided by a local magistrate, points out that the emperor had contributed to the treasury, Roman plebeians, and discharged soldiers no less than 600 million denarii (=2,400 million sesterces). It also lists twenty buildings at Rome and notes his restorations at Rome, including 82 temples.

There was, of course, a splendid funeral. On a couch of ivory and gold, with purple and gold coverings, lay a wax image of the emperor in triumphal garb; his body was in a coffin underneath. Senators carried the couch and coffin to the Forum; behind it came other images of him and of his ancestors

[2] Suetonius, *Tib.* 21, 1.

[3] Tacitus, *Ann.* 1, 11.

[4] Ed. C. Volkmann, *Res gestae divi Augusti* (ed. 2, Berlin, 1964).

[5] R. Syme, *The Roman Revolution* (Oxford, 1939), 523. This whole book may be regarded as a magisterial analysis and revision of the official statement. See also R. MacMullen, *Enemies of the Roman Order* (Cambridge, Mass., 1966).

[6] In *ca.* 29 he speaks of military standards recovered from enemy troops but does not refer to the loss of three legions in Germany in A.D. 9. Two standards were recovered under Tiberius (Tacitus, *Ann.* 1, 60; 2, 25), one only under Claudius (Dio 60, 8, 7).

and relatives, except for Julius Caesar, already deified, and of prominent Romans, including Pompey, as far back as Romulus. Two eulogies followed, one by Tiberius' son Drusus, the other by Tiberius himself. According to Dio, Tiberius compared him with Hercules and pointed out that a democratic form of government could not preserve the empire. "It is fitting that we should not mourn for him but, while now giving his body back to nature, should forever glorify his soul as that of a god."[7] In the presence of a vast crowd his body was next carried to the Campus Martius and placed on a pyre. Around it marched all the Roman priests; then came all the equestrians, with cavalry and the praetorian guard, throwing on the pyre their military decorations. Centurions lighted the pyre with torches, and as the corpse and wax image were consumed an eagle flew upward from the pyre to carry the emperor's soul to heaven. The senator Numerius Atticus took oath that he had seen the emperor ascending. He was given a fee of a million sesterces by the emperor's widow Livia, who with the most prominent equestrians remained by the pyre for five days before placing his bones in his tomb.[8]

The senate met on September 17 and voted to include Divus Augustus in the state cult, instructing Livia and Tiberius to erect a temple dedicated to him (it was not completed until the reign of Caligula). In addition, a *flamen* (priest) and a priestess were appointed in his honor; these were Livia's grandson Germanicus and Livia herself. The senate provided for a college of senators, for the annual celebration of his birthday, and for the institution and continuance of the games called *Augustalia* in October.

During Augustus' lifetime he had often been hailed as divine in provincial cities, where temples of Augustus and Rome had been built and altars erected in honor of the emperor himself. Tiberius now gave permission, and impetus, for the building of temples of Augustus and other monuments to him throughout the empire. He recognized that the memory of the great emperor would perform a function not unlike that which the emperor himself had exercised.

II-THE EMPIRE AFTER THE DEATH OF AUGUSTUS

The Roman empire had come into existence during a period of expansion which had lasted nearly three centuries, beginning with Rome's conquest of Italy and continuing with conquest of the whole Mediterranean world. Commercial and military rivalry with the city of Carthage, settled by Phoenicians on the African coast across from Sicily, had resulted in a series of bitter wars, all of which ended in Roman victory and in the expansion of Roman rule.

[7] Dio 56, 36, 4-5; 39, 5; 41, 9.
[8] *Ibid.*, 56, 42; 56, 46, 2. Cf. L. R. Taylor, *The Divinity of the Roman Emperor* (Middletown, Conn., 1931), 224-38.

Sicily, Sardinia, and Corsica were annexed during the struggle with the Carthaginians in the third century B.C., and in 197 two more provinces, Hither and Further Spain, were created, again because of military necessity in dealing with Carthage. By the middle of the second century the Romans actually controlled almost the whole of the Mediterranean world, chiefly by means of treaties with kings who became "allies and friends" of the Roman republic. In 148, however, annexation began again after a series of campaigns proved that Macedonia could be pacified in no other way. Two years later Greece was placed under the control of the proconsul of Macedonia, and at the same time Carthage was destroyed and the small province of Africa was created.

As early as 155 the king of Cyrene had made a will leaving his kingdom to his "friends and allies" the Roman people if he should die without an heir.[9] The will did not take effect at once, for he was succeeded by a son; but in 133 Attalus III, king of Pergamum, actually left his kingdom to the Roman people.[10] The system of alliances with client kings had thus resulted in the incorporation of a new province into the Roman framework, although much of Attalus' territory was placed under the rule of the kings of Pontus and Cappadocia.

For many years the Greek city of Massilia in southern Gaul was an ally of Rome, but repeated barbarian invasions resulted in Rome's annexation of the whole area and the creation of the province of Gallia Transalpina in 120. About 102 the activities of pirates in the eastern Mediterranean led to Roman occupation of southern Asia Minor and the formation of the province of Cilicia, while within a few years the province of Cisalpine Gaul was created. In 96 the kingdom of Cyrene was finally left to Rome, but it was not organized as a province until 74, the same year in which the kingdom of Bithynia, on the south shore of the Black Sea, was also received by bequest and made a province. Further trouble with the pirates resulted in the capture of Crete in 68 and its attachment to Cyrene, and to the capture of Cyprus, made part of Cilicia, ten years later.

In 62 the Roman general Pompey reorganized many of the eastern Roman provinces and created the new province of Syria, leaving part of the former kingdom of Judaea in the hands of the high priest John Hyrcanus. Julius Caesar was responsible for the conquest of Gaul and the annexation of further provinces there. By defeating Cleopatra VII in the year 30 Octavian (Augustus) obtained Egypt for himself—and the Roman people.

By the time of Augustus' death the empire consisted of Italy and more than thirty provinces of varying size and importance. Ten were under the control of the senate; their governors were called proconsuls, and in the case of Africa and Asia they were ex-consuls. The other proconsuls had attained only

[9] *L'année épigraphique* 1932, 80 (p. 32).
[10] *OGIS* 338.

praetorian rank.[11] The other provinces were administered by legates of the emperor, ex-praetors except in the most important areas where ex-consuls served, or by equestrian officials known as prefects or procurators. The ex-consular legates, in command of legions, governed provinces on the western, northern, and eastern frontiers.[12] On the other hand, prefects or procurators controlled only small bodies of troops since their duties were chiefly related to civil administration.[13]

III·THE ARMY

The provinces were protected by about twenty-five legions, each of which if at full strength consisted of six thousand officers and men. Tacitus, relying on a report of Tiberius to the senate at the beginning of the year 23, provides a survey of the armed forces at that time.[14] Italy, he says, was protected by the fleets based at Misenum, near Naples, and Ravenna; another fleet was based at Forum Iulii in southern Gaul.[15] The main strength of the legions—eight in all—was concentrated along the Rhine, ready to move into either Germany or Gaul. Three legions were stationed in the Spanish provinces, two in Africa (one had been brought from Pannonia because of border raids in Numidia), two in Egypt, and four on the eastern frontier from Syria as far as the Euphrates. The Danube was defended by two legions in Pannonia and two in Moesia; these four were supported by another two based to their rear in Dalmatia. In addition, Rome itself was protected by three urban and nine praetorian cohorts, elite troops chiefly Italian in origin. As Tacitus points out, there were also allied fleets, cavalry forces, and auxiliary cohorts, approximately equal to the legions in size.

In later times the number of legions steadily increased. An inscription which reflects the situation about A.D. 150 contains the names of thirty-three of them, beginning with three now stationed in Britain.[16] The growth of the army led directly to the military anarchy of the third century and to other consequences analyzed by MacMullen.[17] It gained a position in the Roman world in which its power far outweighed that of either the senate or the emperor himself; and when it proved too weak to defend the frontiers the empire in the west collapsed.

[11] Achaea, Baetica, Bithynia-Pontus, Crete-Cyrene, Cyprus, Gallia Narbonensis, Macedonia, Sicilia.

[12] Dalmatia, Germania Superior, Germania Inferior, Hispania Tarraconensis, Moesia, Pannonia, Syria; later Britannia, Cappadocia, Dacia, Palaestina.

[13] For example in Judaea (A.D. 6-41, 44-70).

[14] Tacitus, *Ann.* 4, 5.

[15] C. G. Starr, *The Roman Imperial Navy* (ed. 2, Cambridge, 1960).

[16] *ILS* 2288; five of the 33 are from the early third century.

[17] R. MacMullen, *Soldier and Civilian in the Later Roman Empire* (Cambridge, Mass., 1963).

The expenses of maintaining the legions and their auxiliaries made up a major part of the imperial budget, as the following table will indicate.[18] (All figures are in denarii.)

	soldier	centurion	primi ordines	praetorian
Augustus	225	3,750	7,500	750
Domitian	300	5,000	10,000	1,000
Commodus	375 ⎫	6,250	12,500	⎧ 1,250
Sept. Sev.	500 ⎭			⎩ 1,700
Caracalla	750	12,500	25,000	2,500

To be sure, the purchasing power of the denarius almost steadily declined during this period, but soldiers' pay more than compensated for the loss.

It would appear that under Augustus the "normal" expenses of the state treasury or *aerarium* amounted to about 100 million denarii a year; of this about two-thirds went for military expenses. The income of the *aerarium* was somewhat in excess of this figure,[19] though Augustus himself subsidized it on four occasions with a total of 37½ million denarii and also established a special *aerarium militare* with 42½ million for soldiers' bonuses (to this were added funds from inheritance and sales taxes).[20] During his lifetime the emperor gave to the *aerarium,* the Roman people, and discharged soliders no less than 550 million denarii, and he left 150 million in his will.[21] By astute management Tiberius increased the imperial estate to 675 million denarii, a total not reached again until the death of Antoninus Pius—if Dio's figure is reliable.[22] To be sure, the estate of Trajan must have been remarkably large if his successor Hadrian was able to remit debts of 225 million denarii due to the *fisci.*[23] But times of trouble naturally depleted *aerarium* and *fiscus* alike: Vespasian said he needed ten billion denarii to set the state upright.[24] Perhaps, as has been suggested, he had a capital sum in view; perhaps he was simply exaggerating, for the sum could have yielded a billion denarii. Herodian says that in 211 Septimius Severus left his sons more money than anyone else had ever left;[25] but the historian probably did not take into account the sharply higher price level or the decline in silver content.[26]

[18] J. Kromayer and G. Veith, *Heerwesen und Kriegsführung der Griechen und Römer* (Munich, 1928), 526.

[19] Cf. T. Frank, *An Economic Survey of Ancient Rome,* V (Baltimore, 1940), 4-7. On *aerarium* and *fiscus* cf. A. H. M. Jones, *Studies in Roman Government and Law* (New York, 1960), 99-114 (=*JRS* 40, 1950, 22-29).

[20] *Mon. Ancyr.* 17, pp. 30-33 Volkmann.

[21] *Ibid.,* App. I, pp. 60-61, corrected by Frank, *op. cit.,* 14-15.

[22] Suetonius, *Gaius* 37, 3 (cf. Dio 59, 2, 6); for Antoninus, Dio 73, 8, 3.

[23] *CIL* VI 967=*ILS* 309.

[24] Suetonius, *Vespasian* 16, 3.

[25] Herodian 3, 15, 3.

[26] Rostovtzeff, *SEHRE²* 413-14; on the coinage cf. L. C. West, *Gold and Silver Coin Standards in the Roman Empire* (New York, 1941).

Throughout the history of the Roman empire government expenses and revenues followed Parkinson's law; Tenney Frank guessed that the budget of Vespasian was perhaps three times that of Augustus. It would appear that in Augustus' time about one-fifth of the revenues of the empire came from the I per cent sales tax and the 5 per cent tax on inheritances, while the rest came from provincial levies of various kinds. This is why "customs-collector" is virtually a synonym for "sinner" in the gospels. Revolts were less frequent than might be expected because the army did protect the frontiers and in many areas the emperors conducted lavish building programs which, in turn, upheld the idea of the majesty of Rome. The imperial estates in the provinces provided employment and resulted in a measure of loyalty.

Given the Roman concern for the army, it might be expected that military technology would have been encouraged. Indeed, Hero of Alexandria insisted about A.D. 100 that the philosophy taught by weaponry provided a sense of security in peace or in war.[27] This sense of security rarely existed, however, for the more sophisticated devices existed only on paper.[28] Indeed, the high point of military technology seems to have been reached in 212 B.C., when Archimedes used cranes against the Roman ships attacking Syracuse.[29] In the fourth century A.D. an unknown author proposed governmental reforms and the use of twelve military machines in order to save manpower, but none of them was employed.[30] It should be said, however, that something like chemical warfare was represented by a spontaneously igniting mixture of sulphur with other ingredients; this is first described by the Christian author Julius Africanus.[31] Biological warfare of a crude sort was known: when the inhabitants of Hatra in Arabia were defending their city against Septimius Severus they dropped clay pots, filled with poisonous insects, on the attackers.[32]

Generally speaking, technology either military or civil did not flourish in antiquity. Perhaps the existence of slavery blocked technological advance.[33] Another cause is suggested by a story about Vespasian. Offered an invention for lifting stone columns at Rome, he rewarded the inventor but refused to use the device, stating that he had to "feed the poor" by providing employment.[34]

[27] H. Diels and E. Schramm, *Herons Belopoiika* (*Abhandlungen der preuss. Akad. zu Berlin, Philol.-hist. Kl.*, 1918, no. 2), 5-6.

[28] A. Neumann in *KP* II 782-83.

[29] Polybius 8, 5-6; Livy 24-25; Plutarch, *Marcellus*, 14, 4—17, 3.

[30] E. A. Thompson, *A Roman Reformer and Inventor* (Oxford, 1952).

[31] J. Vieillefond, *Jules Africain: Fragments des Cestes* (Paris, 1932), 62.

[32] Herodian 3, 9, 5. Trajan's troops at Hatra had been bothered by flies, but not in clay pots; cf. Dio 68, 31, 4.

[33] Cf. M. I. Finley, ed., *Slavery in Classical Antiquity* (Cambridge, 1960), 234.

[34] Suetonius, *Vesp.* 18, 2.

IV·CITIES AND PEOPLE

A significant feature of life in the Roman empire was the important role played by the big cities, a role fully recognized by rhetoricians. Their praise of the cities was conventional, but it was more than that. The provincial cities were seats of government and centers of cultural and religious life, supported by the rich and generous provincials of the second century and even the third. The largest of the cities outside Rome were Alexandria, called by Strabo "the greatest emporium in the world,"[35] Antioch in Syria, which he says is little inferior to Alexandria,[36] and Carthage. According to Herodian Carthage vied with Alexandria for second place in the empire.[37] These cities were nearly matched by such others as Ephesus, Smyrna, and Pergamum in Asia Minor,[38] Lyons in Gaul, and the ancient and greatly revered city of Athens.[39] The apostle Paul proudly identified himself as a citizen of Tarsus, "a not undistinguished city" (Acts 21:39).

Above and beyond them all stood Rome, founded according to tradition in 753 B.C. Not just a city but the center of a world government, Rome was praised by rhetoricians, above all by Aelius Aristides in the second century, as the "common town" of the whole civilized world.[40] With a population of about 700,000, this was the city which the apostle Paul said he had to see (Acts 19:21).[41] Indeed, everyone who could do so visited the city—a fact noted without enthusiasm by the Roman historian Tacitus, who claimed that everything disgusting arrived there.[42]

Tacitus was not the only Roman to view with alarm the steady flow of foreigners into the capital city. Seneca describes it with a little more moderation; Juvenal expresses his distaste for the Greeks at Rome and says that "the Syrian Orontes discharges into the Tiber."[43] La Piana cites only one comment from the other side: the second-century African Fronto claimed that simplicity, continence, truthfulness, and honor were Roman virtues, though warmth in affection was not Roman.[44] Fronto's sometime pupil, the emperor Marcus Aurelius, acknowledged the truth of his objection: "generally speaking those whom we entitle 'patricians' are somehow rather wanting in the natural

---

[35] Strabo, *Geog.* 17, 1, 13.
[36] *Ibid.*, 16, 2, 5.
[37] Herodian 7, 6, 1.
[38] D. Magie, *Roman Rule in Asia Minor* (Princeton, 1950), 583-85.
[39] Cf. J. H. Oliver, *The Civilizing Power* (*TAPS* 58, 1, Philadelphia, 1968).
[40] Oliver, *The Ruling Power* (*TAPS* 43, 4, Philadelphia, 1953).
[41] Cf. Acts 23:11; Rom. 1:13; F. M. Heichelheim in *KP* I 879.
[42] Tacitus, *Ann.* 15, 44.
[43] Seneca, *De consol. ad Helv.* 6; Juvenal, *Sat.* 3, 62-118; G. La Piana in *HTR* 20 (1927), 183-403, especially 193-95 and 227-32.
[44] La Piana, *op. cit.*, 227.

affections."[45] This is to say that though Fronto became a senator and even consul he never felt that he was fully accepted by the older senatorial group.

Throughout the empire, however, there was a steady process not so much of leveling as of the ascent of new groups and classes to power. The emperors relied not only on senatorial families but also on the equestrians; when Egypt became a province, Augustus placed it under the rule of an equestrian prefect, who proudly noted the fact on an inscription. "C. Cornelius, son of Cnaeus Gallus, after the kings were defeated by Caesar, son of the god, first prefect of Alexandria and Egypt."[46] Throughout the history of the empire "new men," from the provinces and from the classes below the senatorial, kept coming to the fore.[47] Under Claudius freedmen began to occupy positions of importance in the administration at Rome.

At the top of the Roman social structure stood the senatorial order, since the times of Sulla and Caesar made up not only of the old Roman aristocracy but also of other rich Romans and provincials. Under Caesar the senate had grown to include about nine hundred members, and soon after his death reached a thousand. Augustus revised the roll of the senate three times, reducing its numbers to six hundred and providing regular requirements for admission: personal integrity, a term of military service, and economic independence based on property worth 200,000 denarii (a sum later raised to 250,000). The equestrian order, whose members "preferred comfort, secret power and solid profit to the burdens, the dangers and the extravagant display of a senator's life,"[48] was given similar requirements, but the property qualification was only 100,000 denarii. New members were steadily recruited from the army and from among wealthy freedmen; they continued to command troops and govern provinces, including Egypt, though the senatorial provinces were administered by senators—with equestrian assistance. The two orders worked together to maintain the imperial state. Among the upper class, the *honestiores,* were also included the veterans of the Roman legions and the *decuriones,* those who had held public offices including priesthoods in various municipalities and met property qualifications, often of 25,000 denarii. At Rome and elsewhere the *plebs* or body of free citizens at first enjoyed the right of electing magistrates, but lost it during the third century. Augustus noted the growth of all these classes in his *Res gestae:* in 28 B.C. there were 4,063,000 Roman citizens; twenty years later there were 4,233,000; in A.D. 14 there were 4,937,000.[49] It is hard to make an estimate of the total population of the empire, including slaves, but apparently about 70 million is a reasonable figure for the time of Augustus. The median age of the population was prob-

[45] *Medit.* I, II.
[46] *OGIS* 654=*ILS* 8995.
[47] Cf., e.g., H. G. Pflaum, *Les procurateurs équestres sous le haut-empire romain* (Paris, 1950); *Les carrières équestres* . . . (Paris, 1960-61).
[48] R. Syme, *The Roman Revolution* (Oxford, 1939), 13.
[49] *Res gestae* 8 (pp. 18-21 Vokmann).

ably fairly low, in view of the prevalence of warfare and epidemics, and the primitive state of medicine. Families were usually small; Augustus himself tried to encourage marriage and a higher birth rate. Special privileges were given Romans who produced three children (although the honorary award of these privileges to the childless tended to defeat the emperor's purpose), and penalties were laid on bachelors and married persons without offspring. Bachelors were forbidden to inherit; childless persons were deprived of half of inheritances and legacies.[50] According to Tacitus this legislation resulted only in denunciations by informers and the enrichment of the treasury.[51] Among the lower classes infanticide and the "exposure" of unwanted children, especially girls, was fairly common. In 1 B.C. a husband at Alexandria wrote his pregnant wife at Oxyrhynchus that if she bore a boy she should let the infant live; if a girl, she should "put it out."[52] This practice, according to which "exposed" infants became the slaves of anyone who picked them up (unless they were reclaimed by their parents), was denounced by such philosophers as Musonius and Epictetus,[53] and by Christian apologists,[54] but continued until the sixth century.

A child who was brought up in a fairly prosperous family would ideally learn both Greek and Latin, at first from his nurse, who was often Greek. Later on a slave called a *paedagogus* would take him back and forth from the school in which he would learn reading and writing and then would apply himself to the study of Greek and Latin literature, beginning with the Greeks Homer and Hesiod and the Roman Virgil. In theory he might well study various kinds of literature. The Christian bishop Theophilus seems to be summarizing a school curriculum as he indicates the uselessness of various groups of books: Homer, Hesiod, Orpheus, and Aratus (hexameters); Euripides and Sophocles (tragic poetry); Menander and Aristophanes (comic poetry); Herodotus and Thucydides (history); Pythagoras, Diogenes, Epicurus, Empedocles, Socrates (presumably from Xenophon), and Plato (philosophy).[55] Ideally, again, a Greek student might go on to study music, astronomy, and geometry;[56] but most of his classmates would already have fallen by the wayside. The goal of such education was principally to achieve skill in rhetoric, without which no public career was really possible. If the young man was to influence his contemporaries in the courts or in civic as-

---

[50] Cf. M. Kaster, *Das römische Privatrecht* I (Munich, 1955), 271-74.

[51] Tacitus, *Ann.* 3, 25.

[52] P. Oxy. IV 744; cf. R. Taubenschlag, *The Law of Greco-Roman Egypt in the Light of the Papyri* (New York, 1944), 103-4; earlier: W. W. Tarn, *Hellenistic Civilisation* (ed. 3 with G. T. Griffith, London, 1952), 100-2.

[53] P. Rendel Harris 1; J. E. Powell in *Archiv für Papyrusforschung* 12 (1937), 175-78; Epictetus, *Diss.* 1, 23.

[54] Justin, *Apol.* 1, 27, 1; cf. C. J. Cadoux, *The Early Church and the World* (Edinburgh, 1925), 445; Rostovtzeff, *SEHRE²* 476 and 738 (n. 15).

[55] Theophilus, *Ad Autol.* 3, 2. I owe this point to Professor B. Einarson.

[56] Justin, *Dial.* 2, 4. On the whole subject cf. H.-I. Marrou, *Histoire de l'éducation dans l'antiquité* (Paris, 1950).

semblies or at the senate house in Rome, he needed to acquire fluency in speaking and to turn neat phrases.

Under such circumstances it was inevitable that much instruction was carried on with the use not of the works of philosophers or poets, but of handbooks and anthologies with summaries or excerpts arranged under headings. The writings of the Christian apologists and, for that matter, of Philo of Alexandria are full of quotations from these manuals, although there are also reflections of firsthand acquaintance with philosophical writings. The diversity of the viewpoints presented made it easy for a skeptical theologian to claim that true knowledge could come only from revelation.

At the top of the social scale one might look forward to the career of a typical senator, as expressed in the *cursus honorum*. One might marry the daughter of a distinguished family—or one might not. Out of countless inscriptional examples we may note the career of P. Mummius Sisenna Rutilianus in the second century. After a minor magistracy and service as a military tribune, Mummius was selected to be praetor, tribune of the people, and quaestor. After this point his career was assured; he became legate of a legion, prefect of the treasury of Saturn, and one of the prefects in charge of the Roman food supply. In 146 he was made *consul suffectus*, then with consular rank legate of Upper Moesia. In 160 or 161 he became proconsul of Asia, one of the two great senatorial provinces. By 172 he had been made an augur.[57] This official description of Mummius' career is especially poignant because another aspect is maliciously described by the satirist Lucian. When Mummius was proconsul of Asia the "prophet" Alexander of Abonuteichos produced a disastrously optimistic oracle for a Roman invasion of Armenia.[58] At the age of sixty Mummius himself asked for an oracle about marriage (his first wife had died) and was instructed to marry the prophet's daughter. Apparently he followed this advice in about 165,[59] and through Mummius the prophet was able to influence even the emperor Marcus Aurelius.[60] According to Lucian, this Roman senator and ex-consul "died insane at seventy."[61]

At the other end of the scale there was no *cursus*. Most slaves did not become freedmen, and Augustan legislation discouraged large-scale manumission. On the other hand, the economic and social position of those who did become freedmen steadily improved, and many laws forbade the mistreatment of slaves. As occupations previously reserved for the upper classes were

[57] *ILS* 1101.

[58] Lucian, *Alex.* 27.

[59] *Ibid.*, 33, 54. An inscription from Amastris (*IGR* III 84) mentions L. Lollianus Avitus, "governor of Bithynia and Pontus" around this time (Lucian, *Alex.* 57), as legate in the Pompeian year 229=A.D. 165.

[60] *Ibid.*, 48. On Alexander cf. M. Caster, *Étude sur Alexandre ou le faux prophète de Lucien* (Paris, 1938); M. P. Nilsson, *Geschichte der griechischen Religion* II (Munich 1950), 452-55. Naturally Alexander detested the Epicureans and Christians who scoffed at his "mysteries" (Lucian, *Alex.* 38).

[61] *Ibid.*, 34.

taken up by ex-slaves, so citizens assumed functions earlier performed by slaves alone. Perhaps the most conspicuous example of this change is provided by a famous inscription erected at Rome in 146 by admirers of the Graeco-Roman Spaniard C. Appuleius Diocles, at the age of forty-two just retired from twenty-four years of chariot racing. He had run 4,257 starts and had won a total of nearly 36 million sesterces (9 million denarii).[62] A century earlier a similar sum pointed toward extravagance at Rome in the case of Lollia Paulina, granddaughter of Augustus' first legate in Galatia. Although she was married to the ex-consul C. Memmius, Caligula forced her into a short-lived marriage with himself; a decade later she tried to persuade Claudius to marry her. The elder Pliny stated that at a betrothal banquet she wore emeralds and pearls worth 40 million sesterces.[63]

There is no reason to exaggerate the significance of the great gulf between rich and poor in the Roman world. We note only that it is reflected in the figures provided in the Christian gospels. At one extreme we find debts reckoned in talents;[64] at the other, an *assarion,* a *quadrant* or a *lepton.*[65] Two *lepta* supposedly constituted the whole property of a poor widow.[66]

This is not to say that there was no middle class or upper middle class. As freedmen came to the fore especially at Rome itself, so the equestrian class was given ever-increasing responsibility and power, gradually taking over offices and functions previously senatorial. Roman society became increasingly fluid. As Ramsay MacMullen has shown, opposition to imperial power gradually moved downward from the senatorial class to peasants and barbarians; this movement accompanied a gradual diffusion of Roman power itself, and the formation of a new social structure.[67] MacMullen's own chapter headings piquantly illustrate the change, and now that we have said something about the upper classes and philosophers we too may turn to astrologers, magicians, diviners, and prophets—not so much in order to trace their rise as in order to view them as participants in the life of the Roman empire during the first two or three centuries.

V·RELIGIOSITY

The late Roman republic and the Roman empire as well were characterized by widespread, almost universal belief in the influence of the sun, the moon,

---

[62] *ILS* 5287.

[63] *Nat. hist.* 9, 117-18.

[64] Matt. 18:24; 25:14-30.

[65] Matt. 5:26; Luke 12:59 (smallest coins); Matt. 10:29 (two sparrows for an *assarion*); Luke 12:6 (five sparrows for two *assaria*).

[66] Mark 12:42; Luke 21:2.

[67] R. MacMullen, *Enemies of the Roman Order* (Cambridge, Mass., 1966); conclusions, 242-48.

the other planets, and the stars upon events on earth. Most people, including most emperors, firmly believed that by study of the stars astrologers were able to predict the future, and they paid a great deal of attention to their horoscopes. Occasionally astrologers were expelled from Rome and Italy when political turmoil made it necessary.[68] Supported by Stoic philosophers—all the heads of the Stoic school but Panaetius believed in astrology—and used to confirm the doctrine of predetermined fate, astrology was attacked by a few skeptical philosophers, as well as by Plotinus and the Christians Bardesanes and Origen.[69] Some Christians accepted the reality of cosmic determinism and astrology but claimed that either the coming of Christ or Christian baptism had provided Christians with liberation.[70] Similar ideas were found among the rabbis.[71]

Belief in magic flourished at the same time. Examples of magic in the New Testament are provided by the Samaritan magician Simon (Acts 8:11) and the magical books, worth 50,000 drachmas, burned at Ephesus (19:19). Many magical papyri still extant reflect the use of nonsense syllables (cf. *abracadabra*) and words taken from Jewish and Christian sources in order to work the magician's will by demonic aid. "The magical papyri constantly operate with the debris of other people's religion."[72] Much magic was directed against other people, as we learn from curses still preserved on stone or metal.[73] Learning both astrological and magical was traced back to remote antiquity—precisely to Zoroaster, Ostanes, and Hystaspes—by Greek-speaking enthusiasts for the lore of the Chaldaeans.[74]

VI·RELIGIONS

Religion in the Graeco-Roman world was closely related to both astrology and magic, but both at Rome itself and in the provinces it was most markedly different from either in that it was essentially public, not private; it was supported and regulated by the state. The new cults to which we shall presently turn captured the imaginations of many, but they flourished alongside the great temples of the older gods, built by cities and kings and emperors and

---

[68]Cf. F. Cumont, *Astrology and Religion among the Greeks and Romans* (London, 1912); *Les religions orientales dans le paganisme romain* (ed. 4, Paris, 1929), 151-79; *L'Egypte des astrologues* (Brussels, 1937); F. H. Cramer, *Astrology in Roman Law and Politics* (Philadelphia, 1954).

[69] E. R. Dodds, *Pagan and Christian in an Age of Anxiety* (Cambridge, 1965), 15.

[70] Ignatius, *Eph.* 19; Clement of Alexandria, *Exc. ex Theod.* 78, 1.

[71] S. Lieberman, *Greek in Jewish Palestine* (New York, 1942), 99-100.

[72] Dodds, *op. cit.*, 73.

[73] Cf. A. Audollent, *Defixionum tabellae* (Paris, 1904); R. Wünsch, *Sethianische Verfluchungstafeln aus Rom* (Leipzig, 1898); K. Preisendanz in *KP* I 1423-24.

[74] Cf. J. Bidez and F. Cumont, *Les mages hellénisés* (2 vols., Paris, 1938).

usually maintained at public expense. It need hardly be said that the eighty-two temples which Augustus restored at Rome included none for oriental deities, though he did build a temple for the Great Mother, now Roman. Chief of all the gods was Jupiter, identified with the Greek Zeus; Augustus stated that he had built temples for Jupiter Feretrius and Jupiter Tonans on the Capitol and for Jupiter Libertas on the Aventine.[75] (The notion of so many Zeuses was discussed by Greek and Roman theologians and later ridiculed by Christians.[76]) For this king and father of gods and men Hadrian later brought to completion the great temple of Zeus Olympios at Athens, once aided by Antiochus IV of Syria, and another on Mount Gerizim.[77] For a less splendid example we may mention only the priest of Zeus Propoleos at Lystra in Lycaonia, who tried to offer sacrifice to Barnabas and Paul in the belief that they might be Zeus and Hermes, present among men (Acts 14:13).

At Ephesus in Asia the principal shrine was that of the goddess Artemis; her temple was regarded as one of the wonders of the world. It was supported by the city and also had "large lands of its own," not to mention special police.[78] More important for the Greeks, however, was Athens with its acropolis, itself "an object of worship." Not far away was "the common sanctuary of the Hellenes" at Delphi;[79] still nearer, Eleusis, where the greatest of the mysteries were celebrated.[80] Kings and emperors led the way to initiation there and vied in providing gifts.

The mysteries at Eleusis, which deeply influenced the other "mysteries" moving westward in the Roman empire, were secret, and as G. Mylonas has concluded, their secret was well kept.[81] We know little of what was done in the mysteries there, nothing of what, if anything, was taught. For our purposes the most important feature of the rites is that they were regarded throughout the empire with the utmost reverence. Augustus, Hadrian, and Marcus Aurelius were initiated into them; even the Christian emperor Constantine gave funds to aid the Eleusinian dadouchos (torchbearer at the initiation). The Eleusinian "lesser mysteries" and "greater mysteries" were imitated elsewhere —not least, as we shall see, in the Christian community at Alexandria.

The other religious institution which we have mentioned as being in the vicinity of Athens was the temple of Apollo at Delphi with its renowned oracle. By the second century of our era its influence was actually declining; "it was famous more as a spot for tourists than for the oracle."[82] The treatises

[75] Res gestae 19 (p. 34 Volkmann).
[76] Cf. Theophilus, Ad Autol. 1, 10.
[77] Cf. R. P. Bull and G. E. Wright in HTR 58 (1962), 234-37.
[78] Rostovtzeff, SEHRE² 656 n. 6; 739 n. 17.
[79] J. H. Oliver, The Civilizing Power (Trans. Amer. Philos. Soc. 58, 1, 1968), 69= Aelius Aristides, Or. 13, 142-43. Dindorf.
[80] Ibid., 87=Or. 13, 257.
[81] Eleusis and the Eleusinian Mysteries (Princeton, 1961); cf. Nilsson, op. cit., II, 85-91.
[82] Nilsson, op. cit., 448.

of Plutarch clearly show that this oracle and others were losing their power over men's imaginations. As late as the year 84, however, the emperor Domitian had restored the temple of Apollo "at his own expense."[83] The oracle did not long survive the restoration, however. Christians and others provided naturalistic explanations of the ecstasy of the prophetic priestess.[84]

We have offered no more than a few examples out of many which show that in the time when Christianity arose traditional paganism was still a living force. Its vitality was further evidenced in the new cult of the goddess Roma, encouraged in the provinces along with the even newer cult of the dead and deified "good" emperors after Julius Caesar. Though Tiberius was not deified, since the young Caligula failed to press this question before the senate,[85] Caligula's self-deification before death led to the senate's condemnation of his memory. Claudius was deified; Nero was forced to commit suicide. Galba, Otho, and Vitellius were obviously unworthy of consecration. Vespasian and Titus became gods after death; Domitian, an enemy of the senate, did not. Once the succession was secure, all the great emperors of the second century were deified, and even Commodus, condemned after his death, was given *consecratio* by Septimius Severus. In the third century, with its rapid successions of emperors, not all received this honor. (It should be noted that the father of Philip the Arabian, an emperor whom Eusebius claimed as a Christian, was deified at least at Philippopolis in Arabia.[86]) As for Diocletian and the other tetrarchs who ruled with him in the early fourth century, he was the only one of the four not to be deified; and he was the only one to die in retirement. His successor Constantine, as we shall see, was finally deified by a grateful senate.

The religions we have thus far discussed were those which were attached to particular places or were diffused from the center of the empire in all directions. An equally powerful movement in the realm of religion was taking place from the east to the west.

Foreign cults had been accepted at Rome since the crisis of the second war with Carthage, late in the third century B.C., when political necessity had caused the introduction to Rome of the cult of the Venus of Eryx in western Sicily and the cult of the great Mother of the Gods from Pessinus in the realm of Attalus, king of Pergamum. From Mount Eryx on a clear day Roman observers could watch the Carthaginian fleet, and in Asia Minor the priests of the Mother proved useful allies to the Roman armies. Unauthorized cults provided severe difficulties, however, and most notably in the case of the Greek rites of Bacchus which were flourishing and causing alarm in Etruria when, in 186, the senate moved against them. The situation was so critical

[83] *ILS* 8905=*SIG*³ 821A.
[84] Origen, *C. Cels.* 7, 3 (pp. 396-97 Chadwick); cf. H. W. Parke and D. E. W. Wormell, *The Delphic Oracle* (Oxford, 1956), I, 19-30.
[85] Taylor, *op. cit.*, 240.
[86] *ILS* 8806.

that the consuls were authorized to arrest and put to death participants in the Bacchanalia even if they were on allied territory, not Roman.

According to the senate's decree, the Bacchants were forbidden to hold common funds, to participate in politics, to take oaths among themselves, to practice secret rites, or rites of any kind with more than two men and three women present. Exceptions could be granted only by the urban praetor with the approval of the senate.[87]

The case of the Bacchanalia provided a precedent for later times; according to Livy 7,000 initiates were punished, most of them by death.[88] His own account, written under Augustus, seems aimed at showing the danger of orgiastic, non-Roman cults, and reflects the Augustan attitude toward foreign religions. This attitude was hostile toward oriental religions, which at the time were spreading westward and gaining adherents not only in the provinces but at Rome itself.[89]

The old Roman attitude toward the worshipers of Dionysus did not long survive the collapse of the republic. Tertullian in 197 could speak of "Bacchus now Italian,"[90] and inscriptions show that the situation of the Dionysiacs was one of full recognition. One contains a letter of Marcus Aurelius in 147, expressing his thanks for the congratulations sent by Dionysiacs at Smyrna the year before, when his son was born; their message had been transmitted by the proconsul of Asia. There is also a letter from Antoninus Pius, addressed in 158 to the "synod of the *mystae* at Smyrna."[91] The great Dionysiac inscription from Campania, now in the Metropolitan Museum of Art, shows that among the initiates was the wife of M. Gavius Squilla Gallicanus, proconsul of Asia about 165.[92] Indeed, the process of assimilation as regards the Dionysiacs was similar to what happened to most of the other religious groups.

The attitudes of the early emperors toward the foreign cults which were moving into Rome can be briefly summarized. Augustus respected the Eleusinian mysteries, into which he had been initiated, but thought little of the religions of Egypt and Judaea.[93] Tiberius actually abolished the Egyptian and Jewish cults at Rome.[94] Under Caligula, however, a great temple of Isis Campensis was erected in the Campus Martius,[95] and Claudius actually permitted a festival of the god Attis to be celebrated at Rome.[96] The reason

[87] *ILS* 18; Livy 39, 18, 8-9.
[88] Livy 39, 17, 6.
[89] The kind of trouble that could be expected is reflected in Pompeian wall-inscriptions noting candidates for the office of *aedile* of whom the Isiacs approved (*ILS* 6419c, 6420b).
[90] *Apol.* 6, 10.
[91] *SIG*³ 851.
[92] Cf. M. P. Nilsson, *Geschichte der griechischen Religion* (Munich, 1950), II, 343.
[93] Suetonius, *Augustus* 93.
[94] *Tiberius* 36; cf. Josephus, *Ant.* 18, 65-84.
[95] F. Cumont, *Les religions orientales dans le paganisme romain* (ed. 4, Paris, 1929), 78.
[96] *Ibid.*, 51.

for accepting these cults, even though with some reluctance, was that their adherents came from the provinces within the empire and were offering no resistance to Roman rule. Such was not the case with the Druids of Gaul and Britain, notorious for the practice of human sacrifice.[97] Augustus forbade Roman citizens to participate in the Druid religion; Tiberius "checked" the Druids; and Claudius "completely abolished the religion of the Druids." He executed a Roman knight from Gaul who was carrying a Druid magic egg.[98] The problem was in part political, for in distant Britain the Druids, who continued human sacrifice, detested the new temple of the divine Claudius erected at Camulodunum.[99] Throughout Gaul and Britain they rejoiced when the Capitol burned in 69 and viewed it as a divine sign of their future triumph.[100]

On the other hand, a Hellenophile like Nero was quite willing to relate himself to religions well to the east of Rome. In the summer of 67 Nero visited Achaea and announced its "freedom" from control by the senate.[101] An inscription from Boeotia provides a version of his address and of the reply by the high priest of the Augusti, speaking of the emperor as "lord of the whole world" and as "the new sun shining upon the Greeks." He was to be identified as Zeus Eleutherios Nero, and an altar was erected to him and to the goddess Augusta Messalina, his third wife.[102]

A year earlier his position in regard to friendly orientals and their religions had been even more dramatically expressed at Rome; he had subsidized a state visit by Tiridates, king of Armenia, so that the oriental monarch could receive his diadem at the emperor's hands. Tiridates knelt before Nero and addressed him as his master, his god like the Persian Mithras, his fate and his fortune. Nero replied by suggesting that indeed he was close to divinity: he was the one who could take away kingdoms and bestow them.[103] We may doubt that Nero became a Mithraic initiate, but his ties with Mithras were potentially close.[104]

The mysteries of the Persian god Mithras had been introduced to Rome, according to Plutarch, by the pirates from Cilicia captured and brought back by Pompey,[105] but they did not become widespread for another century. Then they were propagated by traders, for example at Ostia where sixteen shrines of Mithras have been found, as well as in Rome itself, where there were more than a hundred. The great days of Mithraism were in the second and third centuries, when it was espoused by officers of the Roman legions and

[97] H. Last in *JRS* 39 (1949), 1-5.
[98] Suetonius, *Claudius* 25, 5; Pliny, *Nat. hist.* 30, 13; 29, 54.
[99] Tacitus, *Ann.* 14, 30, 3; 14, 31, 6.
[100] Tacitus, *Hist.* 4, 54; for later times cf. R. MacMullen, *Enemies of the Roman Order* (Cambridge, Mass., 1966), 155.
[101] Dio 63, 11. Vespasian restored the province to the senate (Suetonius, *Vesp.* 8, 4).
[102] *SIG³* 814; cf. Nilsson, *op. cit.,* 496.
[103] Dio 63, 14.
[104] Cf. F. Cumont in *Rivista di filologia* 61 (1933), 146-54.
[105] Plutarch, *Pompey* 24.

spread wherever the legions were stationed. Mithras was identified with the "unconquered sun" whom Aurelian and other emperors recognized as the tutelary deity of the empire.

According to Mithraic legend the god had been born from a "generative rock" from which he emerged, wearing his distinctive Phrygian cap and carrying a knife, as shepherds watched the scene. His greatest labor was his combat with the hostile bull, portrayed on the reliefs typical of Mithraic shrines everywhere. As the bull was slain, wheat was produced from its spinal cord and the vine from its blood. Though the hostile scorpion, ant, and serpent tried to consume what came forth, they failed to prevent the production of all that would be of benefit to mankind. Later on, after a farewell meal with his companions, Mithras crossed the ocean and joined the other gods.[106]

Mithraism not only presented the story of a timeless victory over the bull—who must have signified darkness and evil since the god himself was first related to the sun, then identified with it—but also provided an elaborate system of initiations into various ranks related to aspects of the story and to the seven planetary deities.[107]

The movement of legally recognized cult groups from their native land into the Roman world is well illustrated by two inscriptions from Puteoli near Naples. The first contains a vow for the security of the new emperor Domitian and refers to the place conceded by decree—to the god Helios Areptenos, who sailed from Tyre to Puteoli (Eleim brought him by the god's command) when L. Caesennius and P. Calvisius were consuls, in the Tyrian year 204 (= 78–79). Obviously the god was sent by Tyrians, presumably for Tyrians in the important trading center of Puteoli. Nearly a century later, however, the number of Tyrians there had declined; sailors and merchants provided no contributions, and those who maintained the Tyrian "station" had to write home for funds. They were willing to pay for repairing the station for "the holy days of the Lord emperor," but they insisted on receiving financial aid either from Tyre or from the Tyrian station at Rome. What they said they needed was 250,000 denarii a year.[108]

The contrast between this story and that of the Christian community at Rome is remarkable. Brought from Palestine by private individuals, the Christian cult was not supported by a base at home but presumably made contributions to other communities from a very early date. Christians were not devotees of what the second inscription calls "the ancestral gods" but proclaimers of a new revelation.

[106] M. J. Vermaseren, *Mithras the Secret God* (New York, 1963), 67-106; A. D. Nock in *JRS* 27 (1937), 108-13.
[107] Vermaseren in *RGG*³ IV 1020-22.
[108] *OGIS* 594 (year 79; cf. *L'année épigraphique* 1950, 31b) and 595 (174).

CHAPTER II
ROME AND THE JEWS

I-OUTSIDE PALESTINE

Among the oriental peoples who with their religions were moving westward into the Roman world the Jews were especially prominent. Some were prominent in local and imperial government, but there was a widespread feeling that they were clannish and exclusive; their religious practices kept them from being assimilated. As one example out of many,[1] the semihistorical sketch provided by Tacitus deserves notice.[2] Under oriental despotism the Jews were simply viewed as inferiors, but the Seleucid king Antiochus IV endeavored to improve them by abolishing their superstition and introducing Greek customs; he did not succeed. Later the Jews were able to select their own kings, who maintained their power only as tyrants and promoted Jewish superstition by combining priestly with royal authority. Tacitus is apparently ignorant of the part played by the Roman senate in Palestinian politics during this period, and he goes on to describe Pompey as the first Roman to conquer

[1] Cf. T. Reinach, *Textes d'auteurs grecs et romains relatifs au judaïsme* (Paris, 1895).
[2] Tacitus, *Hist.* 5, 8-9.

the Jews and to enter the temple—where he found no images, even in the "secret shrine." After this episode the historian proceeds to summarize Roman-Jewish relations to the time of the war of 66–70.

The relations between Jews and Romans were actually far more complicated, as is demonstrated by an extensive collection of decrees quoted in the *Antiquities* of Josephus and derived from the archives in the Capitoline library.[3] These come from cities, consuls, proconsuls, and such rulers as Mark Antony, Julius Caesar, Augustus, and Claudius. Naturally they include only the more favorable decisions and do not refer to the occasional expulsion of Jews from Rome and Italy, for example in 139 B.C. and A.D. 19. They do show, however, that Jews had rights based on treaties with Rome and that the exercise of these rights was not confined to Palestine. This and other evidence shows that Jewish *thiasoi* or religious communities had jurisdiction over their own members and could administer their own funds (funds being transmitted to Jerusalem were given protection), including the special distributions occasionally made; their members were exempt from military service and from the obligations of the state cult, while they were not required to appear in court on the Sabbath.[4]

In Judaea itself the high priest had jurisdiction over all religious matters, although it appears that he and his supreme court, the Sanhedrin, could not legally impose the death penalty under the Roman prefects or procurators. He was in charge of the temple, largely rebuilt at the end of the first century B.C., and its elaborate rites which included daily sacrifices. At the great festivals of Tabernacles, Dedication, Passover, and Pentecost he presided with the assistance of large numbers of priests and Levites.[5] He could enter the "holy of holies"; gentiles, on the other hand, were forbidden under penalty of death to enter the inner court of the temple.[6]

Tacitus discussed not only the relations of the Jews with Rome but also the early history and nature of their religion. He had nothing good to say of the ancient Jewish rites: "the Jews regard as profane all that we hold sacred and permit all that we abhor." He was able to treat almost every Jewish virtue as a vice. Their gifts to Jerusalem came from scoundrels to enrich others; their mutual loyalty was only the other side of their hatred for outsiders, exhibited in their circumcision and avoidance of foreign women. Their monotheism was better than Egyptian animal-worship, but somehow wrong.[7]

In spite of attitudes like this, Judaism flourished in the Graeco-Roman world. Jews and their synagogues were to be found in all the principal cities—

[3] Cf. H. St. J. Thackeray, *Josephus the Man and the Historian* (New York, 1929), 70-72.

[4] Cf. J. Juster, *Les juifs dans l'empire romain* (Paris, 1914), I, 213-42.

[5] Cf. B. Reicke, *The New Testament Era* (Philadelphia, 1968), 141-68.

[6] *OGIS* 598; cf. *CIJ* II 1400.

[7] Tacitus, *Hist.* 5, 3-5.

notably, of course, in Rome, Alexandria, and Antioch. They were especially prominent at Alexandria and in Egypt, where the Jewish population could be counted (with some exaggeration?) at a million.[8] It was in Alexandria that a vigorous attempt to correlate Judaism with Graeco-Roman culture, especially in philosophy, was made; Philo was the most conspicuous leader of the movement, but he had predecessors. The Greek version of the Old Testament was produced there as early as the second century B.C. At Rome the fairly numerous synagogues known from inscriptions bore titles related to their dedications (Augusteans, Agrippians, Volumnians, Herodians), to districts of the city (Campesians, Suburesians), to the origins of the communities (Vernaculi [Jewish slaves born at Rome], Calcarensians [lime-kiln workers], Tripolitans, Elaeans, Sekeni [from Galilee?]), and perhaps from conservative traditions (Hebrews).[9] Whereas at Alexandria the Jewish community as a whole was headed by an ethnarch, at Rome there was no such officer, presumably because of the diversity reflected in the names of the synagogues.[10] On the other hand, the rather numerous cemeteries at Rome were the property of the whole Jewish community.[11]

The functions of the synagogue are well described in an inscription from Ophel near Jerusalem, built early in the first century A.D. "for the reading of the law and for the teaching of the commandments." In addition, there was an inn with a good water supply for the use of those from abroad, presumably on pilgrimage to the temple.[12] A synagogue could be established wherever there were ten adult male Jews; their leader was known as the *archisynagogos* or presiding officer.[13] Relatively late inscriptions from Smyrna and from Myndos in Caria show that women sometimes held this office.[14] The man who built the synagogue at Ophel described himself as a priest and *archisynagogos;* both his father and his grandfather had earlier held the latter office. The synagogue at Doura-Europos, on the other hand, was built in 245 by a certain Samuel who described himself in Greek as "presbyter of the Jews" and in Hebrew as "priest" and "archon" (= ruler).[15] By "priest" he must have meant that he was descended from priests, for by his time no sacrifices were being offered.[16] Synagogues, schools, and their officers thus flourished in the Graeco-Roman world and provided antecedents for later Christians to follow, as we shall see.

The presence of synagogues outside Palestine, and the existence of Jewish propaganda literature as well, produced a favorable impression on some

[8] Philo, *In Flaccum* 43.
[9] Cf. G. La Piana in *HTR* 20 (1927), 352.
[10] *Ibid.*, 361-62.
[11] *Ibid.*, 364.
[12] *CIJ* II 1404.
[13] Cf. Mark 5:21-43 (Luke 8:49); Luke 13:14; Acts 13:15, 18:8, 17.
[14] *CIJ* II 741; 756.
[15] *CIJ* II 828-29.
[16] Cf. *CIJ* II 1514 (Egypt, 27 B.C.); a woman is described as of priestly descent.

Greeks and Romans who became proselytes or, at times, "God-fearers."[17] Not everyone was repelled by Judaism. We have already noted that Tacitus had to admire Jewish monotheism and their cult without images. Seneca, writing *On superstition,* shared this appreciation.[18] The Augustan geographer Strabo combined praise of Moses with criticism of his successors, apparently following the earlier ethnological studies of the Stoic Posidonius.[19] Moses, he says, was an Egyptian priest opposed to animal worship and devoted to the one God who could be called "heaven" or "cosmos" or "the nature of what exists." He led a large group of Jews to the site of Jerusalem and there erected a temple where the virtuous could receive revelations through dreams. This ideal religion, however, was corrupted—like all other religions, in Strabo's view—by his superstitious successors, who introduced dietary laws and circumcision. Tyrants among them led robbers against Syrians and Phoenicians.

Such a picture of Judaism may have been related to the ideas of emancipated Hellenistic Jews who viewed their religion as universal and in some cases abandoned its particular injunctions. Such Jews were denounced by Philo of Alexandria, but his own tendency to explain away the law by allegorizing its ritual requirements pointed in the same direction. In general, Jews who lived outside Palestine, at least before the war of 66–70, were loyal subjects of the Roman empire and were often deeply concerned with Graeco-Roman culture. Within Palestine, however, Jewish attitudes toward Rome were often more hostile.[20]

II·PALESTINIAN PROBLEMS

Like most of the eastern Mediterranean world, Palestine had been deeply troubled during the years in which Rome rose to mastery. The Seleucid king Antiochus IV Epiphanes had endeavored to make himself king of Egypt as well, but in 168 a Roman legate ordered him to withdraw and he did so. On his way back through Palestine he decided to reform the Jewish religion and to unite his kingdom on the basis of Hellenism; at first he was given encouragement by the Hellenizing high priests at Jerusalem. In 167 he went further. The practice of Judaism was forbidden, and over the altar in the temple court was placed a new Greek altar, dedicated to Zeus Olympios. The temple thus became a temple of Zeus Olympios—to whose worship the king was devoted; he had been trying to complete the great temple at Athens,

---

[17] Cf. K. Lake in K. Lake and F. J. F. Jackson, *The Beginnings of Christianity* V (London, 1933), 74-96.
[18] Seneca, frag. 42 Haase (from Augustine, *De civ. dei* 6, 11).
[19] Strabo, *Geog.* 16, 2, 35-37.
[20] Cf. R. Loewe in *Journal of Jewish Studies* 12 (1961), 123.

finally finished only under Hadrian.[21] Resistance arose with guerrilla warfare under the leadership of Judas Maccabaeus ("the hammer") who was able to recapture Jerusalem and rededicate the temple on 25 Chislev 164.[22]

These events were described not only by Jewish historians but also by the author of the apocalyptic book of Daniel, in which current events were depicted under the guise of prophecy. Antiochus' rebuke by the Roman legate is described thus: "ships of the Kittim shall come against him, and he shall be afraid and withdraw, and shall turn back and be enraged and take action against the holy covenant" (11:30). As Epiphanes he "shall magnify himself above every god" (11:36), and the daily sacrifices will be abolished for 2,300 evenings and mornings; "then the sanctuary shall be restored to its rightful state" (8:14). The book is important not only for its picture of contemporary history but also for its predictions of the future. After the rededication of the temple "the kingdom and the dominion and the greatness of the kingdoms under the whole heaven shall be given to the people of the saints of the Most High; their kingdom shall be an everlasting kingdom, and all dominions shall serve and obey them" (7:27). The author also predicted attacks from Egypt and from the north (11:40 ff.) and therefore wrote before Antiochus' death, east of the Euphrates, in 163.

For our purposes we need not describe the struggle of the Jewish state to maintain its independence during the century after the death of Antiochus. It is enough to say that many Jews were not satisfied with the political character of the high priests who ruled at Jerusalem, some with the title of king. Among those who withdrew from ordinary social life were the covenanters who established an ascetic community at Qumran by the Dead Sea, denounced the wicked priests of Jerusalem, and awaited the coming of the true anointed king.[23] In 63 there were two contenders for power in Jerusalem, one the high priest Hyrcanus II, the other his brother Aristobulus II. The Roman general Pompey took the city, abolished the monarchy, and subordinated Hyrcanus to the legate of the new province of Syria. Once more, apocalyptic writings reflected some of these events. The 17th of the *Psalms of Solomon* criticized the last of the kings, killed or exiled by a foreign conqueror. This conqueror himself would be driven out, however, by a Jewish monarch, the coming "son of David." The second psalm alluded to Pompey even more clearly. A ruler came from the west and broke down the wall of Jerusalem with a battering-ram (in 63); later he himself was killed in a boat (off Pelusium in 48). These

---

[21] Polybius 26, 1, 10; Livy 41, 20, 8; Velleius Paterculus 1, 10, 1.

[22] Cf. E. Bickermann, *Der Gott der Makkabäer* (Berlin, 1937).

[23] For a factual summary with English bibliography cf. M. Mansoor, *The Dead Sea Scrolls* (Grand Rapids, Mich., 1964); for the important point that the covenanters' expectations were already realized in part in their community, see H.-W. Kuhn, *Enderwartung und gegenwärtiges Heil. Untersuchungen zu den Gemeindeliedern von Qumran mit einem Anhang über Eschatologie und Gegenwart in der Verkündigung Jesu* (Göttingen, 1966).

psalms, like the others, look forward to the rise of a new national ruler, a descendant of David.

The king who came, however, was not Jewish but Idumaean. He was the son of the finance minister of the high priest Hyrcanus—a finance minister important enough to be murdered in 43 B.C. after the death of his protector Julius Caesar. The son, Herod, had already been made governor of Galilee in 47, and after Caesar's death he continued to advance. Mark Antony made him tetrarch in 41; the triumvirs gave him the title of king in 37. For nearly a decade he maintained and increased his influence while Octavian and Antony struggled for supremacy; he gave Antony the highly practical advice: "kill Cleopatra."[24] Within a few years after Actium he was able to persuade Octavian that he would be a valuable ally, and his kingship was confirmed at Rome. The value of his kingdom was considerable; estimates based on Josephus suggest that it was about 1,200 talents[25] or about 5½ million denarii.[26] The income of his grandson Herod Agrippa was slightly more than twice as large,[27] reflecting some currency depreciation and more prosperity.

The reign of Herod was long and bloody. It is fully described by Josephus but is also touched upon in an apocalypse, the *Assumption of Moses*. This book depicted first a dynasty of kings and priests, then the thirty-four-year reign of an "insolent king" (37–4 B.C.) and the reign of his children, during which a great king of the west would bring terror upon the land. Various signs and portents would then precede Israel's reign over all mankind. Expectations of this kind were not confined to Palestinian Jews alone. The Alexandrian philosopher Philo clearly set forth his expectation of God's coming victory over men and wild beasts alike,[28] and of divine vengeance on the enemies of the Jewish people. A divine sign, visible to the Jews alone, would appear, and they would be given their freedom. Cities would be rebuilt, the desert would be inhabited, and all the land would be fertile.[29] Some of what Philo says about the future form of government is close to what Polybius had said of the Roman state, but in his view the law of the future would be that of Moses.[30]

At Herod's death, probably in 4 B.C., his kingdom was divided among his three sons. Herod Antipas was given Galilee and Peraea (east of the Jordan) while Herod Philippos received Gaulanitis, Trachonitis, Batanaea, and Panias. Herod Archelaus was made tetrarch of Judaea, Samaria, and Idumaea, with

[24] Josephus, *Ant.* 15, 191.
[25] *Ibid.*, 17, 318-23; cf. F. C. Grant, *The Economic Background of the Gospels* (Oxford, 1926), 89; F. W. Heichelheim in T. Frank, ed., *An Economic Survey of Ancient Rome* IV (Baltimore, 1938), 235.
[26] Cf. Heichelheim, *op. cit.*, 211, citing Pollux 9, 86.
[27] Josephus, *Ant.* 19, 352.
[28] Philo, *Praem.* 79-94.
[29] *Exsecr.* 165-71.
[30] H. A. Wolfson, *Philo* (Cambridge, Mass., 1947), II, 419-26.

Augustus' half-promise that he might hope to receive the title of king. In A.D. 6, however, a mission from Jerusalem accused him of mismanagement, and the emperor took steps against him at once, confiscating his property.

Two Roman officials with their administrative staffs immediately arrived in Jerusalem. The more important of them was P. Sulpicius Quirinius, legate of the province of Syria to which Judaea was once more attached. He had been consul in 12 B.C. and subsequently legate of Galatia, there engaged in subjugating fierce mountain tribes.[31] Now he had just been made legate of Syria; one of his duties was to take a census not only in Judaea but elsewhere in Syria as well. An inscription tells how a military prefect under his orders took the census in Apamea, finding 117,000 local citizens.[32] Though Quirinius was a senator, he was charged with the task of expropriating Archelaus' estate. Presumably much of the work was done by the other official, an equestrian named Coponius, who had been named prefect of Judaea.[33] Like other prefects empowered to maintain law and order and to collect taxes, he had the right to impose the death penalty, as Josephus notes.[34] He also issued coinage of his own presumably at Caesarea; a coin from the 36th year of Augustus (A.D. 5–6) bears the legend "of Caesar" and depicts a palm tree with two bunches of fruit.

Many Jews naturally viewed this census without enthusiasm, even though earlier censuses must obviously have been taken under Herod. Now a certain Judas from Gaulanitis, joined by a Pharisee named Saddouk (= Zadok), called for freedom from the slavery being imposed by the Romans. Their supporters even threatened to burn the temple, presumably because the high priest did not join them. Another rebel was Judas of Galilee, an Essene probably related to the Dead Sea covenanters. He insisted that the only ruler and master was God; no human being could be regarded as "master" (cf. Matt. 23:8-10). He resolutely refused to make a poll tax declaration or to pay "tribute" to the Romans.[35] In spite of resistance, put down by Roman troops, the census was completed in 6–7 and the high priest, whose position had been ambiguous, was removed from office. In his place Quirinius appointed Ananos, son of Seth, who remained in office for nine years.[36] The period immediately subsequent was one in which prefects and high priests seem to have been seeking a *modus vivendi,* without much success. In the year 15, however, the new emperor Tiberius sent Valerius Gratus to Judaea as

[31] Cf. R. K. Sherk, *The Legates of Galatia from Augustus to Diocletian* (Baltimore, 1952), 21-24.

[32] *ILS* 2683.

[33] A. H. M. Jones, *Studies in Roman Government and Law* (New York, 1960), 115-25, especially 119; for Pontius Pilate as prefect, see below.

[34] Josephus, *Bell.* 2, 117.

[35] Josephus, *Bell.* 2, 118; *Ant.* 18, 23.

[36] *Ant.* 18, 26.

prefect, and he, after appointing three high priests in as many years, finally settled on a reliable candidate, Josephus also known as Caiaphas. He was a son-in-law of Ananos and held office until the year 36.

During this period and thereafter the functions of the high priest were both liturgical and political. Josephus lists twenty-eight high priests who held office from the reign of Herod until the destruction of the temple in the year 70.[37] Of these, six were appointed by Herod the Great, three by his son Archelaus, and one by the legate of Syria. Four more were appointed by the prefect Valerius Gratus, two by Lucius Vitellius, legate of Syria between 35 and 39. Thereafter, the appointments were made by kings descended from Herod: three by Agrippa I, two by Herod of Chalcis, and six by Agrippa II. Of these high priests no fewer than seven were members of the family of Ananos, obviously in high favor with Romans and client kings.

A popular reaction to this family and a few others like it was expressed in the Babylonian Talmud. "They are high priests and their sons are treasurers and their sons-in-law are superintendents, and their servants beat the people with sticks."[38] During the early years of their ascendancy a military expert among the Dead Sea sectarians was preparing a document entitled "The War of the Sons of Light against the Sons of Darkness." As a son of light, he expected a period of mobilization which would last for six years, followed by twenty-nine years of fighting. The army of the Sons of Light would comprise 28,000 infantry and 6,000 cavalry and, in addition, countless angels. After an extended series of campaigns the final battle would result in complete annihilation of the enemy—Romans and their supporters—and in the victory of God.[39]

It would appear that the earlier Roman prefects were not unduly perturbed by nationalist aspirations among the Jews. On the other hand, the prefect Pontius Pilatus, sent out in 26 when Tiberius' adviser Sejanus, militantly anti-Jewish, was at the peak of his power, seems to have understood his mission as one of pacification. That he ruled entirely on behalf of Rome is clear enough from the Tiberieum which he dedicated at Caesarea, a building which bore his own name: [PON] TIVS PILATVS/[PRAEF] ECTVS IVDA [EA]E.[40] And unlike his predecessors, who struck coins with religiously neutral or ambiguous representations, he did not hesitate to offer depictions of a *simpulum* (a ladle used for sacrificial libations) and a *lituus* (the staff used by an augur).[41] He brought Roman standards bearing images into the city of Jerusalem and

---

[37] *Ant.* 20, 250. The 28th was chosen by "the people" during the siege.

[38] *Pesachim* 57a.

[39] On this document see Y. Yadin, *The Scroll of the War of the Sons of Light Against the Sons of Darkness* (Oxford, 1962).

[40] A. Frova in *Rendiconti dell' Istituto Lombardo, Classe di Lettere* 95 (Milan, 1961), 419-34; cf. *L'année épigraphique* 1964, 39; J. Vardeman in *JBL* 81 (1962), 70-71.

[41] A. Reifenberg, *Ancient Jewish Coins* (ed. 2, Jerusalem, 1947), 56 (nos. 131-33, from the years 29-30 to 31-32).

placed Roman votive shields in the old palace of Herod; he compelled the priests to contribute the sacred Korban money, trust funds belonging to the temple, for the construction of an aqueduct into Jerusalem.[42] According to Luke 13:1–2 Jesus had heard of men from Galilee whose blood Pilate had mingled with their sacrifices.

Another disturbance while Pilate was prefect was concerned with the case of Jesus of Nazareth in Galilee. Jesus had been asked by Jewish officials what the source of his authority was, and he replied by referring to John the Baptist, executed by Herod Antipas in about the year 28. Adherents of the Herodian family had asked him whether or not the poll tax should be paid to the Romans; his answer could at least be understood as indicating that Jews who were willing to use Roman money bearing the emperor's image and titles should pay Roman taxes. He had cleansed the temple in a manner reminiscent of Judas Maccabaeus and had predicted its destruction. His opponents therefore accused him of leading the nation astray, of forbidding the payment of the Roman poll-tax, and of claiming to be the anointed king.[43] Jesus was arrested. According to the relatively late Gospel of John, Pilate was still willing to release him, since the evidence was conflicting, but Jesus' opponents insisted that if Pilate did so he would not be "Caesar's friend."[44] John describes the chief priests as stating, "We have no king but Caesar." Whatever the phrasing may owe to the evangelist, the attitude depicted is historically correct. Jesus was therefore crucified by the Roman authorities, with the cooperation of the high priest their appointee, probably in the year 30.[45]

Six years later a Samaritan prophet gathered a great crowd on Mount Gerizim, claiming that there Moses had buried sacred vessels.[46] Pilate immediately sent troops against them, killing many and imprisoning more. L. Vitellius, legate of Syria and father of a later emperor, intervened, sending Pilate to Rome (thence to exile) and removing Caiaphas from office. At the Passover festival in 37 he gave back the high priest's robe to the temple; it had been in Roman custody since A.D. 6. He retained his right of appointing the high priests, however, and exercised it three times.

Thus far we have considered the fate of the territories left by Herod to his son Archelaus. His two brothers at first fared better. Herod Philip was loyal to the Romans; thus he rebuilt Paneas by the source of the Jordan river and named it Caesarea (Philippi, cf. Mark 8:27) and colonized Bethsaida by the lake of Galilee, calling it Julias after the wife of Tiberius. He was the

[42] Josephus Bell. 2, 169-77; Ant. 18, 55-62; cf. C. H. Kraeling in HTR 35 (1942), 263-89.

[43] Answers and actions of Jesus: Mark 11:15-17, 27-33; 12:13-17; 13:2; accusations: Luke 23:2.

[44] John 19:12; but the title philokaisar was reserved for client kings.

[45] John 19:15. On the many problems involved cf. P. Winter, On the Trial of Jesus (Berlin, 1961).

[46] Josephus, Ant. 18, 85-90; a political-eschatological move, 2 Macc. 2:4-8.

first Jewish ruler to portray the Roman emperor on his coins, doing so at the time when Archelaus was being deposed. He died peacefully, apparently in 37. Herod Antipas had a stormier career. He too built cities in the emperor's honor, but his marital troubles aroused criticism. At first married to an Arabian princess, he became infatuated with his sister-in-law Herodias and married her. For this reason he was denounced by the prophet John the Baptist, whom he executed, and acquired the enduring hostility of his first wife's father, Aretas IV of Arabia. In 39 the ambitious Herodias persuaded him to ask the emperor Caligula for the title of king. At this point her brother Agrippa, grandson of Herod the Great and successor to Herod Philip, brought charges against him before the emperor. It could be shown that he had conspired with Sejanus against Tiberius and that he was now undertaking negotiations with the king of Parthia. Investigations showed that the arsenals of Antipas contained arms for 70,000 troops, and he was thereupon exiled to Gaul, voluntarily accompanied by his wife. His territories and revenues were assigned to Agrippa.

The career of Agrippa was almost as dramatic as that of his grandfather. He was born in 10 B.C. and at the age of three lost his father, executed by Herod the Great. In spite of this adversity, he was brought up at Rome with Drusus, son of the emperor Tiberius, and remained there until the death of Drusus, in A.D. 23. During the next thirteen years he sought for patrons and ran up enormous debts, finally becoming tutor to the future emperor Caligula. Despised by Tiberius, he was imprisoned when he expressed his hope that Caligula would soon come to the throne but freed six months later when his hope was realized. At this point Caligula gave him the tetrarchy of Herod Philip with additional lands to the west of Damascus. He also received the title of king and a gold chain equal in weight to the iron chain he had borne in prison. In the autumn of 38 he went to Palestine, passing through Alexandria and inadvertently arousing anti-Jewish outbreaks there. Agrippa's intrigues resulted in the exile and eventual execution of the prefect of Egypt who, in his opinion, had not dealt strongly with the anti-Jewish mobs.

The accession of Gaius Caligula had been hailed with unrestrained enthusiasm: an inscription from Cyzicus on the sea of Marmara described it as the rising of the new sun and mentioned prayer for his everlasting reign.[47] Jews too had offered congratulations, and the temple at Jerusalem was the scene of the first sacrifice made in his behalf.[48] The situation began to change in the summer of 38 when his favorite sister Drusilla died and was deified as the goddess Panthea; a Roman senator swore that he had witnessed her ascent into heaven.[49] By 40 Caligula had become convinced of his own deity.

[47] *SIG*³ 798; cf. the loyalty oaths, *ibid.*, 797 and *ILS* 190.
[48] Philo, *Leg. ad Gaium* 231-32.
[49] Dio 59, 11, 3; she is called *diva* in *ILS* 196 and 197, "the new Aphrodite" in *ILS* 8789.

He tried to convert the temple of Apollo at Miletus to worship of himself, and at Rome he erected two temples of his own.[50]

Not unnaturally he was displeased when his prefect at Jamnia in Palestine reported that Jews had destroyed a brick altar erected to him there. His response was to order a colossal gilt statue of himself set up in the temple at Jerusalem.[51] Instructions to this effect were sent to P. Petronius, the new legate of Syria; he was ordered to have the statue cast outside Judaea (Petronius chose Sidon for the manufacture) and brought to Jerusalem under the escort of two legions.[52] That spring a great crowd of Jews met Petronius near Ptolemais and begged him to delay while they sent an embassy to the emperor. The legate agreed on condition that he himself would report to Caligula, and in a letter he argued that delay was essential, both for finishing the statue and for harvesting the crops; riots were to be expected.[53] Though the emperor was enraged, he replied diplomatically, merely urging Petronius to expedite matters.[54] (Josephus adds that he also threatened the legate with the death penalty.)[55] In the autumn Agrippa was at Rome again and was able to persuade Caligula to abandon or at least postpone his scheme. Petronius was instructed not to make any innovations in regard to "the temple of the Jews" but to protect imperial altars, temples, and statues anywhere outside Jerusalem.[56]

Caligula's letter to the legate crossed one in which Petronius asked permission not to erect the statue, and the furious emperor ordered him to commit suicide because of his insubordination.[57] Fortunately for him, this order reached him at Antioch only after news of the murder of the emperor on January 24, 41. The last days of Caligula were marked by insane schemes. According to Philo, he ordered a new colossal statue made at Rome, intending to land it himself on the Palestinian coast and rededicate the temple at Jerusalem in honor of Zeus Epiphanes Neos Gaios.[58] Suetonius also mentioned this journey, claiming that before embarking he intended to put to death a select group of senators and equestrians. Among his effects were found lists of those destined for the sword and the dagger, along with a huge chest full of poisons which, when dumped into the sea by Claudius, killed many fish.[59]

Agrippa, still at Rome, was among those who urged the senate to recognize Claudius as emperor. In the spring of 41 he received his reward when the senate confirmed Claudius' decision to maintain him as ruler of all the ter-

[50] Dio 59, 28, 1-2.
[51] Philo, *Leg.* 200-203.
[52] *Leg.* 207; 222.
[53] *Ibid.*, 246-53.
[54] *Ibid.*, 260.
[55] *Bell.* 2, 203.
[56] Philo, *Leg.* 333-34.
[57] Josephus, *Ant.* 18, 304.
[58] *Leg.* 337-38.
[59] *Gaius* 49, 2-3.

ritories given him by Caligula and, in addition, Judaea and Samaria as well. He returned in triumph to Jerusalem and placed in the temple the gold chain once given him by Caligula. At the same time he offered sacrifices in the temple and paid the expenses of many Nazirites, thus demonstrating his devotion to the national religion.[60] One of his coins, presumably issued at this time, shows how he viewed the source of his power. On the obverse the king is portrayed as veiled and sacrificing, crowned by two female figures of whom one is Victory. The superscription reads "King Agrippa, Caesar's friend [*philokaisar*]." On the reverse there are two clasped hands within a wreath. The wording is nearly illegible, but it certainly contains references to king Agrippa, the Roman senate and people, and an alliance.[61] On this alliance was based the peace and prosperity of his kingdom.

Agrippa's domestic policy was one of almost complete success. He showed favor to the Pharisees and was hailed by temple worshipers as their brother; the occasion was his reading from the law at the festival of Tabernacles in the autumn of 41.[62] When young pagans at Dora on the coast erected a statue of Claudius in a synagogue he persuaded the legate of Syria to punish them and to remind the city council to enforce Claudius' new decree on religious liberty for the Jews.[63] (Claudius was concerned with maintaining peace, not religious freedom for Jews as such. He permitted Jews to observe their customs at Alexandria but refused to admit Jews to sail there from Syria or Egypt.[64] "Since the Jews constantly rioted at the instigation of Chrestus, he expelled them from Rome."[65]) On the other hand, Agrippa encountered some difficulties within his kingdom. A Pharisee stirred up trouble while the king was at Caesarea and claimed that as a violator of the law he should not be allowed to enter the temple. The king summoned him to Caesarea and gave him a seat in the theater next to himself. Unable to cite evidence, the Pharisee remained silent and was rewarded with gifts.[66] Harsher treatment was given to two of the principal followers of Jesus. During "the days of unleavened bread" Agrippa had James the son of Zebedee beheaded; when this move met with popular approval, presumably because Christian Jews refused to join others in recognizing Agrippa as the true king of Israel, he proceeded to have Peter put in prison, though he soon escaped (Acts 12:2-19).

Agrippa's plans for the defense and extension of his kingdom were frustrated by the unsympathetic legate of Syria C. Vibius Marsus, in office from 42 to 44. After the legate reported that the king was planning to build

[60] Josephus, *Ant.* 19, 293-96.
[61] Reifenberg, *op. cit.*, 47, no. 63.
[62] Mishnah, *Sotah* 7, 8 (cf. *Bikkurim* 3, 4).
[63] Josephus, *Ant.* 19, 299-311.
[64] H. I. Bell, *Jews and Christians in Egypt* (London, 1924), 1-37.
[65] Suetonius, *Claudius* 25, 4; Acts 18, 2 (in either 41 or 49). The word "Chrestus" suggests messianic conflicts.
[66] Josephus, *Ant.* 19, 332-34.

a new wall to the north of Jerusalem, the work was halted by an imperial letter.[67] When Agrippa convened a conference of the client kings of the eastern frontier at Tiberias, the legate suspected that they were discussing not only mutual friendship but mutual security as well. He abruptly intervened and ordered them to return home.[68] In 44 the king instituted games at Caesarea, perhaps in honor of Claudius' triumph over the Britons and thus in proof of his loyalty. On the second day he was hailed as divine but a fatal ailment soon ended his reign.[69]

Lamentation over Agrippa's death was not universal. Christian Jews were not unhappy, and according to Josephus the people of Caesarea and the Roman troops garrisoned there greeted the news with undisguised pleasure. As a client king, Agrippa had been rather too independent; and though Claudius had intended to confer the kingdom upon the seventeen-year-old Agrippa II, then at Rome, his secretariat of freedmen persuaded him that Judaea could best be administered by equestrian procurators. Presumably Vibius Marsus gave the same counsel.

The first procurator under the new arrangement was Cuspius Fadus, who immediately suppressed incipient revolt by the employment of execution, imprisonment, and exile. He also proposed to demonstrate Roman mastery by taking into custody the high priest's robe, in Jewish hands for the past eight years. Revolt threatened, but the situation was eased when Fadus, consulting with a new legate of Syria, allowed a Jewish embassy to proceed to Rome. There the young Agrippa supported the ambassadors, and Claudius issued a rescript on June 28, 45, permitting "the whole nation of the Jews" to retain the robe.[70] This move did not bring social unrest to an end. A few years later a prophet named Theudas gathered many followers by the Jordan river, since at his command the waters would part and they could march through, presumably toward Jerusalem. Fadus did not wait but sent a detachment of cavalry to the scene. Many of Theudas' followers were killed before crossing the river; his own head was displayed at Jerusalem as a warning against revolt.[71] It would appear that he had intended to duplicate the feat of the Old Testament hero Joshua, who crossed the Jordan on dry ground (Josh. 3:7-17). As Joshua had conquered the Canaanites, so Theudas probably intended to drive out the Romans.

Around the same time Christian prophets left Jerusalem for Antioch, perhaps in order to dissociate themselves from Theudas' revolt, and there one of them exercised his powers by predicting a great famine "over all the world" (Acts 11:27-30). He may have been assisted by observation of the sharply

[67] Ibid., 326-27.
[68] Ibid., 338-41.
[69] Ibid., 343-50; Acts 12:20-23.
[70] Josephus, Ant. 20, 11-14.
[71] Ibid., 97-98. He is mentioned but misdated in Acts 5:36. On him and other "Zealot prophets" see M. Hengel, Die Zeloten (Leiden-Cologne, 1961), 235-318.

rising price of wheat as speculators in Egypt and elsewhere anticipated shortages.[72] The famine actually took place under Tiberius Julius Alexander, nephew of the Alexandrian philosopher Philo,[73] and was probably accompanied by revolt: the procurator crucified two sons of the old rebel Judas of Galilee.[74]

Unrest continued under Ventidius Cumanus (48–52), whose troops twice offended Jewish religious sentiment and provoked rioting. His term of office came to an end after Galileans were murdered by Samaritans and Samaritans made reprisals. The legate of Syria found that Cumanus had been taking bribes from Samaritans. He impartially executed leaders both Samaritan and Jewish and banished the procurator from Judaea.[75]

At this point the high priest Jonathan, on embassy to Rome, appealed for the influential freedman M. Antonius Felix as procurator. Formerly married to the granddaughter of Mark Antony and Cleopatra,[76] Felix tried to consolidate his power in Judaea by marrying the young daughter of Agrippa I—even though she was already wife of the king of Emesa. His administration, however, was not a success. "Dagger men," according to rumor instigated by Felix himself, murdered the high priest.[77] Religious-minded rebels led crowds into the desert, promising them "wonders and signs" or "signs of freedom."[78] Another prophet from Egypt led a crowd to the Mount of Olives near Jerusalem, promising them that at his command the city walls would fall and they could enter. Cavalry and infantry sent by Felix, however, killed 400 and captured 200 of them. The Egyptian himself fled. This is why a Roman tribune who later arrested the apostle Paul supposed that he might have caught "that Egyptian who recently stirred up revolt and led the four thousand 'dagger men' out into the desert" (Acts 21:38). The pattern the Egyptian was following was derived, once more, from the Old Testament. There it was Joshua who could make a city's walls collapse (Josh. 6:20) so that it could be taken and its inhabitants put to the sword. If the Egyptian is the "ben Stada" of rabbinic tradition, it is significant that he was confused with Jesus (Joshua) of Nazareth. After the failure of his revolt, says Josephus, charlatans and bandits worked together and attracted followers who were concerned with revolt and freedom.[79]

Under Felix's successor Porcius Festus (ca. 55–61) cavalry and infantry

---

[72] For papyrus evidence cf. K. S. Gapp in HTR 28 (1935), 258-65; on famines in general, R. MacMullen, Enemies of the Roman Order (Cambridge, Mass., 1966), 249-54.

[73] He was later prefect of Egypt (66-69) and Titus' chief of staff before Jerusalem in 70.

[74] Josephus, Ant. 20, 102.

[75] Ibid., 118-33.

[76] Tacitus, Hist. 5, 9, 3.

[77] Josephus, Bell. 2, 255-56; Ant. 20, 163-64.

[78] Bell. 2, 259; Ant. 20, 167-68.

[79] Bell. 2, 261-64; Ant. 20, 169-72.

once more sallied forth against a group which had expected to find "salvation" in the desert.[80] It was Festus who sent Paul to Rome because he was a Roman citizen (Acts 25:12). During his time there was a measure of tranquillity in Palestine; he was the only procurator who died in office.[81]

Perhaps around this time Christian Jews were being warned against taking part in movements of revolt. Mark 13:22 gives counsel against false messiahs and false prophets who show signs and wonders. Matthew 24:26 adds a warning against those who say, "Lo, he is in the desert," and instructs Christians not to go out.[82]

In 62, perhaps during the interval between the death of Festus and the arrival of his successor Lucceius Albinus in Judaea, the long-awaited portents began to appear. Before the feast of Passover a bright light illuminated the altar in the temple. Several weeks later, chariots and armed troops were seen in the clouds. At Pentecost the priests heard many voices saying, "Let us remove hence." At Tabernacles a peasant named Joshua began pronouncing apocalyptic woes against Jerusalem and the temple.[83] Certainly it was during the interregnum that Agrippa II, since 50 king of Chalcis, appointed Ananos, son of the earlier high priest, as high priest in Jerusalem. He convened an illegal meeting of the council and executed James the brother of Jesus.[84] A second-century Christian writer says that James had been accustomed to pray in the temple for divine forgiveness of the Jewish people. At Passover he openly proclaimed the coming of Jesus from heaven on the clouds; he was therefore thrown down from a height and stoned to death.[85] Though there are legendary details in the story, it reflects the circumstances of Jerusalem at the time.

When Albinus came on the scene he had the new high priest deposed, and his regime was marked by no more than the usual unrest. When he was recalled in 64, however, he proclaimed a general amnesty except for prisoners already under sentence of death; as Josephus pointed out, he thus filled the country with robbers and rebels.[86]

His successor Florus, whose wife was a close friend of the empress Poppaea, was primarily responsible for the outbreak of revolution.[87] In the spring of 66 the legate of Syria, C. Cestius Gallus, was informed that Florus had stolen seventeen talents from the temple treasury; at the same time baskets were being carried about Jerusalem with the ironic request to provide gifts for Florus. The procurator angrily entered Jerusalem with two cohorts, there

[80] *Bell.* 2, 259-60; *Ant.* 20, 188.
[81] *Ant.* 20, 197.
[82] See also Matt. 24:5; Luke 21:8.
[83] Josephus, *Bell.* 6, 290-306.
[84] *Ant.* 20, 200-202.
[85] Eusebius, *H.E.* 2, 23, 4-18; cf. Mishnah, *Sanhedrin* 6, 4.
[86] *Ant.* 20, 215.
[87] *Ibid.*, 20, 257.

crucifying a number of Jews including some of equestrian rank. Tension increased, and in July the son of a former high priest halted the daily sacrifices offered on behalf of the Roman emperor.[88] This action divided the Jewish community in two. Both Sadducees and Pharisees urged that the sacrifices be restored, but their appeal was disregarded. They then warned Florus of impending revolution, but he did not respond. Agrippa II sent three thousand cavalry to Jerusalem, but in August they laid down their arms.[89] Fire destroyed the palaces of the high priest and of three members of the Herodian family, and in September the high priest himself was murdered. Ten days later the Roman forces in Jerusalem surrendered. Only their commander escaped the subsequent massacre by promising to be circumcised.[90]

It was not until October that Cestius Gallus left Antioch with the Twelfth Legion and many auxiliaries, and early the next month his attempt to take the temple citadel was a failure. On his way back to Antioch he was attacked by Jewish guerrillas who let him escape only because he abandoned much of his equipment, later used by them against Rome. He lost 5,680 of his 33,000 troops, and his request that Rome remove Florus from office was answered by an order for his own recall.[91]

The revolt was far more serious than had been supposed, and greater force was obviously needed. The experienced general Vespasian, who had successfully fought the Britons and had been proconsul of Africa, was given command of three legions and their auxiliary troops, about 40,000 men in all. In addition, the client kings of Chalcis, Commagene, Emesa, and Nabataea supplied another 15,000 troops. In the spring of 67 Vespasian advanced along the coast from Antioch to Ptolemais, where he awaited the arrival of his son Titus with the Legio XV Apollinaris from Alexandria. During the subsequent six months all Palestine north of Caesarea was recaptured. Two legions went into winter quarters at Caesarea, another at Scythopolis, south of Galilee on the Jordan.

Jerusalem meanwhile suffered a reign of terror, and the revolutionists spent much of their force in internecine warfare. Vespasian counted on this development and, though his generals urged him to take Jerusalem, preferred to wait while simply reducing the countryside. An expedition begun in March 68 carefully avoided Jerusalem while capturing almost all the surrounding area. Early in the summer news came to him—perhaps not unexpectedly—that Nero had committed suicide on June 9 and had been succeeded by Galba. As Galba was replaced by Otho, and then by Vitellius, Vespasian watched and waited, leaving Caesarea only in June 69 to put down

[88] Josephus, *Bell.* 2, 409; cf. Mishnah, *Taanith* 4, 6; C. Roth in *HTR* 53 (1960), 93-97.
[89] *Bell.* 2, 411-21. The surrender was investigated at Rome without result (Josephus, *Vita* 407-9).
[90] *Bell.* 2, 454.
[91] *Bell.* 2, 558.

the vestiges of revolt in Judaea. "His friends were most ready and even urgent," says Suetonius,[92] but he took no action until, on July 1, Tiberius Alexander, now prefect of Egypt, followed the lead of troops in Italy and ordered his legions to swear allegiance to Vespasian. Within a fortnight all the legions in Syria had followed this example, and the king of Parthia offered 40,000 archers. Vespasian refused the offer but moved to Alexandria where, in control of Rome's grain supply, he could wait once more while his supporters in Italy brought Vitellius' reign to an end.

By the spring of 70 his power was sufficiently secure for him to give his son Titus command of four legions and the troops of the client kings; Tiberius Alexander was Titus' chief of staff and presumably liaison officer for the emperor. Shortly before Passover the Roman army reached the city. A long siege, punctuated by assaults with battering rams, ended when Roman troops entered the sanctuary of the temple and, intentionally or not, destroyed it by fire. On the 9th-10th of Ab (= approximately August) the temple burned; resistance continued in the upper city for another month, but the victory was complete.[93] John of Gischala, leader of the most extreme revolutionists, was sentenced to life imprisonment as a penalty harsher than death. In the summer of 71 Vespasian and Titus jointly celebrated a great triumph at Rome.[94]

Three fortresses still had to be reduced. Those at Herodeion, near Jerusalem, and Machaerus were soon taken, but Masada, where the Roman garrison had been massacred as the war begun, held out until April 73, when the last defenders committed suicide.[95]

The coinage issued during the war presumably reflects the rebel's aspirations. On the silver of the years 1-5 (= 66/67-70/71) we find the superscriptions "Jerusalem the Holy" and "Shekel of Israel." On the bronze of years 2 and 3 there is "Freedom of Zion," while in the year 4, when bronze was driving out silver, there are references to "Redemption of Zion." It has been suggested that the "redemption" coins were struck by the party of the rebel leader Simon bar Gioras; in the year 4 he "had taken over most of the territory still in the hands of the insurgents." "Redemption" may well imply the existence of messianic hopes among his followers.[96] If there were such hopes, they were broken when the city fell. Simon was taken to Rome and strangled during the imperial triumph.

Certainly apocalyptic eschatology played a role in the events of the war. It

[92] *Vespasian* 6, 1; cf. G. E. F. Chilver in *JRS* 47 (1957), 29-35.
[93] Temple worship may have continued later, however; cf. K. W. Clark in *New Testament Studies* 6 (1959-60), 269-80.
[94] According to Josephus (*Bell.* 6, 420), 97,000 Jews had been taken prisoner and there were more than a million dead.
[95] Cf. Y. Yadin, *Masada* (London-New York, 1966).
[96] A. Reifenberg, *Ancient Jewish Coins* (ed. 2, Jerusalem, 1947), nos. 137-150, for earlier discoveries; B. Kanael in *Biblical Archaeologist* 26 (1963), 59, for later.

was noted that a sword-shaped star stood over the city and that a comet appeared for a whole year.[97] At the end there were prophets in Jerusalem who urged the people to climb to the roof of the temple, where God would provide miraculous signs of deliverance.[98] There had been predictions, perhaps based on Old Testament prophecy, that from the orient would come a king to reign over the world. The captured Jewish general Josephus seems to have been the first to refer the prediction to Vespasian.[99]

In any event, it was Vespasian who came to the throne and issued a remarkable number of coins to commemorate the triumph, with superscriptions such as IVDAEA CAPTA and DEVICTA IVDAEA.[100] They belonged to the systematic publicity which Rome provided for the victory. Along with it went the inscription once carved on the triumphal arch of Titus: "With his father's instructions, advice, and favor, he conquered the people of the Jews and destroyed the city of Jerusalem, either attacked in vain or not attempted at all by all previous generals, kings, and nations."[101] The inaccuracy of the claim doubtless meant little to those who read it. In fact, Titus had taken Jerusalem.

According to Eusebius, the Christians had left the city, warned by a divine revelation, even before the war.[102] Presumably they shared the views of those Essenes who when taken prisoner by the Romans refused "to blaspheme their legislator or to eat what was forbidden them."[103] Presumably they would have welcomed the selection of a high priest by lot[104]—but not, perhaps, under Zealot auspices. If they now lived at Pella in Peraea, they were safe from the struggles in Jerusalem and could enjoy Roman protection after the summer of 68, when Vespasian's troops occupied the area and destroyed Qumran.

It is questionable, however, whether the departure of the Christian community as a whole has any basis in fact. More probably, there were some Christian refugees from Jerusalem who settled at Pella, while the community as a whole remained and survived the war. Apart from other arguments,[105] it seems significant that Hegesippus, well acquainted at least with the legendary traditions about the church of Jerusalem, viewed the church as continuing there without a break and becoming involved in heresy because of its close

---

[97] *Bell.* 6, 289. At Rome the comet was taken to portend doom for Vitellius; cf. Dio 64, 8, 1; F. H. Cramer, *Astrology in Roman Law and Politics* (Philadelphia, 1954), 135.
[98] *Bell.* 6, 285-86.
[99] *Ibid.*, 3, 400-402; 351-52; 6, 312-13; cf. Tacitus, *Hist.* 5, 13; Suetonius, *Vesp.* 4, 5.
[100] H. St. J. Hart in *JTS* 3 (1952), 172-98.
[101] *ILS* 264.
[102] *H. E.* 3, 5, 3.
[103] Josephus, *Bell.* 2, 152.
[104] *Ibid.*, 4, 154.
[105] S. G. F. Brandon, *Jesus and the Zealots* (New York, 1967), 208-20.

relations with Jewish sectarianism.[106] According to Eusebius, perhaps after Hegesippus, all the bishops of Jerusalem to the year 135 were Jews.[107] We may suppose, then, that the Jewish-Christian church of Jerusalem continued to exist after the year 70, but that its influence was greatly diminished.[108]

After Vespasian's triumph at Rome he provided that the annual tax of half a shekel previously paid by adult male Jews to the temple at Jerusalem was to be valued at two denarii and paid to the treasury of Saturn in the capital.[109] As long as the fortresses in Judaea held out, however, the idea of revolt remained alive. At Alexandria rebel leaders urged Jews to assert their freedom, to view the Romans as no better than themselves, and to look upon God as their only master.[110] In Cyrene a weaver led a group of visionaries into the desert to see "signs and apparitions." What appeared was the Roman police.[111] Thereafter, Jewish ideas of revolt were in abeyance until the time of Trajan.

Among Jewish or Judaizing Christians, however, veneration for Jerusalem as the holy city continued to be expressed. The Ebionites practised circumcision and observed the Jewish law and traditions; they venerated Jerusalem as being the "house of God."[112] It may that the Gnostic teacher Cerinthus held that the kingdom of Christ would be made manifest at Jerusalem,[113] although the critic who stated that this was his view was probably attacking the book of Revelation and ascribing a parody of its teaching to the Gnostic. More often Christians, following the precedent set by Paul (Gal. 4:26), thought of the true Jerusalem as "above"; Valentinian Gnostics called the heavenly Ogdoad by the name of Jerusalem."[114]

[106] Eusebius, *H. E.* 4, 22, 4.
[107] *Ibid.*, 4, 5, 1-4.
[108] We cannot agree with Brandon (*op. cit.*, 219) that it "disappeared without trace."
[109] *CPJ* II 160-229; a *procurator ad capitularia Iudaeorum*, *ILS* 1519; in the third century, Origen, *Ep. ad Africanum* 14 (PG 11, 81B).
[110] Josephus, *Bell.* 7, 409-11.
[111] *Ibid.*, 437-50.
[112] Irenaeus, *Adv. haer.* I, 26, 2; cf. H. J. Schoeps, *Theologie und Geschichte des Judenchristentums* (Tübingen, 1949), 141 (prayer toward Jerusalem).
[113] Gaius in Eusebius, *H. E.* 3, 28, 2.
[114] Irenaeus, *Adv. haer.* I, 5, 3. In addition, Gnosticizing Ebionites opposed the temple cultus, the temple itself, and the idea of a kingdom; cf. Schoeps, *op. cit.*, 219-47.

CHAPTER III
CHRISTIAN ORIGINS

I·JESUS

The Christian movement came into existence soon after the fifteenth year of the Roman emperor Tiberius Caesar when, according to the evangelist Luke (3:1-2) "the word of God came upon John the son of Zechariah in the wilderness." In Luke's view the date was so significant that he also mentioned the rulers of the various parts of Palestine. Pontius Pilate was governor of Judaea; Herod (Antipas) tetrarch of Galilee, his brother Philip tetrarch of Ituraea and Trachonitis, and Lysanias tetrarch of Abilene. The high priests were Annas (Ananos) and Caiaphas. Luke thus set the Christian movement, which he intended to describe not only in his gospel but also in the Acts of the Apostles, in a context provided by Roman administrators, client princes, and Jewish temple authorities. The fifteenth year of Tiberius lasted from August 19 in the year 28 to August 18 in 29. It was at this point that John, whose father was a priest at Jerusalem, began to announce the necessity of baptism in view of the impending judgment of God. His baptism was not unlike that already practiced by the Qumran sectarians, except that it apparently took place only once. It also resembled the later baptism of proselytes to Judaism; perhaps he was claiming that Israel needed repentance and cleansing as much as the gentiles did.[1] According to Luke, he also gave explicit directions for the behavior of those who came to him. He told the "crowds" to give what they did not need to those who needed it; he told collectors of poll taxes to exact no more than their instructions required; he told soldiers not to practice looting or extortion but to be content with their wages (3:10-14). Since he also criticized the marital mixup of Herod Antipas of Galilee, he was imprisoned and later beheaded.

Among those who came to be baptized by him was Jesus from Nazareth in Galilee. As he came up from baptism in the river Jordan he underwent an experience in which he came to recognize himself as called by God for a task not unlike that of John. The evangelist Mark summarizes his preaching thus: "The time has been completed and the reign of God has drawn close; repent and believe in the message" (1:15).

What Jesus taught, at first among the disciples whom he gathered, later more publicly, was the imminent coming of God's reign, so close that it could be viewed as already inaugurated and expressed in his miracles of healing (Matt. 12:28; Luke 11:20). Like other Jews, Jesus was concerned almost exclusively with God's relation to Israel, though much of his preaching was delivered in the half-Hellenized cities near the lake of Galilee. Ultimately it was unsuccessful there, and he pronounced woes upon Chorazin and Bethsaida. Had his miracles been worked in Tyre or Sidon, he believed, their pagan inhabitants would have repented. Similarly he rebuked the city of Capernaum, where he had spent much of his time (Matt. 11:20-24; Luke 10:13-15).

It was chiefly to the small group of disciples who followed him as he went through the countryside, and on some occasions were sent out on their own, that he spoke of the need for forgiveness and reconciliation, for love of enemies, for abandoning family and property, for becoming "like children." He encountered opposition among rigorist adherents to ritual laws, though in some respects his teaching (for example on marriage and in general on obedience to moral absolutes) was more rigorous than theirs. Much of what he said was expressed in short pronouncements or in parables, brief stories which caught the hearer's attention and challenged his imagination.

Jesus' proclamation of the coming reign of God provided impetus and sanction for his moral teaching, though in the later tradition it was complicated by references to a "son of man" perhaps identified with the being "like a son of man" in Daniel 7:13—a passage in which this personage symbolizes the Jewish people. There is a celestial "son of man" in the apocalyptic Book of Enoch, but he may reflect Christian speculations. In

[1] Cf. W. H. Brownlee in K. Stendahl, ed., *The Scrolls and the New Testament* (New York, 1957), 33-53.

any event, Jesus himself does not seem to have spoken of the future coming of the "son of man"; it was in later tradition that he was given this title.[2]

It would appear that the earlier stages of his mission took place only in Galilee, and that there he attracted the attention but perhaps not the support of many Jews. His proclamation of the immediate coming of the reign of God was presumably related, at least in the minds of many hearers, to the message of Judas of Galilee, little more than twenty years earlier. Judas too could be regarded as having announced the kingship of God—as against Roman rule and its attendant taxation. It cannot be said that Judas' proclamation was political while that of Jesus was religious. In both cases political and religious ideas were interwoven. As Brandon puts it, the principle on which Judas based his movement was "the absolute sovereignty of Yahweh, the god of Israel."[3] This principle was precisely the one proclaimed by Jesus. The difference, as far as our records inform us, was that Judas tried to prevent the taking of the Roman census while Jesus, at least during his Galilean ministry, paid no attention to the question of Roman rule. He was concerned with preparing the Jewish people for the coming of God's reign. It is true, as Brandon points out, that he is not said to have criticized those who advocated revolution or, for that matter, the sectarians at Qumran;[4] but this silence does not imply complete assent.

The mission of Jesus, it would appear, had more in common with the message of the book of Daniel, with its insistence upon the future action of God, than with the military activities of the Maccabees. Indeed, he had more in common, at least in this regard, with the visionaries of first-century Judaism than with such men as the Zealots and the followers of Judas of Galilee. C. H. Kraeling made the interesting though unprovable suggestion that the significant episode when Pilate had Roman standards brought into Jerusalem occurred in November or December of the year 26. The spring of 30, when Jesus was put to death in Jerusalem, was nearly three and a half years after this date; and the book of Daniel predicts the triumph of God after such a period of time. Be this as it may, we know that the Jewish revolts of 66-70 and 132-135 lasted for the same period of time. The coincidence may be that and nothing more; it may be due to one of the motifs of Jesus' mission forgotten by later Christians.[5]

One should also beware of claiming that the eschatological ideas of Jesus can be explained entirely in sociopolitical terms. As they are reflected in the gospels they do not give an impression of complete consistency, and the observations of C. F. D. Moule on "the influence of circumstances on the use of eschatological terms" should be applied not only to New Testament docu-

2 On this problem cf. N. Perrin, *Rediscovering the Teaching of Jesus* (London, 1967), 164-99 (also 259-60).

3 S. G. F. Brandon, *Jesus and the Zealots* (New York, 1967), 32.

4 *Ibid.*, 200-201.

5 Cf. C. H. Kraeling in *HTR* 35 (1942), 263-89.

ments but to New Testament traditions.[6] What we are about to say of his final mission is subject to such qualifications.

The climax of Jesus' mission was reached when with his disciples he went up from Galilee to Jerusalem, apparently soon before the feast of the Passover in the year 30. The purpose of this expedition has been endlessly debated, for the accounts in the gospels are contradictory. The materials presented in the Gospel of Mark, however, confirm the statement of Luke 19:11: "they supposed that the kingdom of God would appear immediately." Jesus predicted "hundredfold" rewards, including houses and fields; two disciples asked him for positions of honor in his "glory"; outside Jericho a blind beggar hailed him as "son of David," and as he entered the city in the manner of the king foretold by the prophet Zechariah his companions announced "the coming kingdom of our father David."[7] He cursed a fig tree which had not miraculously produced fruit out of season,[8] and proceeded to drive out those who sold and bought goods in the outer court of the temple, overturning the tables of the money-changers and the seats of those who sold doves for sacrifice.[9] With faith, he told his disciples, they could move the Mount of Olives, in conformity with the prediction of Zechariah.[10]

After his final meal with the disciples, apparently on the eve of the Passover, he was arrested by troops either belonging to the high priest or combined with Roman forces. A preliminary investigation by a Jewish court led to his arraignment before Pontius Pilate, the Roman prefect of Judaea, who sentenced him to death by crucifixion on the ground of sedition. Like even Herod Agrippa at Alexandria, and like the Jewish rebel-king under Trajan, he was mocked by the soldiers who hailed him as "king of the Jews."[11] Presumably the two "thieves" between whom he was crucified—with the *titulus* "the king of the Jews"—had something to do with the recent insurrection which Mark mentions (15:7). The word *lēstēs* translated "thieves" or "brigands" is frequently used of revolutionists by Josephus. The context of Jesus' execution was thus clearly the suppression of Jewish revolt against the rule of Romans and their collaborators in Judaea. Any proclamation of the coming reign of God immediately suggested to the Jerusalem authorities that the restoration of a Jewish kingdom was involved. Indeed, it may even be suggested that Jesus had accepted a preliminary anointing as king of Israel at Bethany, though in the tradition this anointing was reinterpreted as preliminary to his burial.[12] It is almost certain that at least one of Jesus' closest disciples was a

[6] *JTS* 15 (1964), 1-15.
[7] Mark 10:30, 37, 47-48; 11:7-10 (Zech. 9:9); cf., e.g., my article in *JBL* 67 (1948), 297-303.
[8] Mark 11:13-14.
[9] Mark 11:15-16.
[10] 11:23 (Zech. 14:4).
[11] Mark 15:16-20; cf. Philo, *In Flacc.* 36-39; H. A. Musurillo, *The Acts of the Pagan Martyrs* (Oxford, 1954), 49, 184.
[12] Mark 14:3-9.

Zealot, a member of the Jewish revolutionary group,[13] though this fact does not imply that Jesus advocated revolutionary action.

A most difficult feature in the tradition has to do with the conduct of Jesus' disciples at the time of his arrest. Those who arrested him were armed with swords and staves "as against a brigand," and one of his disciples cut off the ear of a slave of the high priest. According to Luke he had told them that two swords (apiece?) were enough; at the arrest they asked him if they should use them.[14] This evidence suggests that at least the disciples envisaged armed resistance. After the arrest, however, all of them took flight, and Peter denied knowing who Jesus was.[15] This aspect of the narrative strongly resembles the accounts of later religious opponents of Rome.

Though Jesus' disciples had fled, within a few days some of them became convinced that he had been raised from the dead by God. The oldest extant account of this conviction is provided by the apostle Paul in 1 Corinthians 15:3-8. Christ died and was buried; on the third day he was raised. The list of appearances Paul provides may perhaps come from two different sources, named at the beginning of each section.[16]

He appeared to Cephas,
then to the Twelve;
then he appeared to more
than five hundred brothers
at once, most of whom still
survive although some have
died.

He appeared to James,
then to all the apostles.

The whole list ends with the appearance of Christ to Paul himself. In the gospels different emphases are present: in Mark and Matthew the place of resurrection is clearly Galilee, not Jerusalem, while in Luke and John the appearances take place in the capital city or near it.[17] An appended chapter in the Gospel of John adds an appearance in Galilee.[18] In the gospel accounts much emphasis is laid on the disciples' finding that the tomb of Jesus was empty, whereas while Paul mentions the burial he says nothing about the empty tomb. From this evidence it is not possible to create a convincing historical reconstruction. All that can be said is that Jesus' disciples were convinced that he had been raised, and that the event marked the foundation of the Christian movement. As Paul expressed it, "if Christ was not raised, our preaching is in vain and your faith also is in vain" and "you are still in your

[13] Luke 6:15; Acts 1:13; cf. S. G. F. Brandon, *Jesus and the Zealots* (New York, 1967), 41-47, 243-45.
[14] Mark 14:47-48; Luke 22:35-38, 49-50.
[15] Mark 14:50-52, 66-72.
[16] Cf. E. Bammel in *TZ* 11 (1955), 401-19.
[17] E. Lohmeyer, *Galiläa und Jerusalem* (Göttingen, 1936); cf. F. C. Grant, *The Earliest Gospel* (New York-Nashville, 1943), 125-47.
[18] John 21:1-14.

sins"; in addition, "those who have died in Christ have perished."[19] Without this belief, Christianity would not have survived the death of Jesus.

The event necessitated vast changes in the disciples' way of thinking about Jesus and about themselves, even though these modifications came slowly; Luke depicts two of them as having hoped that Jesus was the one who would redeem Israel (24:21) and apparently supposes that this meant that he would "restore the kingdom to Israel" (Acts 1:6). Now, after receiving the gift of the Holy Spirit (Acts 2:1-4), the followers of Jesus continued to live at Jerusalem or in Galilee while claiming that through resurrection and exaltation God had made the crucified and risen Jesus both "lord" and "anointed one" (2:36). He would remain in heaven until a future date appointed by God (3:21).

It is likely that the New Testament accounts present the period between Easter and Pentecost rather more systematically that the events warranted. In all likelihood there was a series of resurrection appearances concurrent with experiences of the presence of the Spirit, without much differentiation. Thus Paul was able to view the appearance of Jesus to himself as analogous to the appearances to other apostles, although Luke viewed the resurrection appearances as ending with Christ's ascension. Both are systematic pictures based upon later reflection.

What was coming into existence during this period was the Christian community or church. It had been anticipated in Jesus' preaching of the eschatological gospel and in his calling of his disciples. It did not fully exist, however, until the combination of revelation and response reconfirmed the disciples' faith and prepared them to continue the mission. Twenty-five years later the apostle Paul was still describing these primary events as central to the tradition. In I Corinthians 11:23-25 he told of the supper on the night when Jesus was betrayed; in I Corinthians 15:3-7 he reiterated traditions about Jesus' death, burial, resurrection, and appearances to his disciples. In Romans 1:3-4 he stated that the gospel of the Son of God included his human descent from David and his designation as "Son of God in power in relation to the Spirit of Holiness by his resurrection from the dead." In addition, Paul knew sayings of Jesus as transmitted in the oral tradition, though for him the most important matters were the events.

II·PAUL

The significance of Paul for early Christianity was second only to that of Jesus. In his view God had called him to be a missionary of Christ not just at the time of his conversion but even before he was born (Gal. 1:15-16). He

[19] I Cor. 15:14, 17-18.

had been born into a devoutly Jewish family, proud of its membership in the tribe of Benjamin (hence his name "Saul") and its adherence to Pharisaism. Paul had been circumcised a week after birth, in accordance with Jewish law. Later on he had zealously studied ancestral traditions and, indeed, had made more progress in study and action than most of his contemporaries.[20] He had left his native city of Tarsus in Cilicia and had gone to Jerusalem to study "at the feet of Gamaliel," a famous Pharisee of the time.[21] By the standards of the law itself he could claim to be "blameless" (Phil. 3:6). It was his very zeal for the law that led him to be an active persecutor of the Christian communities.

Within a few years after the death of Jesus, however, God "was pleased to reveal his Son to me that I might proclaim him among the gentiles" (Gal. 1:16). What he had regarded as profit turned into loss because of Christ (Phil. 3:7). The revelation made him not only a Christian but also an apostle, entrusted with the mission to the gentiles.[22] He was now aware of possessing "the mind of Christ" (1 Cor. 2:16) or the Spirit of God (7:40); it was now Christ who spoke through him (2 Cor. 13:3; Rom. 15:18). Many "revelations of the Lord" were given him (2 Cor. 12:1, 7). He could work "signs and wonders" (2 Cor. 12:12) in order to produce "the obedience of the gentiles" (Rom. 15:18).

Paul's sense of identification with Christ was so complete that he could regard his experience of conversion as analogous to death and even to crucifixion (Gal. 2:19, 6:14). Christ's death came to provide a model for all members of the community. All Christians, in Paul's view, had been baptized "into" the death of Christ Jesus and had been symbolically buried with him in their baptism. They were "united with the pattern of his death" (Rom. 6:3-8). Not all Christians had visions of the risen Lord; indeed, Paul claimed that he himself was the last to whom he appeared (1 Cor. 15:8). All Christians, however, could be united with Christ, who was in all of them (2 Cor. 13:5); all had been baptized into the one body and had been "made to drink of the one Spirit" (1 Cor. 12:13).

The emphasis Paul placed on work and achievement in his earlier days remained present in his life as a Christian. God's favor enabled him to work harder than all the other apostles (1 Cor. 15:10). Others might claim to be servants of Christ; he did more than they (2 Cor. 11:23). He could do anything by the power God gave him (Phil. 4:13). At the same time, he insisted that he had not really achieved anything or had become perfect. He continued to press on toward the final divine prize (Phil. 3:12-14: cf. 1 Cor. 9:24-27). Sometimes he used athletic metaphors in describing tasks and goals, some-

[20] Gal. 1:13-14; Phil. 3:5-6.
[21] Cf. W. C. van Unnik, *Tarsus or Jerusalem* (London, 1962). According to later legend Gamaliel was a Christian himself (*Clem. rec.* I, 65).
[22] Cf. 1 Cor. 9:1, 15:8-11.

times military ones, as in Thessalonians 5:8 and 2 Corinthians 10:3-6. The words he employed in speaking of being in winter quarters and of being sent forward to battle (1 Cor. 16:6-7; Rom. 15:24) occur in an inscription referring to Trajan's Parthian war.[23]

Paul's description of his career, including the explicit mention of his escape from the ethnarch of King Aretas IV of Nabataea (2 Cor. 11:32-33), has been compared and contrasted with similar records left by Hellenistic and Roman kings and generals.[24] The point is much the same: triumph through power, though Paul's power is not his own but Christ's and is expressed not in military victory but in suffering. Such parallels can be carried even further. If one considers the ways in which Paul refers to his relations with the communities to which he writes, one finds some striking parallels between them and the statements made by Dio Chrysostom when describing the ideal Graeco-Roman ruler.[25] The good king, like Paul, has been appointed by God and resembles Zeus himself. He is like a father to his subjects and like a shepherd in his care for them; he confers benefits on all instead of receiving them; he gives aid to the weak. He is a king for others, not for himself. His life is marked by self-control and by incessant labor for the good of mankind. There is no reason to suppose that Paul had read any treatises on kingship. His picture of himself as an apostle, however, is close to that of Dio's king.

The differences are equally striking. The role of the apostle involves hunger, thirst, nakedness, persecution, wandering, manual labor (1 Cor. 4:11-12). It involves incessant suffering (though without despair[26]), and the episodes in it can be listed. It is meaningful suffering, however, because it is undergone for Christ[27] and because it leads to a future reward.[28]

Sociologically it is worth noting that the sufferings Paul mentioned included manual labor. In his view he had the right, based on apostolic military, and agricultural analogies, on the Old Testament law, on priestly parallels, and on a saying of Jesus,[29] to be supported by the community. He did not exercise the right but supported himself by manual labor.[30] This labor set an example for the Christian community and if imitated by others could prevent criticism by outsiders.[31] Paul had no sympathy with those who supposed that the reign

[23] *OGIS* 544.
[24] A. Fridrichsen in *Symbolae Osloenses* 7 (1928), 5-29; 8 (1929), 78-82 with references, e.g., to the *Res gestae* of Augustus and *OGIS* 383 (Antiochus I of Commagene); cf. *OGIS* 199 and 201.
[25] Dio Chrysostom, *Or.* 1-3. The 4th oration provides fewer parallels, though it develops the picture of the king as like the Cynic wise man.
[26] 2 Cor. 4:8-10; cf. 1 Cor. 4:12-13; Phil. 4:12.
[27] Phil. 1:29; cf. Col. 1:24.
[28] 2 Cor. 4:16-18; Phil. 3:8-11.
[29] 1 Cor. 9:3-14.
[30] 1 Thess. 2:9; 1 Cor. 9:15.
[31] 2 Thess. 3:8-10; 1 Thess. 4:10-12.

of God had already arrived and therefore lived in idleness. His idea that work was an unpleasant duty probably comes from the creation story in Genesis, where God forces Adam to work in punishment for his disobedience.

On the other hand, Paul's insistence upon the necessity of work for all was probably related not only to his Jewish upbringing—students of the law were expected to practice a trade—but also to the circumstances of his family. From the book of Acts we learn that he was not only a Jew but also a citizen of Tarsus in Cilicia (21:39) and a Roman citizen by birth (22:28).[32] Presumably his father, a Cilician Jew, had acquired Roman and Tarsan citizenship during the civil wars or the Augustan peace. Dio Chrysostom, early in the second century, said that at Tarsus citizenship could be acquired for 500 drachmas. He also spoke of dyers, cobblers, and carpenters as among the citizenry.[33] Perhaps Paul's father, certainly Paul himself, belonged to this group, for by trade he was either a cobbler or a tentmaker; the word *skēnopoios* (Acts 18:3) can bear either meaning.[34]

As a member of the "petty bourgeoisie" Paul criticized others for their claims to exalted social status or for attempting to eat without working.[35] He was rather piqued by criticisms of his personal appearance and speaking ability, but proud that his critics had to admit that his letters were forceful.[36] As a Roman citizen he was firmly convinced of the rightness of Roman authority and justice, and he insisted that Roman taxes be paid.[37]

Paul and other Christians not only looked back to the life, death, and resurrection of Jesus and lived within the Christian community but also looked forward to their Lord's imminent return from heaven, where he was seated in glory at the right hand of God. This expectation, expressed in gospel predictions of the coming of the Son of Man, was shared with Jewish apocalypticists to whom Christians owed not only the hope in general but many details as well. It is reflected in Paul's statement that gentile Christians had "turned from idols to God, to serve the living and real God and to await the advent from heaven of his Son Jesus, who delivers us from the wrath to come" (1 Thess. 1:9-10). At times Paul predicted the future more fully, relying on a prophetic "word of the Lord" or an eschatological "secret."[38]

The Lord himself will descend from heaven with a cry of command, with the archangel's call, and with the sound of the trumpet of God. The dead in Christ will rise first; then we who remain alive shall be caught up together with them in the clouds to meet the Lord in the air; and so we shall always be with the Lord.

[32] He therefore possessed a birth certificate like those collected by F. Schulz in *JRS* 32 (1942), 78-91; 33 (1943), 55-64.
[33] *Or.* 34, 23.
[34] J. Jeremias in *ZNW* 30 (1931), 229.
[35] 1 Cor. 1:26; 2 Thess. 3:8-10.
[36] 2 Cor. 10:10; cf. 11:6.
[37] Rom. 13:1-7.
[38] 1 Thess. 4:16-17; 1 Cor. 15:51-52.

We shall not all sleep, but we shall all be changed, in a moment, in the wink of an eye, at the last trumpet. For the trumpet will sound and the dead will be raised imperishable, and we shall be changed.

This apocalyptic hope provided the impetus for the early Christian mission, and the synoptic evangelists beginning with Mark included detailed predictions, again from Jewish sources, of the signs which would precede the end (Mark 13:3-36 and parallels). To be sure, Christians insisted that the Lord would come "like a thief in the night" (1 Thess. 5:2)[39] and transmitted a saying of Jesus to the effect that no one but the Father knew when the end would arrive.[40] It could still be claimed that salvation was nearer than it had been when Christians experience conversion; the night was far advanced, the day was near (Rom. 13:11-12).

The existence of the gospels, however, itself suggests the need for reinforcing faith as the night continued, and in the Gospel of Luke and the book of Acts it is clearly suggested that the earliest disciples' expectations were not fully justified.[41] The Gospel of John indicates that the return of Christ was somehow to be identified with the coming of the Holy Spirit upon the community (John 14-16), although the hope is still maintained in 1 John 2:18: it is "the last hour" and many antichrists have already come.

The expectation of an imminent end was generally maintained more firmly among Jewish Christians than among gentiles. It is to be found in the book of Revelation, the *Didache*, the Epistle of Barnabas, 2 Clement, and the fragments of Papias. On the other hand, 1 Clement, relying on Hellenistic Jewish sources, speaks only occasionally of the end; the providential government of the cosmos is more important. Ignatius of Antioch says that "these are the last times,"[42] but for him the past advent of Jesus Christ was the supreme eschatological event. The apostle Paul sometimes spoke of his own going to be with the Lord (Phil. 1:21-26) but still awaited the Savior's coming from heaven (3:20); Ignatius knows only that he must soon die and be with God. It is therefore not surprising that around 160 the apologist Justin could admit that while he expected the coming of God's kingdom on earth his expectation was not shared by all Christians.[43]

No description of early Christianity can do justice to it unless some emphasis is laid on the personalities of those who became leaders. Some were doubtless phlegmatic, calculating, unenthusiastic. Without such men the movement would not have survived; nor would it have come into existence. Little is known of the elusive personality of Jesus, but the impression he made can be inferred from such passages as Mark 10:32: "they were on the road up to Jerusalem, and

---

[39] Cf. Mark 13:34-35; Matt. 24:43; Luke 12:39.
[40] Mark 13:32 and parallels.
[41] Luke 19:11, 24:21; Acts 1:6; cf. H. Conzelmann, *The Theology of St. Luke* (London, 1960).
[42] *Eph.* 11, 1.
[43] *Dial.* 80, 5.

Jesus was leading them, and they were astonished, and those who followed were afraid." He was a person who could be regarded as having said, "I and the Father are one" (John 10:30) or "he who has seen me has seen the Father" (14:9). At the very least the stories of his miracles indicate that he was regarded as extraordinary. Paul too effected signs and wonders, as we have pointed out; he could do or endure anything because of the power of God (Phil. 4:13). He proclaimed the coming of Jesus from heaven, and he himself had been "taken up" to the third heaven, to the celestial paradise, where he had heard "ineffable words."[44] This "rapture" was only one of many revelations. An angel of Satan attacked him; the Lord himself assured him that his grace was sufficient for him (2 Cor. 12:7-9). There is thus little reason for suspposing that the "word of the Lord" about the coming of Christ was given him by anyone else; he himself was a medium of revelation. "Do not quench the Spirit; do not despise prophecies" (1 Thess. 5:19-20). The author of the book of Revelation was "in the Spirit on the Lord's day" (1:10). Ignatius of Antioch could speak "with God's own voice" and could regard himself as about to be sacrificed, like Jesus and Paul, on behalf of Christians.[45]

III·ESCHATOLOGY

It is obvious that there was a difference between the expectation that God would immediately take up his power and reign and the actual establishment of Christian communities in many parts of the Roman empire. What is obvious to us, however, does not seem to have been obvious to the early Christians, and there is little evidence to show that the question disturbed them. In the Gospel of Matthew we find both the expectation of the coming of the Son of Man and rules for church discipline. The situation is no different in the first-century *Didache* or, for that matter, in the letters of Paul. Perhaps the relation between expectation and actuality can best be termed "anticipation." The Christian at eucharistic worship or engaged in prophecy was expected, like adherents of other religious groups, to behave "decently and in orderly fashion" (1 Cor. 14:40).[46] What he was celebrating, however, was "the Lord's death—until he comes" (11:26) and the present gift of the Spirit as an anticipation of the future resurrection (2 Cor. 5:5). His worship, Revelation suggests, was a foretaste of the worship in the new Jerusalem to come. He had "tasted the heavenly gift" (Heb. 6:4). The Christian commu-

---

[44] 2 Cor. 12:1-4; "taken up," 1 Thess. 4:17.
[45] Ignatius, *Philad.* 7, 1; sacrifice: my *Ignatius of Antioch* (*The Apostolic Fathers*, IV, Camden, N.J., 1966), 13-15.
[46] *SIG*[3] 742, line 42 (regulations for the Andanian mysteries, 92 B.C.)

nities, then, could be regarded as scouts and raiders, selected by God to infiltrate before the day of the divine invasion. It was necessary for them to be highly trained and disciplined before the invasion actually began. During the first two centuries of the church's life this expectation of coming triumph was not lost, and thereafter it was merely translated into terms more fully political and theological.

The mission of Jesus himself found its center in the proclamation that the reign of God was coming very soon and in the appeal to follow him and take part in making the proclamation. To some extent, it would appear, he regarded the reign of God as having been inaugurated already and finding expression in his words and works. His crucifixion brought the mission in this form to an end. It was no longer possible simply to proclaim the coming kingdom; instead, an explanation of his death had to be provided. Such an explanation is reflected in the Pauline epistles. The death and resurrection had, indeed, inaugurated the new age, but although Christians already live by faith in something like God's kingdom, the general resurrection, the last judgment, and Christ's final victory have not yet taken place. What seemed to be the defeat of the mission was now paradoxically regarded as a vindication of it: the Lord's resurrection was an anticipation of the resurrection of all.

Apart from individual emphases, the proclamation of Christ's death and resurrection as pointing ahead toward God's triumph remained central to the Christian mission for at least a century and a half after the death of Jesus. It was the expectation of God's impending action that gave impetus to the mission. Those who became Christians before the latter half of the second century believed that martyrdom might come to them but, if so, they would not face God much sooner than their contemporaries would. A sharp division on this point is first noted by Justin in his *Dialogue with Trypho* (80, 4-5). Unorthodox Christians, not really Christians at all, deny the resurrection of the dead and suppose that at death their souls ascend into the heavens. Orthodox Christians accept the resurrection of the flesh and a thousand years' stay in a rebuilt and enlarged Jerusalem. It was just in the time when Justin wrote that the Montanists in Phrygia were beginning to insist upon the absolute importance of the same doctrines, presumably in question among others.

Though the emphasis on eschatology as providing motivation and, to a considerable extent, content for the mission had diminished earlier, especially in Gnostic circles, it did not fade away generally among theologians until the end of the second century. By this time Christianity had become a fairly well-established movement, with a clearly defined organization, some degree of unformity in rites and accepted books and credal formulas. There was a heightened emphasis on tradition as well as on a semiphilosophical theology. This was the age of the apologists, who believed that Christianity had a place in the Roman world and should be accepted as the true religious philosophy of the state. The apologists' arguments were often derived from Hellenistic

Judaism but were carried further because Christianity was more aggressively missionary. In addition, the Logos doctrine borrowed from Judaism became more concrete in Christian treatments, for the incarnate Logos was Jesus. This Logos doctrine was important to the mission, for it provided a bridge for the convert to cross from right reason in general to Christian right reason in particular.

When we consider the Christian mission at the end of the second century and the beginning of the third, we must remember the difference between the administrators like Irenaeus, who was conscious of living among barbarians and taught a traditional theology, and the more modern theologians, especially at Alexandria, who made use of all the resources of Graeco-Roman culture they could baptize. Clement and Origen were frequently in difficulties with the "simpler believers," and presumably the bishop of Alexandria was one of them. The bishop's idea of Christianity, if we may judge from his actions, was concentrated upon discipline and obedience to authority. He had the responsibility of guiding the "simpler believers" and, at the same time, of checking what he regarded as the excesses of speculative theologians. These theologians endeavored to set forth a Christianity fully, or largely, relevant to the concerns of urban intellectuals. It is no coincidence that when Origen finally composed an answer to an anti-Christian treatise by a cultivated author concerned with Greek culture, including philosophy, and with the safety of the Roman state, he found himself often in agreement with him. By the time of Origen, then, there were at least two major approaches which Christian missions took. On the one hand, the more traditional picture of the coming reign of God continued to exist, although in its extreme form it was present only among Montanists; among the more orthodox the church itself was an anticipation of the kingdom and, indeed, provided the only entrance to the kingdom. On the other hand, speculative theologians employed the traditional formulas but, especially by using the allegorical method, tended to dissolve them into philosophy. A large majority of Christians was traditionalist and orthodox;[47] there were few speculative theologians, though they were highly influential and impressed outsiders favorably.

From the second century onward many of those who became Christians were born of Christian parents, and apparently for this reason infant baptism came to be widespread early in the third century.

---

[47] Tertullian (*Adv. Prax.* 3, 1) rather bitterly points this out: "the simple, not to say imprudent and uneducated, always a majority among believers. . . ."

CHAPTER IV
CHRISTIAN ORGANIZATION

I·SOCIAL GROUPS

The Christian mission required at least a minimal organization in order to provide some structure for the communities coming into existence. According to the gospels, the earliest disciples of Jesus followed him about Galilee and up to Jerusalem and under these circumstances there was no emphasis on group organization. The evangelists depict Simon Peter as somehow the spokesman for the disciples, and he is often associated with James and John, the sons of Zebedee; but the extent to which their accounts are based on postresurrection traditions cannot be determined. It would appear that there were twelve leading disciples, for in 1 Corthinthians 15:5 Paul could mention "the Twelve" without explanation. If so, it is likely that they were intended to be missionaries to the twelve tribes of Israel. The synoptic tradition describes Jesus as telling them, "You will be seated on [twelve] thrones, judging the twelve tribes of Israel."[1] The synoptic evangelists also provide lists of the

[1] Matt. 19:28; Luke 22:30.

names of the twelve,[2] although no such group is known to the author of the Gospel of John. Their mission is portrayed as eschatological. According to Mark 6:7-13, they were sent out in pairs to exorcise unclean spirits, to heal the sick, and to preach repentance. Nothing is said about establishing communities. Indeed Matthew is the only evangelist to mention the *ecclesia* or church; he refers to it as in the future (16:18) and gives a rule for its future conduct (18:15-17).

Christian communities as such came into existence only after the death and resurrection of Jesus. In Acts 1:12-26 we find a clearly defined group remaining in Jerusalem and replacing the traitor Judas by the early disciple Matthias. Though the author may well be placing the definite organization of the community too early, similar concerns reflected at Qumran show that apocalyptic-minded groups were not averse to such structures.[3] The chief of the community at this point was Simon Peter, presumably in virtue of the appearances of the risen Jesus to him.[4]

Reliable statistics about the early church of Jerusalem are not available, though Acts states that before Pentecost there were about 120 "brothers" (1:15), joined at Pentecost by 3,000 more (2:41), and soon reaching a total of 5,000 (4:4), then an unstated number of myriads (21:21). Whatever the numbers may have been, it is clear that some form of organization was imperative as soon as communal sharing was practiced.[5] Difficulties immediately arose when converts concealed the extent of their property (Acts 5:1-10) and when "Hellenist" widows complained of unfair treatment in the daily distribution (6:1). Leaders like Peter or converts who had been customs collectors[6] could deal with the question of property declarations. The daily distributions, however, consumed more time, and the leaders therefore appointed a group of seven to "serve tables" (Acts 6:2-6). Unlike the apostles, the seven bore Greek names, and it may be that they were not waiters but financial officials concerned with the banking operations of the community. The "tables" involved may have been those of money-changers and bankers, as often in the Graeco-Roman world.[7]

These practical matters, along with the rapid growth of the communities (soon extended to Judaea, Samaria, and Galilee, Acts 9:31) and the problem of instructing converts, soon led to a considerable measure of disunity within the church. In response to this disunity, fresh analysis of the nature of political unity was called for—since the church was a body politic.

Even within the oral tradition common to Matthew and Luke we find

[2] Mark 3:16-19; Matt. 10:2-4; Luke 6:13-16; Acts 1:13.
[3] Cf. S. E. Johnson and B. Reicke in K. Stendahl, ed., *The Scrolls and the New Testament* (New York, 1957), 129-56.
[4] Cf. 1 Cor. 15:5; Luke 24:34.
[5] For Qumran cf. W. R. Farmer in *TZ* 11 (1955), 295-308.
[6] Cf. Mark 2:13-15 and parallels.
[7] Cf. E. J. Goodspeed, *Problems of New Testament Translation* (Chicago, 1945), 126-27.

political analysis of the consequences of disunity: "every kingdom divided against itself is laid waste, and no city or house divided against itself will stand" (Matt. 12:25; cf. Luke 11:17). The same rejection of division, along with a more detailed account of the functions of individuals or groups, is provided by the apostle Paul in 1 Corinthians 12:12-26. Paul compares the Christian community with a body, which is one though consisting of many members with diverse functions. The functions are different, but each member has a role to play; if all played the same role the functions would be in-adequately performed. On the one hand, the inferior members cannot say they do not belong to the body because they are not the same as others; on the other hand, superiors cannot say to other members, "I have no need of you." Actually, "the parts of the body which seem to be weaker are indispensable," and the modesty with which the less presentable members are treated shows how valuable they are. Everything is arranged so that there may be mutual care without discord; "if one member suffers, all suffer to-gether; if one member is honored, all rejoice together."

The theme is repeated in Romans 12:4-5. "As in one body we have many members, and all the members do not have the same function, so we, though many, are one body in Christ, and individually members one of another."

It is essentially a political theme, not one peculiarly Christian. Paul does state that Christians constitute the body of Christ because they were baptized by one Spirit (1 Cor. 12:12-13), and he clearly holds that God arranged and adjusted the body and its members (12:18, 24); his conclusion is that "you are the body of Christ and individually members of it" (12:27). The whole picture of the body politic as analogous to the physical body, however, is common enough in Greek political thought from the early fourth century B.C. onward, when Xenophon ascribed to Socrates the comparison of two brothers, made by God to serve each other, to pairs of hands, feet, and eyes, made by God for mutual aid.[8] Closer to Paul is the story which, according to Livy and Dionysius of Halicarnassus, was told to Roman plebeians by the senator Menenius Agrippa in 494 B.C.[9] A conspiracy against the belly was undertaken by hands, mouth, and teeth; what resulted was weakness not only in the belly but in all the members of the body. This analogy was popular in the late republic and the early empire. Cicero used it in defending private property; echoes recur in Philo, Seneca, and Epictetus.[10] The comparison was widespread, and even Paul's ideas about the appropriateness of modesty in regard to the members performing the most necessary functions are to be found in Cicero.[11] Paul's analogy is thus essentially political.

In Colossians and Ephesians the community is described as a body with Christ as its head, from which the body is given health and growth (Col. 2:19;

[8] Xenophon, *Mem. Socr.* 2, 3, 18-19.
[9] Livy 2, 32; Dionysius 6, 86; W. Nestle in *Klio* 21 (1927), 350-60.
[10] *De offic.* 3, 22; cf. W. L. Knox in *JTS* 39 (1938), 243-46.
[11] *De offic.* 1, 126-27.

Eph. 4:16). Just so, Seneca in writing to the young Nero in 55-56 speaks of him as the *animus* or mind of the state, his body, and refers to his *animus* as diffused throughout the "whole body of the empire." Good health comes from the head; through it "all the parts are lively and alert or languid and drooping."[12] According to Ephesians 1:22-23, God has made Christ "the head of all things for the church which is his body, the fulness of him who fills all in all." So Seneca insists that "all this universe which surrounds us is one, and it is God; we are his associates and members."[13]

Admittedly Christian and Stoic theology are quite different in their starting points and some of their conclusions.[14] The pictures of the church and the state as bodies politic are much the same, as is the goal of unity in such bodies. In this realm of ideas Christians did not innovate.

In many respects the social outlook of the apostle Paul was essentially conservative. His conservatism was partly based on the idea of the church as a body politic, partly on a basically hierarchical picture of the world,[15] and partly on the belief that since the end was at hand no social changes were desirable.

In writing to the Corinthians he insisted that Christians were to remain in the social situation in which God had placed them and in which he had "called" them to Christian faith. If a man had been called as a slave he was not to be disturbed by his condition; if he could become free he was to make use of his slavery instead.[16] "For a man who has been called by the Lord as a slave is a freedman of the Lord, and similarly the one who has been called as a free man is a slave of Christ" (1 Cor. 7:22). Paul goes on to describe the life of the Christian as that of an emancipated slave who has been bought (by means of a fictitious sale) by a temple but still has to work for the god of the temple under a binding contract.[17] The metaphor he uses reinforces his conservative line of argument.

II-SPHERES OF INFLUENCE

One of the principal occasions of disunity within the early church was provided by the conversion and mission of the apostle Paul. Although Acts portrays the church at Jerusalem as having sent out evangelists to various

[12] *De clem.* 1, 5, 1; 2, 2, 1.

[13] *Ep.* 92, 30; cf. 95, 52.

[14] J. N. Sevenster, *Paul and Seneca* (Leiden, 1961), 167-73.

[15] See my article in *Myths and Symbols: Studies in Honor of Mircea Eliade* (Chicago, 1969), 279-89.

[16] Cf. the argument of Epictetus 4, 1, 33-40.

[17] Cf. A. Deissmann, *Light from the Ancient East* (rev. ed., London, 1927), 318-30; W. L. Westermann in *Proceedings of the American Philosophical Society* 92 (1948), 55-64.

areas nearby, and insists that a mission to gentiles was actually first under-taken by the Jerusalem apostles, especially Peter,[18] Paul's appearance on the Jerusalem scene meant that the whole question of jurisdiction had to be brought up. Apparently the question had not been faced before this point.

When he became a Christian, Paul writes (Gal. 1:16-24), he did not immediately confer with those who had been apostles before him; instead, he went due south to Arabia and then returned to Damascus. Only after three years did he visit Jerusalem for a fortnight's conference with Cephas (Peter); among the apostles he saw only their leaders, Cephas and James the Lord's brother. Presumably in consequence of this meeting, he then went to "the regions of Syria and Cilicia," avoiding "the churches of Judaea" even though they had been informed of his conversion and his mission work. Paul implies that the Jerusalem leaders agreed with him that he should confine his activities to the gentile mission; at any rate, he was not to work under the direct jurisdiction of Jerusalem or in proximity to it. He also implies that there was no question about the right of the apostles at Jerusalem to govern the churches of Judaea.

The church of Jerusalem was the church of the twelve apostles. From 1 Corinthians 15:5-7 it appears that their jurisdiction was based on appearances of the risen Christ—on the one hand, to Cephas, the Twelve, and a large group of disciples; on the other, to James and to "all the apostles." The list of appearances seems to reflect the combination of two groups of appearances which were especially related to Cephas and to James, and the authority of the Jerusalem church thus rested on a double foundation. Paul's own claim to apostolic authority was obviously parallel not to that of Cephas, who had been a disciple of Jesus in Galilee and at Jerusalem, but to that of James, a convert only after the resurrection. From the account in Galatians it is by no means clear that Cephas and James recognized Paul's apostolate when he first visited them. Indeed, it looks as if they waited for fourteen years before explicitly recognizing that by divine favor he had been entrusted with the mission to the gentiles (Gal. 2:7-9). If this is so, the leaders of the church of Jerusalem must have enjoyed a primacy not only in Judaea but also among Jews in other areas of the Christian world.

What happened after fourteen years was that Paul went to Jerusalem from Antioch, taking with him both Barnabas and a Greek convert named Titus. The purpose of the visit was to hold a private conference with the Jerusalem leaders and to set before them Paul's gospel to the gentiles (Gal. 2:1-10). The results of this conference were extremely important for the later history of the Pauline mission and of the Christian church. Jewish Christians continued to advocate the practice of circumcision; Paul indignantly rejected it and refused to have Titus circumcised. The leaders of the church agreed with his position, and from them he apparently won the definite al-

[18] Cf. M. Dibelius, *Studies in the Acts of the Apostles* (New York, 1956), 109-22.

location of spheres of influence described in his letter. The "pillar" apostles laid no additional requirements upon him, he says, and they recognized that by divine favor he had been entrusted with the gospel for the gentiles, just as Peter had been given it for the Jews. Paul and Barnabas were henceforth to work with gentiles; James, Cephas, and John with Jews. In ratifying this agreement they shook hands with him and also required that he take up a collection in support of the Jerusalem community, presumably thus sealing the concordat. This collection was evidently analogous to the tax which Jews paid for the support of the temple in Jerusalem.

Difficulties arose immediately after Paul's return to Antioch, for the concordat was unworkable in communities consisting of both Jews and gentiles. Cephas came to Antioch and at first observed the local Christian custom of eating meals, as a Jew, with gentiles. Since there were evidently many Jews in the congregation, the more conservative among them presumably informed James, at Jerusalem, that Jewish Christianity was being undermined. James sent emissaries to insist that Jews should not eat with gentiles, and his concern was respected not only by Cephas but also by Barnabas and the other Jewish Christians (Gal. 2:11-13).

At this point Paul could see that his own mission to the gentiles was being endangered. He had successfully claimed that circumcision was not to be required of gentiles, but if the Jewish dietary laws were to be observed—even by Jews in a mixed community—both "freedom in Christ Jesus" (Gal. 2:4) and the unity of the churches would be destroyed. He therefore denounced Peter's action and asked him, "If you as a Jew live in gentile, not Jewish, fashion how can you compel the gentiles to practice Judaism?" Unfortunately he does not report Peter's answer, although the rest of his letter to the Galatians may imply that Peter ultimately agreed with him. It may be that the agreement involved some compromise which Paul does not discuss.

Such a compromise is reflected in the account of a council at Jerusalem provided in the book of Acts (15:1-35). In many respects the account runs parallel to Paul's narrative in Galatians, but the two stories are basically different. According to Acts, the apostles and presbyters of the Jerusalem church held a public discussion on the question of circumcision. Peter made an address in which he pointed to his own work among gentiles and insisted that circumcision was unnecessary. Paul and Barnabas described their work. Finally James proposed that, in view of Mosaic precedents, gentile converts should be given four requirements based on Leviticus 17-18. The apostles and elders agreed with James and composed a decree containing his four points.

This "apostolic decree" is very important as the first pronouncement made by a Christian synod. The first item, abstinence from meats sacrificed to idols, seems to be based on Leviticus 17:8-9 and was understood, at least by Paul (1 Cor. 10:28), to refer to foods known to have been consecrated to pagan gods but not to meals eaten at temples.[19] The second, abstinence from blood, probably had to do with the dietary regulations of Leviticus 17:10-12, and was so interpreted later;[20] at one point, however, Tertullian took it in regard to murder.[21] The third, abstinence from the meat of animals which had been strangled, without their blood being drained; was an ordinance certainly Jewish in origin (cf. Lev. 17:13-14) and enforced among Jewish Christians,[22] but it was not discussed by Paul; it is absent from the text of Irenaeus, Tertullian, and Cyprian. The fourth item, abstinence from "fornication," seems strange in this context, although Paul may refer to it in letters from and to Corinth.[23] Among Jewish Christians, as Molland has shown, it was referred to rules about marital intercourse and ritual washings (cf. Lev. 18:6-19).[24]

By the early second century two versions of the decree were in circulation. One of them contained the four items listed above; the other omitted any reference to "things strangled" and added the "golden rule" that "whatever they do not wish done to themselves they should not do to others" (cf. Tobit 4:15; Didache 1, 2).[25] Witnesses to the third item include both Clement and Origen at Alexandria. The other version was known to Irenaeus and Tertullian, probably also to Theophilus of Antioch.[26]

What this modification indicates is that the decree was seriously regarded as Christian legislation—and for this reason was modified. It was to be transmitted to Antioch and throughout Syria and Cilicia by two Jerusalem "prophets," Judas Barsabbas and Silas, who were to accompany Barnabas and Paul in order to make sure that it was delivered. Later on, we learn that Judas and Silas delivered the decree at Antioch and then returned to Jerusalem (Acts 15:30-33); in Cilicia both Paul and Silas insisted upon its observance, and Paul went so far as to circumcise the son of a Jewish mother and a Greek father (15:40-16:4). Indeed, Silas accompanied Paul through Asia Minor to Macedonia and Achaea, disappearing from the picture just before Paul's extended stay at Corinth (18:5).

The precise extent to which Paul may have regarded such a decree as binding upon gentile converts—for example, outside Syria and Cilicia—is problematical. He and Silas (Sylvanus) wrote a letter from Corinth, insisting that God wills holiness and specifically referring to "abstaining from fornication" (1 Thess. 4:3). He does not speak of dietary regulations, perhaps be-

---

[19] Jewish Christians might not have agreed with him; but cf. Mishnah, 'Aboda Zara 3, 4.
[20] Eusebius, H. E. 5, 1, 26; Tertullian, De monog. 5, 3; later examples, E. Molland in Studia Theologica 9 (1955), 35-37.
[21] De pudic. 12, 4-5.
[22] Clem. hom. 7, 8; 8, 19; Clem. rec. 4, 36.
[23] 1 Thess. 4:3; 1 Cor. 5:1, 6:13; 7:2.
[24] Molland, loc. cit., 37-38.
[25] Positive in Matt. 7:12, Luke 6:31.
[26] Ad Autol. 2, 34.

cause they create no difficulties, but he praises "the churches of God in Judaea in Christ Jesus" as persecuted by the Jews just as the Thessalonians are persecuted by gentiles (1 Thess. 2:14). It is likely that he had told them of the apostolic decree, for the substance of it seems to appear in 1 Corinthians. Sections of practical counsel in that letter begin with discussions of "fornication" (5:1, specifically related to Lev. 18:7) and of "meats sacrificed to idols" (8:1). At the same time, it is evident that he cannot accept the legal principle underlying the decree. Free Christians are not bound by dietary regulations, though they may observe them for the sake of others (10:23-29). If Silas continued to adhere to the Jerusalem regulations, it is no wonder that he left Paul at Corinth. According to Acts 21:25, the elders at Jerusalem were still concerned with observance of them when Paul last visited the church there; they had heard that Paul—"everything to everyone," as he wrote himself (1 Cor. 9:22)—was even urging Jewish Christians not to observe the law (21:21). Acts 21:26 states that Paul purged himself by the Nazirite vow of consecration (Num. 6:9-20). This picture may well be historically correct. At Jerusalem, one would suppose, Paul accepted the practices of the church there. He was under Jerusalem jurisdiction.

It must be admitted that to try to coordinate Paul's account in Galatians with the "literary" narrative in Acts leads to many difficulties. The attempt reflected in what has just been said cannot be regarded as having led to any final solution.[27] It is most unlikely that in the long run Paul regarded the Jerusalem decree—if he really knew of its existence—as binding upon his converts or himself.

If the decree did exist and was known at Antioch, problems arose there as soon as Cephas (Peter) visited the city. Swayed by emissaries from James of Jerusalem, he withdrew from table fellowship with gentiles and was followed by other Jews, including even Barnabas. Paul insisted that his action was inconsistent and irresponsible (Gal. 2:11-14).

To the Corinthians Paul had to insist that even if he was not an apostle to others, he was one to them; they provided the "seal" of his apostolate (1 Cor. 9:2); he had begotten them in the gospel (4:15). To be sure, some Corinthians were appealing to the authority of Apollos, who came to Corinth after Paul, and even to that of Cephas (1:12; cf. 3:22), but Paul carefully pointed out not only that he and Apollos were in basic agreement (Apollos was with him at Ephesus as he wrote, 16:12) but also that his own work was more fundamental than his. He had planted, while Apollos had watered the plant; he had laid the foundation upon which Apollos had raised the

27 On the points involved see K. Lake in F. J. F. Jackson and K. Lake, eds., *The Beginnings of Christianity* V (London, 1933), 195-212; E. Haenchen, *Die Apostelgeschichte* (Göttingen, 1959), 381-414 (especially 404 ff.); H. Conzelmann, *Die Apostelgeschichte* (Tübingen, 1963), 81-87; W. Schmithals, *Paul and James (Studies in Biblical Theology*, 46, 1965).

building (3:6-10). In 2 Corinthians a more acute crisis is reflected. Paul vigorously attacks Jewish Christians (11:22-23) who evidently appeal to apostolic authority (12:11-12). And in this letter he explicitly refers to the infringement of his jurisdictional areas (10:13-16). He is the founder of a church essentially gentile (1 Cor. 12:2)—which is, and must remain, under his control. His concern is reflected not only by the letters themselves but also by his sending first Timothy, then Titus, to Corinth.

From the Pauline epistles it is quite clear that Paul had jurisdiction over the churches he founded and that he maintained control over them not only by personal visits but also by writing letters and by sending his lieutenants especially Timothy and Titus, to them. Though he had been prominent in the churches of Syria and Cilicia (Gal. 1:21), especially in the church of Antioch (Gal. 2:11-14), he had not founded them and did not exercise jurisdiction over them. On the other hand, he founded the churches of Galatia (Gal. 4:13-15) and governed them, at least for a while (1 Cor. 16:1, Gal. 1:2). He also founded the churches of Asia and spoke in their name while he was at Ephesus (1 Cor. 16:19). At some point in his career he exercised control over the communities at Colossae and Laodicea (Col. 4:16-17), though he had not established them; and he differentiated the church at Hierapolis in Phrygia from these two (4:13).

It would appear from Acts 16:6-7 that at first he was excluded from Asia, though he later went there, and that he was never admitted to Bithynia, whether or not he wanted to go there. Northern and northwestern Asia Minor may have lain under another jurisdiction somehow related to Peter, for 1 Peter is addressed to the Christians of Pontus, Cappadocia, and Bithynia. Since it is also addressed to Galatia and Asia we may assume that these churches were removed from Paul's jurisdiction as he moved west. It is significant that when he speaks of the collection for Jerusalem he says that he has asked the churches of Galatia to contribute (1 Cor. 16:1) but in later letters does not refer to any gift of theirs; and he does not mention any contribution by the churches of Asia. The gifts come from two provinces definitely under his control.

These two provinces are Macedonia, where he founded the churches at Philippi and Thessalonica (relying on funds from Philippi, Phil. 4:15-16), and Achaea, where he worked at Athens (1 Thess. 3:1) and founded the church at Corinth (relying on Macedonian funds, 2 Cor. 11:9). Both Macedonia and Achaea definitely contributed to the collection (Rom. 15:26). To be sure, the question of infringement arose in these provinces, at least at Corinth, where he speaks of others as proclaiming "another gospel" (2 Cor. 11:4), using the same language as that employed in the Galatian controversy (Gal. 1:6-9). He speaks of measures and a rule, and of boasting of other men's labors (2 Cor. 10:15).

What he means becomes fairly clear in his letter to the Romans, composed as he is about to take the collection to Jerusalem.[28] He insists that he is an apostle to all the gentiles (1:5; cf. 11:13), the Romans included (1:6-7, 13). He does not create discord but advocates the unity of Jews and Christians alike in Christ. He admits, indeed, a certain primacy of Jewish over gentile Christianity (1:16, 2:10, 3:1) and is deeply concerned with Jewish believers (9-11). As he proceeds to set forth his understanding of the gospel, he tells the Romans that he has long desired to see them and confirm them in their faith (1:9-13). At the end of the letter his hope is expressed somewhat differently, and with less confidence. He knows that opponents await him in Judaea and he is not sure that his gift will be acceptable to the church, but he hopes that he will be able to visit Rome on his way to Spain and perhaps be aided by the Roman church. He is anxious not to infringe upon the jurisdictions of others. He has worked "from Jerusalem roundabout as far as Illyricum" (15:19) on the Adriatic, but only "not where Christ was named, so as not to build on another man's foundation" (15:20). His reason for going to Spain is that he "no longer has a place in these regions" (15:23). In other words, his mission in Greece has been completed, and he must move westward. A generation later, Clement of Rome doubtless reflected his intention accurately: he went "to the limits of the west" (1 Clem. 5, 7).

Perhaps about A.D. 75 the author of the book of Acts provided something of a description of the mission of the early apostles "in Jerusalem and all Judaea and Samaria and to the end of the earth" (1:8) when he described the Jewish witnesses to the gift of the Spirit at Pentecost as coming "from every nation under the heaven" (2:5). He went on to speak of them as Parthians, Medes, Elamites; inhabitants of Mesopotamia, Armenia (?)[29] and Cappadocia, Pontus and Asia, Phrygia and Pamphylia, Egypt and the regions of Libya about Cyrene; Romans, . . . Cretans and Arabs" (2:9-11). This listing seems to be based on astrological geography, according to which various lands were especially related to the twelve signs of the zodiac.[30] This is not to say that either the author of Acts or some Christian predecessor was concerned with astrological geography as such.[31] It is only to say that in using geographical materials some early Christian took them from sources related to astrology. It was only among the Valentinian Gnostics that it was held that "the apostles replaced the signs of the zodiac, for as birth is governed by them, so rebirth is directed by the apostles."[32]

[28] On this collection cf. D. Georgi, *Die Geschichte der Kollekte des Paulus* (Hamburg, 1965).

[29] "Judaea" in the text of Acts does not seem to be correct; Tertullian (*Adv. Iud.* 7, 4) replaces it with "Armenia."

[30] E. Haenchen, *Die Apostelgeschichte* (Göttingen, 1959), 133-34; cf. S. Weinstock in *JRS* 39 (1949), 43-46. Both rely on F. Cumont in *Klio* 9 (1909), 263-73. Cf. also F. Boll, C. Bezold, and W. Gundel, *Sternglaube und Sterndeutung* (Leipzig, 1926), 64 and 157-58.

[31] Among other traces of astrological ideas, however, cf. Rom. 8:39 and Matt. 2:1-12.

[32] Clement, *Exc. Theod.* 25, 2.

A similar concern for "territorial" arrangements is found among Alexandrian Christians at the end of the second century and the beginning of the third. Eusebius reports that Pantaenus was said to have visited India, where he found that Bartholomew had long before proclaimed the gospel, leaving there a copy of the gospel of Matthew in Hebrew.[33] It is conceivable, though not provable, that both Pantaenus and the earlier apostle did visit India, for there was considerable commercial and cultural interchange between India and the Roman world.[34] Origen's statement that Thomas was assigned Parthia, Andrew Scythia, John Asia, and Peter Pontus, Galatia, Bithynia, Cappadocia, and Asia[35] is obviously based on Revelation and I Peter as far as the last two apostles are concerned, perhaps on apocryphal acts for Thomas and Andrew. Once more, however, the traditions underlying his possible sources may have been justified by fact. Though we know next to nothing about early oriental missions, there is no reason to assume that all the apostles turned westward or that all missions were finally successful. Presumably some of them worked among the large Jewish communities east of the Euphrates.[36]

III·THE QUESTION OF APOSTLES

According to the apostle Paul "God set in the church first apostles, second prophets, third teachers." After mentioning these three kinds of officers, Paul listed a rather heterogeneous group of functions: "then miracles, then gifts of healing, assistances, administrations, various kinds of tongues" (I Cor. 12:28). In his view the apostles are obviously primary. The fourteenth chapter of I Corinthians is the statement of an apostle to the effect that prophecy is superior to talking ecstatically in tongues. Nothing is said about miracles (characteristic of an apostle, according to 2 Cor. 12:12) or the other functions. Evidently the apostle holds that all Christians are potentially capable of the various functions, though they should aim at the higher offices, especially by prophesying (I Cor. 14:1). Elsewhere he urges them to exercise various kinds of special offices without confusing them (Rom. 12:6-8). But the office of the apostle is obviously superior to the others, and includes them. Paul is an apostle; he can also prophesy and teach, as well as speak in tongues (I Cor. 14:18-19). He proclaims the gospel and baptizes, although the preaching is more important than baptizing (I Cor. 1:14-17).

What makes him an apostle is his commission from God through Christ

[33] *H. E.* 5, 10, 2-3.
[34] Cf. M. Wheeler, *Rome Beyond the Imperial Frontiers* (London, 1954); J. D. M. Derrett in *KP* II 1388-93.
[35] *Gen. comm.* 3, in Eusebius, *H. E.* 3, 1, 1-3.
[36] Cf. J. Neusner, *A History of the Jews in Babylonia* I (Leiden, 1965), especially 166-69.

to proclaim the gospel, specifically among the gentiles (Gal. 1:1, 16). Others were apostles before him (Gal. 1:17; cf. 1 Cor. 15:7), and he knows apostles who were not among the Twelve. The implication of 1 Corinthians 9:5-6 is probably that Barnabas and "the brothers of the Lord" were also apostles. Barnabas, we learn from Acts 4:36-37, gave his property to the church at Jerusalem; the author of Acts calls him an apostle (14:14), but gives no explanation of the presence of James, presumably the Lord's brother, at Jerusalem (12:17; cf. 15:13). Presumably he was somehow commissioned by the risen Christ (cf. 1 Cor. 15:7).

The New Testament evidence leaves the position of Barnabas somewhat uncertain. Was he really an apostle? If so, was he an emissary (cf. Acts 11:22, 30) of the church at Jerusalem or Antioch, or of Christ? Was he called to be an apostle directly through a vision of Christ, or by other apostles? The uncertainty suggests that there was some vagueness about the use of the term "apostle," as there is in 2 Corinthians 8:23, Philippians 2:25, and Romans 16:7.

If we turn back to the gospels, we find that the term is used by the evangelists in relation to the Twelve, but that it is fairly clearly read back by them into the early narratives. In other words, while it is highly probable that there was a group of twelve and that their functions were those later assigned to apostles, they were not originally given this title; and from Paul's language we infer that the primary apostolic commissioning was a post-resurrection event, attested by the lists in 1 Corinthians 15.

IV·PROPHETS AND TEACHERS

In second and third place after the apostles, Paul says, were the prophets and the teachers of the church. Paul makes no mention of individuals who are prophets or teachers, though he recognizes prophesying and teaching as distinguishable gifts of divine favor. In Acts, on the other hand, we hear of the prophet Agabus who went from Jerusalem to Antioch, predicting a famine in the future (11:28), and later went from Judaea to Caesarea to predict Paul's troubles at Jerusalem (21:10-11). Other prophets at Jerusalem included Judas and Silas, sent out to convey the apostolic decree (15:32). The Jerusalem prophets were either rather independent, like Agabus, or under the control of the apostles and elders, like Judas and Silas. At Antioch, on the other hand, it appears that prophets and teachers, among them Barnabas and Saul, actually governed the community. The others commissioned Barnabas and Saul for their mission to the northwest (13:1-3).

According to Acts 11:19-26, the church at Antioch had been founded from Jerusalem; at first it consisted only of Jews, but later disciples from

Cyprus and Cyrene made converts among Greeks, and Barnabas was sent from Jerusalem to investigate the situation. As the numbers grew he needed assistance, and he therefore sought out Saul in Tarsus and brought him back to Antioch. After Agabus' prediction of famine the church at Antioch demonstrated its solidarity with Jerusalem by sending relief. The funds were transmitted to the presbyters there by Barnabas and Saul (11:29-30).

V·PRESBYTERS

The term "presbyter" or "elder" is not related to any sacerdotal status or function. It simply refers to an older man, who by virtue of age and experience was given respect in the Jewish synagogue or the Jewish-Christian church. In the indubitably genuine Pauline epistles no mention of such officers occurs. According to Acts, on the other hand, there were presbyters at Jerusalem (as we have just seen), and with the apostles they governed the church there (15:2, 4, 6, 22-23). They must have corresponded roughly to the Jewish Sanhedrin. No explanation of their origin is provided, although Acts 14:23 states that in Cilicia Paul and Barnabas "appointed presbyters in the churches." Since both of them have just been designated—for the first time—as "apostles" (14:4, 14), it would appear that they made the appointments in virtue of their office. By analogy, then, the presbyters at Jerusalem would be apostolic appointees.

The absence of presbyters from the Pauline epistles can be explained as due to the presence of officers equivalent to them. In 1 Thessalonians Paul commends "those who labor among you and are in charge of you in the Lord and instruct you" (5:12). Such men are evidently equivalent to presbyters. At Corinth the analogy becomes even clearer, for Christians are to be subordinate to the household of Stephanas (presumably primarily to Stephanas himself) and to other such persons who labor on behalf of the community. This household is especially commended as being "the first fruits of Achaea" (1 Cor. 16:15-16; cf. 1:16); it was therefore important that its members had been Christians for a relatively long time. They were presbyters at least in relation to Christian service.

When such leaders of the churches were sent out to preach the gospel or to maintain Christian communications they too could be called "apostles." Such was the situation in regard to Epaphroditus, sent from Philippi to Paul in prison; Paul called him "your apostle" (Phil. 2:25) and elsewhere spoke of "apostles of churches" (2 Cor. 8:23). Andronicus and Junius, mentioned in Romans 16:7, may have had the same function.

What this brief survey shows is that in early times the terminology of Christian office was highly fluid. It suggests that the functions of leadership, primary and secondary, existed but had not yet been crystallized. The most common early terms—apostle, prophet, teacher, presbyter—were derived from Judaism, in which they were currently employed.

VI·BISHOPS AND DEACONS

Philippians begins with mention of the "bishops and deacons" of the church. Such officers are not mentioned elsewhere in the genuine Pauline epistles and are named only once in Acts: the presbyters of Ephesus are also called "bishops" (20:28). The word we usually translate as "bishop" (*episcopos*) originally meant no more than "overseer"—and an overseer was in charge of the work of any kind of servant (*diakonos,* "deacon"). The language comes from the most ordinary kind of Greek and refers to any kind of administration. Indeed, in 1 Corinthians 12:28 Paul speaks of assistants and administrators (see also Rom. 12:7-8).

By the time when the Pastoral Epistles were written in Paul's name—to his two chief lieutenants, Timothy and Titus—the functions of bishops and deacons were so well established that lists of their qualifications, comparable to contemporary qualifications for Hellenistic administrators, could be provided. The requirements for a bishop are listed in 1 Timothy 3:1-7 and Titus 1:7-9; those for deacons, much the same, occur in 1 Timothy 3:8-13. Most of them are self-evidently necessary, as are those for presbyters given in Titus 1:6; the only one that might seem strange is that any candidate for any of the offices be "the husband of one wife." Presumably this refers to the case of a widower, who should not have remarried, although the author recommends the remarriage of young widows on practical grounds (1 Tim. 5:14-15).

Timothy is represented as having been left in charge of the church at Ephesus by Paul (1 Tim. 1:3), in accordance with the "prophecies" that pointed him out (1:18). He possesses the spiritual gift of governing and teaching, given him "through prophecy with the laying on of the hands of the presbytery" (4:11-14). In turn, he is not to "lay hands hastily" on anyone (5:22). The church he governs has a ministry consisting of one bishop, along with presbyters (some of whom "govern well" and are worthy of double honor, perhaps a wage of some sort, 1 Tim. 5:17-18) and deacons. Apparently ordination is effected by the bishop along with the presbyters. Timothy's charismatic gift came at the hands of Paul too (2 Tim. 1:6).

It is not quite clear what is meant when he is called an "evangelist" (2 Tim. 4:5). Evangelists are mentioned in Acts 21:8 and Ephesians 4:11, and they appear to have definite functions; but we do not know what they were. From

2 Timothy it appears that the primary function was not only to preach the gospel but to explain it and defend it.

Titus is represented as having been left in Crete by Paul in order to appoint presbyters and, indeed, bishops throughout the island's cities (Tit. 1:5-6; cf. 7-9). In this letter nothing is said of deacons, but it is likely that all three were intended to be read together.

As a whole, the letters reflect the fusion of the "bishops and deacons" mentioned in Philippians with the "presbyters" of Acts; the role of the bishop is not clearly differentiated from that of the presbyter who governs well, and the situation thus resembles what we shall find in the Roman church toward the end of the first century. We should assume that the Pastoral Epistles reflect the organization of the churches, at least in Asia as well as in Rome, around the time when Acts was written—or, roughly, in A.D. 75-80. The picture is different from the one we shall find in the contemporary *Didache*.

VII-ORGANIZATION AND SUCCESSION

It is obvious that, like Luke, the author of the Pastorals was concerned with continuity. He wrote in Paul's name and traced the authority of Timothy and Titus back to the apostle. Looking forward, he depicted both of them as appointing and ordaining others. Such concern with organization and succession is notably absent from the Gospel and Epistles of John, apparently composed either in Syria or in Asia, perhaps around the same time. In the Gospel the technical term "apostle" does not appear, and there is no mention of the Twelve, even though Jesus is described as sending forth his disciples (John 4:38, 13:16, 17:18). Their mission really begins after the resurrection, when the risen Lord sends them forth as the Father sent him, imparts the Holy Spirit to them, and commissions them to forgive and retain sins (20:21-23; cf. Matt. 16:19, 18:18). In 1-2 John there is no mention of any Christian officers. Only in 3 John do we find a problem related to authority. The author addresses "the beloved Gaius," who welcomes visitors and therefore is favorably mentioned "before the church." He commends a certain Demetrius, although he does not say why. On the other hand, he severely criticizes Diotrephes because, with his self-aggrandizement, he "does not receive us" or other Christians and expels more hospitable members from the church. It seems unlikely that the author, who calls himself "the presbyter," was an apostle, for Diotrephes thought he could exclude him from the community he controlled. But what office can Diotrephes have held? Some have thought that he was an early monarchical bishop, exalting himself at the expense of elders. Perhaps this is correct, but if so it should be noted that "the presbyter" does not deny the existence or appropriateness of a first rank; he simply criticizes Diotrephes for his abuse of the office. What this letter suggests is that the situation is one in which the organization of the communities was not clearly determined. It reflects, in fact, the need for a clearly defined structure. One might almost claim that if the church involved was in Asia Minor, it provided an example of the situation Ignatius of Antioch was later trying to correct.

CHAPTER V
SOME CHRISTIAN
CONTROVERSIES

If we look only at the expansion of the Christian movement and the development of offices in it, we gain the impression of a rather straight-line movement from Jerusalem to the edges of the Roman world, with few difficulties that could not be solved in conferences. A closer look at the Pauline epistles, however, allows us to see something of what the early Christian converts thought was going on. Through Paul's agreements, criticisms, and condemnations we can see what a variety of interpretation was actually present within the churches. It must be recalled that though Paul regarded these Christians' views and actions as largely mistaken, they themselves obviously believed that they were correctly interpreting the gospel.

All the major letters of Paul were concerned with controversy. Those addressed to the Christians at Thessalonica in Macedonia dealt with problems related to the return of Jesus from heaven and to Christian behavior during the time before his return. There were those who held that "the day of the Lord" had come[1] or was coming in the very near future. For this reason they believed that they could live in idleness and, perhaps, in sexual promiscuity.

[1] Cf. 2 Thess. 2:2.

Conceivably they thought they were following the command of Jesus to seek God's kingdom and receive food and clothing as gifts.[2] The eschatological problem was obviously primary. In reply, Paul argued that while the Lord would come down from heaven, the time of his coming was not known.[3] In the interval the Thessalonians were to obey the will of God and try to attain sanctity in sexual matters.[4] In a second letter he explained that the coming of Christ would be considerably delayed; meanwhile "if anyone does not wish to work he is not to eat."[5] This discussion reflects not the presentation of a carefully worked-out doctrine but an attempt to work out the doctrine in the face of obvious difficulties.

Paul's letters to the church at Corinth in Achaea (especially I Corinthians) provide the clearest picture we have of life in any of the early Christian communities. This seaport town had been razed in 146 B.C. but was re-established by Augustus as a Roman "colony" with an autonomous local government, tax exemption, and a Roman administration. It was a center for sailors, prostitutes sacred and secular, and Cynic philosophy; indeed Dio reports that the Cynic Diogenes felt he should go to Corinth (where he later died) because a wise man ought to go where there are the most fools.[6] Religiously the situation was mixed, with old temples intermingled with shrines of oriental gods and at least one Jewish synagogue.

Corinth was the capital of the Roman senatorial province of Achaea, and in the book of Acts (18:12) is mentioned the arrival of Gallio as proconsul. This official, L. Iunius Gallio Annaeanus, was brother of the emperor's tutor Seneca and became consul suffectus between 53 and 55. The date of his proconsulship is provided by an inscription from Delphi. Gallio is named as proconsul of Achaea; the emperor Claudius has been acclaimed as imperator for the twenty-sixth time. This event occurred in the year 52. Gallio was therefore in office either in 51-52 or in 52-53.[7]

After some earlier correspondence, Paul wrote to the Corinthians from Ephesus in the hope of terminating the divisions which were rending their community. Almost everything in his letter illustrates the problems presented not only by the Jewish-Christian eschatological preaching but also by the presence of both Jews and gentiles in the church. The very formula with which the letter begins is a Greek version of a blessing used in synagogues.[8] Somewhat further on, there may be echoes of a Jewish homily

---

[2] Matt. 6:19-34; Luke 12:15-34.

[3] I Thess. 4:13—5:11.

[4] I Thess. 4:1-8.

[5] 2 Thess. 2:1-12; 3:10.

[6] Dio Chrysostom, *Or.* 8, 5; see also D. R. Dudley, *A History of Cynicism* (London, 1937).

[7] *SIG*³ 801; cf. K. Lake in F. J. F. Jackson and K. Lake, *The Beginnings of Christianity* V (London, 1933), 460-64.

[8] H. Lietzmann in *TU* 68 (1958), 284-87.

on wisdom (1:16-31),[9] while the term "Lord of glory" (2:8) comes from Jewish apocalyptic.[10] Such examples might easily be multiplied. What Paul has to say finds parallels in Jewish writings and in Hellenistic and Roman documents as well.

Those whom Paul criticized, on the other hand, seem to have turned their backs on Judaism—just as, to some extent, he had done. They had an exalted opinion of their own status, for they possessed wisdom and perhaps a special form of knowledge (gnōsis). They claimed to be powerful, well-born, intelligent, strong, and famous. They could argue that they were filled or even satiated; they were rich; they were kings. They were free and possessed authority; everything had become permissible for them. Their own conscience, or consciousness of being right, was their guide. They were spiritual beings ("pneumatics"), while others were merely "psychic" (animate) or perhaps "sarkic" (fleshly). As inferences from their wisdom they drew practical conclusions. No one could be judged by another's conscience, and no action even though regarded as sinful by others could affect a man's essential nature. Dietary regulations, Jewish in origin, were matters of indifference; since there is only one God, idols have no real existence and one can eat meats sacrificed to them. Like eating, sex is a natural function and is not bound by regulations.[11]

Many of these ideas were clearly related to the Cynic-Stoic picture of the ideal wise man, presented at Corinth in Paul's time by the Cynic philosopher Demetrius. The doctrine obviously led to anarchy in state and church alike. Nero banished Demetrius from Rome; Vespasian deported him to an island.[12] Paul argued with the Corinthian Christians and made use of Roman political analogies.

To a considerable extent Paul was in agreement with the Corinthians, but he had to point out that they were providing an unreal picture of themselves and their situation. They were describing themselves as already living in the circumstances of the kingdom of God; they were speaking as if it had already come. It had not come, however, and the life of the Christian in the present situation was one of suffering, not of success.[13]

One of the Corinthians' main points suggests that they were acquainted with sayings of Jesus about life in the kingdom. They believed that they were already "filled," rich, and reigning.[14] To reign and to be rich was character-

---

[9] E. Peterson in *Biblica* 32 (1951), 97-103.
[10] 1 Enoch 22, 14 and *passim*.
[11] In spite of attempts to relate the Corinthians' views to Gnosticism (e.g., by W. Schmithals, *Die Gnosis in Korinth*, Göttingen, 1956), better parallels are provided in Cynicism; cf. A. Oltramare, *Les origines de la diatribe romaine* (Lausanne, 1926).
[12] Philostratus, *Vit. Apollon.* 4, 42; Dio 65, 13; cf. R. MacMullen, *Enemies of the Roman Order* (Cambridge, Mass., 1966), 46-94.
[13] 1 Cor. 1:18—2:5; 4:9-13.
[14] 1 Cor. 4:8.

istic both of the ideal wise man and of the Christian in God's kingdom.[15] The word "filled," however, recalls the promise of Jesus that the hungry would be "filled."[16] Apparently his promise was taken by the Corinthians to refer to their present state. Paul argues against this notion that the apostles are actually hungry and thirsty, not "filled."[17] The kingdom of God is going to be inherited; it lies in the future.[18]

There is no reason to suppose that the Corinthians were adherents of a sect like the Gnostic sects of the second century (see Chapter VIII). It is worth pointing out, however, that something like their attitude clearly recurs later among the followers of a certain Prodicus.[19] This man's disciples, who called themselves "Gnostics," held that they were "by nature" sons of a First God. As sons of the supreme King they were princes or "royal sons." Indeed they claimed to be kings and therefore to live free to do as they pleased; they quoted the Greek proverb, "For a king, law is unwritten."

Though the followers of Prodicus were clearly Gnostics, since they taught that they had come into the world as into an alien land not under the control of their Father or themselves, they certainly relied on sayings of Jesus to make their point. They referred to themselves as "lords of the Sabbath" and thus had in mind the saying that "the Son of Man is lord of the Sabbath"; they must have understood the term "Son of Man" as referring peculiarly to themselves.[20] They also spoke of sexual intercourse as an obligation; it was a "mystical union" which lifted them into the kingdom of God. Such a saying does not occur in the Christian gospels but may well have circulated in apocryphal tradition.[21] Indeed, according to Clement, a disciple of Prodicus approached a Christian virgin and cited the text, "Give to everyone who asks you."[22] She replied that if he was interested in marriage he should ask her mother for her hand.

What differentiates Prodicus from the Corinthians is the fact that as a second-century Gnostic he had a system and a detailed myth of origins. There is no reason to suppose that he was the heir of the Corinthians.[23] We have referred to him only to show how under later circumstances the approach the Corinthians took could rise again.

Corinth was not the only place in which Paul encountered difficulties, nor

[15] Cf. especially Luke 6:20-21.
[16] Matt. 5:6; Luke 6:21.
[17] I Cor. 4:11.
[18] I Cor. 6:9-10; 15:50.
[19] Clement, *Str.* 3, 27-33; cf. Tertullian, *Adv. Val.* 3, 6; *Scorp.* 15, 6.
[20] Cf. Mark 2:28 and parallels.
[21] Cf. Valentinians in Irenaeus, *Adv. haer.* 1, 6, 4; a verbal parallel in I Clem. 49, 4.
[22] Cf. Matt. 5:42; Luke 6:30.
[23] His followers used secret "Zoroastrian" books (Clement, *Str.* 1, 69, 6); cf. H.-C. Puech in *Entretiens sur l'antiquité classique* 5 (1957), 165-67.

were the views of the Corinthians the only ones to provide trouble for him. (In addition, other difficulties at Corinth are reflected in 2 Corinthians.[24]) Among the churches of Galatia in northern Asia Minor he had to argue against Jewish-Christian missionaries who claimed that he was, or should be, subordinate to the apostles at Jerusalem, that the Jewish calendar ought to be observed, and that gentile Christians had to be circumcised. In Paul's opinion these missionaries were teaching what amounted to "another gospel"—a gospel which obviously involved "another Jesus" and "another Spirit."[25] Those who preserved his letters clearly thought that he was right. At the time when he wrote, however, the situation was by no means so settled. It was quite possible that Paul's opponents would win the day.

To cite only one more example, we may refer to the situation at Colossae in Asia Minor, either in Paul's time or somewhat later. Some Christians seem to have advocated a "philosophy" which involved Jewish ritual observances and some kind of compulsory asceticism, perhaps related to ecstatic visions.[26] The answer of the author of Colossians is to remind his readers of Christ's all-sufficient cosmic functions and of the redemption given them in baptism.[27]

What these examples show is the difficulty encountered by early Christians in determining just what the Christian gospel was. The eschatological problem provided many occasions for difficulty; so did the relation of Christian thought to popular philosophy, toward which it was moving, and to Judaism, which it was in danger of abandoning. Paul tried to lay emphasis on the coming return of Jesus and of the kingdom of God while insisting that the kingdom had not yet come. He tried to make use of the more stable elements in Hellenistic moral philosophy, usually as mediated by Hellenistic Judaism, while maintaining that to the Israelites belonged "the adoption, the glory, the covenants, the legislation, the worship, the promises, and the Christ as a human being" (Rom. 9:4–5). What he was working out was a new expression of Christianity.

It is by no means clear that, in spite of the difficulties which Paul and other Christian leaders encountered in dealing with Jewish communities in Palestine and outside, there was a definitive break with Judaism before the fall of Jerusalem in 70. Admittedly Paul could use violent language about other Jews, and could even speak of them generally as having killed the Lord Jesus and the prophets and persecuting himself and displeasing God and men (1 Thess. 2:15). The evangelist John depicts Jesus as constantly engaged in controversy with "the Jews," and claims that it had been decided that anyone

[24] On these cf. D. Georgi, *Die Gegner des Paulus im 2. Korintherbrief* (Neukirchen-Vluyn, 1964).

[25] Gal. 1:6-7; cf. 2 Cor. 11:4.

[26] Col. 2:8, 16-23; cf. G. Bornkamm, *Das Ende des Gesetzes* (Munich, 1952), 139-56.

[27] Cf. E. Käsemann, *Essays on New Testament Themes* (London, 1964), 149-68; also H. M. Schenke in *Zeitschrift für Theologie und Kirche* 61 (1964), 391-403.

who acknowledged Jesus as the Messiah would be expelled from the synagogue.[28] If there ever was such a decision, however, it came long after Jesus' lifetime.[29] Originally Christianity was a sect like others within Judaism. The success of the gentile mission led to separation, which we see reflected in Ignatius' use of the term "Christianism" as opposed to "Judaism."[30]

[28] John 9:22; 12:42; cf. 16:2 (future).
[29] Justin, *Dial.* 16, 4.
[30] *Magn.* 10, 3; *Philad.* 6, 1. "Judaism" occurs in 2 and 4 Maccabees and in Gal. 1:13-14.

PART TWO·CHRIS-
TIANITY IN THE
SECOND CENTURY

CHAPTER VI
ROME AND THE CHRISTIANS

I. ANTECEDENTS AND PRECEDENTS

The first and most important encounter between Christianity and the Roman government took place in the year 30 when Jesus himself was brought before the Roman prefect of Judaea, who condemned him to death and had the title "the king of the Jews" affixed to his cross. The responsibility of the prefect for Jesus' death was minimized by later Christian writers who endeavored to make it appear that "the Jews" alone brought it about. The official Roman position as reflected by Tacitus, however, clearly shows that Jesus was viewed as the founder of a novel and pernicious superstition and that the prefect's decision was approved.[1]

We have already seen that the crucifixion of Jesus occurred in a frontier province constantly on the verge of revolt. Roman administrators found it difficult to differentiate the early Christian movement from the groups which shared a "love of freedom" and claimed that no man could be called master

[1] Tacitus, *Ann.* 15, 44.

because the only ruler and master was God.[2] As tension increased during the period before war finally broke out in 66, there were doubtless Christians who like the Essenes suffered torture rather than "blaspheme the Lawgiver or eat any unsuitable food."[3] They certainly agreed with the Jewish rebels in Egypt who refused to acknowledge "Caesar as their master" (*Kaisara despotēn*).[4]

Suspicion was attached to Christians in spite of the professed loyalty of leaders like the apostle Paul, a Roman citizen who about the year 60 was sent from Jerusalem to Rome only because he had appealed to Caesar (Acts 26:32). The book of Acts ends with Paul at Rome, preaching and teaching "without hindrance" and apparently awaiting the outcome of his appeal to Caesar. No doubt the author of Acts is strongly emphasizing Paul's status as a Roman citizen, but according to Paul's own letter to the Romans (13:1–7) he was a loyal subject of the emperor and, like Jesus himself (Mark 12:13–17 and parallels) advocated the payment of Roman taxes.

The relation of the Jerusalem Christians to the Roman state at the time of the Jewish revolt is not absolutely clear, but the execution of James the brother of Jesus at a time when there was no Roman procurator in Judaea does not suggest that the Christians of Jerusalem were viewed as hostile to the Roman state. All the evidence we have indicates that they would have responded to the oracle of a peasant named Joshua, who at Tabernacles in 62 pronounced woes upon Jerusalem—not upon the Romans.[5]

Before 64, it would appear, Christian martyrs suffered chiefly because of tensions arising between Jews and local Roman administrators or directly between Jews and Christians. In 64, however, Christians were directly confronted by the imperial power at Rome. On July 19 in that year a fire destroyed a large part of the city and it was suspected by many that the emperor Nero was responsible for it. Many of the buildings destroyed were in the area where he was building a great new palace. In order to quell the rumor, Nero accused the Christians of arson. According to Tacitus, who wrote about fifty years later but relied on earlier documents, the Christians were already the object of popular hatred because of their "crimes." He does not specify what these were, though he speaks of their "hatred of the human race," an accusation which he elsewhere directs against Jews.[6]

With what Syme calls "documentary precision" Tacitus explains how the name "Christian" arose. It was derived from Christus, who had been put to death under Tiberius by the procurator Pontius Pilatus. Though the pernicious superstition which Christus established was checked for a time, it broke out again not just in Judaea but at Rome itself, "the common

[2] Josephus, *Bell.* 2, 118; *Ant.* 18, 23.
[3] *Bell.* 2, 152.
[4] *Ibid.*, 7, 418-19.
[5] Josephus, *Bell.* 6, 300-9.
[6] Tacitus, *Ann.* 15, 44; see *Hist.* 5, 5.

receptacle of all that everywhere was vile."[7] Tacitus' contemporary Suetonius also notes that Christians were punished in Nero's time, but lays emphasis only on their "new and criminal superstition."[8]

Convicted on the charge of arson and possibly also of such crimes as holding Thyestean feasts (cannibalism) and engaging in magic, some Christians were dressed in animal skins and lacerated by dogs; others were crucified and burned in Nero's gardens while the emperor, dressed as a charioteer, drove among the audience. Clement of Rome, writing perhaps a generation after this massacre, almost certainly has it in mind when he describes the martyrdoms of Peter and Paul and of Christian women who suffered as Danaids and Dircae (cc. 5–6). The daughters of Danaus, according to myth, were awarded to victors in a gymnastic contest; Dirce was bound to the horns of a bull, as represented at Naples by the Toro Farnese. The kind of bloody realism that would produce such spectacles was favored by Nero, according to Suetonius. In his shows he seems to have had a bull mount a real Pasiphae who was concealed in a wooden heifer; and an Icarus, attempting flight, spattered his blood over the emperor.[9]

Whatever the gory details may be, it is noteworthy that Nero set a precedent for dealing with Christians in the city of Rome, not outside it, and the precedent was binding only during the rest of his reign.[10] His persecution cannot therefore explain the later anti-Christian policy. The case was unique.

This is not to say that the problem for the state was unique. Under Nero the aristocrat Thrasea Paetus was forced to commit suicide, and among the charges brought against him were several with which Christians, at least later, were confronted. Thrasea would not take the solemn oath of loyalty to the emperor at the beginning of the year; he never offered sacrifice for the safety of the emperor (or for his "heavenly voice" as a singer); he did not believe in the deity of the late empress Poppaea. As Tacitus sums up the situation, he rejected religious rites and broke the laws.[11] But the religious disaffection which in Thrasea's case was apparently a symptom of his political attitude was, for Christians, the heart of the matter. They could not accept the gods or the rites of the Graeco-Roman world. They were not concerned with restoring the Roman republic or with any particular form of governmental order. On the practical question of cultus, however, they rejected the demands of Roman civic life.

If there was a persecution under Domitian—and the evidence for it is tenuous—it was not directed against Christians as such. First we possess a story told a hundred years later, by Christians, concerning Domitian's in-

[7] R. Syme, *Tacitus* (Oxford, 1958), 469; see 533 n. 5.
[8] Suetonius, *Nero* 16, 2.
[9] *Ibid.*, 12, 2; 11, 2.
[10] A. N. Sherwin-White in *JTS* 3 (1952), 208-9.
[11] Tacitus, *Ann.* 16, 22; cf. C. Saumagne in *Revue des études latines* 33 (1955), 241-57.

vestigation of tax matters in Palestine. Since the destruction of the temple in 70 the temple tax had been paid to the imperial treasury; widespread evasion had resulted. According to the story, two grandsons of Jude were asked about their ownership of land and, in passing, about their political views. Their property, worth 9,000 denarii, consisted of 39 plethra of farm land from which they supported themselves and paid real estate taxes. They looked forward to a "kingdom of Christ," but it had nothing to do with Jewish expectations; it would be "heavenly and angelic" and would come only at the end of the age. Since they were obviously not liable for the temple tax, they were released.[12]

Second, both Suetonius and Dio Cassius[13] say something about a plot against Domitian which was put down in 95. The emperor arrested Flavius Clemens, consul in that year, his wife Domitilla, and Acilius Glabrio, consul four years earlier. Clemens and his wife were accused of "godlessness, for which many others also were condemned because they had drifted into the practices of the Jews." So says Dio; Suetonius, on the other hand, describes Clemens as suspected of conspiracy, Glabrio with others as a genuine revolutionary. The church historian Eusebius thought that Clemens and his wife were Christians,[14] but—even though there was a Christian catacomb of Domitilla—there is no sufficient reason for agreeing with him. The question involved was (at least in part) adherence to Judaism. Under Nerva, Dio tells us, no one was allowed to bring charges of the adoption of Jewish ways of life,[15] and this statement is confirmed by coins of Nerva bearing the inscription FISCI IUDAICI CALUMNIA SUBLATA. When Dio spoke of Judaism he did not mean Christianity.

Third, it is highly probable that the Apocalypse of John, with its prediction of persecutions, was written "toward the end of Domitian's region," as Irenaeus states.[16] The actual events to which the author refers, however, consist only of a famine and the legislation provided in order to mitigate its effects.[17] There have been sporadic martyrdoms, to be sure, but no general persecution has occurred. The anticipations of the author do not prove that such a persecution took place.

[12] Eusebius (Hegesippus), *H. E.* 3, 20, 1-6; cf. Suetonius, *Domitian* 12, 2.
[13] Suetonius, *Domitian* 15; Dio 77, 14.
[14] *H. E.* 3, 18, 4.
[15] Dio 78, 2.
[16] *Adv. haer.* 5, 30, 3.
[17] Rev. 6:5-6; cf. Suetonius, *Domitian* 7 and 14; Philostratus, *Vit. soph.* I, 21, p. 520; J. Moffatt in *Expositor* VII 6 (1908), 359-69; Rostovtzeff, *SEHRE*² II 599-600.

II-PLINY AND TRAJAN; HADRIAN

Probably in 110, however, Christians were certainly punished as Christians by Plinius Secundus, legate of Trajan in Bithynia and Pontus on the south shore of the Black Sea. After accusations were brought against Christians he proceeded to hold an investigation (*cognitio*), though he had never been present when similar inquiries were made at Rome or elsewhere. Those who insisted that they were Christians, even after being warned three times that the penalty was death, were either executed or, if Roman citizens, sent to Rome. Their "stubbornness and inflexible obstinacy," always punishable under Roman law, was equivalent to *contumacia*,[18] something like "contempt of court."

After this first inquiry had been concluded, he received an anonymous accusation containing many names. Obviously the discovery of the Christian "core group" led non-Christians to attack those less closely affiliated with the movement.[19] Two types of defendants came before the legate. First, there were those who said they had never been Christians. Second, there were those who had once been Christians but no longer adhered to the group; of these some had left it as long as twenty years before, while others had withdrawn after Pliny himself banned the existence of sodalities (*hetaeriae*) in the province. Both kinds of defendants had to pass a test which Pliny provided by leading them in an invocation of the gods and the offering of incense and wine to an image of the emperor Trajan; he also required them to anathematize Christ, since he had heard that genuine Christians could not be compelled to perform these actions.

In an effort to discover exactly what Christian cult practices were he discovered that

they were accustomed to meet on a fixed day before dawn, to say an antiphonal hymn to Christ as to a god, and to bind themselves with an oath—not for performing any crime but for abstaining from theft, robbery, adultery, and the violation of oaths, and the refusal to repay a deposit on demand. After this they were accustomed to depart and then meet again for a meal which was ordinary and harmless.

The torture of two slaves whom the Christians apparently called "deaconesses" added evidence of nothing but "a crude and exaggerated superstition."

Pliny's concern for details of the Christians' oath and meals was doubtless based on his reading of Livy, who told of the earlier investigation of the Bacchanalia in Etruria, or on similiar accounts of the Druids or other groups. The Bacchants took an oath to perform "every crime and act of lust"; their

---

[18] A. N. Sherwin-White, *The Letters of Pliny* (Oxford, 1966), 699.
[19] Compare the "envy" related to persecution according to Tacitus and Clement of Rome.

common meal combined wine with feasting and perhaps with cannibalism. Pliny found that the Christian practices were quite different.

The real danger presented by Christianity lay not in immoral behavior but in the spread of this superstition from town to country and into all levels of society. It threatened other religions and the suppliers of animals for sacrifice, as Pliny pointed out. With the arrest of suspected Christians, temple attendance improved along with the sale of animals.

In spite of the changed situation, Pliny still doubted that he had followed exactly the correct procedure, and he wrote to the emperor for guidelines. (1) What was to be investigated and punished? The name "Christian" or the crimes associated with the name? If the latter, Pliny's investigation itself strongly suggested that there were no crimes. (2) To what extent should the investigation be carried out? Pliny himself was in doubt as to whether or not he should have accepted an anonymous accusation. (3) What penalty was to be inflicted? Should there be allowances for age and physical condition? (4) Could the charge of being a Christian be dismissed upon proof supplied by public recantation? Pliny himself strongly favored this course because of the return to religion already under way.

In reply, Trajan approved what the legate had already done. In his view, there was no precise precedent for dealing with Christians. "Nothing can be established as a universal principle with a fixed form." He gave no answer at all to Pliny's first question. As for the second, Christians were not to be sought out, and anonymous accusations, characteristic of Domitian's reign, were never to be used in criminal cases. Third, if brought to court and convicted, Christians had to be punished, one way or another. Fourth, recantation if demonstrated by sacrifice to "our gods" (not the emperor's image) was to result in a free and full pardon.

Writing nearly a century later, the Christian apologist Tertullian denounced the confusion implicit in this decision. If Christians were to be condemned, why were they not sought out? If they were not sought out, why were they not pardoned?[20] The answer to Tertullian's question must surely be that like Pliny himself the emperor was trying to provide a workable administrative answer to a question that demanded a more basic analysis. To give such an analysis, however, would have demanded a close look at religious and political presuppositions which Roman administrators preferred to accept without question.

At the beginning of Hadrian's reign a similar question arose in the province of Asia, and again the administrators discussed only operational matters, not the substance of the charges. Probably in 121-122 the proconsul Silvanus Granianus, disturbed by growing numbers of false accusations, asked Hadrian for instructions. The emperor replied to his successor, Minucius Fundanus. In essence his reply was the same as Trajan's. He worked out the implications of what we have called the second and third answers. Accusa-

[20] Tertullian, *Apol.* 2, 7-8.

tions were to be made only before a magistrate; no attention was to be paid to "the turbulent methods of a fanatical multitude when trying to influence the normal procedure of the court."[21] For this reason it would be best for the proconsul to conduct his own investigation. Of course convicted Christians were to be punished; but calumniators—those who accused non-Christians of being Christians—were to be punished too. On this basis there was no change whatever in the legal position of Christians, even though Justin, who quoted the emperor's rescript (*Apol.* 1, 68), claimed that there was.[22]

It is obvious that Roman administrators could clearly differentiate Christians from Jews, and it is not surprising that when Jewish revolts took place under both Trajan and Hadrian the Christians were not subject to prosecution. They were not involved in these uprisings, both of which seem to have had messianic overtones.

In 115 a violent revolt broke out among the Jews of Cyrene and the province suffered devastation. During the following year it spread to Cyprus and to Egypt. The Roman forces had to withdraw to Alexandria, and there both the temple of Nemesis and the principal Jewish synagogue were destroyed. What seems to be an edict of the prefect M. Rutilius Lupus denounces Jews and Greeks impartially for their acts of violence.[23] Whether or not this was a "messianic" revolt, it is significant that it was led by a Jewish "king" named either Lukuas or Andreias.[24] His guerrilla forces ravaged the Egyptian countryside, as papyrus letters attest,[25] until Q. Marcius Turbo arrived with military and naval forces and killed the Jewish king in 117.[26] There was also trouble in Palestine and in Mesopotamia and this was suppressed by Lusius Quietus, another of Trajan's generals.[27]

The revolt was accompanied by massacres of gentiles and Jews alike and by the destruction of pagan temples.[28] It obviously possessed religious implications, presumably recognized in the stage mime at Alexandria ridiculing the "king" in 117.[29] A few years later the Jewish population of Alexandria was somehow redistributed;[30] Jewish property elsewhere in Egypt was subject to confiscation.[31] At the end of the second century the victory over the Jews was still being celebrated.[32]

[21] W. Schmid in *Maia* 7 (1955), 9, to be qualified by the remarks of E. J. Bickerman in *Rivista di filologia* 96 (1968), 290-315.
[22] Even before Pliny's time Christians *had* to be punished; cf. J. Crook, *Law and Life of Rome* (Ithaca, N.Y., 1967), 335.
[23] Cf. H. A. Musurillo, *The Acts of the Pagan Martyrs* (Oxford, 1954), 59-60, 194-95.
[24] Eusebius, *H. E.* 4, 2; Dio 68, 32.
[25] *CPJ* II 436-37.
[26] Eusebius, *H. E.* 4, 2, 4.
[27] E. M. Smallwood in *Historia* 11 (1962), 500-10; R. Syme in *JRS* 48 (1958), 9.
[28] A. Fuks in *Aegyptus* 33 (1953), 131-58; A. Applebaum in *JJS* 13 (1962), 31-43.
[29] *Acta Pauli*, col. i (p. 49 Musurillo).
[30] *Ibid.*, col. vi (p. 52).
[31] *CPJ* II 445, 448.
[32] *CPJ* II 450=Wilcken, *Chrest.* 153.

Christians could not possibly have participated in this revolt against Rome, and their feeling of separateness from Jews and Judaism must have been intensified. At Alexandria the tendency among Christians to regard their religion as purely spiritual and, indeed, Gnostic was undoubtedly strengthened.

Another Jewish revolt, this time with definite messianic overtones, broke out in the spring of 132. Hadrian had visited Palestine in the summer of 130 and had given orders for the creation of a Roman colony, Aelia Capitolina, on the site of the ruined Jerusalem. A temple of Jupiter Capitolinus was to be built there and one of Zeus Hypsistos on Mount Gerizim in Samaria.[33] War broke out as soon as resistance to the emperor's plans could be organized. With rabbinic support, Simon son of Kosba proclaimed himself "prince of Israel." Some of the coins he struck bear this title and refer to the liberation of Israel or the liberty of Jerusalem. The famous rabbi Akiba believed that this son of Kosba ("bar Kosba") was fulfilling the prediction of Numbers 24:17—"a star shall arise out of Jacob"—and he was therefore often known as "bar Kochba" (son of the star).[34] His guerrillas seem to have annihilated one Roman legion, and the revolt was not suppressed until 135, probably in August, when he and the remnant of his supporters were killed. Hadrian had found it necessary to summon Sextus Julius Severus, legate of Britain, to command of the Roman troops in Judaea, and late that year a triumph was celebrated at Rome.[35] Dio Cassius, presumably relying on official records, says that the Romans had destroyed fifty camps and 985 villages and had killed no fewer than 580,000 men.[36]

Christians took no part in the revolt. The Epistle of Barnabas, perhaps written or published as work on the temple began, insists that the true temple is a spiritual one.[37] The Gnostic teacher Basilides referred to "prophets" by the names of Barkabba and Barkoph, perhaps parodying the name of Bar Kochba as he also ridiculed dietary laws and confession during persecution.[38] Indeed, Justin states that Bar Kochba "ordered the Christians, and them alone, to be led off to terrible punishments unless they denied that Jesus was the Christ and blasphemed him."[39]

Apparently it was soon after the revolt that the Gnostic teacher Marcion

---

[33] Dio 69, 12, 1; R. J. Bull in *Biblical Archaeologist* 31 (1968), 58-72.

[34] The prediction had been important at Qumran; cf. J. M. Allegro in *JBL* 75 (1956), 174-87.

[35] *Ornamenta triumphalia* for the general, *ILS* 1056; Hadrian was not Imperator II on April 14, 135 (*CIL* XVI 82) but had received the title before December 9 (*IG* XII Suppl. 239); cf. F. M. Heichelheim in *Jewish Quarterly Review* 34 (1943-44), 61-63.

[36] Dio 69, 14, 1.

[37] Barn. 16:4; cf. H. Bietenhard in *Judaica* 4 (1948), 94-100. On the date of the revolt see J. A. Fitzmyer in J. L. McKenzie, ed., *The Bible in Current Catholic Thought* (New York, 1962), 149-51.

[38] Agrippa Castor in Eusebius, *H. E.* 4, 7, 7.

[39] *Apol.* 1, 31, 6. A papyrus letter from Simon ben Kosba refers to "Galilaeans," but they are not Christians (P. Benoit, J. T. Milik, and R. de Vaux, *Les grottes de Murabba' at* [*Discoveries in the Judaean Desert*, II, Oxford, 1961], 159).

came from Pontus to Rome and tried to propagate his gospel there. A prominent feature of his doctrine was that the Old Testament predicted the coming of a Jewish messiah, who was to be a warrior and would capture Damascus and Samaria.[40] Obviously Bar Kochba had not been such a messiah, but Marcion wanted to make sure that Christians were not associated with any Jewish nationalist hopes. The Roman church seems not to have expelled Marcion until 144, and his initial success must be ascribed to the wave of anti-Jewish sentiment which followed the revolt.

Around the time when Marcion came to Rome the bishop Telesphorus may have suffered death as a martyr,[41] but nothing whatever is known of the circumstances of his martyrdom. It cannot be definitely related to problems within the community or to Roman policy in regard to the Christians.

III-CHRISTIANS UNDER THE ANTONINES

For a time, it would appear, Christians were virtually ignored by the Roman state, but around 150 they again came to the attention of judges. This fact is suggested by the appearance of the *Apology* of Justin about that time and confirmed by a case he describes in an appendix.[42] A woman converted to Christianity came to be alienated from her husband and finally divorced him. He thereupon denounced her as a Christian; she presented a petition to the emperor, asking for time to settle her affairs[43] before presenting her defense. This request was approved; Justin says nothing about the outcome. Meanwhile her husband denounced her Christian teacher Ptolemaeus, who was cast into prison and tortured presumably so that he would recant. Finally he was brought before the urban prefect Q. Lollius Urbicus, former legate in Britain and builder of the Antonine wall.[44] Urbicus asked only whether or not he was a Christian, and then sentenced him to death. Another Christian in court protested the decision on moral grounds. "It seems to me," said the judge, "that you too are one of them." The Christian's confession, followed by that of another bystander, immediately resulted in the death penalty. The only question, as Justin rightly pointed out, was that of the name "Christian." Justin and other apologists attacked this procedure as immoral, but it followed the precedent in existence before Trajan and Hadrian.

The precedent established by Trajan when he ordered search not to be made for Christians was broken toward the end of the reign of Antoninus Pius

[40] Tertullian, *Adv. Marc.* 3, 21, 1; 4, 20, 4; cf. A. von Harnack, *Marcion: das Evangelium vom fremden Gott* (ed. 2, Leipzig, 1924), 117 n. 1, 289*-90*.
[41] Irenaeus, *Adv. haer.* 3, 3, 3 (Greek in Eusebius, *H. E.* 5, 6, 4).
[42] *Apol.* 2, 2.
[43] For a similar request cf. P. Giss. 41=*Select Papyri* II 298 (about 120).
[44] Prefect by March 146: W. Hüttl, *Antoninus Pius* (Prague, 1933), I, 370.

when, after several executions had taken place at Smyrna in the province of Asia, mob enthusiasm led to a search for the bishop Polycarp.[45] This new precedent was followed in Gaul about twenty years later and is taken for granted by the anti-Christian writer Celsus.[46] As Bickerman points out, however, it was a concession to the mob and did not reflect imperial policy.[47]

Probably in 156 or 157 the eighty-six-year-old Polycarp, bishop of Smyrna, was arrested by police after slaves under torture had betrayed his hiding place in the countryside. In prison, he was urged to say "Caesar is lord" and to offer sacrifice, but he refused to comply and was therefore brought before the proconsul L. Statius Quadratus in the stadium at Smyrna. The proconsul tried to persuade him to recant and to consider his age; he could do so by taking an oath by the Fortune ("genius") of the emperor and by saying, "Away with the godless." Polycarp did say, "Away with the godless," but indicated that he had the crowd in the stadium in mind. Changing the formula to the one used in Pontus by Pliny, the proconsul asked him to take the oath and to curse Christ. Polycarp refused. After a third request to take the oath, Polycarp accused the proconsul of pretending not to know who he was and explicitly stated that he was a Christian; he was willing to explain the nature of Christianity should occasion be given. Like his predecessor Severus, the proconsul suggested that the accused should persuade the people.[48] Polycarp refused to do so; he did not regard them as worthy of hearing his defense. After threatening him with death by wild beasts or by fire, the proconsul sentenced him and he was burned alive.

This is the first account of a martyrdom in which the taking of an oath by the emperor's *tychē* is mentioned, though such oaths certainly go back to the reign of Augustus and were compulsory in the time of Caligula.[49] The earliest example on papyrus comes from August 10, 69, six weeks after the prefect of Egypt had ordered his legions to take an oath of allegiance to Vespasian.[50] After this time such oaths became common,[51] and during the reign of Antoninus Pius the situation was doubtless aggravated, as far as Christians were concerned, by the occasional designation of the emperor as *kyrios*, "lord."[52] Polycarp refused either to refer to Caesar as lord or to take an oath.

The question of the date of Polycarp's martyrdom deserves some attention, since in recent years the date February 23, 156, seemingly established by

---

[45] *Mart. Polyc.* 3, 2.
[46] Origen, *Contra Celsum* 8, 69.
[47] *Rivista di filologia* 96 (1968), 290-315, especially 314-15.
[48] Aelius Aristides, *Orat.* 26, 87, p. 447, 17 Keil.
[49] Horace, *Epist.* 2, 1, 16; Suetonius, *Gaius* 27, 3.
[50] *Pubblicazioni della Societa Italiana: Papiri Greci e Latini* XIV (Florence, 1957), no. 1433.
[51] E. Seidl, *Der Eid im römisch-ägyptischen Provinzialrecht* I (Munich, 1933), 11-13. For Latin examples cf. *ILS* 6088-89; 9059=Wilcken, *Chrest.* 463. Jews took them; cf. J. Juster, *Les juifs dans l'empire romain* (Paris, 1914), I 344.
[52] *Ibid.*, 13 and 36, with references to papyri of 144, 151, and 156.

the arguments of E. Schwartz, has often been rejected in favor of 177 or 167.[53] The later the date is set, of course, the more difficult it becomes to explain Polycarp's relation to Ignatius (unless Ignatius himself was martyred not under Trajan but under Hadrian) and the more necessary it becomes to reject the testimony of the *Martyrdom* to the effect that the proconsul was Statius Quadratus (c. 21). It is hard to see what purpose or "tendency" would be served by wrongly naming the proconsul, however, and we therefore adhere to a date around 156 or 157.[54] The date was important not only in regard to Polycarp himself but also because eleven other Christians from Philadelphia were martyred with him.[55] The impression made both on Christians and on pagans must have been pronounced, and conceivably it helps account for the contemporaneous rise of the Montanist movement.

Between 162, when Q. Junius Rusticus was consul for the second time and probably became urban prefect, and 168, when his successor probably took office, the apologist Justin with six companions came before the urban tribunal. The Acts of his martyrdom, evidently based on court records, have been handed down in two forms: the common, and apparently interpolated, version, and a shorter, more trustworthy version provided by one manuscript of the tenth century.[56] In the shorter version Justin still tries to argue with the prefect, but he takes less time. At the end of the discussion Rusticus asks him where the Christians meet, and Justin seems to say that some of them meet at his home, "above the Tiburtine bath." He acknowledges being a Christian, and Rusticus then turns to the others. They too acknowledge being Christians, some of them because they were instructed by their parents.

According to the longer version, the climax of the interrogation comes when Rusticus insists that they offer sacrifice to the gods. This note, while present in the shorter version, is a minor one. The basic question is simply whether or not Justin and the others persist in remaining Christians in the face of punishments. When they do persist, Rusticus orders their execution. The longer version thus probably reflects the time of Decius, in the third century; the shorter version is in conformity with second-century practise. Being a Christian was the basic offense. No compromise was possible either on the Christian side or on that of the Roman state. Rusticus was a Stoic of some repute and indeed had taught philosophy to Marcus Aurelius. In his eyes, as

---

[53] E. Schwartz, *Christliche und jüdische Ostertafeln* (Berlin, 1905), 125-38; H. Grégoire–P. Orgels in *Analecta Bollandiana* 69 (1951), 1-8; H.-I. Marrou, *ibid.*, 71 (1953), 5-20.

[54] P. Meinhold in *RE* XXI 1662-93; T. D. Barnes in *JTS* 18 (1967), 433-37.

[55] Cf. W. R. Schoedel, *Polycarp, Martyrdom of Polycarp*, etc. (Camden, N.J., 1967), 76.

[56] P. Franchi de' Cavalieri in *Studi e Testi* 8 (1902), 33-36, and 33 (1920), 5-17. My attention was drawn to this text by Mr. T. D. Barnes; cf. *JTS* 19 (1968), 509-31, with his reference to G. Lazzati in *Aevum* 27 (1953), 473.

in those of governors before him, Christianity was a superstition; more important, its adherents refused to obey the duly constituted authorities of the Roman state.

Around the time of the martyrdom of Justin a popular philosopher named Peregrinus Proteus demonstrated his contempt for death by setting himself afire at Olympia in 166. The antiquarian Aulus Gellius describes Peregrinus as a sober and consistent philosopher; he was banished from Rome by the prefect of the city under Antoninus Pius because of his attacks on the emperor. For us he is important because of a satire by Lucian which stresses the ease with which he could impose upon the Christians. According to Lucian, he joined the Christian movement in Palestine and soon won a reputation as prophet, president, and synagogue chief, interpreting and composing Christian books. When he was thrown into prison as a Christian, he was visited day and night by old women, widows, orphans, and men of rank. They had suppers in prison with him and read their "sacred discourses." Christians in the cities of Asia sent gifts from the common funds of the churches.

In Lucian's view

those wretches have persuaded themselves that they are all going to be immortal and will live forever, so that they despise death and voluntarily give themselves up—most of them. Furthermore their lawgiver . . . persuaded them that they are all brothers and that once converted and having denied the Greek gods they should worship that executed sophist and live in accordance with his laws. They therefore despise everything equally and hold everything in common, having accepted such ideas without a soundly based faith.

Lucian's picture of Christianity resembles the ideas expressed by the prefect Rusticus, and his view of Christians as essentially irrational will be repeated by the anti-Christian writer Celsus and by Galen, court physician to Marcus Aurelius and Commodus.[57]

Given the situation in which Christians suffered from widespread hostile suspicion and were subject to the death penalty if legal precedents were followed, their only recourse was to try to obtain a new precedent from the emperor himself. Their appeals are preserved in the major "apologies" of the second century.

Under the Roman system, private petitioners could address libelli either to the emperor or to his provincial representatives such as legates or the prefect of Egypt. (In theory proconsuls represented the senate; in fact they too were servants of the emperor.) Answers to such petitions, apparently read by the emperors themselves, were made through the secretariat a libellis. The original versions of petition and rescript, approved by the emperor, were

---

[57] Lucian, *De morte Peregrini* 11-16; cf. H. D. Betz, *Lukian von Samosata und das Neue Testament* (*TU* 76, Berlin, 1961). On Galen see R. Walzer, *Galen on Jews and Christians* (Oxford, 1949).

published at Rome and then filed in the *liber libellorum rescriptorum* in the imperial archives. Copies could be obtained by the petitioner.[58]

The two apologies of the Christian teacher Justin, composed soon after 150, were *libelli* of this sort. At the beginning of the first, its author describes it as a "declaration" and a *libellus*; later on he uses the equivalent term *axiōsis*.[59] His knowledge of the procedure is proved by what he says of a libellus presented to the prefect of Egypt—who refused to subscribe to it.[60] His awareness that imperial letters provided precedents is indicated by his quoting an *epistula* of Hadrian.[61] The so-called "second" apology was actually an appendix to the first, bringing it up to date by describing inequitable proceedings under the prefect Lollius Urbicus. Justin explicitly petitioned the emperor to subscribe to his *biblidion* (*libellus*) and publish it, thereby alleviating the Christians' situation.[62]

Several later apologies had the same function. Melito of Sardis described his own work as a petition, and Eusebius rightly called it a *libellus*.[63] Toward the beginning of the so-called "embassy" of Athenagoras we find verbs related to nouns for petitions, and it too was therefore a *libellus*.

The reason for our discussing this point in so much detail is to argue that with these apologies or, rather, *libelli,* we encounter the first moves made by Christians to try to change the legal and administrative circumstances under which they were suffering the death penalty. (The apology of Aristides, perhaps about 140, does not come to the same point.) In essence the claim of all is the same. Christians alone are punished simply because of their name; their actual doctrines and behavior are not investigated. If an investigation were to be made it would show that their ethical outlook is far superior to that of pagan religions or of Gnostic groups which are not Christian. It would also show that they are loyal to the best philosophical traditions of the empire. They refuse only to worship false gods or human beings such as emperors. The apologies are thus an appeal for justice and for truth in the face of a situation in which both are being perverted by the state in the name of religious tradition.

Whether or not the emperors actually saw any of these petitions, they did not subscribe to them. The Christian petitions therefore had no effect except upon the morale of Christians themselves, although it is possible that the anti-Christian treatise of Celsus, about 178, was in part a reply to the petition of Justin.[64]

[58] See H. F. Jolowicz, *Historical Introduction to the Study of Roman Law* (ed. 2, Cambridge, 1954), 379, 381; A. N. Sherwin-White, *The Letters of Pliny* (Oxford, 1966), 716-17; F. Millar in *JRS* 57 (1967), 9-19.
[59] *Apol.* 1, 1; 56, 3. Cf. A. A. T. Ehrhardt in *JEH* 4 (1953), 1-12.
[60] *Apol.* 1, 29, 2-3.
[61] *Apol.* 1, 68.
[62] *Apol.* 2, 14, 1.
[63] Eusebius, *H. E.* 4, 26, 5-6.
[64] Cf. C. Andresen, *Logos und Nomos* (Berlin, 1955).

The imperial rescripts on the subject of Christianity do not seem to have been collected before the early third century,[65] and under these circumstances some Christians evidently tried to produce forged imperial letters. One was a letter to the "assembly of Asia" which was circulated in two versions. One was ascribed to Antoninus Pius and apparently dated between December 10, 160, and March 7, 161; the other, to Marcus Aurelius and set between March 7 and December 9, 161. In both versions the assembly was instructed not to make trouble for Christians.[66] Another document was a letter from Marcus Aurelius to the Roman senate and people, reporting a recent miracle produced by the prayers of Christian legionary soldiers. We shall presently discuss the event; here we note only that the letter, apparently known to Tertullian,[67] gave orders for accusers of Christians to be burned alive, and for confessing Christians to be set free. The author's idea of what Marcus would have written is obviously quite mistaken. Finally, another letter, probably much later, represented the same emperor as sending for Abercius, bishop of Hieropolis, because of his skill in exorcism and healing.[68] Since the emperor did not believe in exorcism, as he himself said in his *Meditations,* the picture is obviously false.[69] Such documents must have circulated only among small groups of Christians.

In the spring of 175 the seemingly endless wars against the Quadi and the Marcomanni to the north of the river Danube were punctuated by a revolt against Marcus Aurelius which was led by his ablest general, Avidius Cassius.[70] The emperor's poor health had led to rumors that he was dead, but when faced with revolt he and his generals in Asia Minor acted vigorously and within a few months had the situation under control. Avidius Cassius, according to rumor secretly supported by the empress Faustina, was put to death against the emperor's wishes. In 176 the imperial couple undertook a tour of the eastern empire while coins bore the legend PAX AETERNA AUGUSTI.

The new peace clearly involved the suppression of groups within the empire which were regarded as endangering it, and from this time we possess the remains of three apologetic treatises composed by Christian leaders. The first of them was addressed "to Antoninus" by the loyalist bishop Apollinaris of Hierapolis in Phrygia. In this work he told the story of the "thundering legion" which defeated Germans and Sarmatians on the Danube because of the prayers of Christian soldiers. Lightning drove the enemy back, while

---

[65] By Ulpian, according to Lactantius, *Div. inst.* 5, 11, 19.

[66] Cf. E. Schwartz, *Eusebius: Kirchengeschichte* II (Leipzig, 1903), 326-30; J. B. Lightfoot, *The Apostolic Fathers,* Part II, I (London, 1885), 465-69.

[67] *Apol.* 5, 6.

[68] Cf. Lightfoot, *op. cit.,* 469-70 and 476; C. R. Haines, *The Correspondence of Marcus Cornelius Fronto* II (London–New York, 1920), 298-305.

[69] *Medit.* 1, 6.

[70] For the dates of the revolt (mid-April to mid-July) as determined from papyri and ostraca cf. R. Rémondon in *Chronique d'Égypte* 26 (1951), 364-77.

rain supplied water for the Roman troops.[71] This miracle, depicted on the column of Marcus Aurelius at Rome, took place in either 172 or 174. The *Historia Augusta* ascribes it to the prayer of the emperor himself, while Dio Cassius gives credit to an Egyptian magician.[72] The legion itself was XII Fulminata (not Fulminatrix), loyal to the emperor in 175 and therefore given the appellation *certa constans*.[73] By claiming this legion for Christianity, Apollinaris was showing how loyal the Christians were.

Another work was addressed to the emperor by Melito, bishop of nearby Sardis, in 175 or 176. Recent decrees in Asia, Melito writes, have led to a novel situation: Christians are being persecuted by the confiscation of their property and sometimes by death. He asks whether or not these decrees have been authorized by the emperor himself. Conceivably they reflect the critical situation when Avidius Cassius tried to seize power, though they may come from the period just after the revolt. Melito explicitly argues for official recognition of Christianity. It is a philosophy which at first flourished among barbarians: what he has in mind must be Judaism as the forerunner of Christianity. The philosophy appeared in the empire during Augustus' reign and clearly aided the growth of the empire. Church and state grew up together.

The successor of Augustus, therefore, must protect this philosophy just as his predecessors protected it, for "the prayers of all" have prevented any harm to the state. (Perhaps Melito too has the Twelfth Legion in mind.) To be sure, at times Christians have been persecuted. The only persecutors, however, have been ignorant emperors who were under the influence of "certain malignant persons." The emperors were Nero and Domitian; presumably Melito is aware that Roman officialdom viewed them without enthusiasm.[74] Hadrian and Antoninus Pius, on the other hand, sent rescripts to governors and cities in Asia, Macedonia, and Greece on behalf of the Christians.[75] Marcus Aurelius should follow the example of these (adoptive) ancestors, since he possesses "greater love of mankind and wisdom." His reign will continue and his son Commodus will succeed him if he will only protect Christianity.[76]

Melito's allusion to Commodus as heir to the throne serves not only to indicate the probable date of his apology but also to denote its main purpose. After the revolt broke out, the emperor abandoned the tradition of adopting the best available successor and reverted to the hereditary principle; Avidius Cassius himself had been the most likely candidate. Melito is arguing that the

[71]Eusebius, *H. E.* 5, 5, 1-4.

[72] *M. Aurelius* 24, 4; Dio 71, 8-10.

[73] See Ritterling in *RE* XII, 1710. The legion had been known as Fulminata since the time of Augustus.

[74] For Nero see Marcus Aurelius, *Medit.* 3, 16.

[75] There is no mention of Trajan's letter to Pliny; Melito does not know it or, more probably, prefers not to discuss it.

[76] Eusebius, *H. E.* 4, 26, 5-11. On Commodus as heir cf. J. Keil in *Klio* 31 (1938), 293-300.

interests of the monarchy will best be served by providing it with Christianity as its religious foundation. Christians are loyal to the throne. In turn, the throne owes them protection.

The third apologist was Athenagoras, perhaps an Alexandrian, who wrote between 176 and 180 and lavished extravagant praise upon the emperor and his son. Such praise of rulers was common enough in the Roman world, as elsewhere; a striking example of it already occurs in an address to a procurator of Judaea described in the book of Acts (24:2-3). In Trajan's time the philosopher Epictetus could speak of imperial benefits thus: "you see that Caesar seems to provide us with great peace, for there are no longer wars or battles or brigandage or piracy; at all times it is possible to travel, to sail from east to west."[77] Another example was provided under Antoninus Pius by the rhetorician Aelius Aristides, friend of all the Antonines, in his florid oration *To Rome*.[78] Such praises of Roman rule were reiterated and even intensified by Athenagoras.

To the emperor and his son the Christian apologist can say that "your inhabited world" makes use of various customs and laws, and "both you and your laws" allow this diversity to all (1, 1-2). He refers to the imperial attitude as mild, merciful, peaceable, and humane. There is equity throughout the empire, especially as regards the claims of various cities. The whole inhabited world "enjoys deep peace" because of the imperial plan (1, 2—2, 2). Precisely the same points had been made by Aelius Aristides.

Just as the pagan rhetorician ended his address with a prayer to all the gods and sons of gods to perpetuate the empire, so Athenagoras too says at the end of his apology that Christians pray for the succession of imperial rule and the growth of the empire. He has already said that the authority of government comes "from above" and has compared the relation of Marcus to Commodus with that of the Father to the Son (18, 2).[79]

In the *Oration* of another Christian named Tatian, who perhaps wrote at about this time, we hear a dissident voice. Tatian believed that he had rejected nearly every aspect of Graeco-Roman culture when he turned to Christian "barbarism"—although modern studies have shown that he gave up neither philosophy nor rhetoric. In his view both Greek and Roman legislative systems ought to be condemned; the whole world should live under one and the same rule (c. 28). Presumably he had in mind the Christian law. In any event, notions like his were dismissed by the anti-Christian Celsus, writing about 178: "Would that it were possible to unite under one law the inhabitants of Asia, Europe, and Libya, both Greeks and barbarians even at

---

[77] Epictetus, *Diss.* 3, 13, 9; a Christian parallel in Irenaeus, *Adv. haer.* 4, 30, 3.
[78] *Or.* 26, ed. B. Keil; see J. H. Oliver, *The Ruling Power* (*TAPS* 43 [1953]), 87-103.
[79] Similar ideas recur in Eusebius' oration on the thirtieth anniversary of Constantine's reign (*Laus Const.* 3, 6; 10, 6); cf. N. H. Baynes in *JRS* 34 (1944), 140.

the farthest limits." The ideal is acceptable—but impossible. "He who thinks this knows nothing," and all one can do is maintain traditions.[80]

It appears that the idea of a Christian empire was being promoted rather openly at this point. Celsus claims to have heard Christians discussing its difficulties. If the reigning emperors were to become Christians and then (inevitably?) were captured by their enemies, and if the same fate overtook their successors, sooner or later an emperor would arise who would use his intelligence and destroy the Christians before they destroyed him.[81] This passage clearly shows that in non-Christian circles the Christian goal was having some impact, as well as within the church.

The idea of accommodation between church and state received a drastic setback, however, within a very short time. The martyrdom of many Christians at Lyons, probably in 177, showed how illusory the hope was, at least in relation to mob action and to officials who would not protect Christians.[82] At first popular hostility resulted simply in keeping Christians off the streets, but violent mob action soon ensued. A military tribune took Christians into protective custody until the imperial legate could arrive, and only somewhat later was there a general search for others. Some household slaves when interrogated claimed that their Christian masters were given to "Thyestean banquets" (involving cannibalism) and "Oedipodean intercourse" (involving incest). In consequence, even the more moderate-minded citizens of Lyons became hostile toward their Christian neighbors.

After some time the legate began a series of trials. One Christian started his defense with the statement that "there is nothing godless or irreligious among us." He was interrupted by shouts from the bystanders, and the legate immediately put the question to him: was he or was he not a Christian? When he declared that he was, he was put in prison. There was a brief delay in the proceedings while the legate requested definite instructions from Rome in regard to the punishment of Roman citizens. In reply the emperor stated that they were to be released if they abjured Christianity, executed if they did not. The legate thereupon proceeded to take the Festival of the Three Gauls as the occasion for the executions required. Roman citizens were beheaded. The others were killed by wild animals, suffocated in prison, or burned to death.

The emperor's attitude may seem surprising, but it was no different from that of his tutor Junius Rusticus.[83] Christianity as such was forbidden by the state; those who professed it were necessarily subject to the death penalty. In his *Meditations* (11, 3) he clearly stated his view. Men should always be willing to face death, but they should not do so "out of simple

---

[80] Origen, *C. Cels*, 8, 72.
[81] *Ibid.*, 8, 71.
[82] Eusebius, *H. E.* 5, 1-4.
[83] On his attitude toward Rusticus, *Medit.* 1, 7; SHA *M. Aurel.* 3, 4.

obstinacy, like the Christians."[84] Apologists had flattered him or had claimed that one of his legions had been saved by Christian prayers, but they had written in vain. His own philosophy was the philosophy of the state. There was no place in it for Christianity.

So that the martyrs might not have even a hope of resurrection (wrote Irenaeus), the bodies of those suffocated were cast to dogs and kept from being buried by Christians. The remains of those eaten by animals or burned were scattered or burned to charcoal. The heads and trunks of the beheaded citizens were kept under guard. The Christians made petition for the corpses, offered money for them, tried to steal them at night. After six days everything remaining was totally consumed by fire and the ashes were scattered in the river Rhone, presumably near the temple of Rome and Augustus which stood at the confluence of the river Saône. This temple was the meeting-place for the council of the Three Gauls, whose presiding officer was priest of the temple.

It has been argued that the martyrdoms were specifically related to a special privilege recently allowed to priests of the imperial cult in the Three Gauls: they were allowed to use condemned prisoners at their festival instead of expensive gladiators. This was "a concession to ancient religious customs . . . demanded for economic reasons by the big landowners of Gaul." Hence the martyrs were killed at the festival, fought as gladiators, and were killed by wild beasts.[85] Such punishments of Christians occurred elsewhere, however, and although Irenaeus does mention "what passed for a sacrificial rite" he is referring to the Christian sacrifice, not a pagan one.[86] Though the occasion of the martyrdoms doubtless lies in the social and economic conditions of Gaul and of the war-weary empire, it is not to be sought in legislation concerning gladiators.

A widespread attitude toward Christians is reflected in the *True Doctrine* which their vigorous opponent Celsus produced about this time. Toward the end of his elaborate treatise, Celsus severely criticizes the Christians for their refusal to offer "due honors," including rites of worship, to the emperors and their representatives. It looks as if they deliberately seek martyrdom. They refuse to take oaths by the Fortune or Genius of the emperor, though "earthly things have been given to him, and whatever you receive in this life you receive from him."[87]

If everyone were to do the same as you, there would be nothing to prevent him [the emperor] from being abandoned, alone and deserted, while earthly things

---

[84] See F. Martinazzoli, *Parataxeis: le testimonianze stoiche sul cristianismo* (Florence, 1953). The emperor's word may be equivalent to *contumacia;* see A. N. Sherwin-White, *The Letters of Pliny* (Oxford, 1966), 699.

[85] J. H. Oliver and R. E. A. Palmer in *Hesperia* 24 (1955), 320-49, especially 325.

[86] Irenaeus in Eusebius, *H. E.* 5, 1, 40 and 56. For Irenaeus as the author see P. Nautin, *Lettres et écrivains chrétiens des iie et iiie siècles* (Paris, 1961), 33-64.

[87] Origen, *Contra Celsum* 8, 55-67.

would come into the power of the most lawless and savage barbarians, and nothing more would be heard among men either of your worship or of the true wisdom.[88]

Christian self-interest should coincide with loyalty toward the state which protects them. It would change the situation in which they are now "sought out and condemned to death."[89] And Celsus ends with a direct appeal for cooperation in the business of government.

[You should] help the emperor with all [your] power, and cooperate with him in what is right, and fight for him, and be fellow-soldiers if he presses for this, and fellow-generals with him. [You should] accept public office in our country if it is necessary to do this for the sake of preserving the laws and piety.[90]

We have already seen that several Christian leaders shared Celsus' attitude. The actual persecutions necessarily meant, however, that cooperation was practically impossible. Christians came to agree with Tatian that they could not hold any public office under an anti-Christian government which protected paganism and insisted upon emperor worship.

In effect an official Christian reply to Celsus was made by Theophilus, bishop of Antioch early in the reign of Commodus. He drew a sharp distinction between worship, to be offered only to the true God, and honor, legitimately due to the emperor, who owes his authority to God. Just as there is only one emperor and his subordinates cannot be given his title, so there is only one God, and only he can be worshiped. The honor due to the emperor is expressed through obeying him and praying for him.[91] Theophilus thus adheres to the political monarchy, giving it a divine sanction by analogy, while subordinating it to the supreme God. Elsewhere in his treaties he explicitly states that the development of Roman rule has been due to God, though he points out that Roman power has been abused, for example in the time of Tarquinius Superbus. He seems to view this king as a prototype of some later rulers, for he says that Tarquin exalted himself, exiled Romans, and favored immorality. He was the last of the kings.[92] The loyalty of Christians, one would assume, is due only to emperors who subordinate themselves to God, treat their subjects with equity, and like Christians uphold morality.

Inspite of statements like this, persecution continued, at least sporadically, during the reign of Commodus, as Theophilus himself indicates.[93] Indeed,

[88] *Ibid.*, 8, 68 (tr. H. Chadwick).
[89] *Ibid.*, 8, 69.
[90] *Ibid.*, 8, 73-74.
[91] *Ad Autolycum* I, 11; for imperial power as given by God cf. Dio 71, 3, 4, ostensibly citing Marcus Aurelius. W. Ensslin (*Sitzungsberichte der Bayerischen Akad. der Wiss., Philos.-hist. Abt.*, 1943, no. 6, 45 and 57) cites both passages but does not connect them.
[92] *Ibid.*, 3, 27.
[93] *Ibid.*, 3, 30.

the first examples of persecution ever to occur in the province of Africa took place very early in his reign. On July 17 at Carthage twelve Christians were condemned. The proconsul had told them that "we swear by the Genius of our Lord emperor and make supplication for his security." The martyrs refused to join him. One said that he did not recognize the *imperium* of this age. Another stated that he feared no one but "our Lord God who is in the heavens."[94] The proconsul urged them to return to "the Roman way of life" (*mos Romanorum*) but they were not in sympathy with it. Again perhaps in 183 the martyr Apollonius was ordered by the urban prefect Perennis to take an oath by the Fortune of "our Lord Commodus the emperor." He replied that though Christians had been commanded not to swear at all but to speak the truth with everyone, he was willing to swear by the true God that Christians did honor the emperor and pray for his power. Perennis rejected this offer and proceeded to try to persuade him to offer sacrifice. He refused and was condemned to death.[95]

The question of the oath, originally secondary, was obviously becoming more important, and Christians were insisting on taking literally the prohibition of oaths found in Matthew 5: 33-37 and James 5:12. It is reiterated by Justin, Irenaeus, Tertullian, Clement, and Origen.[96] Sympathetic pagans, or perhaps Christians, claimed that "fortune" was simply a conventional expression which did not involve theological implications. To this claim Origen replied: "We do not swear by something which does not exist, as though it were a god." It could be argued, too, that "people who swear by the Genius of the Roman emperor are swearing by his daemon"; but Christians could not possibly take an oath by a demon![97] No compromise seemed possible.

The *Acts of Apollonius* contain many echoes of the points made in various apologetic treaties of the second century, and scholars have therefore suspected that the *Acts* constitute an apology, not an account of Apollonius' martyrdom.[98] In any event, the story of the martyr has been transformed into a Christian apology. Its chief purpose is the same as that of Theophilus—to show that Christians are loyal to the state and to the emperor, who reigns by God's will, although they reject pagan idolatry and mythology. They thus resemble Socrates, loyal to Athens although condemned on the ground of religious innovation. This is to say that Christians accept the best features of Graeco-Roman society but reject Graeco-Roman religions, proposing that Christianity itself be regarded as the spiritual foundation of the culture.

[94] *Acts of the Scillitan Martyrs* 3-8, p. 29 Knopf-Krüger.
[95] *Acts of Apollonius*, pp. 30-35 Knopf-Krüger.
[96] Justin, *Apol.* 1, 16, 5; 21, 3; Irenaeus, *Adv. haer.* 2, 32, 1; Tertullian, *Apol.* 32, 2-3; Clement, *Str.* 7, 51, 8; Origen, *Exh. mart.* 7.
[97] Origen, *Contra Celsum* 8, 65; cf. Tertullian, *loc. cit.*
[98] Cf. R. Freudenberger in *ZNW* 60 (1969), 111-30.

IV-SEPTIMIUS SEVERUS

From the very end of the second century comes the famous *Apology* written in Latin by Tertullian of Carthage and based on the works of such Greek predecessors as Justin, Apollinaris, Melito, Tatian, and Theophilus. The points he makes are essentially the same as theirs, but with the acumen fortified by legal training he directs them to the theme of the injustice of persecution.

Tertullian wrote two apologetic treaties in 197. The earlier, two books *Ad Nationes*, was a rather traditional compilation of materials on mythology, philosophy, and religion. Later in the year he rewrote it completely and produced the *Apology*. The occasion for both works was provided by the end of four years of civil wars and the triumph of Septimius Severus. It was possible that persecution would begin again; it was also possible that a new age was dawning. Tertullian hoped that his defense of the Christian position would bring about the reconciliation of the state with the church.

Early in the *Apology* Tertullian speaks of Septimius Severus as "most conservative of princes" and refers to his attempts to reform contradictory legal traditions. For the emperor, then, he produces a fairly complete account of the various earlier rulers and their relations to Christianity. According to Tertullian, Tiberius received a report about Jesus from Pontius Pilate, who himself was practically a Christian. He endorsed the report and transmitted it to the senate. Unfortunately, among the Romans no god could be consecrated by an emperor or a general without the senate's prior approval, and the senate therefore rejected this message since it confirmed the deity of Christ. Tiberius continued to believe in Christ's deity and threatened accusers of Christians with punishment. (Tertullian's picture of Tiberius' attitude in contradicted by Tacitus, but Tertullian calls him "most eloquent of liars.") Nero and Domitian, the latter only temporarily, were the only persecutors. Vespasian was tolerant, though he made war on the Jews; Trajan forbade searching for Christians. Their tolerant policy was followed by the emperors of the later second century. Marcus Aurelius, most praiseworthy of emperors, wrote letters attesting the miracle wrought by Christian soldiers prayers and imposed a heavy penalty on accusers. In turn, no Christians supported the revolts of Avidius Cassius or Niger or Albinus and none took part in the murder of Commodus. Non-Christians, on the other hand, have frequently plotted against the emperors: "at this moment the accomplices in plots and the sympathizers are daily being revealed" (35, 11). Such is Tertullian's argument.

Tertullian's insistence upon Christian loyalty and his revision of past history were especially appropriate in 197, when Septimius Severus—from Africa, though not notably African in outlook[99]—condemned twenty-nine rebels and their sympathizers to death[100] and proceeded to deify the dead Commodus, thus reversing the senate's earlier decision. One of Tertullian's chief purposes was to provide a picture of Roman imperial history which would show how close an ally of the state Christianity could be and must have been. Fifteen years later he quoted Caecilius Capella, who lost Byzantium for Niger to Septimius Severus, as having cried out, "Christians, rejoice!"[101]

He was not alone, of course, in expressing his loyalty to the newly victorious emperor. An inscription from Kasyoun in Palestine reveals that the Jewish community there was eager to attest its devotion to the emperor, his two sons, and the empress Julia Domna—in 197.[102]

But it must be admitted that there was a minority view, reflected in the *Sibylline Oracles*, in which history and mythology seem to be combined.[103] As the passage now stands, it seems to combine the rise of Niger to power in Asia with the apocalyptic expectation of the return of Nero. In any event, the Antonine rulers would come to an end,[104] and the new king would take Rome by force after the city had existed for 948 years (= 195-196).[105] Obviously a Christian who cherished this oracle would be no revolutionary as he awaited the collapse of Rome. On the other hand, he could hardly be counted among the supporters of Septimius Severus.

Tertullian, who did not know this book of the *Oracles*, had no sympathy with such a view. He held that the Roman state and Christianity could coexist. He objected, however, to the idea that Roman power was due to pagan religion. His argument is that Roman religion is a strange amalgam of Greek and Tuscan elements; historically it arose after the period of the first kings. Empires are the result of war, not of religiosity, and war often involves the destruction or violation of the sanctuaries of pagan gods. It is the one God who ordains the rise and fall of empires, who raises them up and brings them down in ruin. For this reason Roman Christians do not, and need not, offer sacrifice to the gods. They cannot accept pagan religion (cc. 25-27).

Indeed, there is no reason why the Roman state itself should accept religions deserving of persecution. The African worshipers of Saturn were prevented from sacrificing children to their god by a proconsul; human sacrifice was forbidden to the devotees of Mercury in Gaul and of Jupiter at Rome itself (c. 9). On the other hand, the state is also free to revise its

---

[99] Cf. T. D. Barnes in *Historia* 16 (1967), 87-107.
[100] Dio 75, 4; *SHA Septimius Severus* 13-14 lists 43.
[101] *Ad Scap.* 3, 4.
[102] *CIJ* II 972.
[103] *Orac. Sib.* 8, 138-59.
[104] *Ibid.*, 132-33.
[105] The figure is based on the numerical values of the Greek letters R (100) O (800) M (40) E (8).

opinions of religions previously rejected. Thus in ancient times the Bacchanalia were driven out of Rome and all Italy; the worship of Serapis, Isis, and Harpocrates was excluded from the Capital, and two consuls overturned the altars erected to them. Nowadays, however, Serapis is a Roman and Bacchus an Italian (c. 6). Why should not the Roman state accept a religion which promotes virtue?

Doubtless it will be charged that Christians slight the majesty of the emperor (cc. 28-34). But Christians, as their books prove, pray for the security of the emperors (1 Tim. 2:2). They pray to the one God who bestowed authority upon the emperors, and they pray for the continuation of the empire. As long as it lasts the end of the world will be postponed. What they refuse to accept is the fusion of politics with pagan religiosity. They cannot take an oath by the Genius of the emperor, for to them "genius" is simply another word for "demon." Instead, they gladly take oaths by his health (*salus*). They cannot call him God, for he is only a man. They are willing, though reluctant, to use the term "Lord" (*dominus*) of him— although Augustus himself refused the name—but it must be understood as an ordinary expression without any implication of deity.

If this statement suggests that there are few occasions for conflict between church and state, why does persecution arise? Tertullian claims that it is the urban mob from which it comes: "none more apt to demand the death of Christians" (35, 8). This mob attacks them with stones and fire and digs up the Christian dead (37, 2). When natural disasters take place it cries out, "Christians to the lion" (40, 2). Magistrates win favor with the mob if they put Christians to death (50, 12). In passages like these Tertullian is trying to align the magistrates with Christians against the lowest classes of Roman society and to appeal to the morality the magistrates profess. Like the apostle Paul and Melito of Sardis, to name no others, he stands with the state against mob anarchy.

Finally, however, he speaks on behalf of a movement which has to resist the state if it usurps the place of God. Christians fear God, he says, not the proconsul. Against false religion they have to be "obstinate," for they win pardon for their sins through their blood. At the end, it may well be, they are condemned by Rome but acquitted by God himself.

It is hard to tell what effect, if any, the *Apology* produced among the magistrates to whom it was addressed. In his later treatise *Ad Scapulam*, sent in 212 to the proconsul of Africa, Tertullian claimed that Septimius Severus summoned a Christian healer to the palace, employed a Christian nurse for his son Caracalla, and rescued Christians of high rank from mob violence (4, 6-7). In Africa itself C. Iulius Asper, probably proconsul in 200–201, released a Christian who was brought before him (4, 3). On the other hand, in March 203 a Christian catechist and some of his pupils were executed at Carthage, as we learn from the *Acts of Perpetua and Felicitas*.

Around the same time other martyrdoms took place at Antioch, Corinth, and Rome. Hippolytus of Rome gives a vivid description of the situation there, though the exact date of his *Commentary on Daniel* is unknown.[106]

Men watch for the accustomed day [Sunday] and slip into the house of God when all are praying there and singing hymns to God. They seize certain individuals, take them out, and tell them, "Come, agree with us and worship the gods; otherwise we will testify against you." They take them before the tribunal and accuse them of violating Caesar's decree and get them condemned to death.

This decree is sometimes supposed to have been issued around 202 by the emperor, forbidding both Jews and Christians to make converts and imposing the death penalty for disobedience.[107] It is true that the *Acts of Perpetua* describe converts and their teacher as being executed, though not on this ground, and that several of Origen's pupils were put to death. But Hippolytus' "decree" has nothing to do with converts, and Origen's father, a martyr in 201-202 under Q. Maecius Laetus, prefect of Egypt,[108] was not a recent convert or an active missionary. Persecution at Alexandria continued in 202-203, according to Eusebius; but he wrongly supposes that Subatianus Aquila was prefect in that year. Papyri speak of Aquila as prefect between the autumn of 206 and July 23, 210.[109] If he persecuted Christians his activities were not simply continuous with those of his predecessor. It should also be noted that Origen himself, though head of the training school for converts, was not even arrested. The so-called edict of Septimius Severus, therefore, did not exist, and persecution at this time was due to private and/or local initiative.[110]

Around the same time, or a little later, the famous jurist Domitius Ulpianus began publishing a series of treatises "to cover the whole field of law and to make direct references to previous authorities unnecessary."[111] One such treatise was *De officio proconsulis,* written for the guidance of provincial governors. In the seventh book of this treatise, says Lactantius,[112] he "collected the nefarious rescripts of emperors in order to teach what penalties were to be imposed on those who acknowledged that they were worshippers of God." It is possible that this was a semiofficial reply to Tertullian's attempt at modifying the history of legal precedents. It is also possible that a Tertullian whom Ulpian mentioned was the Christian writer; but the evidence is entirely inconclusive.[113]

[106] *Dan. comm.* I, 20.

[107] *SHA Septimius Severus* 17, I.

[108] Cf. E. Schwartz, *Eusebius: Kirchengeschichte* III (Leipzig, 1909), ccxx. The last papyrus under Laetus (*PSI* III 199) is dated Feb. 26, 203.

[109] P. Oxy. VIII 1100; P. Flor. 6. Cf. O. W. Reinmuth in *Bulletin of the American Society of Papyrologists* 4 (1967), 106-9.

[110] Cf. K. H. Schwarte in *Historia* 12 (1963), 185-208.

[111] H. F. Jolowicz, *Historical Introduction to Roman Law* (ed. 2, Cambridge, 1954), 402.

[112] *Div. inst.* 5, 11, 19.

[113] Jolowicz, *op. cit.,* 401.

CHAPTER VII
THE APOLOGETIC MOVEMENT

By the end of the reign of Hadrian (117–138) the Christian movement had been in existence for a century. The explosively creative apostolic age, with all its experiments and innovations, lay in the past. The apologist Quadratus could speak of men healed or raised from the dead by "our Savior" as having lived on for a long time after his departure, "so that some of them even reached our times." Simply because of the passage of time there were tendencies toward stabilizing the life and thought of the communities, toward a relative fixity expressed in common creedal formulas, in common usage of sacred books, and in a common order of ministers related to common orders of worship. It was to be expected that there would be a general conservative movement toward consolidation; and such a movement found expression in Asia Minor and Greece as well as at Rome.

The new Christian century was not to be conspicuous for its tranquillity, however, for the churches lay under the constant threat of persecution by the Roman state. Whether or not any definite edict had been directed against them in earlier times, the letter of Trajan to Pliny in 110 had the force of law, and in it the emperor definitely stated that confessed Christians had to be punished by death. The state's position, irrational and inhumane though it seemed to Christians, was clear. Even though conservative Christian leaders might, and did, protest their loyalty to the emperor, the fact that they remained Christians was proof to the state of their disloyalty.

Under these circumstances, the apologetic movement of the second century, with its attempt to work out the relationships between Christianity and Graeco-Roman culture, was bound to have more effect within the Christian communities than upon the government officials to whom the apologies were usually addressed. At the beginning of the century the Romans who we know were concerned with Christianity were opposed to it simply on the grounds that it was a foreign superstition alien to the best traditions of the senatorial class. Later on, this ground of hostility was reinforced by the peculiarly Roman Stoicism to which some leading officials, and especially the emperor Marcus Aurelius, were devoted. No matter how an apologist like Justin might point to Heraclitus, Socrates, and Musonius Rufus as preChristian Christians, the leaders of the state were not convinced.

This is not to say, of course, that the only ground for working out a philosophical theology lay in the attempt to improve church-state relations. From very early times the Christian movement had looked toward GraecoRoman culture as providing a medium of expression for the gospel, and as its ties with Judaism gradually loosened the need for some kind of cultural accommodation became even greater. Generally speaking, the leaders responsible for the direction of the major communities were in favor of a positive relation both with the state and with the best elements (chiefly philosophical and literary) in the culture of the empire. The hostility of the state toward the church certainly hindered the movement in this direction. Justin's pupil Tatian produced a fierce diatribe against Graeco-Roman culture and society, and turned away from the church to a militantly ascetic, antiworldly sect. As a whole, however, the church continued to seek for a place in the culture and did not abandon its hope for a reconciliation.

I·BEGINNINGS

Under the leadership of the apostle Paul, the Christian community very early became aware that the gospel had universal implications. It was addressed to Greeks as well as to Jews; Paul himself had been called by God to proclaim Christ among the gentiles and to free them from their enslavement to their nonexistent gods (Gal. 4:8), the mute and lifeless idols (I Cor. 12:2) of paganism. They were to be converted to God from idols, to serve the living and real God (I Thess. 1:9). Though there were many so-called gods, Christians had recognized the one God who was the source of all creation and the one Lord Jesus Christ, his agent in creation and redemption (1 Cor. 8:6). God had made his eternal power and deity known to men, though they had turned away to the idolatry from which they were now recalled (cf. Rom. 1:19-23).

The approach to gentiles which Paul and other missionaries took involved entering into the thought world of the gentiles. Christians could not accept the recognition or the worship of idols, any more than other Jews could, but in Paul's view it was necessary to "become everything to everyone" for the sake of the gospel (1 Cor. 9:22-23).

Under these circumstances is is not surprising that in Acts we find three key scenes, set at Lystra in Asia Minor, at Athens, and at Ephesus, in which Paul vigorously rejects idolatry but (in two instances) sets forth the gospel in terms which at least part of his audience found comprehensible. At Lystra (Acts 14:8-17) a miracle of healing was followed by a crowd's acclamation of Barnabas as Zeus and of Paul as Hermes; the local priest of Zeus was eager to offer sacrifices with the people. The apostles therefore tore their clothing, because of the expression of blasphemy, and stated that they were not gods but men, proclaiming the gospel of the living God, the creator and providential governor of the universe. God was calling upon men to turn from idols to himself. At Athens (Acts 17:16-33) Paul also rejected the worship of idols and seized upon an inscription which he read as "To an unknown god" in order to set forth his teaching concerning the true God, the creator and providential governor who is "not far from each one of us." The apologetic nature of his discourse is especially clear from Acts 17:28. "In him we live and move and have our being" may be an allusion to a line from Epimenides; "for we are indeed his offspring" is explicitly ascribed to "some of your poets" and actually comes from the *Phaenomena* of the Stoic Aratus. The discourse is not purely apologetic; Paul does not hesitate to speak of God's command to repent, of future judgment, and of the resurrection of Jesus. But in this address at Athens we see prefigured the later work of Christian apologists.

The scene at Ephesus (Acts 19:23-41) clearly shows that in the matter of idolatry there could be no compromise. The silversmiths of Ephesus recognize the danger to their business from Paul's rejection of idols, and they provoke a riot in favor of the great Artemis of the Ephesians. The city clerk is able to quiet the mob only by insisting that regular legal procedures must be used against the Christians. The story ends on this note, but Paul soon leaves Ephesus. Acts does not say so, but it is obvious that a conflict on this point could be settled only by the abandonment of idolatry—or the triumph of paganism.

After Paul's time, it is clear, the Christian movement continued to reject Graeco-Roman religion while at the same time making use of Graeco-Roman cultural themes which could be assimilated. Such use is especially prominent in the letter addressed by the Roman church to that at Corinth at the end of the first century. Just as in Paul's earlier letter to the Corinthians we find the Christian community described as a body politic in language characteristically Stoic (1 Cor. 12:12-26), with a few Christian additions, so in 1 Clement 20 the providential and harmonious operation of the universe is set forth in Stoic terms, with a few additional notes derived from Hellenistic Judaism. The chapter offers what Werner Jaeger called "a perfect example of Hellenization." Similarly in 1 Clement 25 there is a "proof" of resurrection from the story of the wonderful phoenix, from whose corpse comes a worm that turns into a new bird. In urging the leader of sedition at Corinth to seek exile, Clement explicitly uses pagan examples. "In times of plague, many kings and rulers, in response to oracles, have given themselves up to death so that their people might be rescued through their blood; many have left their own cities to keep revolt in them from going farther" (c. 55). The theme is typically Graeco-Roman.

We should not exaggerate the extent of Clement's Hellenism, however. In his 37th chapter he uses military analogies to the life of the church.

We should consider those who serve our generals and note the order, readiness, and obedience with which they follow orders. Not all are prefects or tribunes or centurions or captains of fifty, but each according to rank follows the orders of the king and the generals.

These generals are not Roman but "ours," and the army is not the Roman army, in which there were no "captains of fifty," but an imaginary one based on Old Testament models.[1] Again, in his final exhortatory prayer he asks for obedience to "our rulers and governors on earth" to whom God has given power and sovereignty. They are to administer the rule which God has given them. Clement may have the governors of the Roman empire in mind, but in the light of his whole letter his attention must certainly be devoted to the governors of the Christian church, whose authority he discusses in several chapters. He is concerned with the internal administration of the Christian churches.

The apologetic movement as such really got under way when circumstances demanded its appearance. According to the *Chronicle* of Eusebius, the apology of Quadratus appeared in 125–126, when the Hellenizing emperor Hadrian visited Athens and was initiated into the Eleusinian mysteries. It is by no means certain that Eusebius' date is correct; Weber suggested the year 132, when the emperor dedicated the great temple of Zeus Olympios at Athens, begun by Antiochus Epiphanes but completed only by Hadrian.[2] In any event, Hadrianic Hellenism was bound to result in a Christian response, for his

[1] Cf. R. M. Grant and H. H. Graham, *First and Second Clement* (New York, 1965), 65.

[2] W. Weber, *Rom: Herrschertum und Reich im zweiten Jahrhundert* (Stuttgart, 1937), 224.

program brought him into headlong collision with the Judaism out of which Christianity had arisen. Like Antiochus, who in the second century B.C. had tried to unite his kingdom on the basis of Greek culture and religion, Hadrian favored the worship of Zeus (Hypsistos) in Samaria and of Zeus (Capitolinus) at Jerusalem, where he proposed to rebuild the destroyed city and name it Aelia Capitolina, in honor of himself and/or Zeus.

Christians had to take a stand in relation to this policy, and it appears that at this point their leaders decided to accept its cultural implications while rejecting the cultic-religious ideas involved. Such an outlook is clearly implied by the surviving fragment of the apology of Quadratus, cited by Eusebius to demonstrate its author's "antiquity."[3]

But the works of our Savior were always present, for they were real—those who had been healed, those who rose from the dead, who were not merely seen when they were healed and arose but were always present, not only while the Savior was present but also for a long time after his departure, so that some of them even reached our own times.

The authentic miracles of Jesus are obviously being contrasted with the impermanent miracles effected by others, perhaps with the miracles supposedly worked by some other "savior"—such as Hadrian himself. Did the apologist have Hadrian or Zeus, or both, in mind? Was he thinking of saviors more generally and recalling the skeptical view that the deeds of men do not outlast their lifetime?[4]

No matter what Quadratus may have meant, the Jewish revolt under Bar Cochba's leadership was not supported by Christians, who in Palestine were persecuted by the "messiah." Christians turned toward Greek culture and rather rapidly abandoned the original Jewish context of their religion. Justin's *Dialogue with Trypho* reflects the Christian effort to reinterpret the Old Testament for the benefit of Hellenistic Jews who had fled from Palestine during the war of 132–135.[5]

Another attempt at apologetic writing is to be found in the work which Marcianus Aristides of Athens apparently addressed to the emperor Antoninus Pius early in his reign (138–161). This work, extant in full in a Syriac version along with some Greek fragments, begins with a philosophical definition of God, essentially Middle Platonist in origin. After a sketch of the "four races of men in this world, barbarians and Greeks, Jews and Christians," Aristides preceeds to show what is wrong with non-Christian religions. In essence, the barbarians worship the four elements, all of which are mutable and therefore not divine; the Greeks worship immoral and changeable human beings; the ignorant Egyptians worship animals. The Jews are much closer to

[3] *H. E.* 4, 3, 2.
[4] Cf. Sextus Empiricus, *Adv. math.* 9, 35.
[5] *Dial.* 1, 3. Note that the Hellenistic Jew Trypho has just described himself as a pupil of the Socratic Corinthus at Argos.

Christianity but their worship is really directed toward angels. Christians alone worship God rightly; their religion began with Jesus Christ, the Son of God who came down from heaven and taught his twelve disciples concerning the true God and pure morality. The world continues to exist by virtue of their prayers.

The principal theological difficulty in Aristides' apology arises in relation to his statements about God and Christ, and this is the problem with which his successors were to be confronted. How was it possible to make use of philosophical definitions in speaking of God and then simply to speak of Jesus as Son of God (or, in the Syriac version, as God)—born, crucified, and buried, even though risen and ascended? One would suppose that Aristides' objections to the sufferings of Greek and oriental deities could be raised against the Christian teaching. And it is precisely this problem which later apologists and theologians were to find difficult. Indeed, the whole Logos theology of the second century and after can be viewed as an attempt to solve it.

This is not to say that the problem was not earlier considered within the Christian community. Indeed, Paul's language about God the Father as the source and goal of existence and the Lord Jesus Christ as the agent of creation and redemption (1 Cor. 8:6) implies that Christians had been considering the question. Ignatius of Antioch clearly reflects it when he speaks of Christ as "the eternal; the invisible, visible for us; the intangible; the impassible, passible for us; the one who endured for us in every way."[6] But when addressing the world of Graeco-Roman culture the apologists were unwilling to remain in the world of religious paradox, and they therefore endeavored to explain the mystery along semiphilosophical lines.[7]

II-PHILOSOPHY IN THE SECOND CENTURY

The philosophies with which second-century Christians were acquainted were not the dogmatic systems of the early Hellenistic age. All had undergone modification and even transformation, in part because of the corrosive effects of Academic Skepticism, in part because of the widespread view that philosophy should lead to a goal outside itself, whether toward religion or the service of the state.

Philosophy was eminently respectable. Antoninus Pius subsidized philosophers as well as rhetoricians. Q. Junius Rusticus, the judge before whom the Christian Justin finally appeared, was well known not only as an administrator but also as the tutor who had converted the young Marcus Aurelius from

[6] *Polyc.* 3, 2.
[7] On the earliest theology cf. *The Early Christian Doctrine of God* (Charlottesville, Va., 1966), 14-18.

rhetoric to Stoic philosophy and had lent him the *Discourses* of Epictetus. Marcus Aurelius himself was devoted to the austere morality of Roman Stoicism, as his *Meditations* prove.

The Stoicism of the second century had developed far beyond the notions of its early Hellenistic founders, Zeno, Cleanthes, and Chrysippus, even though their writings were still sometimes used as textbooks. Panaetius and Posidonius had instructed young Romans, and Cicero had put some of their major treatises in Latin garb. During the first century of our era both Seneca and Musonius Rufus had taught ethical philosophy at Rome, and Musonius' pupil Epictetus taught with great success at Nicopolis on the western coast of Greece. Whereas in early Stoicism theology had been merely a subdivision of physics, in later times the religious impulse was predominant.

Platonism too had rather steadily moved closer to religion, especially after Carneades, head of the school in the second century B.C. developed skeptical arguments in his struggle against Stoic doctrine and used them within his own Academy. Though he himself taught that if the gods exist they do not care for men, the Middle Platonists of the first centuries of our era had turned to both monotheism and to a doctrine of providence, in part because of Stoic influence. The school's teaching in the second century is well represented by Albinus (*Eisagogē*), Apuleius (*De Platone*), Atticus (who wrote against Aristotle), and the rhetorician Maximus of Tyre. In the case of Albinus, Platonism was combined with Aristotelian ideas; he thus followed the lead of Antiochus of Ascalon (first century B.C.) and foreshadowed developments in Neoplatonism.[8] Around the same time the Pythagorean or Platonist Numenius of Apamea endeavored to synthesize not only philosophies but religions as well; he was famous for the question, "What is Plato but a Greek-speaking Moses?"

At Delphi the archons expressed their gratitude to Platonic philosophers by means of at least three decrees between 145 and 163 providing awards and exemptions. Among those honored were Bacchius Paphius, a teacher of Marcus Aurelius, and the more famous L. Calvisius Taurus.[9]

During the first century B.C. the Peripatetic school was enjoying a revival which continued through the early Christian period. Aristotle had long been known for the Platonizing works he had written as a young man; the treatises he himself had used in his teaching had descended by bequest to book collectors who kept them locked up. During the reign of Eumenes II of Pergamum (197–159) the owners hid the books underground to keep them out of his hands. Early in the first century a rich bibliophile bought them and had copies made, but these were full of mistakes because the originals had been damaged by moisture and moths. When the Roman general Sulla captured Athens in

---

[8] Cf. R. E. Witt, *Albinus and the History of Middle Platonism* (Cambridge, Mass., 1937); essays in *Entretiens sur l'antiquité classique* (Fondation Hardt, Geneva) III (*Recherches sur la tradition platonicienne*, 1955) and V (*Les Sources de Plotin*, 1957).
[9] *SIG*[3] 868.

84 he took them to Rome, where grammarians worked on the text, and about 70 the Peripatetic Andronicus of Rhodes began producing commentaries on them.[10] By the second century of our era Aristotle's teaching on logic and the categories was playing a considerable role among Middle Platonists, though Christians and others criticized Aristotelianism as excessively subtle. In the third century Plotinus used Peripatetic commentaries; in the fourth century Eusebius of Caesarea provided quotations from them.

During the second century Epicureanism, already brilliantly set forth in Roman dress by Lucretius in his poem *De rerum natura*, continued to flourish, though perhaps chiefly among the upper classes. Plotina Augusta, the widow of Trajan, was much concerned with the school at Athens and obtained legal concessions for it from Hadrian in 121.[11] In the Antonine period a certain Diogenes of Oenoanda in Lycia erected a portico and had carved on it an elaborate summary of Epicurean thought, including criticisms of other schools and an appeal to readers to recognize the ethical superiority of the doctrine.[12] Unfortunately one cannot date the Tunisian tombstone of C. Artorius Celer, *philosophus Epicureus pius*,[13] but it illustrates the same attitude.

These four schools, then—Stoic, Platonic, Peripatetic, and Epicurean—represented the approved philosophies of the second century. It is not surprising that when Marcus Aurelius visited Athens in 176 and was initiated at Eleusis, he promoted philosophical teaching at Athens by subsidizing professors chosen from each of the four. Rhetoricians, perhaps jealous of the subsidies, noted the munificent salaries, set at 10,000 drachmas.[14] The Christian rhetorician Tatian seems even to have exaggerated them by quoting the figure of 600 aurei (= 15,000 drachmas).[15]

Two more schools, less important in official circles and even suspect of disloyalty, must be noted because of their importance for Christian apologetics. The first of these was Cynicism, perhaps more a state of mind than a clearly defined philosophical system. Rhetoricians like Dio Chrysostom and Stoic moralists like Epictetus admired the independence of the first Cynic, Diogenes; we have already argued that the ideal wise man of Cynics and Stoics captured the imaginations of some early Christians at Corinth. About 120 the Cynic teacher Oenomaus of Gadara composed an attack on the immorality, ambiguity, fraudulence, and potential fatalism of oracles, especially the one at Delphi. The fragments of this treatise were preserved by the Christian bishop Eusebius and by the ex-Christian emperor Julian—and quoted with approval

[10] Strabo, *Geog.* 13, 1, 54; Plutarch, *Sulla* 26, 1-2; cf. J. Bidez, *Un singulier naufrage littéraire dans l'antiquité* (Brussels, 1943). For the early Aristotle cf. R. Walzer, *Aristotelis fragmenta* (Florence, 1934); for the later school, F. Wehrli, *Die Schule des Aristoteles*, 8 vols. (Basel, 1944-1956).
[11] *SIG*³ 834 + *ILS* 7784.
[12] A Grilli, *Diogenis Oenoandensis fragmenta* (Milan, 1960).
[13] *ILT* 1614.
[14] Lucian, *Eunuchus* 3; Philostratus, *Vit. soph.* 2, 2, p. 566; cf. Dio 71, 31, 3.
[15] Tatian, *Or.* 19, 1.

and distaste.[16] Related to Cynicism, but found among adherents of other schools, was a widespread criticism of the cult of images,[17] as well as criticism of religion in general. Christians gladly made use of Cynic criticisms.

The other school was that of the Skeptics. Though Skepticism had entered Platonic thought in the time of Carneades (second century B.C.), it was no longer alive there but was maintaining a separate existence. Generally viewed without much enthusiasm, it provided arguments to Christian apologists as they tried to undermine the arguments of "dogmatists" (usually Stoics) or the mythological stories of Greek religion.[18]

Not everyone concerned with philosophy was willing to adhere to the tenets of a particular school, and indeed the history of philosophy in the late Hellenistic and early Roman periods is marked by a strong tendency toward eclecticism. The Roman Stoic Seneca made several statements which were, or became, slogans for this attitude. "What is true is mine"; "the best views are common property"; "whatever has been well said by anyone is mine."[19] The last of these was quoted by the Christian apologist Justin in reference to the ideas of Plato, the Stoics, poets, and historians,[20] and Clement of Alexandria, who also quoted it with approval, referred it to a distinctive "eclectic" school.[21] Diogenes Laertius, writing in Clement's time, made mention of such a school as recently established at Alexandria,[22] but the attitude, like the slogan, was nearly universal.

Though the various schools continued to exist, the common eclectic approach to their doctrines meant that Christians could borrow from Stoic ethics as well as from Platonist (and sometimes from Stoic) metaphysics. The interrelations between second-century Platonism and Stoicism made such borrowing relatively easy.

III·THE GREEK APOLOGISTS

The writings of five of the Greek Christian apologists of the second century are still in existence; they come from Aristides, Justin, Tatian, Athenagoras, and Theophilus, and they reflect a wide variety of purposes and interpretations.

[16] Cf. P. Vallette, *De Oinomao Cynico* (Paris, 1908); H. J. Mette in *RE* XVII 2249-51; K. Latte in *RE* XVIII 864.

[17] C. Clerc, *Les théories relatives au culte des images chez les auteurs grecs du ii*ᵐᵉ *siecle apres J.-C.* (Paris, 1915), 89-123.

[18] Cf. A. Goedeckemeyer, *Die Geschichte des griechischen Skeptizismus* (Leipzig, 1905). There are many parallels to Sextus Empiricus in the treatise *Ad Autolycum* by Theophilus.

[19] *Ep.* 12, 11; 16, 7; cf. R. E. Witt, *Albinus and the History of Middle Platonism* (Cambridge, 1937), 24-26.

[20] *Apol.* 2, 13, 2.

[21] *Str.* I, 37, 6.

[22] Diogenes Laertius I, 21.

Aristides, probably from Athens, addressed a petition to the emperor, as did Justin at Rome and Athenagoras at Alexandria. (The lost petitions of the Asian bishops Apollinaris and Melito were petitions of the same kind, as we shall see.) Tatian in Syria and Theophilus at Antioch wrote treatises of a more general nature.

The most important among these authors was Justin, "son of Priscus and grandson of Baccheius, of Flavia Neapolis in Syria Palestina," who addressed a petition to the emperor and his heirs about 150 and, a decade later, wrote his *Dialogue with the Jew Trypho* in an attempt to produce conversion by showing that Old Testament prophecies had been fulfilled in Christ. The *Dialogue* begins with an account of Justin's own conversion.

This account is one of the most important witnesses to the Christianity of the second century, not so much for its record of events as for the attitudes it reflects. Like other young men in his time, and men not so young, he began his search for the truth by studying with a Stoic philosopher. Just so, in about 143 the young Galen started out in philosophy with a Stoic at Pergamum; just so, the Hermotimus satirized by Lucian took on faith whatever his Stoic master taught. Justin's reason for leaving his first master was different from theirs, however: he found that he was making no progress toward the knowledge of God. This is to say that he shared the view of philosophy expressed in the Hermetic *Asclepius.* "Philosophy is striving through constant contemplation and saintly piety toward the knowledge of God." For a Stoic, teaching about the gods came at the end of one's education, after one knew enough Stoic physics to understand what the gods were. Justin could not wait; he went on to a "subtle" Peripatetic who asked to be paid for his speculations. Once more Justin moved on.[23] This time he came to a Pythagorean, who asked if he was acquainted with music, astronomy, and geometry. The teacher asked him, "Do you think that you can comprehend any of the matters that lead to happiness unless you have first learned these—which take the soul away from objects of sense and suit it for objects of intelligence so that it can view the beautiful and the good?" Justin was unwilling or unable to make these studies. Again the *Asclepius* illustrates his attitude.

Many have made philosophy incomprehensible and confusing . . . mixing it up in various unintelligible studies through their clever treatises on arithmetic, music, and geometry.

Galen held that a physician should know about such matters, but he came from a social environment different from Justin's.

Justin's fourth educational venture took him to a Platonist, with whom he achieved what he calls "great advancement daily." There was an almost pathetic eagerness about the studies of this provincial Platonist and his pupil,

[23] Platonists and Platonizers in the second century claimed to find Aristotelian thought obscure: see Numenius, frag. 2 (p. 119, 4 Leemans) and Atticus in Eusebius, *P. E.* 15, 9, 13.

both devoted to the revelation given by Plato and the mysteries unveiled in the *Timaeus* and the *Phaedrus*. One dialogue explained the origins of the cosmos; the other guided the immortal soul to God.

The knowledge of incorporeal objects overcame me and the contemplation of the Ideas gave wings to my mind; in a short time I seemed to have become wise, and in my stupidity I hoped to have the vision of God at once. This is the goal of the philosophy of Plato.

One might note that the order of the curriculum was partly responsible for the results. Galen went from a Stoic to a Middle Platonist, then on to a Peripatetic and an Epicurean before turning to medicine. Justin ended his philosophical studies with Platonism.

Presumably it was from the Platonist that he learned something of the history of philosophy. It was a divine gift, "sent down to men," and therefore was one by origin and nature. The first philosophers, such as Heraclitus, Pythagoras, and Socrates, had searched for this truth, but their followers merely admired them and were content with a simple traditionalism. By returning to Socrates and Plato, Justin was going back to the sources of revelation.

A mark of a Platonist's advancement was his withdrawal to deserted places for meditation. Justin was following this practice one day by the sea. There he met an old man who struck up a conversation about the meaning of philosophy. The old man (real or ideal) asked him some crucial questions which shattered his Platonism and made him ready for Christianity. The key answers Justin gave were wrong. Throughout the conversation the old man had one end in view. He was determined to undermine the Platonic doctrine of reminiscence, which he saw was holding Justin's system together. He made two principal points. First he asked Justin whether or not the soul remembers the vision of God after returning to the body. Here Justin contradicted the *Phaedrus* of Plato (249 c-d) and said that it did not. The old man could then ask, "What's the use?"—a crushing reply given the shared axiom that God or nature does nothing without purpose. Second, he attacked an inconsistency in Plato himself. Plato had claimed that souls judged unworthy of the vision of God transmigrate into other bodies including those of animals.[24] Can the soul of an animal recall its previous existence? "Do the souls know why they are in bodies of this sort and what their sin was?" Unfortunately Justin, unlike several second-century Platonists, replied, "I think not." The old man had clearly won the debate. "Then there is no use," he said; and he went on to underline his points.

Then souls do not see God nor do they transmigrate.
You are right, I said.
Therefore these philosophers know nothing about these matters.

[24] *Phaedo* 81 f, *Timaeus* 42 b-c, 91 d—92 b.

The old man was free to proceed to annihilate the Platonic doctrine of the soul as a self-moved mover (*Phaedrus* 245 c).

The source of the old man's arguments lies within the history of philosophical debate; it is to be found either in Peripatetic or, more probably, in Stoic arguments against Plato.[25] Perhaps Justin should have stayed longer with his earlier teachers, or should have raised more questions with his last teacher. In any event, he was forced to abandon the doctrine of reminiscence and seek for another epistemological foundation. What could the source of religious knowledge be?

The old man advised Justin to read the writings of the ancient prophets. They were inspired by God; they discussed philosophical questions such as first principles or origins and the goal of life (i.e., creation and eschatology); and their statements are unshakable. They are unshakable first because they are above all rational proof and second because of two facts: prophecy has been fulfilled and the prophets themselves worked miracles. Justin wanted this kind of authority, and when he turned to the prophets his heart was kindled by the spark of revelation. One might wonder how he could so easily forget the claims of Greek philosophy; but Plato himself had admired the wisdom of Egyptian priests, and in Justin's time there was a widespread admiration of "barbarian faith." A little later we find it well expressed by the rhetorician Aelian.[26]

Who would not praise the wisdom of the barbarians? None of them has fallen into atheism; they have no doubts as to whether or not the gods exist and whether or not they really are concerned for us. . . . All their activities prove that their piety and reverence toward the gods is strong.

The gods of Aelian's barbarians foretell the future and exercise providential care, as does the God of the old man's prophets.

What Justin had done when he moved from philosophy to Christianity was to discover a new religious sanction for his inherited and acquired culture. God and the philosophers were to some extent replaced by God and the prophets. The precise nature of his conversion is hard to understand. In his *Second Apology* (c. 12) he says that when he was "taking delight in the doctrines of Plato" he heard of the Christians. They were supposed to be immoral, but when he observed their fearlessness when facing death he knew that "they could not possibly be living in vice or the love of pleasure." Here he came close to Galen, who criticized the Christians for their lack of rationality but pointed out that they despised death and were often devoted to asceticism and the pursuit of justice.[27] But unlike Galen Justin became a Christian.

25 N. Hyldal, *Philosophie und Christentum: eine Interpretation der Einleitung zum Dialog Justins* (Copenhagen, 1966).

26 *Var. hist.* 2, 31.

27 See R. Walzer, *Galen on Jews and Christians* (Oxford, 1949).

As a Christian he read the prophetic writings in a manner not unlike that recommended by Plutarch. Plutarch too made use of a literature national in origin. In his treatise *De Iside et Osiride* (c. 66) he stated that the exegete of the Egyptian myths must go beyond the particular or national elements to look for what is universal. Similarly Justin took the Old Testament stories and found in them prophecies pointing to the universal revelation in Christ. He found Heraclitus, Socrates, and the more recent Musonius Rufus partially inspired by the same universal Logos or divine Reason fully incarnate in Christ.

As a Christian he could use whatever weapons were to be found in his old philosophical arsenal. In the *Timaeus* he could still find a fairly reliable account of creation. He could use the story of Heracles' choice between vice and virtue (from Xenophon's *Memorabilia of Socrates*) to illustrate his own idea of free will, and he could attack fatalism with arguments derived from Carneades, the founder of the New Academy.[28] He argues at length that the pagan gods are really demons who inspired the immoral stories of mythology and demanded worship. Here he probably relies on a theory ultimately from Xenocrates, head of the Academy a generation after Plato. No doubt he never read a page of Xenocrates, but his ideas can be traced back to him.

Indeed, his eclecticism and his combination of Genesis with the *Timaeus* may suggest that he was still directly influenced by the early second-century eclectic philosopher Numenius, who came from Apamea in Syria. Justin continued to make use of Platonic expressions in defining his Christian ideas and thus pointed toward the theology which was to be worked out especially at Alexandria. It has often been claimed that Justin was influenced by the Hellenistic Jewish philosopher Philo, but proof of the claim is difficult to provide.[29] Certainly Justin treated the Old Testament theophanies as Philo did, as manifestations of the divine Logos, and Philo too had used Platonic language in working out his theology. It may be that among Justin's teachers was a student of Philo's writings.

In addition, Justin was deeply influenced by the Christian tradition of interpreting the Old Testament as full of prophecies and prefigurations of Christ.

The new element in Justin's thought is based on his acceptance of the continuous revelation of God through his Logos (reason and word) to the Old Testament prophets—beginning with Adam—and in the incarnate Logos, Jesus. When the old man by the sea insisted to him that the prophets were reliable because their prophecies were fulfilled, he obviously meant that they were fulfilled in the ministry of Jesus. What Justin has accepted is an embryonic philosophy or, rather, theology of history, based in part on

[28] D. Amand, *Fatalisme et liberté dans l'antiquité grecque* (Louvain, 1945).
[29] See E. R. Goodenough, *The Theology of Justin Martyr* (Jena, 1923): H. A. Wolfson, *Philo* (Cambridge, Mass., 1947).

earlier Hellenistic Jewish interpretations of the Old Testament but given full confirmation by the incarnation.

Justin's ideas about how the incarnation took place are rather vague, but the culminating moment was obviously the crucifixion of Jesus. The suffering of the Logos was prefigured by the sufferings of philosophers who recognized him, though only incompletely; these were Heraclitus, Socrates, and Musonius Rufus. The cross was implanted in the nature of the universe, for Plato said (*Timaeus* 36 b-c) that the Demiurge shaped the universe like the Greek letter *chi* (X). It is in man, for his eyebrows and nose form the letter T; it is in his artifacts, such as the mast and sail of a ship, a plow, the banners and trophies of the legions, and the images of emperors borne on standards. The cruciform Logos is thus the clue to nature and history alike.

Incarnate, the Logos was no sophist, even though Lucian of Samosata, a satirist and sophist himself, was to call him "that executed sophist."[30] The accounts of his life were not just wonder stories, for the gospels as "reminiscences of the apostles" were just as reliable as Xenophon's "reminiscences of Socrates." To some degree Justin's conversion can be described as a movement from philosophy to historical reality, and to the living Christian community.

Justin insists that Christians pay taxes and tribute to Roman tax collectors everywhere, as Jesus taught them to do. Though they worship God alone, they rejoice in loyal service to the emperors; they not only acknowledge the authority of the state but also pray that the imperial power may be accompanied by "disciplined reason." At this point, however, he points out that all the earlier emperors have died—a thought that was to pervade the *Meditations* of Marcus Aurelius—and warns of possible punishment in eternal fire. As Christ said, "Of him to whom God has given much, much will be required." What the emperors must do is live up to their reputation as "pious [Antoninus Pius] and philosophers and guardians of justice and lovers of learning" (1, 2). They will not escape the future judgment of God if they persist in injustice.[31]

The essence of injustice is to be found in the persecution of Christians. But when the state acts unjustly it is untrue to its own nature. Justin's basic acceptance of the rightness of Roman power is clearly indicated, as Henry Chadwick has pointed out,[32] in his statement that the cross, symbolized in all nature, is represented by the *vexillae* and trophies of the Roman legions, symbols of Roman power and of divine power at the same time (1, 55).

In spite of the efforts made by Justin and other apologists relatively soon after his time, the apologetic venture did not evoke a favorable response from non-Christians. Around 178 the anti-Christian author Celsus scornfully claimed that Christians never entered into conversation with intelligent pagans;

30 *Vita Peregrini* 13.
31 *Apol.* 1, 17-18 (Luke 12:48); 1, 2; 1, 68.
32 *Bulletin of the John Rylands Library* 47 (1965), 275-97.

instead, they dealt with adolescent boys, crowds of slaves, and groups of fools—thus, as Origen noted, supposedly resembling the Cynic street preachers of the time.[33] In addition, he argued that they got into private houses as wool workers, cobblers, and launderers and there stirred up revolt against family and school traditions.[34] As Dodds points out, Origen does not deny the truth of the charge but simply reports what Celsus said.[35]

If one accepts Celsus' criticism as reliable, it is obvious that in the latter years of the second century there was a significant "generation gap" of which the Christian missionaries were making use. They urged children to pay no attention to their father and teachers, who spoke nonsense and lacked understanding. They claimed that the teachers were stupid and corrupt and controlled the young only by means of punishments. The children should leave these representatives of the older generation and go to the wool shop or the cobbler's or the laundry, where they would learn the right and perfect way to live and "would become happy and make their home happy as well." In Celsus' opinion this approach to the younger generation was often successful.

His picture of rebellion against parental authority as encouraged by Christians is so vivid that it may well be based on the personal experience of Celsus himself or his friends, whose children no longer found meaning in the Graeco-Roman cultural tradition. If such a parent happened to encounter the *Oration* of the Christian critic Tatian, his worst fears would be confirmed. Tatian took positive delight in his own alienation from society and claimed that it was essentially Christian. "I do not wish to rule, I do not wish to be rich, I despise military honors. . . ."[36] Christians like him regarded philosophy and rhetoric as meaningless compared with knowledge derived from revelation and personal experience.

According to Tatian himself, he was "born in the land of the Assyrians" and was later instructed in rhetoric and was even initiated in "the mysteries." He visited many lands and finally went to Rome, where he claims to have found human sacrifice practiced in honor of Jupiter Latiaris and, at Aricia, for Artemis. He also observed the Greek statues which had been taken to Rome. In revolt against Graeco-Roman culture as a whole, he withdrew for contemplation. At that point, he says, he encountered the Old Testament writings and was convinced by them because of their lack of artifice and their teaching about the future, the nature of morality, and their monotheism. He "bade farewell to the arrogance of Romans and the idle talk of Athenians." He accepted a "barbarian philosophy" which he found superior to that of the Greeks; he was freed from the power of the gods whom he now recognized

---

[33] *Contra Celsum* 3, 50.
[34] *Ibid.*, 3, 55.
[35] E. R. Dodds, *Pagan and Christian in an Age of Anxiety* (Cambridge, 1965), 116.
[36] *Or.* 11; cf. Hippolytus, *Apost. Trad.* 16, 17-19.

as demons. He became a pupil of "the most admirable Justin." Perhaps it was after his master's martyrdom (between 163 and 167) that he left Rome and returned to the east, apparently founding a school at Antioch,[37] and becoming a leader of the ascetic Encratites.[38]

Tatian's attitude, though unusual among the rhetoricians of his day, was not unique. When Adrian, a Tyrian pupil of the famous Herodes Atticus, began teaching rhetoric at Athens, he began his inaugural address by saying, "Once again letters have come from Phoenicia."[39] An athlete who was Herodes' companion criticized the decline of Attic Greek in the manner of Tatian and also denounced the immorality of Greek mythology and the pointlessness of athletic contests.[40] Tatian went further, however, and attacked philosophy, medicine, geography, mythology, the theater, gladiatorial contests, grammar, rhetoric, theology, and legislation, not to mention sculpture.

Tatian's *Oration against the Greeks* is the only work by him still extant, though his *Diatessaron,* a synthesis of the four gospels, has been reconstructed from fragments and quotations by later writers. Its title reflects his continuing concern with Greek culture, for it refers to "the fourth concord" in Greek music. The *Oration* may have been written in 177 or thereabouts; the *Diatessaron* cannot be dated.

Tatian's contemporary Athenagoras, who may have written at Alexandria about the same time, addressed Marcus Aurelius and Commodus as co-emperors and attempted to refute the charges of godlessness, cannibalism, and sexual promiscuity which were commonly brought against Christians. He tried to show that Christians were trinitarian monotheists who exhibited a high morality and shared in the best of Graeco-Roman literary culture.

Neither emperor seems to have been moved by this apology or others. Marcus Aurelius had no respect for Christians. The court physician Galen, however, though critical of Jewish and Christian emphasis on "faith," greatly admired their contempt of death, their self-discipline and self-control, and their pursuit of justice. In this regard they were "not inferior to . . . genuine philosophers."[41] His statement shows that he had accepted the apologists' description of Christianity as a philosophy, though not their claim that it was philosophically adequate.

General apologies or diatribes were not the only works of an apologetic nature to be produced by Christian writers addressing non-Christians. A treatise *On the resurrection* ascribed to Athenagoras is intended to defend a doctrine which, derived from Judaism, had presented difficulties for gentile

---

[37] Epiphanius, *Haer.* 46, 1, 8.
[38] Cf. F. Bolgiani in *Atti della Accademia delle Scienze di Torino* 91 (1956-1957), 1-77.
[39] Philostratus, *Vit. soph.* 2, 10, p. 587 Olearius.
[40] *Ibid.,* 2, 1, pp. 553-54.
[41] R. Walzer, *Galen on Jews and Christians* (Oxford, 1949), 15.

Christians almost from the beginning.[42] Earlier Christian writers, following the example of the apostle Paul, had appealed to revelation and had made use of analogies taken from the world of nature. This treatise, however, makes no use of analogies although it implicitly relies on revelation throughout. The first part of it is a refutation of pagan criticisms. (1) God lacks the power to effect resurrection—because he is either ignorant or impotent. But he is neither ignorant nor impotent, for he created the world. Objections based on the consumption of human bodies by animals or other human beings are refuted by the claim that cannibalism is unnatural and therefore men cannot digest the bodies of other men; human bodies do not wear out. (2) God lacks the will to effect resurrection—because he is either unjust or not concerned with the matter. But he is just when he raises some men and not others, and he must be concerned because he created the world. The second part is intended to confirm the faith of Christians. (1) Man was created so that he could perpetually view the work of divine wisdom. (2) His life as a rational being requires immortality. (3) God's providence and justice require a last judgment. (4) Man's final end is not found in this life. Therefore resurrection is not only possible but necessary.

Whether or not Athenagoras wrote this treatise, the theme was important at Alexandria soon after his time. Clement certainly intended to produce a discussion of the resurrection,[43] and Origen wrote a treatise on the subject, extant only in fragments. From a different point of view Tertullian also wrote a work De resurrectione carnis. The doctrine continued to create difficulties both inside the church and outside it.

A similar emphasis on resurrection occurs in the first book Ad Autolycum, composed by Theophilus, bishop of Antioch, around 180. All three of Theophilus' books reflect the attempted fusion between Christianity and culture which was being made in his time. The first book deals chiefly with the nature and attributes of God and makes use of precedents provided in Hellenistic Judaism and popular philosophy. The second book, like the third, relies on handbooks to show the inconsistencies of Greek poets and philosophers and provides exegesis, largely Jewish in origin, of the opening chapters of Genesis. The third book claims, against Marcionites and outside critics, that the prophets agree with the sayings of Jesus, and then offers a chronology, chiefly biblical, from creation to the death of Marcus Aurelius. Excerpts from Josephus accompany the discussion. It is hard to tell just what place remains for primitive eschatology in Theophilus' thought. Certainly there is a resurrection before the last judgment, and after the judgment either Adam or man in general will return to Eden, an earthly paradise.[44] Since 5,695 years have

[42] Acts 17:32; I Cor. 15:12-58; I Clem. 24-27; 2 Clem. 9.
[43] Paed. I, 47, 1; 2, 104, 3.
[44] Ad Autol. 3, 26; cf. 24.

elapsed since creation, however, it would appear that the time of the resurrection is not a matter of immediate concern.

For the apologists as for other Christians the resurrection, like the creation, was of cardinal importance because it was an expression of the absolute power of the one God whom Christians worshiped. Sooner or later he would reveal his power and would act on behalf of those who had known him by faith.

One more aspect of the work of the apologists merits consideration at this point, for it reflects their relationship to the world of Graeco-Roman religion. From early times the prophetic books of the Sibyl had been treasured at Rome, and since the first century B.C. a collection of her oracles had been preserved on the Palatine hill. After the fire at Rome under Nero they were consulted.[45] The Christian prophet Hermas mistook the aged Church, who appeared to him in a vision, for the Sibyl.[46] Justin appealed to the authority of the Sibyl and the Persian sage Hystaspes in support of the view that the world would be destroyed by fire.[47] It is therefore not surprising that the Jewish *Sibylline Oracles* were quoted by Athenagoras, Theophilus, Clement of Alexandria, and Tertullian (among others) as the work of a Greek "prophetess." After all, in 162 the emperor Lucius Verus either visited or was expected to visit the temple of the Sibyl at Erythrae in western Asia Minor.[48] The Sibyl had received official sanction among Greeks as well as in the city of Rome. Similarly both Athenagoras and Tertullian made use of the writings ascribed to the supposedly Egyptian Hermes Trismegistus—and late in the third century a prayer from the Hermetic *Poemandres* made its way into a collection of Christian prayers.[49] By the fourth century both kinds of literature were frequently quoted by Christians.

An example of less specifically religious assimilation is to be found among the authors of apocryphal acts of the apostles, beginning in the second century. In these romances the popular tales of the Graeco-Roman world found their way into the Christian consciousness. In the *Acts of Paul,* for example, we find a Christianized version of the story about Androcles and the lion. In official circles these romances were not highly favored, but they were widely read anyway.

It may seem that by speaking of the apocryphal acts along with the apologists we have passed from the relatively sublime to the relatively ridiculous, but our purpose in doing so is to reemphasize the fact that what Harnack called (in reference to Gnosticism) the acute Hellenization of Christianity occurred on all sorts of levels during the second century. The later apologists

45 Tacitus, *Ann.* 15, 44, 1.
46 Hermas, *Vis.* 1, 2, 2—2, 4, 1.
47 *Apol.* 1, 20, 1 (cf. 44, 12 and J. Bidez and F. Cumont, *Les mages hellénisés*, Paris, 1938, II, 361-62).
48 Cf. P. Corssen in *Athenische Mitteilungen* 38 (1913), 1-22.
49 A. D. Nock and A.-J. Festugière, *Corpus Hermeticum* I (Paris, 1945), 18 bis.

and the authors of the apocryphal acts alike had no real place in their thought for the eschatology of an earlier era. The political views of the apologists, which we have already discussed, are almost uniformly expressions of loyalty to the Roman state.

Perhaps the apologists' statements were not wholly ingenuous. In his *Apology* Justin clearly claims that Christians do not expect a "human kingdom" but are allies of the Roman emperors.[50] What he must mean, however, is simply that the future kingdom will be given by God, for in his *Dialogue*—not addressed to the emperors—he says that "Christ said . . . that he would come again to Jerusalem and then would eat and drink again with his disciples." He agrees with other "right-minded" Christians that there will be a resurrection of the flesh and a period of a thousand years' duration in a rebuilt, beautified, and enlarged Jerusalem.[51] Such a motif is completely absent from the writings of the other early Greek apologists, and it obviously could hardly be reconciled with their concern for Graeco-Roman culture and philosophy. It was this concern, combined with political factors, which proved decisive during the latter years of the second century.

The apologetic movement, implying a serious concern for the relation of the church to the Graeco-Roman world, cannot be viewed as the achievement of only a few Christian intellectuals or would-be intellectuals. The apologists often held responsible positions within the churches. Justin was not an isolated teacher but obviously stood close to the bishop and the church life of Rome. The later apologists Apollinaris and Melito were bishops in Asia Minor; Theophilus was bishop of Antioch and his treatise, like Justin's, was used by Irenaeus, bishop of Lyons in Gaul.

Though Irenaeus' extant works were directed specifically to problems within the church, he expressed a positive attitude toward the empire, both implicitly and explicitly. God's reign would come, and the Roman empire would be divided into ten parts, but only after six thousand years from the creation.[52] Meanwhile the Romans provided peace in the world. Christians. could walk the roads without fear and sail wherever they wished.[53] Christian leaders were not hostile to the empire as such.

[50] *Apol.* I, II, I-I2, I.
[51] *Dial.* 51, 2; 80, 5.
[52] *Adv. haer.* 5, 26, I; 38, 3.
[53] *Ibid.*, 4, 30, 3.

CHAPTER VIII
THE GNOSTIC CRISIS

In large measure, though not entirely, Gnosticism seems to have originated out of the crisis of apocalyptic eschatology in Judaism and in early Christianity. Once the victories promised in eschatological doctrine proved illusory, one could settle down to work in the world (in the manner of more orthodox Jews and Christians) or else seek for escape from a world in which one felt oneself to be an alien. (One could also reiterate the eschatological promises; the Montanists, who did so, will be discussed in the next chapter.) There were resemblances between the Montanists and the Gnostics. Both expected to enjoy the life of heaven, the Montanists when it appeared on earth, the Gnostics when they escaped to it. Both groups were thus radically alienated from the life of the Graeco-Roman world. Both found inspiration in the ecstatic mystical utterances of prophets and prophetesses. Both also claimed to represent neglected aspects of primitive Christian tradition. Both actually developed teaching which Christian leaders generally found wholly unacceptable.

What Christian theologians found wrong in Gnostic doctrine was the denial of the reality and the potential goodness of the created world and of human life. For the Gnostics, God was completely unknown except to themselves; they refused to come to terms with the traces of divine providence for which most of the apologists had looked. They denied the reality of the incarnation and of the future resurrection as well. In other words, they were almost diametrically opposed to the main lines of Christian theological development in the second century, especially in so far as it was coming close to philosophical ideas generally accepted in the Graeco-Roman world. To be sure, the Gnostics shared some of their conceptions with some philosophers. It must not be forgotten, however, that the Neoplatonist Plotinus denounced them for their rejection of the world.[1]

Generally speaking, the Gnostics differentiated themselves from other Christians by their claim to possess a saving *gnosis* or knowledge, secretly revealed to their predecessors (usually disciples of Jesus) and transmitted to them alone. This knowledge concerned the supreme God, superior to the Creator, who was known only to them because, as spiritual beings, they had emanated from him. They would be saved by recognition of him and of themselves and would return to him after death, escaping from the alien world which belonged to the Creator. Their spirits were temporarily imprisoned in fleshly bodies; Jesus—for Christian Gnostics the Revealer—had merely seemed to possess such a body. Since their real selves were spiritual, they could express their alienation from merely human existence through either extreme asceticism or the opposite.

The Gnostic movement presented a threat to ordinary Christianity because its leaders could provide highly subtle exegesis of the mysterious sayings of Jesus and isolated texts from the Pauline letters; in addition, they used books purporting to contain the authentic sayings of Jesus, known only to a select group of disciples. Their spirituality appealed to men and women alienated from Graeco Roman society and from conventional education and morality. The sheer novelty of the doctrines doubtless attracted some adherents. We may suppose that in some measure Gnosticism was a parody of Christianity, but in its time it evidently looked like an alternative. One aspect which may have attracted adherents was the view of many Gnostics—though not the Marcionites[2]—that martyrdom should be avoided because the spiritual Christ was different from the Jesus about whom investigators inquired.

I·SYSTEMS

In spite of modern discoveries of Gnostic documents, especially at Nag Hammadi in Egypt,[3] the oldest sources we possess for Gnostic teaching are

---

[1] *Enn.* 2, 9; cf. *Gnosticism: an Anthology* (London-New York, 1961), 235-39.

[2] Eusebius, *H. E.* 5, 16, 21.

[3] For a survey of these documents see J. M. Robinson, "The Coptic Gnostic Library Today," *New Testament Studies* 12 (1967-1968), 356-401.

still the writings of the early church fathers who militantly opposed the Gnostics but rather accurately described their views. The first account we have is in the *First Apology* of Justin Martyr (*ca.* 150), who briefly criticized Simon Magus, Menander, and Marcion and referred his readers to a treatise *Against all heresies* for more details.[4] Irenaeus, writing against the same sectarians a generation later, probably made use of Justin's treatise, which is now lost.

Irenaeus began his sketch of early Gnostic developments[5] by describing the system of the Simonians, whom he regarded as followers of the Simon of Acts 8:9-24. In their view Simon himself was the Highest God; at creation he emitted a Thought which generated a group of spiritual beings who in turn made the universe. Because of their desire to be regarded as supreme, they imprisoned their mother, Simon's Thought, in a succession of female bodies beginning with Helen of Troy and ending with a prostitute at Tyre also named Helen. All religions were essentially manifestations of the Simonian revelation. The Simonians venerated statues of Simon as Zeus and of Helen as Athena, for in Greek mythology Athena had sprung from the head of Zeus and she was often interpreted as his Forethought. Simon, they said, was known as Father among the Samaritans and as Holy Spirit among the gentiles; he had descended as Son in Judaea and had been crucified though only in appearance. Evidently, since he was finally able to rescue his Thought in Helen of Tyre, he also descended as Father in Samaria.

It is hard to escape the conclusion that this picture is in part based upon some form of the Christian doctrine of the Trinity and therefore presumably does not date from a time before the end of the first century. In addition, when the Simonians said that laws were conventional and had been ordained by the angels who made the world, they seem to have been relying on Galatians 3:19; when they said that by Simon's grace men were saved, not by works of law, they were apparently distorting Ephesians 2:8-9. It looks as if the system described by Irenaeus was in part a modification of Christian doctrine and therefore does not go back to Simon or, at any rate, to the early years of his ministry.

The essence of Simonian Gnosticism lies in the revelation of a god, otherwise unknown, who did not create the world, which was made and governed by beings hostile to him and to his Thought. The unknown god who finally revealed himself also revealed the spiritual history of mankind and showed that salvation was to be found in the rejection of convention and, presumably, in an escape analogous to the eventual escape of his own Thought from the

---

[4] *Apol.* I, 26. According to Justin, a statue of Simon was officially erected on the *insula Tiberina* in Claudius' reign; it bore the inscription SIMONI DEO SANCTO. Such an inscription exists (*ILS* 3474), but it is dedicated SEMONI SANCO DEO FIDIO, to an old Sabine deity. Other Roman inscriptions combine SANCO with SANCTO (*ILS* 3472-73). The error was due to poor eyesight or to the power of suggestion.

[5] *Adv. haer.* I, 23-31.

world. He really had nothing to do with the material world; as Jesus, he merely seemed to suffer but did not actually do so.

At a fairly early date, probably within the first century, Simonianism seems to have produced a heresy of its own. At Antioch Menander, said to have been Simon's disciple, replaced the figures of Simon and Helen by a First Power, unknown to all, and the Thought of this Power—and by himself, who was the Savior sent from above. The means of salvation was a baptism which, in Menander's view, was to produce perpetual youth. (In succeeding generations, for obvious reasons, we hear little about Menander's followers.) Conceivably he did not intend his teaching about baptism to be taken literally—any more than Ignatius of Antioch literally regarded the Eucharist as a "drug of immortality"—but his disciples evidently thought they would live forever.

Toward the beginning of the second century another Gnostic teacher at Antioch came even closer to Christianity, though of course with a peculiarly Gnostic interpretation. Like Menander, Saturninus held that the Supreme Being (*authentia*) was completely unknown, but he spoke of Christ rather than himself as the Savior. This Being made the spiritual beings who made the world. They then glimpsed a "luminous image" which came down from above and returned, and they tried to make a copy of it (Saturninus read Genesis 1:26 as "Let us make man after *the* image and likeness"). Their attempt was not altogether successful, for the product remained inanimate until a "spark of life" (cf. Gen. 2:7) came down from above; this spark, present in good men, is the element which is saved. Another descent took place when Christ, who merely seemed to be a man and was probably the luminous image which appeared earlier, came down to destroy the spiritual beings hostile to the highest Being. Since ordinary human existence, including marriage, procreation, and eating meat, is evil, the followers of Saturninus were to have nothing to do with it. They were also to have nothing to do with Judaism or Jewish Christianity, for the Old Testament prophets were inspired by the inferior spiritual powers, including both Satan and "the god of the Jews."

This system reflects a kind of Gnosticism quite different from that of the Simonians or Menander, at least in its ethical consequences. These earlier Gnosticisms include a female principle, the Thought of God, perhaps derived from the Sophia of Jewish wisdom literature. Their ethical ideas are antinomian and libertarian. On the other hand, for Saturninus there is no female principle and he advocates extreme asceticism. He doubtless agreed with the apocryphal *Gospel of the Egyptians* that Jesus "came to destroy the works of the female."

In these two classes of Syrian Gnosticism we find foreshadowed most of the later Gnostic developments. There is a supreme unknown God revealed by a redeemer, come to liberate men from the bondage of the tangible world. Redemption comes through knowledge rather than through worldly morality of any kind. The followers of Simon were free to live as they pleased; those of Saturninus were pleased to live in freedom from the world. Both kinds of freedom were based on the assumption that the world was under the control of evil powers and that victory could come only through escape.

The notion that the Highest God was completely unknown apart from his revelation in Jesus, and that the prophets were inspired by an inferior being, was taken over and developed by the famous heretic Marcion, who was a member of the Roman church between 137 and 144. In his view the Highest God, the Father of Jesus, was good whereas the Creator-God of the Jews was merely just and was responsible for eschatological prophecies. Jesus came, as a life-giving spirit, to make manifest a new revelation and a new way of life. Unfortunately his message was not written down at first, and when it was written it was immediately interpolated by false apostles who were under the spell of Judaism. Only Paul understood the gospel, and his letters too were interpolated. Making use of the gospel of Luke (written by a follower of Paul), Marcion proceeded to cut out the interpolations and restore the authentic, non-Jewish gospel. His lack of enthusiasm for Judaism was probably increased by the disastrous Jewish revolt of 132–135; his rejection of the Jewish law was characteristic of Gnostics. He himself was expelled by the Roman church.

Inferences as to Marcion's social status and Roman church finance have sometimes been drawn from Tertullian's statements about a gift of money he gave when he arrived and received back when he left.[6] The figure is usually given at 200,000 sesterces,[7] but Tertullian actually speaks of 200 (*ducenti*), and this word is used by Latin writers simply to refer to "a large number." It is clear that Marcion was well to do, but we know nothing in detail.

About the same time, another Gnostic teacher, Valentinus by name, came to Rome and developed a complicated mythological picture of the emanation of various spiritual beings or aeons from the supreme deity. The twelfth and lowest of these aeons, emitted in pairs like the male and female of Genesis 1:27, included the female Sophia or Wisdom. Her instability led her to fall into the outer darkness, where she conceived spontaneously and brought forth a premature infant who then created the universe we know. He used materials which were the solidification of his mother's emotions (thus her grief produced tears which became water). This creator, called Ialdabaoth in similar systems, regarded himself as the only god there was; he constantly struggled with his mother Sophia for control over mankind, his creation into which she had inserted a divine spirit or spark. In order to redeem both her and mankind, Jesus was sent down to collect the scattered spiritual seeds and to restore them to the "pleroma" (cf. Col. 1:19, etc.) or "fulness" of spiritual

---

[6] *Adv. Marcionem* 4, 4, 3 (*pecunia*); *De praescr.* 30, 2 (*ducenti sestertii*).

[7] E. g., A. v. Harnack, *Marcion: das Evangelium vom fremden Gott* (ed. 2, Leipzig, 1924), p. 17*.

being, the twelve aeons above. For Valentinians, human marriage was a symbolic imitation of the unions in the spiritual world, and we are not surprised to learn that a sacred marriage formed part of their ritual.

The Valentinian system is dualistic, but it is less dualistic than that of Saturninus or the *Apocryphon of John,* with which it has points of contact. In the *Apocryphon* there is a primeval struggle between Ialdabaoth (the creator) and Christ. Ialdabaoth made paradise and gave man a wife in order to chain him to the material world; Christ, however, persuaded man to eat from the tree of knowledge (*gnosis*). In the course of this ageless struggle Christ came again and gave his true teaching (the content of the myth) to his disciple John—hence the title, the "secret doctrine" of John.

Even within a single system there is considerable variety, and we know that Ptolemaeus, a Roman disciple of Valentinus, presented his teaching in one way to initiates and in another to prospective converts from ordinary orthodox Christianity. Ptolemaeus also differed from Valentinian teachers at Antioch. And in another work probably Valentinian, the *Gospel of Truth,* there is much less emphasis on aeons and, indeed, on cosmology than in other fragments of his teaching. It remains a question whether this difference is to be explained by doctrinal development or by different occasions for the works. The *Gospel of Truth* is more poetic, more mystical, than other Valentinian documents.

Valentinianism is important in the history of Christian exegesis, since Ptolemaeus provided elaborate allegorical explanations not only of the parables of Jesus but also of events in his life. He also wrote an allegorical explanation of the opening verses of John, claiming that the aeons were symbolized there. Another Valentinian, Heracleon, prepared exegetical notes on at least the first eight chapters of John; these were later used by Origen in his commentary.

A different type of Gnostic thought is represented by an older contemporary of Valentinus, Basilides. He taught that originally there was absolutely nothing. A nonexistent God then produced a nonexistent seed out of nothing, and from this seed proceeded various kinds of existent things, including a "threefold Sonship" whose goal was to return to the nonexistent God. The goal of history is this return. When the spiritual elements have all gone back above, oblivion will come over the earth and there will be no further salvation. Perhaps because of this nihilistic emphasis, Basilides did not attract as many followers as Valentinus did; indeed, the church fathers tell us of only one, his son Isidore, who wrote treatises on ethics and on the allegorical interpretation of Greek and oriental literature.

Later Gnostic systems represent permutations and combinations of the elements found earlier. In the third and fourth centuries efforts were made to find the systems prefigured in Greek and oriental history, philosophy, and mythology, but much early Gnosticism was supplanted by the rise of Manichae-ism, which spread from Persia to the Roman empire, in spite of official con-demnation and Christian opposition.

Both Gnosticism and Manichaeism threatened the growth of Christianity because they were Gnostic; in other words, their teachers knew an elaborate mythological cosmology toward which Christianity was either agnostic or openly hostile. The Gnostic, like the Manichee, knew that he was essentially a part of God, a divine spark, and that nothing he did in the world made much difference. Moreover, the Gnostic use of the allegorical method meant that Gnostics could claim to have the true explanations of difficult passages.

Probably the best example of a syncretistic Gnostic system occurs in the book *Baruch,* summarized by Hippolytus.[8] The system clearly has roots in pagan religion and philosophy, in Judaism, and in Christianity. According to these Gnostics, the universe originated from three primary principles analogous to God, the world of ideas, and matter. The first principle, above the other two, is the Good, the male creative force, identified with the Greek fertility god Priapus. The other two are the male Elohim and the female Eden. After they experienced mutual desire, Eden produced twelve paternal and twelve maternal angels; all together they constituted the "paradise" of Genesis 2:8: "God planted paradise in Eden." These angels are the trees of the creation story. The tree of life is the paternal angel Baruch; the tree of knowledge is the maternal angel Naas (serpent). The angels made man from the best earth, i.e., the best, anthropoid parts of Eden, and fashioned animals from her inferior, theriomorphic parts.

Since man is a "symbol of their unity and love," Eden gave him soul and Elohim gave him spirit. Eve too was a symbol, but more specifically of Eden. They were given the command to "increase and multiply and inherit the earth" (cf. Gen. 1:28). This meant that they were to inherit Eden by imitating her marriage with Elohim. In addition, women were to provide dowries for their husbands just as Eve had given all her "substance" to Elohim.

When, as in Genesis, everything had been created, the twelve maternal angels, divided into four "sources" as in Genesis 2:10-14, were given rule over the world and became equivalent to the signs of the zodiac. Elohim, on the other hand, ascended with his angels to behold the world (Gen. 1:31) and left Eden below. He came to the light of the Good and said, "Open the gates for me so that I may enter and acknowledge the Lord [Ps. 118:19]; for I thought that I was the Lord." A voice from the light replied, "This is the gate of the Lord; the righteous enter through it" (Ps. 118:20). Elohim went in with his angels, and the Good said to him, "Sit at my right hand" (Ps. 110:1, ordinarily applied to Christ). Elohim asked the Good to let him overturn the world, for his spirit was imprisoned among the sons of men

[8] *Ref.* 5, 26-27.

(cf. Gen. 6:1-13). The Good instructed him to leave the world to Eden and himself remain above.

Eden knew that Elohim had abandoned her, and after adorning herself (cf. Gen. 2:1-2) without avail she ordered her angel Babel (= Aphrodite) to introduce adultery and divorce among men in order to grieve Elohim's spirit present among them (cf. Gen. 6:6). Naas was to assist Babel. Elohim thereupon sent Baruch to give aid to his spirit; he stood in the midst of paradise and told man not to eat of the tree of knowledge (Gen. 2:17), i.e., of Naas. Men could experience the passions (the other trees) but not transgression (Naas). Naas, however, committed adultery with Eve and pederasty with Adam. Thus evil originated for mankind.

In order to save the spirit, Elohim sent Baruch to Moses and spoke to the children of Israel through him, but Naas used the soul to make his own commandments heard. The same obstacle prevented the prophets from clearly enunciating the message of Baruch. Elohim then chose the gentile prophet Heracles; he performed twelve labors against the twelve maternal angels but was seduced by Omphale (= Babel = Aphrodite). Last of all, in the days of king Herod (Luke 1:5), Baruch was sent to Jesus, son of Joseph and Mary, who was twelve years old (Luke 2:42) and was tending sheep (David in 1 Sam. 16:19). Baruch told Jesus the whole history of the world and warned him not to be led astray. Jesus then proclaimed the gospel but was crucified at the instigation of Naas. Leaving his body on the cross, he then ascended to the Good. To Eden he said, "Woman, you have your son" (cf. John 19:26; the "psychic and earthly man"). Bearing the spirit of Elohim in his hands (cf. Luke 23:46), he ascended to the Good.

The Gnostic who understands this system has a key to the interpretation both of Greek mythology and of the Old Testament. In some respects Zeus is to be identified with Elohim, for Elohim is the swan that came upon Leda and the gold that came upon Danaë. In others, he is Naas, as in the case of the eagle and Ganymede (= Adam). Isaiah 1:2-3 is to be allegorized thus: "Hear, O heaven [= spirit], and give ear, O earth [= soul], for the Lord[= Baruch] has spoken. . . . Israel [= Eden] did not know me."

It would appear that the system is essentially derived from Jewish-Gnostic exegesis of the Old Testament, combined with current allegorizations of Greek mythology and a Christian-Gnostic doctrine of Jesus as the revealer. It illustrates the powerful syncretistic movement in the Gnosticism of the second and third centuries. Irenaeus tells us, for example, that the Simonians not only found their divine female principle in Helen of Troy but also worshiped statues of Simon as the Lord Zeus and of Helen as the Lady Athena. The Carpocratian Gnostics, more philosophically minded, put crowns on images of Christ supposedly made by Pilate and on those of Pythagoras, Plato, Aristotle, and others.[9]

[9] Irenaeus, *Adv. haer.* 1, 23; 1, 25, 5.

This is to say that many Gnostics desired to conform to the ways of Graeco-Roman religion and thus to abandon the distinctive claims of both Judaism and Christianity. According to Irenaeus, the Valentinians "eat meats sacrificed to idols and consider that they are not harmed by them; they are the first to assemble at every gentile festival in honor of idols; and some of them do not abstain from the murderous spectacle of beast-fighters and gladiators, abhorred by God and men."[10] For Christians such laxity was intolerable.

II·REVELATION AND WORSHIP

The problem created by the Gnostic movement was not only external but internal as well, for several Gnostic groups—perhaps especially the Valentinians—related their theology to their liturgical practices. Some introduced new sacraments; others laid much emphasis upon prophecy, thus resembling the Montanists whom we shall presently discuss. Irenaeus evidently knew Valentinians who had come to Gaul from Asia Minor and were followers of Valentinus' disciple Marcus,[11] and he describes their prophetic activities at some length.

Marcus himself had received a revelation of the highest Tetrad, which came down to him in female form, manifesting "what she was, and the origin of all things, which she had never revealed to anyone, whether gods or men, but only to him." She said to him, "I wish to show you the Truth herself, for I have brought her down from the abodes above so that you may see her bare and learn her beauty and hear her speaking and marvel at her understanding." As Irenaeus relates, "When she had said these things, while the Truth looked at him she opened her mouth and spoke a word; the word became a name." After uttering the name of Christ Jesus, the Truth became silent. Marcus "expected that she would say something further, and again the Tetrad came forward and said, 'You considered contemptible the word which you heard from the mouth of the Truth.'" The Tetrad showed him that it was not to be despised, for it contained deep numerological meanings.[12]

This account of Marcus' vision is important, for it gives us a picture of the kind of spiritual experience which lay at the heart of Gnosticism and other contemporary movements. Like the Montanist prophetess Priscilla, Marcus received his vision from a female revealer. (He thus differed from his teacher Valentinus, to whom the Logos appeared as a little child.[13]) The feminist emphasis of the revelation corresponds with the emphasis on the liturgical function of women in this sect.

[10] *Ibid.*, I, 6, 3; cf. W. H. C. Frend in *JEH* 5 (1954), 25-37.
[11] Irenaeus, *Adv. haer.* I, 13, 7 (p. 126 Harvey).
[12] *Ibid.*, I, 14, 1-4 (pp. 128-36).
[13] Hippolytus, *Ref.* 6, 42, 2.

Irenaeus provides a fairly complete description of the Marcosian eucharist, and from it we learn that there was an extended invocation before the communion proper, with prayers that the Grace over all might come and flow upon the worshipers.[14] (With this may be compared the words of the *Didache*: "Let grace come and let this world pass away.") Cups of wine mixed with water were given to the women, who gave thanks over them. Then Marcus himself would pray thus:

May the pre-existent, incomprehensible and ineffable grace fill your "inner man" [cf. Eph. 3:16] and multiply the knowledge of it in you, sowing the grain of mustard seed in the good earth.[15]

At this point the chalice he was holding would overflow, symbolizing the abundance of the grace that was present.

After the eucharist would come the rite of ecstatic prophecy. To an individual woman Marcus would say:

I wish you to share in my grace, since the Father of the All sees your angel constantly before his face [cf. Matt. 18:10]. The Place of Greatness is in us; we must become one. First, receive grace from me and through me. Adorn yourself as a bride expecting her husband [cf. Rev. 21:2], so that you may be what I am and I what you are. Establish the seed of the Light in your bridechamber. Receive the bridegroom from me and hold him and be held in him. Behold grace has descended upon you; open your mouth and prophesy.

The woman might reply that she had never prophesied and did not know how to do so. Marcus would then offer further invocations and say, "Open your mouth and say anything at all, and you will be prophesying." She would then go into a trance and, according to Irenaeus, give Marcus her property and person.

The sexual imagery of this Gnostic worship is striking.[16] Equally striking is the fact that early Christian eschatological ideas are being reinterpreted as realized in the actuality of worship. The parables about the sower and the mustard seed conclude with pictures of the miraculous fertility and productivity to be expected in the reign of God; for Marcus they referred to the miraculous outpouring of grace, actually effected in worship when the chalice overflowed. Christians who looked to the future for the coming of the kingdom could not accept such views.

Marcosian prophecy, too, presented difficulties for those who were not Gnostics. One of Irenaeus' teachers held that the Gnostic prophetesses' in-

[14] Irenaeus, *Adv. haer.* I, 13, 1-4.
[15] This is a combination of the parables of the sower (Mark 4:1-20 and parallels) and the mustard seed (Mark 4:30-32 and parallels) with sayings about faith like a grain (Matt. 17:20; Luke 17:6).
[16] See *After the New Testament* (Philadelphia, 1967), 173-94. At least in the Gospel of Philip, however, the rite may have been reserved for the dying; cf. H.-G. Gaffron, *Studien zum koptischen Philippusevangelium* (Bonn, 1969), 191-219.

spiration was due to their souls' heat when warmed by "empty air"; Irenaeus himself attacked their immorality. His basic complaint, however, was that the prophetic Spirit could not be controlled as Marcus controlled it. True prophets spoke where and when God wished, not at a Gnostic's command.[17] Prophecy as such could not be rejected; to reject it was an unforgivable sin.[18] But Christians had to keep away from the Marcosian assemblies or, if need be, blow away the evil spirits and curse them.[19]

Could such objections be raised against a movement in which Gnostic ideas, including sexual imagery, were not present? This was the problem raised in the second century when the movement called Montanism sprang up in Phrygia and claimed that the Spirit was at work among its adherents. Our evidence suggests that Gnosticism was in some ways simply one of the two types of responses that could be made to the early Christian apocalyptic eschatology. Montanism was the other.[20]

[17] Irenaeus, *Adv. haer.* I, 13, 3-4.
[18] *Ibid.*, 3, 11, 9, balanced by 4, 33, 6.
[19] *Ibid.*, I, 16, 3.
[20] Both Valentinians and Montanists spoke of ordinary Christians as merely "psychics" (Clement, *Str.* 4, 93, 1).

CHAPTER IX
THE MONTANIST CRISIS

In time when Irenaeus wrote against it, Gnosticism was still flourishing but, at least outside Alexandria, it was generally regarded as a distorted expression of Christianity. An emphasis on common tradition, common organization, and common faith had generally prevailed, under the leadership of the bishops of Rome, Ephesus, and Antioch. Several problems had not been fully settled, however, and among these were questions related to the work of the Holy Spirit among individual Christians and to the doctrine of the last things, including the descent of the heavenly Jerusalem. On the first point, the popularity of both the Apocalypse of John (not to mention the apocryphal apocalypses) and the *Shepherd* of Hermas show how highly the function of prophecy was still regarded; and on the second, the same apocalypses usually dealt with the imminent coming of the kingdom of God on earth. The two points were obviously bound together.

As the church had to draw organizational and doctrinal lines in the conflict with Gnosticism, it was almost inevitable that difficulties would arise over individual prophecy and eschatological doctrines. Against Gnosticism the church was insisting upon the supremacy of the whole community over individuals and upon the importance of the links between past and present as opposed to speculations about the future. Under these circumstances it was natural for a reaction to take place.

I·ORIGINS

When the reaction occurred it was at first confined to Phrygia in Asia Minor; indeed, its opponents stigmatized it as "the Phrygian sect," thus trying to indicate that it was a purely local phenomenon. There had been Christians in Phrygia from very early times. The church at Hierapolis is mentioned in Colossians 4:13, Phrygian Christians in Acts 18:23. The fragments of Papias of Hierapolis, early in the second century, reveal that in spite of the Hellenistic veneer evident in a preface and a discussion of literary questions there existed a firmly tradition-minded Jewish-Christian community. Papias was devoted to oral tradition rather than to the written word; he apparently venerated the Asian apostle John and certainly obtained oral traditions from various disciples of the apostles and from the daughters of Philip, who according to Acts 21:9 were virgin prophetesses.[1]

The fact that some of his sources were prophetic in nature helps explain his strongly apocalyptic eschatology. Papias was convinced that Jesus had said, "The days are coming when vineyards will grow up, each with ten thousand vines, on one vine ten thousand branches, on one branch ten thousand shoots, on each shoot ten thousand clusters, on each cluster ten thousand grapes; each grape when pressed will yield twenty-five measures of wine." All other plants would be equally productive; animals would no longer be carnivorous. Only the traitor Judas doubted this prediction.[2] Actually a similar prediction about wine occurs in Jewish apocalypses.[3]

The combination of prophecy and apocalyptic prediction reflected in Papias' ideas provided precisely the setting in which a revival of prophecy could have been expected; and this is what took place.

The much-debated question of the date of Montanism is highly important in this regard. Our sources give us two dates for the time when it arose. (1) In his *Chronicle* Eusebius placed the date in 172 and, when writing his *Church History,* he quoted an anonymous writer against Montanism who set it in the year "when Gratus was proconsul of Asia."[4] Unfortunately there is no extant record of Gratus or of the year when he held office. (2) On the other hand, Epiphanius (who unlike Eusebius had access to authentic Monta-

---

[1] Eusebius, *H. E.* 3, 39; for other fragments cf. W. R. Schoedel, *Polycarp, Martyrdom of Polycarp, Fragments of Papias* (Camden, N. J., 1967), 89-127.

[2] Irenaeus, *Adv. haer.* 5, 33, 3-4 (Schoedel, *op. cit.,* 94-96).

[3] *2 Baruch* 29, 5-6; I Enoch 10:19 (Schoedel, *op. cit.,* 94-95).

[4] Eusebius, *H. E.* 5, 16, 7.

nist documents) sets it "about the nineteenth year of Antoninus Pius," or about 156–157.[5] The two dates can be explained as marking the origin of the movement in the earlier year and its condemnation by church leaders in Asia Minor in the latter. We know that Claudius Apollinaris, bishop of Hierapolis about 175, was a militant opponent of the movement.

If 156–157 is approximately the correct date, we may proceed to see in Montanism a reaction against any attempt to correlate Christianity with the life of the Graeco-Roman world. It probably arose in a time of crisis, and such a crisis seems to be provided by the execution of the most famous Christian leader in Asia Minor, Polycarp of Smyrna, in February 156.[6] Few Christians, upon learning of Polycarp's death, could believe that rapprochement with Rome was either possible or desirable.

The anonymous author to whom we have referred ascribes Montanism to a recently baptized Christian named Montanus, who at the village of Ardabau on the Mysian-Phrygian border began to go into trances and "utter strange sounds." Though some fellow Christians rebuked him and warned against false prophets, possibly relying on Matthew 7:15, others accepted his prophesying as "a prophetic gift of the Holy Spirit" and gave him encouragement and support. Two women, the prophetesses Priscilla and Maximilla, soon shared his gift and joined him.

The place name Ardabau cannot be found on a map, though it may have existed. More probably it gives us some insight into Montanus' background. In the Jewish apocalypse known as 2 Esdras or 4 Ezra, a work popular among second-century Christians, we read that a place of revelation and, indeed, the location for the future "Zion" is named Ardab (9:26).[7] What is meant by "Ardabau," then, is probably not the village where Montanus began prophesying but the place where he awaited the coming of the new Zion.

The place where Montanists actually expected Zion or Jerusalem to come down from heaven is named by the anti-Montanist writer Apollonius as related to both Pepuza and Tymion, villages in Phrygia.[8] Presumably the spot was located not only by Montanus but also by Priscilla, from whom we have an oracle discussing it. "Christ," she declared, "came to me in the form of a woman clad in a shining robe; he set wisdom in me and revealed to me that this very place is sacred and that here Jerusalem will descend from heaven."[9] Her ideas were in part influenced by something like the book of Revelation, where the bride of the Lamb wears a shining robe (19:7-8) and as the new Jerusalem descends from heaven (21:2). 2 Esdras also provides a good

---

[5] Epiphanius, *Haer.* 48, 1, 1.
[6] For the date of Polycarp see p. 86; for that of Montanism, G. S. P. Freeman-Grenville in *JEH* 5 (1954), 7-15.
[7] On Ardab and Ardabau see E. Preuschen in *ZNW* 1 (1900), 265-66; H. Kraft in *TZ* 11 (1955), 249-71, especially 260-61.
[8] Eusebius, *H. E.* 5, 18, 2; for possible locations see *MAMA* IV, p. xv.
[9] Epiphanius, *Haer.* 49, 1.

parallel. The woman who appeared to the seer had a shining face and was immediately replaced by a city which was the new Zion (10:25-27). The "place" was sacred because there were no buildings on it—as in the Phrygian mountains—and there the Most High would show forth his city (10:53-54).

Montanus and the prophetesses alike insisted upon the divine origin of their prophecies. Two oracles from Montanus himself produced scandal among his opponents.[10]

Behold, man is like a lyre and I hover over him like a plectrum. Man sleeps, while I awake. Behold, it is the Lord who makes men's hearts ecstatic and gives [new] hearts to men.

It is I, the Lord God Almighty, who am present in a man. I am neither an angel nor an emissary; I, the Lord God the Father, have come.

Evidently Montanus was speaking in ecstasy and in his view God was speaking through him. To be sure, Ignatius had been able to say that he spoke "with God's own voice" (*Philad.* 7, 1), but Ignatius was bishop of Antioch, not a Phrygian neophyte.

Similarly Priscilla, as we have already seen, held that Christ had come to her in order to give revelation. Presumably she included herself among those for whom "continence results in harmony and they see visions and, bowing their heads, hear distinct voices, at once salutary and mysterious."[11] The "harmony" was doubtless that of the lyre mentioned by her leader.

Maximilla's picture of her mission seems to owe something to Paul.

The Lord sent me as a devotee, revealer, interpreter of this labor and promise and covenant; I was compelled, willing or unwilling, to learn the knowledge of God.[12]

Just so, Paul had been sent by God and preached the gospel whether willing or unwilling (1 Cor. 9:17). And just as Paul had proclaimed not himself but Christ (2 Cor. 4:5), so Maximilla exclaimed, "Do not hear me but hear Christ."[13] When Christians refused to listen, however, and described Montanists as wolves in sheep's clothing (Matt. 7:15), she lamented over them.

I am driven from the sheep like a wolf. I am not a wolf; I am word and spirit and power.

As Christ had lamented over Jerusalem (Luke 19:41), so Maximilla grieved over the Christians who did not recognize her revelation. Like Christ, she predicted future wars and revolutions.[14]

[10] Epiphanius, *Haer.* 48, 4, 1; 11, 1; 11, 9.
[11] Tertullian, *Exh. cast.* 10, 5.
[12] Epiphanius, *Haer.* 48, 13, 1.
[13] *Ibid.*, 48, 12, 4.
[14] Mark 13:7-8; Matt. 24:6-7; Luke 21:9.

Montanus' public message encouraged Christians to take a stand against the state and accept martyrdom.[15]

Are you publicly defamed? It is good for you, for he who is not defamed among men is defamed in the Lord (cf. Luke 6:22, 26). Be not dismayed: justice leads you into the presence of all. Why be dismayed when you are gaining glory? Power arises when you are viewed by men.

Do not desire to die in bed or in abortions or in debilitating fevers, but in martyrdom so that he who suffered for you may be glorified.

This message won enthusiastic response among the "voluntary martyrs" whose actions were not encouraged by the church as a whole.

Desire for martyrdom was naturally accompanied by emphasis on ascetic behavior, and opponents of Montanism claimed that the leader persuaded the prophetesses to leave their husbands; he "advocated the dissolution of marriages" and "laid down laws on fasting."[16] He explicitly stated, "The church is able to remit sins, but I will not do so lest others sin."[17]

The prophetess Priscilla, who was called a "virgin" in the Montanist community,[18] certainly advocated continence, as we have seen, for it led to ecstatic utterance. It is not so clear why she said, "They arc flesh and they hate the flesh."[19] Perhaps she was speaking of ascetic Gnostics.

II-OPPOSITION

The reaction of the Christian leaders of Asia Minor, like the Montanist movement itself, seems to have crystallized only after a considerable lapse of time. Two Phrygian bishops tried to cast out the "false spirit" from Maximilla; others attempted to exorcize Priscilla—but without success. Opposition arose in Phrygia itself and in Asia and nearby Thrace.[20] The most vigorous critic of the movement seems to have been Apollinaris, bishop of Hierapolis. According to Eusebius, he wrote an encyclical letter "while Montanus with his false prophetesses was still taking the first steps in his error."[21] Presumably this statement means that hc still had hopes of bringing the Montanists back into the church.

Other writings of Apollinaris clearly show that he was loyal not only to

15 Tertullian, De fuga 9, 4.
16 Eusebius, H. E. 5, 18, 2.
17 Tertullian, De pudic. 21, 7.
18 Eusebius, H. E. 5, 18, 3.
19 Tertullian, De res. carn. 11, 2.
20 Eusebius, H. E. 5, 16, 10; 19, 3.
21 Ibid., 4, 27.

the Roman church, whose date for Easter he accepted against the usual Asian custom, but also to the Roman state. In an apology now lost he told the story of a legion miraculously victorious after Christian soldiers had knelt in prayer.[22] Such a bishop inevitably frowned upon Montanist ardor and disorder. His contemporary Melito of Sardis followed Asian tradition in regard to Easter but was equally devoted to the Roman administration.[23] He too must have rejected Montanism, for Tertullian, writing as a Montanist, said that most Christians thought he was a prophet though he was really a rhetorician.[24] We must suppose that these two bishops were among the leaders of those who convened synods throughout Asia and condemned the movement.

This is not to say that all Christian leaders were anti-Montanist. Irenaeus, who had come to Lyons from Asia, did not regard Montanus as the sole instrument of the Spirit, and he vigorously argued that the Spirit was at work among the episcopal successors of the apostles. At the same time, when he wrote the *Letter of the Churches of Vienne and Lyons* he used language like that of the Montanists to describe a martyr who "had the Paraclete in himself."[25] Irenaeus could not condemn the "new prophecy." Indeed, in writing against heresies he criticized the anti-Montanists for opposing both the gospel and the prophetic Spirit and argued that they were driving prophetic grace out of the church. In I Corinthians, he said, the apostle Paul had discussed the prophetic gifts which both men and women exercised in the community.[26]

Before 189, however, and possibly a decade earlier, Eleutherus of Rome must have condemned the Montanist movement. Tertullian, writing about 213, says that a bishop of Rome (who must be Zephyrinus) was persuaded to honor the decisions of his predecessors taken against the Montanists;[27] and these predecessors can only be Eleutherus and Victor. Eleutherus died about 189.

At this point militant opposition to Montanism arose. About 192–193 Serapion became bishop of Antioch; he circulated the earlier work of Apollinaris, along with a letter of his own, in order to show "that the working of the lying organization called the New Prophecy is held in abomination by the whole brotherhood in the world."[28] And from just the same time there survive fragments of a lengthy work by an anonymous bishop in Asia. His name was either unknown to Eusebius or suppressed by him; it has plausibly

22 *Ibid.*, 5, 5, 4.
23 *Ibid.*, 4, 26, 5-11.
24 Jerome, *De vir. illustr.* 24.
25 Eusebius, *H. E.* 5, 1, 10; for the author see P. Nautin, *Lettres et écrivains chrétiens des ii*e *et iii*e *siècles* (Paris, 1961), 54-59.
26 *Adv. haer.* 3, 11, 8-9 (false prophets criticized 4, 33, 5).
27 *Adv. Prax.* 1.
28 Eusebius, *H. E.* 5, 19, 2.

been suggested that he was Polycrates of Ephesus.[29] This work was addressed to Avircius Marcellus, probably the bishop of Hieropolis (not Hierapolis) in Phrygia.

The Anonymous vigorously combines gossip with his arguments against the Montanists. He suggests that Montanus and Maximilla, like Judas Iscariot, hanged themselves, though he admits that he is not sure of his facts. The Montanist "trustee" Themison may have been borne aloft while in ecstasy and then killed in the ensuing crash—or so rumor says. In general the Montanists have certainly not fulfilled gospel prophecies, for none has been either persecuted by the Jews or crucified (Matt. 23:34). They claimed that Maximilla and Priscilla inherited their gift of prophecy from the daughters of Philip, from the later Quadratus, and from Ammia of Philadelphia. This is not the case, he argues, for the early prophets did not speak in ecstasy; furthermore, after the death of Maximilla no new prophetesses had arisen. Maximilla herself had predicted the coming of wars and then the end, but during the thirteen years after her death (179–192) there had been no wars either local or universal and Christians had enjoyed a lasting peace. To be sure, some Montanists had been martyrs, but this fact proved nothing. There were many Marcionite martyrs too, and true Christian martyrs always avoided the company of Montanist confessors.

The dedication to Avircius Marcellus and most of the content of the fragments indicate that the author's concerns are chiefly with the life of the church—even though at one point he states that "by the mercy of God the Christians have enjoyed continuous peace" during the reign of Commodus. He has long been opposed to Montanism, but has not hitherto written against the heresy "lest perchance I might seem to some to be adding a new article or clause to the word of the new covenant of the gospel" (5, 16, 3). The explanation suggests that up to this point Montanism had not been universally condemned. Since he himself had once tried to give exorcism to Maximilla (5, 18, 13), he had long been opposed to it.

The name of Avircius Marcellus in the dedication of the work clearly points toward the kind of group hostile to Montanism. The inscription on this man's tombstone, discovered in Phrygia in 1883, shows that he was devoted to the ideal of a universal church and its eucharistic rites. He had visited Christians in Syria and at Nisibis and Rome and perhaps referred to Rome as queen of the Christian world. The conventional language with which the epitaph ends—a warning to tomb violators that they would be liable to fines assessed by the Roman treasury and by his native city—shows that he viewed himself as under the protection of Roman law.[30] To such men Montanist spirituality was both wrong-headed and dangerous.

Within a few years, probably about 196, a certain Apollonius also wrote a

[29] W. Kühnert in *TZ* 5 (1949), 436-46.
[30] On the inscription see H. Strathmann and T. Klauser in *RAC* I, 12-17.

treatise against the Montanists in which he attacked their founder's ascetic teaching, his ideas about the new Jerusalem in Phrygia, and his provisions for financial agents and their support. In addition, he laid strong emphasis on the misbehavior of Montanist "martyrs" in relation to church and state alike. Themison had bribed his way out of prison; Alexander was jailed not as a Christian but as a robber. The story about Alexander mentions Frontinus, proconsul of Asia under Commodus, and confirms the Anonymous' statement that Christians enjoyed peace during that emperor's reign. When the "martyr" appealed to the name of Christ he was released by the authorities. Apollonius himself mentions "the public archives of Asia" as available for further reading about the case.[31] By this time success had evidently spoiled some of the second-generation prophets. This is clear not only from the numbers of financial agents whose offices are mentioned but also from the rhetorical questions Apollonius asks: "Does a prophet dye his hair? Does a prophet paint his eyelids? Does a prophet love adornment? Does a prophet play at gaming-tables and dice? Does a prophet lend money at interest?" These complaints also show that the movement was continuing to win adherents.

The anti-Montanist efforts of Serapion, the Anonymous, and Apollonius clearly indicate that apocalyptic expectations came to the fore in Christian circles soon after the end of Commodus' reign. A period of relative tranquillity, as far as Christians were concerned, came to an end and was followed by the struggle for power which ended with the triumph of Septimius Severus only in 197. The leaders of the Christian community sided with the future emperor; Tertullian tells us that there were no followers of Severus' rival Albinus among them, and that as Byzantium fell to Severus' forces the defeated defender exclaimed, "Christians, rejoice."[32] In his apology of 197 Tertullian himself, not yet a Montanist, insisted upon Christian loyalty to the emperor.

This is to say that the Montanists took the civil wars of 193–197 as the fulfillment of eschatological prophecy, whereas the leaders of the church as a whole viewed them merely as historical episodes. Their goal had been, and remained, the reconciliation of the state with the church on a non-pagan basis—not the overthrow of the state. They had no sympathy with anarchy.

III·RENEWAL

In 198, however, Montanist claims were lent support by reports from Severus' oriental expedition. Trustworthy pagan witnesses sighted a walled city in the sky over Judaea. Though it would vanish at daybreak, it appeared on forty

[31] Eusebius, *H.E.* 5, 18, 9; cf. K. Gross, "Archiv," *RAC* I 614-31.
[32] Tertullian, *Ad Scapulam* 2, 5; 3, 4.

consecutive mornings.[33] (Evidently the Montanists, or some of them, had now changed the location of the place where the new Jerusalem would come down.) Four years later, intensive local persecution, at least at Rome, Alexandria, and Carthage, broke out again. Once more, the reaction of Christians to these events was not uniform.

There was certainly a revival of apocalyptic expectations. A certain Judas composed a treatise on the "seventy weeks" in the book of Daniel, tracing the fulfillment of prophecy as far as the tenth year of Septimius Severus (202–203) and concluding that the Antichrist was about to appear.[34] In Syria a bishop persuaded many Christians to go out to meet Christ in the desert, and they wandered aimlessly along roads and in the mountains. Only the Christian wife of the governor of Syria was able to prevent their arrest and execution as bandits. In Pontus another bishop received a series of visions which drove him to predict the last judgment in a year's time. "If it does not take place as I said," he insisted, "no longer believe the scriptures but let each of you do as he will." At the end of the year the Christian virgins married, the Christian farmers returned to their deserted farms, and those who had sold their possessions for the adventure were reduced to begging.[35] At Carthage by 206 Tertullian began expressing his sympathy for Montanism and in 212 he openly joined the movement.

At Rome, however, in spite of a vigorous persecution, Christian leaders did not lose their faith in the historical process. The learned presbyter Hippolytus prepared a commentary on Daniel (in which he described the aberrations in Syria and Pontus) to show that though the end would come sometime it was not imminent. The birth of Christ took place five hundred years before the end, which was therefore not due for another three centuries.[36] To be sure, Tertullian suggests that Zephyrinus, bishop at this time and no friend of Hippolytus, "was on the point of recognizing the prophecies of Montanus and Prisca and Maximilla, and as a result of that recognition was offering peace to the churches of Asia and Phrygia." (These churches were not Montanist, however.) At that juncture Praxeas arrived from Asia and prevented the move. He made "false assertions" about Montanism and insisted on the validity of earlier Roman decisions; in consequence the bishop had to recall the conciliatory letters he had already issued.[37] If there is anything to this story it shows that opinion was sharply divided within the Roman church.

Within a few years at Rome the presbyter Gaius went so far as to ascribe the book of Revelation, beloved among Montanists, to the Jewish Gnostic Cerinthus; he denounced the doctrine of an earthly kingdom at Jerusalem and

---

[33] Tertullian, *Adv. Marc.* 3, 24, 4; date in Harnack, *Chronologie* II, 257.
[34] Eusebius, *H. E.* 6, 7.
[35] Hippolytus, *Dan. comm.* 4, 18-19.
[36] *Dan. comm.* 4, 23-24.
[37] *Adv. Prax.* I

held that the notion of its lasting a thousand years was "contrary to the scriptures."[38] At Alexandria Clement could say that the true Christian "thinks little of the promises, divine though they be, of worldly blessings,"[39] and Origen completely rejected apocalyptic eschatology.

Gaius also provided a historical answer to Montanism which reflects the increasing concern of Christians for their own past. This concern was shared by some Montanists, at least, for the Montanist Proclus argued that the tombs of the four daughters of Philip, all prophetesses in New Testament times, were still to be seen at Hierapolis in Asia.[40] Gaius replied that he could point out the "trophies" of the apostles (Peter and Paul) who founded the Roman church; they were on the Vatican hill and by the Ostian Way.[41]

This interest in tombs was fairly widespread among Asian Christians and was certainly present at Rome as early as the middle of the second century.[42] It did not spring into existence at that time, for in the New Testament itself we read of the burial of John the Baptist[43] and of the martyr Stephen.[44] Ignatius of Antioch expected wild beasts to be his tomb, but this was a special case.[45] Polycarp of Smyrna was carefully buried, even though a reference to an annual commemoration in the late second century may be an interpolation in the story of his martyrdom.[46]

The argument of Gaius against the Montanists shows that the argument from historical evidence was becoming important in the face of futuristic eschatology.

It would appear that under such circumstances the Montanists' own ideas were modified. We have already referred to Proclus' concern for the tombs of Philip and his daughters. In addition, some Montanists certainly favored a location for the new Jerusalem outside Phrygia. Tertullian provides the proof when he refers to the hovering of the heavenly city over Judaea. Since he never mentions Pepuza or Tymion, the location of the new Jerusalem has obviously been changed.

It is uncertain whether or not a prophetess who arose in eastern Asia Minor about 235 was a Montanist. In any event, her claims clearly reflect the continuing vitality of apocalyptic prophecy, especially when unsettled political conditions were accompanied by natural catastrophes like earthquakes. The local Roman governor had begun a persecution of Christians;

[38] Eusebius, *H. E.* 3, 28, 2; cf. 7, 25, 2-3 (Dionysius of Alexandria).
[39] *Str.* 7, 74, 7.
[40] Eusebius, *H. E.* 3, 31, 4.
[41] *Ibid.*, 2, 25, 7.
[42] J. Toynbee and J. W. Perkins, *The Shrine of St. Peter and the Vatican Excavations* (New York, 1957).
[43] Mark 6:29; Matt. 14.12.
[44] Acts 8:2.
[45] *Rom.* 4, 2.
[46] *Mart. Polyc.* 18, 2-3; cf. H. von Campenhausen in *Sitzungsberichte der Heidelberger Akademie der Wissenschaften, Philos.-hist. Kl.*, 1957, no. 3, 29-31.

the prophetess, speaking ecstatically, predicted further earthquakes and demonstrated her spiritual power by walking barefoot in the snow, converting a presbyter and a deacon, baptizing many persons, and celebrating the eucharist. In anticipation of the end, she proposed to lead her followers from Cappadocia and Pontus to Jerusalem.[47] The circumstances thus closely resembled those under which Montanism arose.

IV·DECLINE AND FALL

The centers of Montanist activity were, and remained, in central Asia Minor, even though missioners attracted occasional converts at Rome, Carthage, and Byzantium.[48] In general, the larger cities were fairly free of Montanists, chiefly because in them the organized episcopate was strong. Ultimately the problem was settled—in so far as any historical problem is settled—not so much by argument as by the changed situation of the church in the reign of Constantine. An edict which he issued in the year 331 ordered the public "houses of prayer" maintained by heretics, including Montanists, transferred to the Catholic Church, while their private meeting places were simply confiscated by the state.[49] In the new era there was no room for apocalyptic eschatology of the Montanist kind and little for any other.

This is not to say that Montanism itself retained all its pristine vigor. It is difficult to see specifically apocalyptic traits in a fourth-century sect which Epiphanius related to the Montanists. The feminist aspect of the sect was surely Montanist in origin: the women who became bishops and presbyters[50] traced a kind of succession from Eve, who first ate from the tree of knowledge, from the sister of Moses, and from the daughters of Philip, then from "Quintilla" and Priscilla.[51] At their meetings seven torchbearing virgins, clad in white, would enter and prophesy, reducing the congregation to tears.[52] This Montanist group had come to be nearly as formal as the Catholic Church.

It may be added that by 550 Montanism was as tradition-minded as any of its competitors. John, bishop of Ephesus, struck a fatal blow at the movement not only by burning its temples to the ground but also by digging up and burning the bones of Montanus, Maximilla, and Prisca.[53] The movement had already lost its future; John deprived it of its ties with the past.

[47] Firmilian, *Ep.* 65, 10.
[48] For Byzantium cf. Epiphanius, *Haer.* 48, 14, 1.
[49] Eusebius, *Vita Constantini* 3, 64-65.
[50] *Haer.* 49, 2, 5.
[51] *Ibid.,* 49, 2, 1-2.
[52] *Ibid.,* 49, 2, 3-4.
[53] P. de Labriolle, *Les sources de l'histoire du montanisme* (Paris, 1913), 238 (no. 195).

The trouble with Montanism was that it opened the door to problems with which the churches had been wrestling for a long time; it threatened to diminish or destory the orthodoxy precariously achieved. The charges levied by Apollonius prove nothing about Montanism as such. The basic question must have been related to the needs of the whole Christian community, now governed by bishops in succession from the apostles. When Celsus, the opponent of Christianity, described prophets as saying, "I am God" or "the Son of God" or "the divine Spirit," he may not have had Montanists in mind.[54] But the possibility of new revelations of such a kind was not one which the churches' leaders could view with equanimity. These leaders agreed with Celsus that fresh revelations, pinpointing the time and place of the descent of the New Jerusalem, were hardly desirable.

Christian leaders had taken great pains to argue that the revelation was in harmony with philosophy at its best because philosophers had in part been inspired by the Logos. They also insisted that prophecy was a rational matter. The anti-Montanist Anonymous, therefore, claimed that the false or Montanist prophet began in intentional ignorance and proceeded toward unintentional delirium; he thus was different from any prophet under the old covenant or the new.[55] Similarly Origen accused the Montanists of irrationality and spoke of their "intellectual weakness."[56] In his view, the biblical writers were thoroughly rational.[57] Hippolytus called the Montanists "uncritical."[58] In this way Christian leaders dealt with the symptoms of Montanism.

What underlay the symptoms, however, was the Montanists' basic concern. They were reviving the apocalyptic eschatology, based on Jewish and Jewish-Christian documents, from which the churches had gradually been turning away. Their revival of primitive Christian concerns was basically irrelevant for the leaders of late second-century Christianity and for their followers as well. The church was now coming to terms with Graeco-Roman culture and finding a place for itself in the world.

V·MONTANISM AND GNOSTICISM

During the second century two radical answers were thus provided for the problem of eschatology—a problem which involved the whole nature and future of the Christian religion. One answer, as we have seen, was provided

---

[54] Origen, *Contra Celsum* 7, 9.
[55] Eusebius, *H. E.* 5, 17, 2-3.
[56] *Princ.* 2, 7, 3.
[57] Cf. *The Letter and the Spirit* (London, 1957), 97.
[58] *Ref.* 8, 19, 1.

among the Gnostics who generally substituted the ascent of the divine spark after death for the establishment of God's reign on earth. In their view the world was the byproduct of disorder in the spiritual world above, not the result of God's creative act. The other answer was given by the Montanists, who from moment to moment awaited the descent of the heavenly Jerusalem and the return of Christ.[59] It is fairly obvious that the Montanist movement was fairly close to Jewish Christianity, which in essence it attempted to revive. By the time when the movement arose, however, Christianity had already moved far away from its origins. The cumulative effect of the decisions made by Christian leaders was to bring the church into the world and to multiply its numbers until it could win the world to Christian allegiance. The Montanists, like the Gnostics, were at heart sectarians. The church, at least in principle, was catholic.[60] Phrygian Montanism came to an end under Justinian when the Montanists "shut themselves up in their sanctuaries and immediately set them on fire so that they pointlessly perished with their buildings."[61]

The books contained in the New Testament as generally accepted in the second century provided few guidelines in regard to apocalyptic expectations. To be sure, in Mark 13:32 one could read that "of that day or that hour no one knows, not even the angels in heaven, nor the Son, but only the Father." Irenaeus, himself rather enthusiastic about apocalyptic, quoted the saying against Gnostic speculations[62] and did not bother to observe that it could be applied against his own idea that the world would end six thousand years after creation.[63] In any case, however, there would be a long delay of the end.

Two works first accepted at Alexandria were clearly intended to prevent undue emphasis on expectations. According to 2 Peter 3:8–10 the day of the Lord will come but the date cannot be predicted. The *Epistle of Barnabas* (15, 4) explicitly states that "everything will be completed in six thousand years." In either case the point was the same: there was no reason to expect the imminent return of Christ.[64]

Presumably the same purpose lies behind the learned chronologies which Christian leaders provided at the end of the second century and early in the third. Generally speaking these computations are in agreement as to the

---

[59] Other Christians shared these expectations but laid little emphasis on them (see below).

[60] The word "catholic" in a technical sense may appear in the *Martyrdom of Polycarp* (16, 2; cf. 19, 2); cf. Ignatius, *Smyrn.* 8, 2, and W. R. Schoedel, *Polycarp, Martyrdom of Polycarp, Fragments of Papias* (Camden, 1967), 73.

[61] Procopius, *Anecd.* 11, 23.

[62] *Adv. haer.* 2, 28, 5.

[63] *Ibid.*, 5, 28-29.

[64] On the canon at Alexandria cf. *The Formation of the New Testament* (London and New York, 1965), Chapter XI.

basic point: the world is approximately fifty-seven hundred years old and therefore the end cannot possibly occur for another three hundred years. This conclusion is not drawn by all the writers, but it was obviously relevant in their circumstances.[65] An end three hundred years in the future has no bearing on the present.

[65] The chronographers are Theophilus of Antioch, Clement of Alexandria, Hippolytus of Rome, and Julius Africanus.

CHAPTER X
CHRISTIAN ORGANIZATION

I-EARLY DEVELOPMENTS

By the end of the first century the Christian movement had experienced very rapid growth. I Peter shows that there were Christian communities in Asia, Galatia, Bithynia, Pontus, and Cappadocia. The book of Revelation and the letters of Ignatius provide the names of the leading churches in the province of Asia: these were at Ephesus, Smyrna, Magnesia, Tralles, Laodicea, Philadelphia, Sardis, Thyatira, and Pergamum. Farther to the east, the Pauline foundations at Perge, Pisidian Antioch, Iconium, Lystra, and Derbe were probably still in existence. The church of Antioch was flourishing. In Palestine there were several communities, notably at Jerusalem. Apparently the western part of the empire was less subject to Christian influence, though there were certainly communities around the Aegean shore at Troas, Philippi, Thessalonica, Athens, and Corinth with its port of Cenchreae. In Italy churches are known only at Rome and Puteoli, although a mysterious "Sator Arepo" square found at Pompeii probably points to some Christian presence.[1]

It was necessary for a movement so widespread to develop its organization, especially in regard to the forms and functions of its ministry. Evidence for such development is to be found first of all in the *Didache,* or "teaching of the twelve apostles," apparently compiled in Syria in the latter half of the first century.

The ministry in the *Didache* is depicted in two stages. In the earlier stage there are wandering apostles, tested by their behavior. They are to be received "as the Lord" but must not stay in one place for more than two days or ask for money (11, 3–6). The most important ministers are the prophets, who can say the eucharistic prayer as they wish and are not to be tested or examined when they speak in ecstasy. Some prophets, like the apostles, are itinerant. Others settle in particular communities and are viewed as equivalent to the high priests of the Old Testament. They therefore receive "first-fruits" of agricultural products, as well as of money, clothing, and possessions in general (13, 1–7). The *Didache* also mentions teachers as ministers of the community; they are to teach in accordance with what is said in the document itself (11, 1–2). There are thus two orders of ministers in the stage which most of the *Didache* reflects; these are the local prophets and teachers, just as at Antioch according to Acts 13:1–2. The book also reflects an earlier period in which both apostles and prophets were itinerant.

The author of the *Didache* stands, however, at a turning point in church organization. He instructs his congregations to appoint bishops (*episkopoi*) and deacons (*diakonoi*) worthy of the Lord. Such men perform the task of the prophets and teachers. "Do not hold them in contempt, for they are honorable men among you, along with the prophets and teachers" (15, 1–2). The situation is one of transition. On the one hand, the prophets and teachers have been, or are to be, supplanted by bishops and deacons; on the other, the older ministries are not at once to disappear.

There is no concern for future successions in office, for the Didachist's congregations pray for the immediate coming of the Lord (10, 6) and watch for signs of this event (c. 16).

A more complex situation is reflected in 1 Clement, written toward the end of the first century in the name of the Roman church to the church at Corinth. There is a situation of rebellion in the Corinthian church; one rebel in particular has been able to deprive presbyters or bishops of their office (44, 6; 47, 7). Perhaps the Roman church intervenes in the affairs of Corinth just as the Roman government was accustomed to intervene in the affairs of the Roman colony Laus Iulia Corinthus. In any event, the Roman letter

---

[1] For the distribution of Christian churches cf. F. van der Meer and C. Mohrmann, *Atlas of the Early Christian World* (London, 1959), Map 1; on the word-square, D. Fishwick in *HTR* 54 (1961), 39-53.

presents a strong plea for order in the community as based not only on Old Testament prefigurations and philosophical considerations but also on the historical origins of the office of presbyter-bishop. This office is of divine origin because God sent Christ and Christ sent forth the apostles (42, 1–2). In turn, the apostles "appointed their first-fruits, testing them by the Spirit, to be bishops and deacons of future believers" (42, 3–4). They knew that strife would arise in regard to the episcopate, and therefore "added the codicil that if they should fall asleep, other approved men should succeed to their ministry" (44, 2).[2] The succession is to be traced not only from the apostles but also from "those who were later appointed by other eminent men" (44, 3). The cure proposed for the Corinthian situation is that the rebel leader should accept voluntary exile for the sake of the people (54, 2). The Roman church is also sending emissaries to deal with the situation; they will report back to Rome.

Here the situation is more carefully defined than in the *Didache*. The strong practical bent of Roman Christianity is coming to the fore. The underlying situation at Rome, as ideally at Corinth, is one in which presbyters govern the church (54, 2), though only one of them, presumably, exercises the office of administration and offers the "gifts" characteristic of it.[3]

At Rome a few years later the prophet Hermas similarly spoke of apostles and teachers as leaders of the church in the past.[4] In referring to past and present alike he mentioned apostles, bishops, teachers, and deacons;[5] from this statement we may perhaps infer that the ministers with whom he is best acquainted are bishops and deacons. Bishops and hospitable men, he says, welcome the servants of God into their houses and with the deacons give shelter to the destitute, widows, and orphans.[6] There were also teachers both reliable and unreliable, as well as true and false prophets.[7] There seems to be no prophetic office as such, however, for the prophet is one "on whom the angel of the prophetic Spirit rests" during Christian worship.[8]

Of presbyters Hermas had little to say, although in the early *Visions* there are "leaders of the church" who occupy seats of honor.[9] These must be "the presbyters who are in charge of the church," with whom Hermas is supposed to read two books of visions. He is also to send one to Clement for transmission to other churches, the other to Graptē (evidently a woman) for exhorting the widows and orphans.[10] Unfortunately he does not say what office either Clement or Graptē held.

[2] It is not quite clear who "they" are, but the matter of succession is not affected.
[3] I Clem. 44, 1. 4.
[4] *Sim.* 9, 15, 4; 17, 1; 25, 2.
[5] *Vis.* 3, 5, 1.
[6] *Sim.* 9, 26-27.
[7] *Mand.* 11.
[8] *Mand.* 11, 9.
[9] *Vis.* 2, 2, 6; 3, 9, 7.
[10] *Vis.* 2, 4, 3.

Obviously the church was one of rich organizational complexity, and it is not surprising that there was jealousy about status and rank.[11] Presumably it was in response to such a situation that the monarchical episcopate came to the fore at Rome.[12] As late as 144, however, it appears that presbyters and teachers, not a single bishop, expelled the Gnostic teacher Marcion from the Roman community.[13]

The monarchical episcopate certainly existed a generation earlier, for it was attested by Ignatius, himself bishop of Antioch during the reign of Trajan (98–117). This is to say that he attested it for eastern communities, not for Rome; in writing to the Roman church the only bishop he mentioned was himself, "bishop of Syria." Too much weight cannot be laid on his silence, however, for he wrote to the whole church and did not, in fact, mention Roman presbyters either. In writing to Christian communities in Asia he insisted that the unity of the church was based on submission to the local bishop and college of presbyters. In his view the bishop occupied the place of God, of whom he was a "type" or copy, while the presbyters were analogous to God's council and the deacons to Jesus Christ.[14] This series of comparisons is not wholly logical. We should expect the presbyters, superior to the deacons, to be compared with Christ, not with the apostles. It has therefore been inferred that it reflects an earlier stage of the ministry at Antioch or elsewhere; the bishop would be compared with God, the deacons with Christ, while the presbyters, compared with the apostles, would have been introduced later.[15] Perhaps, then, before Ignatius' time there were bishops and deacons at Antioch, as among the Philippians to whom Paul wrote and as in the Didache. With this kind of ministry there would have been combined the presbyter (=bishops) known from Acts and 1 Clement. Their episcopal functions would have been taken by the one bishop, while their apostolic origin would still be recognized.

In Ignatius' view such bishops "have been appointed throughout the world,"[16] but he does not say how they were appointed. Indeed, the Lord has sent them. The Philadelphian bishop, like the apostle Paul, obtained his office "not from himself or through men."[17] Apostolic succession, perhaps claimed by the presbyters, is a matter of indifference.

Ignatius never mentions either prophets or teachers as ministers of the churches. Instead, he refers to his own prophetic utterances and ascribes them to God or the Spirit. The utterances have to do with obedience to the

[11] Sim. 8, 7, 4-6.
[12] H. Chadwick, The Office of a Bishop (London, 1948), 17.
[13] Epiphanius, Haer. 42, 2, 2.
[14] Magn. 6, 1; Trall. 3, 1; Smyrn. 8, 1.
[15] Cf. G. Kretschmar, Studien zür frühchristlichen Trinitätstheologie (Tübingen, 1956), 98.
[16] Eph. 3, 2; Philad. inscr.
[17] Eph. 3, 2; 6, 1; Philad. 1, 1 (cf. Gal. 1:1).

bishop, the presbytery, and the deacons.[18] Thus for Ignatius, as contrasted with the *Didache,* there is no question of despising the bishops and deacons; they have taken over all the functions which prophets and teachers previously held.

From his letters it is clear that the church at Antioch had recently undergone a crisis probably related to the appointment of his successor. As he traveled westward he learned that it was over; now other churches were to send bishops, presbyters, and deacons to Syria,[19] presumably to take part in the new bishop's consecration or to ratify his election. Whether the succession was soundly assured or not, it may be significant that for the next seventy years or so we hear nothing about the church at Antioch. Indeed, no letter to Antioch from Ignatius was preserved. In many respects the ideas of Theophilus, bishop there about 180, resemble those of the "Judaizers" whom Ignatius attacked in his letters. Perhaps Christianity declined after his time and was restored only on a somewhat different basis.

The only bishop to whom Ignatius wrote a letter still preserved was Polycarp of Smyrna. Certainly Polycarp was a monarchical bishop by the time of his martyrdom, about forty years later. It is a question, however, whether or not he occupied such an office in Ignatius' time. Certainly a bishop did not need to refer to his office in the salutation of a letter; thus Polycarp began his letter to the Philippians with the words, "Polycarp and the presbyters with him." He did not refer, however, to bishops at any point in the letter. The officers of Christian churches were deacons (5, 2) and presbyters (6, 1); the latter, not a bishop, had the duty of overseeing (*episkeptomenoi*) the weaker members of the community. Whereas Ignatius had compared the bishop to God, the deacons to Christ, Polycarp used a strikingly different comparison: Christians were to be subject "to the presbyters and deacons as to God and Christ" (5, 3). It is difficult to avoid the conclusion that the church at Philippi was governed by presbyters and deacons, not by bishops—and that Polycarp did not insist on monarchical episcopacy in the manner of Ignatius.

The tone of Ignatius' insistence upon this kind of episcopacy, in addition to the other evidence we have mentioned, suggests that his picture of the ministry was more ideal than real as far as his own time was concerned. To be sure, the monarchical episcopate would eventually triumph and come to be universally accepted. This victory lay far in the future, however.

In Ignatius' view, as we have said, the bishop occupies the place of God. Obedience to the bishop is therefore obedience to God.[20] One may wonder whether, in addition to the practical need for unity, some theoretical factors were not involved in Ignatius' claim. For example, in the Hellenistic Judaism

[18] *Philad.* 7, 2.
[19] *Philad.* 10, 2.
[20] *Eph.* 5, 3; *Magn.* 3, 1.

represented by Josephus the Jewish theocracy was advocated as the perfect form of government, and in it God governed everything, while priests under the direction of the high priest were administrators on his behalf. To disobey the high priest was to be impious toward God himself.[21] Like Ignatius, Josephus insisted upon adherence to the "one temple of God."[22] In addition, during the reign of Trajan prominent Greek orators claimed that monarchy was the best form of government; Dio Chrysostom called it "divine."[23] The king-emperor, said Plutarch, is "the image of God who governs the world." He "forms himself in the likeness of God by his virtue."[24] The prevalence of such ideas meant that Ignatius' view of the monarchical episcopate could at least seem familiar to Greek-speaking Christians in Asia Minor.

II-THE LATER SECOND CENTURY

The only Christian writer from the middle of the second century to say anything about the organization of the community is the apologist Justin (ca. 150). He tells us that at the eucharist a lector read from the "reminiscences of the apostles" (which, he says, "are called 'gospels' "), and bread and wine were brought to "the president [proestōs] of the brethren." After he offered a long prayer or sequence of prayers, the "deacons" distributed the bread and wine to those present and also took them to the absent.

The president's functions were both liturgical and charitable, for he was also the community's administrator of funds for orphans, widows, the sick, prisoners, and visitors from abroad.[25]

Justin is writing at Rome, and it is therefore not surprising that in earlier Roman writings similar functions are described. In the *Shepherd* of Hermas, for example, we have found "the presbyters who preside over the church," and both bishops and deacons—the latter by definition subordinate to the former—concerned with widows and orphans.

Furthermore, what Justin says about the apostles is remarkably similar to what we find in Hermas. He relates, chiefly following Luke and Acts, that the companions of Jesus abandoned him but after he appeared to them and taught them how to read the Old Testament prophecies (Luke 24:45–46), they witnessed his ascension and received power from heaven. They went out into the world from Jerusalem, taught what he had taught them, and were

---

[21] *Contra Apionem* 2, 185-87; 193-94.

[22] *Magn.* 7, 2; Josephus, *Contra Apionem* 2, 193.

[23] *Or.* 3, 50; cf. Plutarch, *De trib. rei publ. gen.* 4, 827B; J. Béranger in *Colloque international sur Les empereurs romains d'Espagne* (Paris, 1965), 39.

[24] Plutarch, *Ad princ. inerud.* 3, 780E.

[25] *Apol.* 1, 65-67.

called apostles.[26] Hermas too lays emphasis on the function of apostles as postresurrection preachers to the gentiles; before dying, he says, the apostles proclaimed the Son of God to the twelve nations of the world (*Sim.* 9, 17, 1).

Neither writer says anything about apostolic succession. In Justin's case the silence is doubtless due to his apologetic purpose, while for Hermas past apostolicity was less significant than present prophecy.

Justin's reticence about presbyters and bishops, contrasting with his explicit mention of "president," lector, and deacons, may also be due to the circumstances. Had he mentioned these officers they might have been subject to arrest by the Roman authorities. In any event, judging from writings both before and after 150, the "president" was one among the Roman presbyters, and he was probably a bishop.

From the important period between about 150 and about 175 we possess little direct evidence concerning the organization of the churches. We do know that in this time Anicetus, Soter, and Eleutherus were bishops of Rome; that Pothinus was bishop of Lyons and Theophilus, of Antioch; and that Polycarp was still bishop of Smyrna. From various sources we learn that Melito was bishop of Sardis and Claudius Apollinaris, of Hierapolis in Phrygia.

For the years around 170 we have the evidence given by Eusebius in describing the letters of Dionysius, bishop of Corinth. Dionysius' letters to the Athenians and to the Romans clearly reflect not only the existence of the episcopate but the fact that it had been long established. To the Athenians he recalled that their first bishop had been Dionysius the Areopagite, mentioned in Acts 17:34. The later "president" (*proestōs,* as in Justin) Publius had been martyred, and after him Quadratus had been made bishop. It is interesting that two early Athenian bishops thus had names Latin in origin. In writing the Romans, Dionysius recalled their "blessed bishop Soter" (presumably deceased), who maintained the tradition of helping other communities already exemplified in 1 Clement. He also spoke of the ties between Corinth and Rome as long in existence, for both Peter and Paul had been present in Corinth and both became martyrs at Rome.[27]

Dionysius clearly knows of bishops elsewhere; he mentions those of Gortyna and Cnossus in Crete and names Palmas as bishop of Amastris in Pontus. In writing on orthodoxy, peace, and unity to the Lacedaemonia church, and on the heresy of Marcion to the Nicomedians, he does not seem to have mentioned bishops; at any rate, Eusebius does not report that he did so. To argue on this ground that there were no bishops in Lacedaemonia or Nicomedia is to make more of Eusebius' silence than is justified.

Five or ten years later a Christian writer named Hegesippus, about whom

[26] *Apol.* 1, 39-40 and 50.
[27] It is not clear how much of this information is based on 1 Clement alone.

we know little more than that he traveled from somewhere to the east through Corinth to Rome, wrote a treatise in which he laid strong emphasis on apostolic succession, perhaps deriving some of his information about it from the leaders of the church of Jerusalem. As A. Ehrhardt pointed out, the idea, or at least the emphasis, seems closely related to the Jewish concern with the succession of the high priests, and Hegesippus believed that James the Lord's brother had worn the high priest's breastplate.[28]

In Hegesippus' view heresy arose in the early church only after the apostolic age, and it did not arise everywhere. At Jerusalem the succession was carefully guarded. After the death of James, brought about by the plotting of Jewish sectarians, another relative of Jesus was made bishop; this was Simeon, "the son of Clopas the Lord's uncle." Heresy arose within the church because of the activities of a certain Thebouthis, a rival candidate for the episcopate. The church ceased to be "a pure virgin," and Jewish-Christian sectarians brought about the crucifixion of Simeon during the reign of Trajan.

At Corinth there was a similar sequence of orthodoxy-heresy. This church has remained in the truth faith until Primus (a Latinate name) was bishop; then it was infiltrated by heresies.

In speaking of the Roman church, however, Hegesippus says nothing about heresy. Evidently he regards Rome as the prime example of the way in which true orthodoxy is preserved in local successions of bishops. Apparently he himself made a succession list upon arriving at Rome. "Soter succeeded to Anicetus; after him came Eleutherus." It should be said, however, that although Rome is obviously significant, Hegesippus says nothing of a Roman primacy.

III-IRENAEUS OF LYONS

The importance of Irenaeus, successor of the ninety-year-old Pothinus as bishop of Lyons about 177, lies in his strong emphasis on tradition as the basis for church order. This emphasis is explained by his struggle against Gnostics of various schools. "When we appeal to the tradition which comes from the apostles and is guarded through the successions of presybyters in the churches, they oppose the tradition, saying that they, not only wiser than the presbyters but also wiser than the apostles, have discovered the genuine truth."[29] Against them Irenaeus argued that the apostolic tradition is not secret like theirs but is known to all; even if there had been a secret tradition it

[28] *The Apostolic Succession* (London, 1953), 63-66. For the fragments see Eusebius, *H. E.* 2, 23, 4-18; 3, 32, 3. 7-8; 4, 22, 2-4.
[29] *Adv. haer.* 3, 2, 2.

would have been committed to those "who by the apostles were appointed [*instituti*] as bishops in the churches."[30]

The foundation of Irenaeus' doctrine therefore lies in the apostolic appointment of the earliest bishops. "The blessed apostles . . . committed the ministry of the episcopate to Linus" at Rome, and at Smyrna to Polycarp. Clement "in the third place from the apostles was given the lot [*klēroutai*, cf. *klēros*, Acts 1:26] of the episcopate," at a time when "many survived who had been taught by the apostles."[31] Indeed, Clement "saw the blessed apostles"— an idea probably derived from 1 Clement 5.[32] Therefore "one must obey those presbyters in the church who have a succession from the apostles . . . , who with succession in episcopal office received a sure gift of grace in accordance with the decree of the Father."[33] The true form (*character*) of the body of Christ is "in accordance with the successions of the bishops to whom the apostles delivered the church which is in every place"[34]—i.e., the Catholic Church.

It is clear that the kind of ministerial succession which Irenaeus upholds is one in which the offices of bishops and presbyters are practically interchangeable. The literature he knows best presents the same picture. He is well acquainted with Acts, which he proves was written by a companion of Paul, and uses Acts 20:25–28 to show that there were both bishops and presbyters in Paul's time.[35] He knows 1 Clement, in which presbyters and bishops are not fully differentiated, and the letter of Polycarp, according to which presbyters govern the church. In his own letters Irenaeus refers to Polycarp as a "blessed and glorious presbyter" and speaks of the "presbyters who governed [*prostantes*] the church before Soter" at Rome.[36] Above all, while he certainly knows Ignatius' letter to the Romans[37] he never mentions him by name and makes practically no use of the letters in which the bishop is elevated above the presbyters. It is most unlikely that he accepted Ignatius' view of the monarchical episcopate.

It is also clear, however, that the existence of a monarchical episcopate at Rome is implied in the list of Roman bishops he provides. In it "episcopate" is mentioned three times, "succeeded" three times, and "apostles" four times. This fact implies that Irenaeus' own view is the older one, according to which some presbyters held episcopal office, but that he is acquainted with the view, held at Rome, that there had always been monarchical bishops. The situation is one of transition.

---

[30] *Ibid.*, 3, 1, 1.
[31] *Ibid.*, 3, 3, 1. 4.
[32] *Ibid.*, 3, 3, 3.
[33] *Ibid.*, 4, 26, 1.
[34] *Ibid.*, 4, 33, 7.
[35] *Ibid.*, 3, 14, 2.
[36] Eusebius, *H. E.* 5, 20. 24.
[37] *Adv. haer.* 5, 28, 3 (*Rom.* 4, 1).

IV·INTERRELATIONS AMONG THE CHURCHES

As Christianity expanded and communities were established in cities and in nearby towns, and as questions arose that seemed to require consistent solutions, it was inevitable that attention should be paid to the interrelations of the communities. The apostles had already dealt with the affairs of churches dispersed over wide areas, and in some measure their role was taken over by the Christian travelers of the second century such as Justin, Hegesippus, and Clement, though their functions seem not to have been "official." Messengers and letters were often sent from one church to another. Ignatius of Antioch, on his way to Rome through Asia, assumed the responsibility of sending instructions to the churches.

The leaders of the churches in the larger cities exercised some measure of control over Christians in areas nearby. Thus Ignatius addressed the Roman church as presiding "in the place of the country of the Romans," the city and its environs. His own see city was Antioch, but he also referred to himself as "bishop of Syria."[38] At a later date Serapion of Antioch exercised authority over the church at Rhosus, twenty-five miles from the metropolis.[39] In addition, authority may have been related to political and economic factors. The Roman church intervened in Corinthian affairs partly because Corinth was a Roman "colony."[40] Dionysius of Corinth dealt with nearby churches in Achaea and Crete but also wrote to Nicomedia in Bithynia and Amastris in Pontus, perhaps because of trade routes between Corinth and the Black Sea.

The idea of convening synods of bishops and other leaders does not seem to have arisen until the latter half of the second century, and in Asia. These first synods were occasioned by the Montanist crisis.

When the faithful in Asia had met frequently and at many places in Asia for this purpose, and on examination of the novel teachings had pronounced them profane and rejected the heresy, these persons were then expelled from the church and shut off from its communion.[41]

The late *Liber synodicus* goes so far as to say that Apollinaris of Hierapolis convoked a synod with twenty-six other bishops and that Sotas of Anchialus brought together twelve other bishops.[42] There is no reason to suppose that its author was acquainted with reliable tradition, but the general picture he gives must be correct.

[38] Ignatius, *Rom.* inscr.; 2, 2.
[39] Eusebius, *H. E.* 6, 12, 2-6.
[40] See R. Van Cauwalaert in *RHE* 31 (1935), 267-306, especialy 282 ff.
[41] Eusebius, *H. E.* 5, 16, 10.
[42] C. J. Hefele and H. Leclerq, *Histoire des conciles* I (Paris, 1907), 128-30.

The controversy over the celebration of Easter also led to the meeting of synods throughout the east and at Rome, and during the third century many local synods were held to discuss liturgical, doctrinal, and disciplinary questions.[43] The first general council in the west was convened at Arles by Constantine in 314, and it was followed by the first "ecumenical" council, that held at Nicaea, in 325.

V·THE ROMAN PRIMACY AND IDEA OF THE EPISCOPATE

Travel, correspondence, and synods did not provide the only means for increasing the unity of the churches. Unity was also provided by the growing power and authority of the church at Rome, the capital of the empire. According to Acts 19:21, the apostle Paul himself had expressed his desire to see Rome, and this statement is confirmed in his letter to the Romans (1:13). Less than half a century later this church had unhesitatingly intervened in affairs at Corinth. Ignatius had praised it without reserve and had referred to its apostolic founders.[44] Irenaeus described it as "the greatest, the most ancient, and well known to all." It had been founded and established by Peter and Paul. And he added the highly controversial sentence which must be quoted from the Latin version of Irenaeus; unfortunately the original Greek is missing.[45]

Ad hanc enim ecclesiam, propter *potentiorem principalitatem, necesse est omnem convenire ecclesiam*—hoc est eos qui sunt undique fideles—*in qua* semper, ab his qui sunt undique, conservata est ea quae est ab apostolis traditio.[46]

Every word and phrase italicized offers matter for debate. The general sense seems relatively clear. Irenaeus is arguing that since it would take a long time to deal with the successions in all the churches he is concentrating on the Roman succession. Because of the very great (comparative for superlative) antiquity and authority of this church, the whole church is necessarily in agreement or conformity with it (the whole church consisting of the faithful "from everywhere"), because in this church (also consisting of those "from everywhere") the apostolic tradition has been preserved. In his con-

---

[43] *Ibid.*, 133-51, 154-206.

[44] *Rom.* 4, 3.

[45] *Adv. haer.* 3, 3, 1-2. For a bibliography on the passage cf. N. Brox, *Offenbarung, Gnosis und gnostischer Mythos bei Irenäus von Lyon* (Salzburg, 1966), 140-41; add F. M. Sagnard, *Irénée de Lyon: Contre les hérésies Livre III* (Paris, 1952), 414-23.

[46] "Because of its very great antiquity/authority, it is with this church, in which the tradition from the apostles has always been preserved by the faithful from everywhere, that every church, consisting of the faithful who are from everywhere, must agree/conform."

text, it would appear, this is what he means to say. He is setting forth what he views as facts, not describing Roman claims to primacy.

Through Irenaeus certainly has Christian Rome and Roman Christians in mind, it is worth noting that the somewhat rhetorical character of his sentence could bring rhetorical parallels to the minds of ancient as well as modern readers. W. L. Knox has well compared the language of rhetoricians in dealing with the glories of ancient Rome, especially when Diodorus Siculus speaks of the greatness of the city in the eyes of those who come from other regions.[47] It is a theme developed at length in the address *To Rome* by the second-century rhetorician Aelius Aristides.[48] It is quite possible that Irenaeus had the theme in mind as he wrote. In addition, he lived among the Celts, as he points out in his preface. This point has suggested to V. White an odd parallel in Caesar where the Roman general describes the succession of chief priests among the Druids. One who has had supreme authority is succeeded by another, and in the middle of Gaul Druids assemble "from everywhere" to decide upon the successor.[49] It is most unlikely that Irenaeus thought of the Roman succession as analogous to that of the Druids. The similarity indicates only that a potential convert from Druidism in his time would not have found Irenaeus' ideas entirely strange.

The emphasis Irenaeus lays on succession from the apostles has seemed strange to critics, in spite of its presence in I Clement nearly a century earlier. It has been argued that he was influenced by Hegesippus, who in turn was influenced by Gnostics. This notion seems untenable. First, no evidence shows that Hegesippus was influenced by the Gnostics; second, it is more likely that Irenaeus derived his ideas from I Clement, a letter which he certainly knew. The kind of succession he describes is like that found in I Clement, where, it would appear, bishops are presbyters who have the special function of governing the community. We have already seen that Hermas speaks of "the presbyters who are in charge of the church." Though writing in the fourth century, Epiphanius does say that the heretic Marcion was expelled by presbyters and teachers at Rome, not by a bishop as such.[50]

The list Irenaeus gives for the apostolic succession at Rome therefore requires careful examination.[51]

The blessed apostles, having founded and built the church, entrusted the ministry of the episcopate to Linus. (Paul mentioned this Linus in the letters to Timothy [2 Tim. 4:21].) Anencletus succeeded him; after him, in the third place from the apostles, Clement was allotted the episcopate, he who had seen the blessed apostles and had been with them, and still had the preaching of the apostles in his ears

[47] Diodorus Siculus 1, 4, 2-3; W. L. Knox in *JTS* 47 (1946), 180-84.
[48] J. H. Oliver, *The Ruling Power* (*TAPS* 43, 4 [1953]), 896 (sec. 11), 901 (61-62), 907 (107-9).
[49] Caesar, *Bell. Gall.* 6, 13; V. White in *Dominican Studies* 4 (1951), 201-3.
[50] Epiphanius, *Haer.* 42, 2, 2 and 6.
[51] Irenaeus, *Adv. haer.* 3, 3, 3.

and the tradition before his eyes; he was not alone in this, for many still then survived who had been taught by the apostles. . . .

Whether or not this passage is based on reliable traditions, its language seems to be derived from earlier works which Irenaeus undoubtedly knew. The mention of "allotting" presumably comes from the account of Matthias' selection in Acts 1.26, while the idea of succession occurs in 1 Clement 44, 2. Clement's work with the apostles may come either from his own description of them in 1 Clement 5 or from Paul's mention of a Clement in Philippians 4:3. Linus and Anancletus are ciphers as far as our knowledge of them goes, though this does not mean that they did not follow the apostles.

There is no reason to question the accuracy of the rest of the list.

Euarestus succeeded this Clement, and Alexander, Euarestus; then, sixth from the apostles, Xystus was appointed, and after him Telesphorus, who suffered a glorious martyrdom; next Hyginus, then Pius, and after him Anicetus. After Soter succeeded Anicetus, Eleutherus now holds in the twelfth place the lot of the episcopate which came down from the apostles. In the same order and succession the tradition from the apostles in the church and the preaching of the truth have come down to us.

We know from 1 Clement that at a very early date the Roman church was concerned with the idea of legitimate succession. For the middle of the second century we have the insistence of Ptolemaeus at Rome that the Valentinians *also* possessed teaching from the apostolic succession.[52] And when the third-century Adoptianists claimed that theirs was the original doctrine of the Roman church, they accepted the episcopal list without quesion.[53]

At Rome, then, there was strong support for the primacy of the Roman church and for the authenticity of its doctrine as derived from the apostles and transmitted through apostolic succession. Episcopacy at Rome certainly became monarchical by the middle of the second century, when Justin referred to a single "president." But nothing in early Christian literature suggests that anything like the later papacy existed. In the third century we hear much of the "Petrine promise" (Matt. 16:17–19). In the preceding century both Peter and Paul were regarded as the founders of the Roman church, and there was no direct mention of the promise. The only trace of it is to be found in the words of Polycrates of Ephesus, rejecting the claims of Victor of Rome: "Those greater than I have said, One must obey God rather than men." The saying is ascribed to the apostle Peter in Acts 5:29, and perhaps Polycrates is quoting Peter against the claims of his successor.[54] Even if he is doing so, however, there is no proof that Victor traced the source of his authority back to Peter alone. Mention of the Petrine promise

[52] Epiphanius, *Haer.* 33, 7, 9.
[53] Eusebius, *H. E.* 5, 28, 3.
[54] Eusebius, *H. E.* 5, 24, 7.

actually occurs for the first time in a work which Tertullian wrote about 220.[55]

This is not to say that the power of the Roman church and the Roman bishop was not growing. Indeed, Victor evidently believed that he could excommunicate "the communities of the whole of Asia, together with the neighboring churches."[56] At Rome itself he excommunicated the Adoptianist Theodotus of Byzantium and deposed a presbyter who advocated Valentinian doctrines.[57]

The Roman idea of the episcopate seems to have been rather different from that advocated in Asia Minor. Polycrates of Ephesus laid considerable emphasis on a kind of family-succession not unlike that advocated in Palestine. In arguing against Victor he relied on the traditions of his family. "Seven of my kinsmen were bishops, and I am the eighth; and my kinsmen always observed the day when the people put away the leaven."[58] Another emphasis both Jewish and familial was expressed in his concern for the fact that the apostle John wore the *petalon* or high priest's breastplate; similarly Epiphanius probably relying on a source related to Jewish Christianity, says that it was worn by James of Jerusalem.[59] At Rome presbyters and bishops were compared with Jewish priests and high priests,[60] but the comparisons are less specific than in Asia; and in Rome there is no trace of family succession.

The *Apostolic Tradition* of Hippolytus, probably written about 215, gives a clear picture of the state of the ministry at Rome soon after Victor's time. When a bishop is consecrated the presbyters stand silent while only the bishops lay hands on the popularly elected candidate. The bishop, it is said, has been chosen by God to feed his flock (John 21:15-17), to remit sins (John 20:23), and "to loose every bond in accordance with the power which thou gavest the apostles" (Matt. 18:18).[61] At the ordination of a presbyter, on the other hand, both bishop and presbyters lay hands on him, though only the bishop pronounces the prayer. The presbyters are merely indicating their approval, not ordaining; the presbyter's power of governing mentioned in the prayer is thus subordinate to the bishop's. Finally, at the ordination of a deacon—not to a priesthood, says Hippolytus, but for service to the bishop—only the bishop imposes hands and prays. If the deacon serves well he may be advanced to the presbyterate.[62]

The presbyters are thus clearly subordinated to the bishop, and Hippolytus goes out of his way to say that though they lay hands on the ordinand they

[55] De pudic. 21, 9.
[56] Eusebius, H. E. 5, 24, 9.
[57] Ibid., 5, 24, 9.
[58] Ibid., 5, 24, 6.
[59] Haer. 29, 4, 4; cf. 78, 14, 1.
[60] I Clem. 44; Hippolytus, Apost. Trad. 3-4; Ref. 1, praef. 6. See also Didache 13, 3.
[61] Apost. Trad. 3, 5. Note that what is said of Peter in the Gospel of John is applied to all the apostles.
[62] Apost. Trad. 8-9.

do not ordain. This point may suggest that at one time the presbyters did ordain, as in the situation described in I Timothy 4:14. It may also point toward a contrast between the procedure at Rome and that at Alexandria or in Gaul. At Alexandria the bishop was consecrated by the presbytery at least as early as about 190, and thereafter to 313. The tradition was abandoned when forbidden by the Council of Nicaea.[63] In Gaul a similar custom seems to have been observed in Irenaeus' time.[64] It may be, then, that Hippolytus is opposing not only earlier procedures but also those of some churches outside Rome in his time.

During the second century, then, and even later at Alexandria, we encounter three forms or expressions of the idea of episcopal succession. At Jerusalem and Asia there was an emphasis on succession within a family— at first within the family of the Lord, later within an "episcopal" family. At Alexandria the presbyters chose a successor to the bishop from among themselves. At Rome the presbyters and the whole people elected the new bishop and other bishops consecrated him. The Roman practice eventually became universal.[65]

In speaking of the Christian ministry up to this point we have been careful to refer to *presbyteroi* as "presbyters," rather than as "priests," even though in English and French the word "priest" or "prêtre" comes from *presbyteros*. In Greek and Latin the words for "priest" are *hiereus* and *sacerdos,* and while as we have seen the Christian bishop or presbyter-bishop early possessed sacrificial-priestly characteristics, in the early church two ideas about priesthood prevented further development, at least at the beginning. First, all Christians were regarded as priests and all constituted a "royal priesthood."[66] Second, Jesus himself was regarded as the only true high priest.[67] It was not until the third century that specifically sacerdotal language was employed in relation to the clergy, first occasionally by Tertullian and Hippolytus and then very frequently by Origen and Cyprian. In the decree of the council at Antioch in 268 the clergy are called a *hieration* or body of priests.[68] Each of these examples suggests that the language employed was not new and that accordingly its rise should be placed toward the beginning of the third century. This is to say that priestly functions preceded priestly language.

---

[63] W. Telfer in *JEH* 3 (1952), 1-13.

[64] E. Molland in *JEH* 1 (1950), 12-28.

[65] The Roman bishop was later called "pope" or *papa,* but the title "father" was originally applied both to bishops (*Mart. Polyc.* 12, 2; Eusebius, *H. E.* 5, 4, 2) and to others, and *papa* was used of bishops (*Mart. Perpet.* 13, 1; Tertullian, *De pudic.* 13, 7), notably of Dionysius of Alexandria (*H. E.* 7, 7, 4); cf. G. W. H. Lampe, *A Patristic Greek Lexicon* (Oxford, 1961 ff.), 1006.

[66] Irenaeus speaks of the apostles as priests (*Adv. haer.* 4, 8, 3) but so also of all Christians (5, 34, 3); cf. Justin, *Dial.* 116, 3.

[67] 1 Clement 36, 1 (from Heb. 2:17, 3:1, 4:15).

[68] Eusebius, *H. E.* 7, 30, 13.

Indeed, when in the *Didache* (15, 1) Christians are instructed to appoint bishops and deacons who "minister the ministry of the prophets and teachers," it has already been said that the prophets are the high priests of the communities (13, 3).

VI-SUPPORT OF THE MINISTRY AND CHARITY

According to the three synoptic gospels, the earliest disciples were to take no provisions for their mission but were to be supported by those who received them.[69] According to Matthew (10:10), Jesus stated that "the workman deserves his food"; Luke (10:7) speaks of a "wage" instead. The same situation obtains in the Pauline epistles, where the apostle insists upon the apostolic right to support by the community, even though he himself works for his living (1 Cor. 9:3-18). Apparently the Corinthians were not absolutely convinced that such a right existed in Paul's case, for he provided the example of other apostles, analogies from other kinds of occupations, and quotations from "the law of Moses" (Deut. 25:4) and the saying of Jesus already mentioned. Similarly in 1 Timothy 5:17-18 the authority of "scripture" is quoted, and it is also said that presbyters who govern well are to receive double compensation. In Acts 20:33 Paul is quoted as saying that he coveted no man's silver or gold or apparel, presumably with reference to the words of Jesus and perhaps to Paul's own insistence upon not laying burdens on his churches.[70]

The burden which he did lay upon them was for the support of "the poor" in the church at Jerusalem. At his meeting with the Jerusalem apostles he had accepted their request for such support (Gal. 2:10) and thereafter had frequently urged his congregations in Macedonia and Achaea to contribute to a collection for "the saints."[71] Romans 15:25-33 shows that he was on his way to Jerusalem to deliver the collection there.

Conceivably such a collection was necessary in order to provide support to Jerusalem not only because of the famine of 46–47 (Acts 11:27-30) but also because of the early experiment in communism at Jerusalem (Acts 2:44-45, 4:32-5:11). It is evident, however, that some churches were accustomed to give support at least to the apostles: the Philippians sent gifts to Paul when he was at Thessalonica (Phil. 4:16), and he expected that the Romans would support his mission to Spain (Rom. 15:24).

The picture of such matters presented in the *Didache* is somewhat different

[69] Mark 6:8-11; Matt. 10:9-13; Luke 9:3-4, 10:4-9.
[70] 1 Thess. 2:5-6, 9-10; 2 Cor. 11:7-12, 12:14-18.
[71] 1 Cor. 16:1-4; 2 Cor. 8-9; perhaps Gal. 2:10 + 6:10; cf. D. Georgi, *Die Geschichte der Kollekte des Paulus für Jerusalem* (Hamburg, 1965).

and is more closely related to Old Testament precedents. Itinerant apostles and prophets are not to ask congregations for money,[72] but resident prophets deserve their food (13, 1). Such prophets, equivalent to the Old Testament high priests, are to be supported with the "first-fruits" of agricultural produce and animals or with tithes of money, clothing, and other possessions.[73] The background of the *Didache* thus lies in Judaism, as does Matthew 23:23, where tithing is recommended.

Irenaeus too discusses first-fruits and tithes but insists that among Christians everything is given to the Lord's use, not just a portion of it.[74] His statement, however, represents the ideal, not the actuality, for in a homily on Numbers Origen has to insist that the laws about first-fruits and tithes still have a literal meaning as well as an allegorical one.[75]

From Syria in Origen's time we have the evidence provided by the *Didascalia Apostolorum*, a revised version of the *Didache* in which the bishop replaces the local prophet. The bishop administers the church's income, derived from the first-fruits of agricultural produce and tithes of other income.[76] These funds supply him with a modest living but are basically intended for the support of orphans, widows, the indigent, and strangers, none of whom are to take undue advantage of this support. At common meals the widow's portion is doubled for deacons, presbyters, and the lector; it is quadrupled in the case of the bishop. The *Didascalia* forbids the bishop to accept payments for admission into the church or for pardoning sins.

In other communities, it would appear, bishops were not so well paid, for Tertullian mentions only a double portion for presiding presbyters—relying on 1 Timothy.[77]

Obviously the funds of the churches were used for maintaining the clergy and for the "hospitality" mentioned by Clement, Hermas, and Justin at Rome.[78] The administration of the funds certainly created problems, for Polycarp speaks of a Philippian presbyter who apparently had become notorious for his avarice (*Phil.* 11). At least at Rome, however, the church was well known for the aid which it continually supplied to other communities and for the relief sent to Christians condemned to work in the mines. According to Dionysius of Corinth, this beneficence was increased under Soter.[79]

During the second century, however, it would appear that no regular salaries were paid to the clergy; otherwise it would be difficult to account for

---

[72] *Did.* 11, 6 and 12.
[73] Num. 15:17-21, 18:11-19; Deut. 18:3-5; Neh. 10:35-39; Sir. 7:31.
[74] *Adv. haer.* 4, 18, 1-2.
[75] *Num. hom.* 11, 2 (p. 79 Baehrens).
[76] On tithes cf. L. Vischer, "Die Zehntforderung in der alten Kirche," *ZKG* 70 (1959), 201-17.
[77] Tertullian, *De ieiun.* 17, 4.
[78] Cf. H. Chadwick in *TU* 79 (1961), 281-85.
[79] Eusebius, *H. E.* 4, 23, 10.

the vigor with which Apollonius (about 196) attacks the Montanists for their financial arrangements.[80] At the end of the second century, with the growth of the churches, the situation was changing. Since Victor could provide Callistus with a monthly pension, it would appear likely that he received some regular wage himself, and Hippolytus criticizes the size of a heretical bishop's stipend, not the fact that he was being paid.[81]

By the middle of the third century the expansion of the Roman church, like that of others, obviously required administrative expansion as well. Cornelius of Rome speaks of 155 Christians at Rome with clerical and semi-clerical functions and of 1,500 cases of charity, all supported by "the grace and philanthropy of the Master."[82] When robbers kidnaped Numidian Christians in 253, Cyprian raised a fund of 100,000 sesterces to ransom them (*Ep.* 72). Charity both at home and abroad obviously led to increased regularization in administration.

In turn, the growth of the churches and the necessity for dealing with larger sums of money inevitably led to concern with administration for its own sake. Origen bitterly criticized bishops who sought to transmit the episcopate to their relatives or, especially in the larger cities, became rich and powerful at the expense of the poor.[83] There is no reason to suppose that Origen misrepresented the situation, although his personal difficulties with the bishop of Alexandria undoubtedly influenced his judgment.

[80] *Ibid.,* 5, 18, 2.
[81] Hippolytus, *Ref.* 9, 12, 13; Eusebius, *H. E.* 5, 28, 10.
[83] Eusebius, *H. E.* 6, 43, 11.
[83] Harnack in *TU* 42, 3 (Leipzig, 1918), 77-78; cf. 136-38.

PART THREE·CHRIS-TIANITY IN THE THIRD CENTURY

By the beginning of the third century the Christian movement had practically completed its most crucial development or metamorphosis. Most of its leaders, the bishops of such leading sees as Rome, Carthage, Alexandria, and Antioch, had taken firm stands against the spiritualizing syncretism of the Gnostics and the apocalyptic revival of the Montanists. They had favored the tendencies already present in the apostolic age toward order and organization.

Toward the end of the second century a strong emphasis on Christian history and tradition had come to the fore, even though it was still expected that the Lord would return and inaugurate the kingdom of God. At Rome, as early as 160, there was a *memoria* of the apostle Peter which served to call to mind the foundation of the church there.[1] At Alexandria and in Palestine and Asia bishops and teachers were concerned with traditions about Christian origins. The same concern is reflected in the writings of Irenaeus of Lyons. At Antioch the apologetic works of the bishop Theophilus contain few echoes of the earlier eschatological hope. The "holy churches" are islands of refuge from

[1] See D. W. O'Connor, *Peter in Rome* (New York, 1969), 158-206.

the sinful world; men can escape to them and avoid both sin and the wrath and judgment of God,[2] but this judgment is viewed as taking place after death and resurrection.[3] Theophilus' concern for the antiquity of divine revelation leaves little room for the old eschatology. This apostle Paul had spoken of his own stewardship; Theophilus applied his words to the Roman emperor.[4]

In spite of this modification, however, the third century was to bring conflict with the Roman government.

[2] *Ad Autol.* 2, 14.
[3] *Ibid.*, 1, 13-14.
[4] *Ibid.*, 1, 11; 1 Cor. 9:17.

CHAPTER XI
ROME AND THE CHRISTIANS

In 208, when Septimius Severus was sixty-two, he crossed the Channel with his sons in order to restore peace in Britain; after three years of campaigning he died at York, leaving the throne to both Caracalla and Geta. The sons provided the army with a donative, and on this occasion a Christian soldier, enthusiastically supported by the Montanist Tertullian, refused to wear a laurel crown and was executed.[1] A year later, Caracalla claimed that Geta was plotting against him and proceeded to murder him. All who mourned Geta's death were executed; his name was eradicated from monuments; agents of the secret police were everywhere. More funds were lavished upon the army, and the funds accumulated by Septimius were dissipated. Apparently Christians were persecuted, at least in Africa, and Tertullian produced another treatise denouncing the majority who either escaped by taking flight or simply bought immunity, sometimes by providing gifts to soldiers.[2]

In 212 (or perhaps two years later)[3] came the *constitutio Antoniana*, ap-

[1] *De corona* I, I.
[2] *De fuga* 5, 5; 12, 1; 13, 3.
[3] See F. Millar in *Journal of Egyptian Archaeology* 47 (1962), 124-31, cited by T. D. Barnes in *JTS* 20 (1969), 122 n. 6.

parently providing citizenship for all the people in the Roman empire, with only a few exceptions. According to Dio Cassius, hardly an impartial witness, Caracalla's purpose was "to increase his revenues by this means, inasmuch as aliens did not have to pay most . . . taxes."[4] On the other hand, an extant papyrus copy of the *constitutio* expresses the emperor's gratitude to "the most holy gods" for his deliverance from danger, and his hope that the extension of the citizenship would provide the gods with more worshipers.[5] The tie between citizenship and Roman religiosity was clear in Caracalla's mind, and at Rome itself he promoted the worship of Isis, a goddess by now not un-Roman.[6] Martyrdoms in North Africa, however, may have been due to religious zeal on the part of governors.[7] No clear evidence suggests that many Christians perished at this time.

The constitution of Caracalla seems to have had no effect on the life of the Christian churches. On the other hand, his visit to Alexandria in the spring of 215 was a disaster for all citizens. He took vengeance on the Alexandrians, who had ridiculed him, by massacring many of the inhabitants. The Christians were not directly harmed; according to Herodian, the chief victims were young men being inducted into the army,[8] and if Alexandrian Christians shared Origen's view of military service, few Christians can have been among them. Origen himself, however, withdrew to Palestine and remained there until, presumably after Caracalla's departure fairly early in 216,[9] Demetrius sent deacons to recall him.[10]

The assassination of Caracalla in 217 and the brief reigns of his praetorian prefect Macrinus (217–218) and the Syrian priest-king Elagabalus (218–222) had little effect on the churches. At Rome Zephyrinus died peacefully in 217 and was succeeded by his archdeacon Callistus. This bishop died in 222, possibly as a martyr to mob violence but not because of imperial persecution. The reign of Alexander Severus (222–235), was marked by closer relations between Christians and the court. The emperor may have kept statues of Christ, Abraham, Orpheus, and Apollonius of Tyana—along with some of the deified emperors—in his private chapel.[11] Certainly the Christian polymath Julius Africanus designed a library for him,[12] and Hippolytus of Rome dedicated a treatise to his mother Julia Mamaea. She herself summoned Origen to discuss religious matters with her at Antioch, probably in 232.[13]

---

[4] Dio 78, 9, 5.
[5] Mitteis, *Chrest.* 377; Wilcken, *Grundzüge*, pp. 116-17.
[6] *SHA Caracalla* 10, 10-11.
[7] Tertullian, *Ad Scapulam* 4, 8.
[8] Herodian 4, 9, 4-8; cf. Dio 77, 22, 1-23, 4; cf. H. A. Musurillo, *The Acts of the Pagan Martyrs* (Oxford, 1954), 229-32.
[9] A. Maricq in *Syria* 34 (1957), 297-302, relying on P. Flor. 382 and Wilcken, *Chrest.* 245.
[10] Eusebius, *H. E.* 6, 19, 15-19.
[11] *SHA Severus Alexander* 29, 2.
[12] P. Oxy. III 412.
[13] Eusebius, *H. E.* 6, 21, 3.

The emperor and his mother were murdered three years later, and the new ruler Maximin, once a shepherd in Thrace, dismissed Alexander's staff and even put to death many of his palace attendants.[14] Eusebius has transformed this episode into a general persecution, based on "ill will toward the house of Alexander, since for the most part it consisted of believers." According to him, the emperor "ordered the rulers of the church to be put to death, since they were responsible for the teaching of the gospel."[15] No evidence confirms this statement. To be sure, the two rival bishops of Rome, Pontianus and Hippolytus, were deported to Sardinia and lost their civil rights. Neither was put to death, even though Hippolytus had dedicated a treatise to Julia Mamaea. Ambrose, Origen's patron, and a presbyter of Caesarea were imprisoned for a time, and to them Origen, not a prisoner, addressed his *Exhortation to Martyrdom*. There were troubles in Pontus and Cappadocia, but these were due not to any imperial decree but to mobs frightened by earthquakes and to the ill will of a local governor. The view that Maximin was a persecutor cannot be substantiated.[16]

This emperor was himself murdered in 238 when protests against new taxes developed into revolt, and his successors Gordian (238–244) and Philip (244–249) were no persecutors. Indeed, Philip was so friendly toward Christian leaders that Eusebius was able to transmit legends pointing toward his active acceptance of Christianity.[17] Once more, Origen maintained a correspondence with the imperial house, writing to Philip and to his wife Otacilia Severa.[18] At the end of 247 Philip celebrated the thousandth anniversary of the founding of Rome with impressive religious ceremonies and, it may be, provided the occasion, in part, for Origen's apologetic treatise *Against Celsus* —a reply to pagan criticism made about seventy years earlier. In this work Origen expressed approval of the empire, though he was apprehensive about the immediate future. Like Melito of Sardis, he noted the coincidence between the birth of Jesus and the reign of Augustus, the emperor who united many kingdoms in the one empire. The Christian gospel could not have been successfully proclaimed unless peace had prevailed under Roman rule.[19] To be sure,

many questions are raised . . . by the existence of those who have ruled savagely and tyrannically, or of those who have drifted from exercising rule into debauchery and wantonness.[20]

But Christians are loyal to "the emperor who reigns righteously," and they support him through their prayers. Their function in the empire is to "educate

[14] Herodian 7, 1, 2-4.
[15] Eusebius, *H. E.* 6, 28.
[16] Cf. G. W. Clarke in *Historia* 15 (1966), 445-53.
[17] *H. E.* 6, 34.
[18] *Ibid.*, 6, 36, 3.
[19] *Contra Celsum* 2, 30.
[20] *Ibid.*, 8, 65.

the citizens and teach them to be devoted to God, the guardian of their city." They lead them to the great city which transcends human empires.[21]

Origen was writing at the end of a long period of peace. In 248, however, rebellion against Philip had broken out, and he was apprehensive for the immediate future. Persecution might well arise

when those who attack Christianity in every possible way regard the multitude of believers as responsible for the rebellion which is so strong at this moment, thinking that it is because they are not being persecuted by the governors as they used to be.[22]

In the past, however, God has prevented opponents of Christianity from being "too violently inflamed against them."[23] His conclusion is optimistic: someday Christianity will prevail, "since the word is continually gaining possession of more souls."[24]

He was also writing on the eve of a new persecution. Perhaps encouraged by the celebration of Rome's millennium in 247–248, enthusiasm for the old religion was fanned by a priest whom Eusebius does not name.[25] He may have been a certain Myron, deputy high priest of Egypt, who is known from an inscription to have been trying to restore local worship in the province; the inscription directs that within fifteen days all the pigs are to be driven out of a village temple.[26] At Alexandria anti-Christian feeling led to rioting and looting and to bloody violence against an old man and a woman, then to murder.[27] The anarchic situation continued for a year as Philip gradually lost control of the empire. In September 249 his general Decius was hailed as a new Trajan who would reestablish the state—on the foundation of traditional paganism. Fabian, bishop of Rome, was executed on January 20, 250, perhaps in consequence of an edict already issued by the new emperor and first enforced at Rome. The edict has not survived, but papyrus copies of more than forty certificates issued in Egypt between June 12 and July 14 make plain what was required. These certificates contain petitions addressed to the local sacrifice commissions; the petition would state that he or she had always sacrificed to the gods and was now doing so in the presence of members of the commission, who then affixed their signatures. The extant *libelli* include petitions from a priestess of the crocodile god Petesouchos, from a proxy for an illiterate woman, and from a man on behalf of his wife, sons, and daughter. (The daughter's name was Thecla, and she *may* have been a Christian.)[28]

[21] *Ibid.*, 8, 73-74.
[22] *Ibid.*, 3, 15.
[23] *Ibid.*, 3, 8.
[24] *Ibid.*, 8, 68.
[25] Eusebius, *H. E.* 6, 41, 1-2.
[26] *OGIS* 210 = Wilcken, *Chrest.* 73.
[27] Eusebius, *H. E.* 6, 41, 3-9.
[28] Cf. J. R. Knipfing in *HTR* 16 (1923), 345-90.

Some Christian leaders refused to offer sacrifice and were therefore jailed: both Alexander of Jerusalem and Fabius of Antioch died in prison. At Caesarea Origen suffered torture but was not put to death. Dionysius of Alexandria was arrested, then released. He later stated that large numbers of the "more eminent" Christians offered sacrifice, though some did so because of imprisonment and torture. Fourteen Alexandrian Christians seem to have been executed, though Dionysius refers to "many others" in Egypt.

In Egypt and elsewhere bishops withdrew from their see cities. Dionysius mentions the aged Chaeremon of Nilopolis as one of them;[29] Cyprian of Carthage was another. At Carthage the church lost most of its members,[30] and later on, "thousands" of renegades sought forgiveness.[31] The Spanish bishops Martialis and Basilides purchased certificates of sacrifice.[32] Even in distant Pontus, the bishop Gregory Thaumaturgus took to flight.[33]

Had the persecution continued for a longer time, the growth of the Christian movement might well have been slowed or even stopped. As it was, conflicts within the church lasted for a decade or more.

During the year that was left to him, Decius did not repeat the demand for universal sacrifice. He had intended to produce not martyrs but apostates, and in large measure he had succeeded.[34] More pressing matters occupied his attention, for the Goths against whom he had been fighting when he was proclaimed emperor continued to move into the empire from the north; in June 251 Decius fell before them, south of the Danube.[35] His successor remained in power for only two years before another general had him killed and, in turn, was put to death by his own troops.

This period of anarchy was accompanied by sporadic, though mild, persecution in the larger cities. Cornelius of Rome was exiled in 253; Dionysius of Alexandria refers to persecution, though not to martyrdoms, around the same time.[36] The basic problems of the church for the next few years were internal. At Rome before Cornelius' exile there had been two claimants for the episcopate. He was one; the other was the presbyter Novatian, who had gained control of the community during the persecution and proposed to lay harsh penalties on Christians, now penitent, who had lapsed. At Carthage, Alexandria, and Antioch there were struggles between the rigorists and the more lenient leaders. It is not surprising that the moderates won the contest. They had the backing of large numbers of Christians, and both Cyprian of Carthage and Dionysius of Alexandria had been absent from their sees when

[29] Eusebius, *H. E.* 6, 41, 11—42, 4.
[30] Cyprian, *Ep.* 11, 1.
[31] *Ep.* 20, 2.
[32] *Ep.* 67, 1.
[33] *PG* 46, 949A.
[34] Cyprian, *Ep.* 24 (*universi*).
[35] Cf. A. Alföldi in *CAH* XII 145.
[36] Eusebius, *H. E.* 7, 1.

sacrifice was required. Fabius of Antioch, however, was doubtless inspired by the death in prison of his predecessor Babylas and favored Novatian in spite of many letters sent him by his colleagues. Upon his death in 252, however, a synod held at Antioch rejected the Novatianist view.[37]

After Valerian came to power in 253 the persecution ended. Dionysius of Alexandria could write that "all his house was filled with godly persons and was a church of God"; at the least this statement means that his advisers were occupied with other matters, such as the Gothic invasions of Greece and Asia Minor. Gregory Thaumaturgus, bishop of Neocaesarea in Pontus, vividly describes the aftermath of the victory of the Goths and the Borani in 255.[38] Writing to another bishop in Pontus, he exonerated Christian captives from blame if they ate food provided by the barbarians, for it had not been offered to the gods; Christian women raped by the barbarians were free from blame. The invasion had led to more difficult problems, however. Some Christians had seized the property of those who had fled or had been killed; others had robbed the refugees or held them captive. Some had actually joined the invaders, forgetting their own Pontic and Christian allegiance, and had killed their own people. During the invasion they had served the invaders as guides, pointing out roads and houses to them. Some had simply broken into the houses belonging to others. Of less consequence were the sins of those who found and kept property left by the barbarians in fields or houses. Even after the invaders' departure there was those who were demanding rewards for information, for saving life, and for finding lost property.

This situation, foreshadowing the divisions within the church in Diocletian's time, demanded the strong disciplinary measures which Gregory took. The Christians of Pontus were obviously in disarray. Perhaps the greatest miracle worked by the Thaumaturge was his preservation of the community.[39]

In the summer of 257, as the military situation momentarily improved, Valerian was persuaded to take steps against the Christians, beginning with their leaders. His motive was primarily religious. To Cyprian the proconsul of Africa said, "The most sacred emperors Valerian and Gallienus have deigned to transmit to me an epistle in which they have ordered that those who do not profess the Roman religion must not refuse to take part in Roman religious ceremonies."[40] The first edict of Valerian therefore required bishops, presbyters, and deacons to offer sacrifice to the gods; in addition, Christian

[37] Ibid., 6, 41-46; cf. P. Nautin, Lettres et écrivains chrétiens des iie et iiie siècles (Paris, 1961), 143-56.

[38] Eusebius, H. E. 7, 10, 3; Gregory in M. J. Routh, Reliquiae Sacrae (ed. 2, Oxford, 1846), III, 256-64; cf. V. Ryssel, Gregorius Thaumaturgus (Leipzig, 1880), 15, 29-31; for the date, A. Alföldi in CAH XII 146-48; in Berytus 4 (1937), 57.

[39] According to Gregory of Nyssa, there were about 17 Christians in Neocaesarea at the beginning of his mission, 17 pagans at the end (PG 46, 953D).

[40] Acta Cypriani 1, 1 (cf. 4, 1; pp. 62-63 Knopf and Krüger); cf. G. E. M. de Ste. Croix in Past and Present, no. 26 (1963), 31.

assemblies either in churches or in cemeteries were forbidden. Cyprian was banished from Carthage on August 30. At Alexandria Dionysius was brought before the deputy prefect of Egypt and urged to worship his own god along with the other "natural" gods known to all. He refused, claiming that the one true God had given authority to Valerian and his son Gallienus, and was thereupon sent into exile.[41]

A year later, as Valerian was at Antioch preparing a campaign against the Persians,[42] a second decree was issued against the Christians. This time the death penalty was provided, not only for the higher clergy but also for Christians of the senatorial and equestrian classes. Matrons were to suffer loss of property and exile; minor officials in the administration were to be reduced to slavery. On August 8, Xystus of Rome with four deacons entered the cemetery; they were apprehended and put to death.[43] Five weeks later Cyprian was beheaded at Carthage. The following February, Fructuosus of Tarragona in Spain was burned alive after refusing to offer sacrifice.[44]

In the summer of 260 Valerian was captured by the Persian king Shapur either in battle or by treachery after offering the Persians an indemnity and attending a peace conference. A monument cut in rock near Persepolis shows Valerian kneeling before the mounted Shapur while Mariada, an Antiochene who betrayed his city to the Persians, stands nearby. After Valerian died in captivity the Persians stuffed his skin and placed it in a temple.

The persecution of Christians had failed to save the emperor, and his son Gallienus immediately took steps toward reconciliation. Only a few days after the election of Dionysius as bishop of Rome (July 20, 260), the new emperor transmitted a copy of an imperial rescript to him, along with an enabling letter. The letter quoted by Eusebius may have been addressed to Dionysius of Alexandria, but the contents would be the same.[45]

The emperor Caesar Publius Licinius Gallienus Pius Felix Fortunatus Augustus to Dionysius and Pinnas and Demetrius and the other bishops. I have decreed that the benefit of my donation should be published throughout the world so that [occupants] will withdraw from the places of worship and therefore you may be able to use the copy of my rescript without molestation. And this, which it is in your power to accomplish, has long since been conceded by me; therefore Aurelius Quirinius, secretary of the treasury, will act in accordance with the copy issued by me.

The decree permitted the bishops to resume their duties and restored the churches to their control. In addition, another rescript soon permitted the

---

[41] Eusebius, *H. E.* 7, 11, 8-10.
[42] G. Downey, *A History of Antioch in Syria* (Princeton, 1961), 259-60.
[43] Cyprian, *Ep.* 80, 1.
[44] *Martyrium Fructuosi* 2, 4 (p. 85 Knopf and Krüger).
[45] Eusebius, *H. E.* 7, 13.

recovery of the cemeteries. A graffito in the catacombs of St. Sebastian gives the date of August 9, 260.[46]

From the time of Gallienus Eusebius mentions only one martyr, who suffered death under exceptional circumstances. This was Marinus, a legionary soldier at Caesarea in Palestine who was forced by the local bishop to choose between sacrificing to the gods while advancing to the rank of centurion, and refusing to sacrifice and being executed.[47] Dionysius of Alexandria had nothing but praise for Gallienus,[48] who put down a revolt led by the anti-Christian Macrianus.

At this point the persecutions which had troubled the church for two centuries effectively came to an end. Under Gallienus and his successors up until 303 there were no general persecutions of Christians, and the church was left free to expand and develop. Its property rights were officially recognized. Only in the army, closely tied to traditional Roman religion, was there any possibility of conflict. To be sure, about 270 the Neoplatonist philosopher Porphyry produced fifteen books against the Christians, denouncing them for abandoning "the ancestral customs" and "the theology always held by all Greeks and barbarians" in favor of "irrational and unexamined faith."[49] Their sacred books were inconsistent and incredible. They themselves were governed by a senate of matrons and wives which made decisions about priestly office.[50] Thousands of them (fortunately) had recently been put to death.[51]

It may be, as the later historian Socrates stated, that Porphyry was once a Christian at Caesarea but was beaten by his fellows and hence turned away to pagan philosophy.[52] His work seems to have had no effect on the politics of his time, though Christians later insisted on burning it.[53]

[46] R. Marichal in *La Nouvelle Clio* 5 (1953), 119; cf. also D. W. O'Connor, *Peter in Rome* (New York, 1969), 151.
[47] Eusebius *H. E.* 7, 15.
[48] *Ibid.*, 7, 23.
[49] Eusebius, *P. E.* 1, 2, 1-4; 1, 3, 1.
[50] A. von Harnack, *Abhandl. der preuss. Akad. der Wiss.*, 1916, no. 1, Frag. 97.
[51] *Ibid.*, Frag. 36.
[52] Socrates, *H. E.* 3, 23; cf. Frend, *Martyrdom*, 357.
[53] Harnack, *op. cit.*, 33-36.

CHAPTER XII
THE PROBLEM OF GROWTH

I·BUILDINGS AND FUNDS

By the early third century Christians had come to expect a long period of life in the world before the end would finally come. It was necessary to make provision for this life as it had not been so necessary earlier. The whole range of circumstances, for individuals as well as for the communities, had to be considered. It is therefore not surprising that now we hear of infant baptism for the first time, and that schools come into existence for both lower and higher education. Discussions arise concerning the kinds of employment in which Christians can engage. Marriage and family life come to be controlled, at least in theory, by the communities and their leaders. The liturgy, though not essentially changed, tends to be elaborated and to lay more emphasis on thanksgiving than on petition for deliverance. Charity is more highly organized. Finally, provision for Christian burial is made in cemeteries belonging to the Christian communities.

These developments necessarily involved a more carefully organized administrative establishment, with more diversity of functions among the administrators. It was necessary for the bishops or their agents to disburse ever larger sums of money and to deal with larger tracts of land. It was also necessary for them to be concerned with buildings in which Christians could meet for baptism, eucharist, and instruction, Krautheimer has indicated what kind of space was needed: a large assembly room, an anteroom for catechumens and penitents, classrooms, a dining room for the *agapē,* storerooms and living quarters.[1] In the first and second centuries Christians had met in houses. In the third century they still did so, but now they had taken over entire houses, often large, and had remodeled them for church use. Near the city wall of Dura-Europus on the Euphrates were a Jewish community house and, close by, a Christian community house as well. The former building was adapted for Jewish use around 200 and completely rebuilt in 245; the latter was remodeled for Christian use in 231. Both were destroyed in 257 when the wall was reinforced against Persian attack.[2]

Krautheimer points out that community houses of this type probably existed in small towns all over the empire, while in the larger cities they would be set in tenement houses, only occasionally in private houses. It is from this practice that the name *titulus* comes for churches in Rome. "The term *titulus* is a legal one, derived from the marble slab which bore the owner's name and established his title to the property." It is therefore likely that the *tituli*—which still survive—go back to the period before Constantine and point toward the original owners of the community houses.[3]

It should not be supposed that such community houses were found only among Christians. At Ostia there are four shrines of the Persian god Mithras which were constructed in houses during the second and third centuries; another example from the second century has been found at Rome.[4] The Mithraeum at Dura-Europus too was originally part of a house and was gradually expanded and rebuilt over a period of seventy years.[5]

In spite of their considerable size the Christian community houses were relatively inconspicuous, and only occasionally did outsiders enter and threaten worshipers with arrest. Tertullian, describing the life of Christians in the world, argues that they are just like everyone else.[6] The same impression—of an almost Epicurean avoidance of publicity—is provided by an

[1] R. Krautheimer, *Early Christian and Byzantine Architecture* (Baltimore, 1965), 5.

[2] For the church see M. I. Rostovtzeff, ed., *The Excavations at Dura-Europos: Preliminary Report of Fifth Season of Work* (New Haven, 1934), 238-88; C. H. Kraeling, *The Excavations at Dura-Europos: Final Report,* VIII, Part 2: *The Christian Building* (Locust Valley, N.Y., 1967).

[3] Krautheimer, *op. cit.,* 8, with a reference to J. P. Kirsch, *Die römischen Titelkirchen im Altertum* (Bonn, 1918).

[4] M. J. Vermaseren, *Corpus Inscriptionum et Monumentorum Religionis Mithriacae* I (The Hague, 1956), nos. 216, 224, 264, 299, 476.

[5] *Ibid.,* no. 34.

[6] Tertullian, *Apol.* 42, 1-3; cf. *Ad Diognetum* 5.

early Christian inscription from Rome.[7] Here we find a description of the career of a certain Marcus Aurelius Prosenes, who began his advancement under Commodus and, after being procurator in various important offices, became a court chamberlain under Caracalla. On the side of the stone there is further information about him. "Prosenes was received before God . . . in the consulship of Praesens and Extricatus II [217] upon returning to the city from the [Persian] expeditions."[8] Only the expression *receptus ad deum* shows that this court official was a Christian.

II·ADMINISTRATIVE PROBLEMS

From this period when Christianity was rapidly expanding come some notices provided by Origen about the inevitable problems that arose. It must be borne in mind, of course, that Origen was a perfectionist and therefore prone to find fault with actual conditions. On the other hand, he could hardly have spoken as he did without reference to actual situations. In his view, there were many preachers who tried to please their congregations by oratory instead of teaching them.[9] There were bishops, especially in great cities, who imitated governmental officials and terrorized the poor.[10] There were clergy who used church funds for themselves instead of the poor.[11] Tyrannical and ignorant bishops, priests, and deacons could be described as "selling whole churches." Deacons, supposed to administer the church's funds well, were actually dipping into them in order to grow rich from funds given for charitable purposes.[12] Presbyters were engaged in business,[13] and bishops bequeathed their sees to relatives and friends, sometimes paying for popular votes.[14] There is no reason to suppose that such situations existed always or everywhere, but there are sufficient grounds for supposing that church administrators did not always, or perhaps even often, come up to Origen's ideal.

[7] *ILS* 1738 = *ILCV* 3332. Cf. H. U. Instinsky in *Abhandlungen der geistes- und sozialwissenschaftlichen Klasse, Akademie . . . Mainz*, 1964, 113-29.

[8] Under Septimius Severus the Christian Proculus Torpaion was also apparently a chamberlain (Tertullian, *Ad Scap.* 4, 6).

[9] *Ezek. hom.* 3, 3. These texts were collected by A. Harnack in *TU* 42, 3-4 (1918-1919).

[10] *Matt. comm.* 16, 8.

[11] *Ibid.*, 11, 9.

[12] *Ibid.*, 16, 22.

[13] *Ezek. hom.* 7.

[14] *Num. hom.* 22, 4.

III·LEGAL SITUATION

The legal situation of the churches during the second and third centuries is very difficult to determine. Who actually held title to the community houses, the cemeteries, and the common funds? Certainly they were under the bishop's control; Ignatius refers to "the common fund" only when writing to Polycarp of Smyrna. (4, 3), and it was the bishop Zephyrinus who put Callistus in charge of the cemetery at Rome. At Antioch Paul of Samosata apparently held title to "the house of the church."[15] It would appear, however, that the bishop ordinarily delegated control, and perhaps title, in the third century. The *Apostolic Tradition* of Hippolytus describes the deacon as ordained by the bishop alone and for his service; the deacon's function is not to counsel the clergy but to take charge of church property.[16] Since the Roman *tituli* may point toward ownership by nominees of the bishop, we venture to suggest that in the early third century church properties were held in the names of deacons, chosen to represent the bishops. The deacons were thus in a position to confuse church funds with their own, as Origen says they did. But since ultimate control rested with the bishop, bishops themselves could try to bequeath churches by will, as Origen again says they did. The title to church properties when held by bishops and deacons made it excessively easy for these officers to mix up church funds with their own—as Hippolytus and Origen say they did.[17]

The churches themselves, subject to persecution by the state, cannot have owned property, and it may be supposed that their leaders were often attacked not only because of their spiritual power but also because of their ownership of property. It should be noted that the rescript of Gallienus in 261 modified this situation at least in principle. By writing to the bishops, the emperor implicitly acknowledged their legal status as officers of Christian communities.[18] By allowing free access to "the places of worship" and by restoring ownership of the cemeteries to the bishops (and presumably to their nominees) he implicitly recognized the right of Christians to exist within the legal structure of the empire. Within a decade the emperor Aurelian received a petition from the Christians of Antioch and assigned the ownership of church property on the basis of a decision by "the bishops in Italy and Rome."[19] From this time onward new churches were constantly being built.

[15] Eusebius, *H. E.* 7, 30, 19.

[16] *Apost, Trad.* 9, 1-2 (presumably against Callistus).

[17] Bishops who withdrew from their sees in times of persecution presumably left control of properties in the hands of their deacons.

[18] Eusebius, *H. E.* 7, 13; compare the earlier letter from the legate of Arabia to Demetrius of Alexandria (p. 204).

[19] *Ibid.*, 7, 30, 19.

Porphyry criticized the practice, claiming that Christians were erecting very large houses, resembling temples, for their worship; they could just as well have prayed at home.[20]

The legal difficulty remained, at least in theory. Under Roman law, temples and their sites were *res sacrae,* consecrated to the gods by the authority of the Roman people, by a law or a decree of the senate; but the "houses" of the church were not temples. Tombs and cemeteries were *res religiosae,* consecrated to the gods below (*dis Manibus*) by legal burials made by persons competent to make them. Christian cemeteries could not be dedicated to the *dii Manes.*[21]

From a canon of the synod of Ancyra it is clear that, by the early fourth century, ownership of church property was vested in the bishop.[22]

Concerning the properties of the church, whatever the presbyters sold while there was no bishop and is to be recovered, the bishop is to decide whether the buyers should recover the price, given that the income from the property has often repaid them the price.

The presbyters could sell the property in the bishop's absence.

When Constantine restored properties to the Christian community in Africa he stated that they were to be given back to "the Catholic Church in various cities or other places" and then referred to individual "churches."[23] Similarly the joint decree of Constantine and Licinius speaks of returning properties to "the Christians," to the *corpus Christianorum,* and to "the Christians, i.e. corpori et conventiculis eorum.*"[24] This language seems intended to express the universality of the restoration of property. The church as a whole is a *corpus* of which the individual churches or *conventiculi* are parts. In 321 Constantine insisted that property could be left by will to "the most holy and venerable council [*concilium*] of the Catholic church," presumably with individual churches in view.[25]

It was easy enough for ascetically-minded Christians or for Romans of the higher classes in society like Cyprian to denounce the avarice of their Christian confrères. No extant evidence suggests that any church writers really understood the social or the economic situation of the third century. It was a time of anarchy and of military oppression, epitomized by Caracalla's program: "No one but me should have money, so that I may give it to the troops."[26] Taxes constantly increased, while the gold and silver content of money constantly declined. In consequence, the middle class, from which

[20] *Ibid.,* 8, 1, 5; Porphyry, Frag. 76 Harnack.
[21] Cf. M. Kaser, *Das römische Privatrecht* I (Munich, 1955), 320-21.
[22] Ancyra, Can. 15 (pp. 316-17 Hefele-Leclerq).
[23] Eusebius, *H. E.* 10, 5, 16; cf. Kaser, *op. cit.,* II (Munich, 1959), 105-7, 175-76.
[24] Lactantius, *De mort. persec.* 48, 7-10.
[25] *Cod. Theod.* 16, 2, 4; cf. Kaser, *op cit.,* 348; H. Dörries, *Das Selbstzeugnis Kaiser Konstantins* (Göttingen, 1954), 183.
[26] Dio 78, 10, 4; Rostovtzeff, *SEHRE²,* 417.

Christian leaders were generally recruited, was engaged in a struggle for economic survival. Only two social groups, apart from the armed forces, could stand aside from this conflict. The ascetic-minded Christian was free from it, for his needs were severely limited and, in any case, were supplied by others. Origen offers a conspicuous example: he was supported not only by various churches but also by individual benefactors. In addition, upper-class Romans, whose wealth was invested primarily in land, suffered less from currency depreciation than other groups did. Here the case of Cyprian is instructive. Though as a Christian he sold much of his land for the poor, he was able to give his executioner no less than 25 aurei. This is not to say that the life of the rich was marked by security. In the turmoil of 238 the prominent men of Carthage were executed, the temples were looted, and both public and private funds were confiscated. Outside the city, farms and villages were looted and burned,[27] though to some extent, no doubt, landowners were able to provide bribes or ransoms. The "military anarchy" affected all classes, but it affected the very poor and the inconspicuous rich less than others.

[27] Herodian 7, 9, 10-11; Rostovtzeff, op. cit., 457. On the army in the third century cf. R. MacMullen, Soldier and Civilian in the Later Roman Empire (Cambridge, Mass., 1963).

CHAPTER XIII
THE CHURCH AT ROME

By the end of the second century the Christian church at Rome was widely regarded as possessing some kind of primacy among the churches. We have already seen the regard in which Irenaeus held it. Because Rome was the center of the empire, it was natural and easy for travelers and communications to appear there and be sent from there. Relations among churches, like those between Rome and Corinth at the end of the first century, were influenced by the situation of the city of Rome itself. During the episcopate of Eleutherus the Gallican martyrs wrote letters on the peace of the church not only to the brothers in Asia and Phrygia but also to the bishop of Rome; this fact implies that he was involved in Asian affairs. His successor Victor made a vigorous attempt to regularize the date of Easter throughout the Christian world, although Irenaeus urged moderation upon him. In addition, both Victor and Irenaeus had to deal with schismatic and heretical movements at Rome itself.[1]

The relationship between Rome and other churches was not merely ideological but was based on a long tradition of practical aid. The apostle

[1] Eusebius, *H. E.* 5, 3, 4; 5, 24; 5, 20, 1.

Paul himself was able to expect the Roman church to contribute to his support (Rom. 15:24), and the letter of Clement shows that Roman Christians went to prison in place of others and even became slaves in order to feed others (55, 2). Ignatius had to urge the Roman Christians not to obtain his release (*Rom.* 4, 1). Both 1 Clement and Hermas strongly emphasized the virtue of hospitality, and Justin spoke of episcopal aid to orphans, widows, the sick, the poor, prisoners, and visitors to the community (*Apol.* 1, 67, 6). Dionysius of Corinth praised the Roman church because from the beginning it sent aid to many churches for the relief of poverty and, in particular, to help those condemned to work in the mines.[2] Much later, Dionysius of Alexandria apparently referred to gifts being supplied to churches in Syria and Arabia.[3]

Such benefits, provided from the center of the Christian world to the peripheral regions, strongly resemble the similar donations provided by the Roman emperor to outlying cities and regions by means of gifts and endowments. Their importance is emphasized by Aelius Aristides in his famous oration *To Rome,* in which he says to the Romans, "Gifts never cease from you to the cities, and it is not possible to determine who the major beneficiaries have been, because your kindness is the same to all."[4] Just as the Roman state gave support to Roman communities within the empire, so the Roman church provided for Christians throughout the world.

Because of the importance of the Roman church as a center not only of Christian orthodoxy but also of Christian finance, it is not surprising that toward the end of the second century much of our information about it has to do with money matters. The career of the slave Callistus, who later became bishop, is described in full and malicious detail by his enemy Hippolytus, and presumably most of the account is true.[5]

Callistus' master, a Christian freedman who was a minor official under Commodus, was impressed by his financial ability and advanced funds to him so that he could open a bank in the Piscina Publica. Christian widows and others made deposits in the bank, but unfortunately it failed. When his master, under Roman law liable for the bank's debts and contracts, asked for an accounting Callistus headed for Portus and boarded a ship there. Upon the master's arrival the slave tried to commit suicide by jumping into the sea, but he was rescued and put to work at a treadmill in a bakery. There he claimed that he had some credits still on deposit, and his master had him released so that he could collect them. On a Sabbath day he entered a synagogue and created a riot by denouncing Jews who refused to pay debts owed to a Christian. His master tried to protect him, but the urban prefect Seius Fuscianus condemned

---

[2] Eusebius, *H. E.* 4, 23, 10.
[3] *Ibid.,* 7, 5, 2.
[4] J. H. Oliver, *The Ruling Power* (*TAPS*, 43, 4, 1953), 906 (section 98).
[5] Hippolytus, *Ref.* 9, 12, 1-14.

him to hard labor in the Sardinian silver mines.[6] The reason why Hippolytus insists upon Callistus' vicissitudes is apparently related to the *Apostolic Tradition* (10, 2) where we read that a confessor who was "by chance derided for the Name" does not automatically become a presbyter but has to be ordained. Perhaps there was some doubt, at least in Hippolytus' mind, as to the regularity of Callistus' orders.

Between 189–190 and 192 the emperor's pro-Christian concubine Marcia summoned Victor, the new bishop of Rome, to her presence and asked him for a list of the Christians who had been deported to Sardinia. Under her influence Commodus issued a rescript for their release; she gave it to a Roman presbyter with orders to sail for the island and make it effective. There he found Callistus—whose name, not surprisingly, was not on Victor's list—and on his own initiative had him released with the other Christians. When Victor heard that Callistus had returned to Rome both he and the slave's master were greatly perturbed, but neither one took steps to send him back. Callistus was now accepted as a martyr, and Victor sent him to Anzio with a monthly pension from the church's funds. In 199 Zephyrinus became bishop. He recalled Callistus from Anzio, ordained him, and placed him in charge of the Roman clergy, presumably as archdeacon. In addition, he put him in charge of "the cemetery," the principal asset of the Roman church and presumably the cemetery now called Sancti Calixti.[7]

According to Hippolytus, neither Zephyrinus nor Callistus was worthy of office in the church. Zephyrinus was "untrained, illiterate, and without experience of the church's rules"; he took bribes and loved money.[8] His situation was therefore quite different from that of Hippolytus himself—it would appear. "When a man is worthy of receiving grace from God and is found to be wiser than the rest, at once all converge to hate him, persecute him, insult him, dishonor him, revile him, disdain him, so that thus they may seem to be something when they are nothing." Behind this use of Pauline language to describe Daniel lies Hippolytus' opinion of himself, presumably an unsuccessful candidate for the episcopate.[9]

It is clear, however, that in Zephyrinus' time financial matters were important at Rome. A leading heretic was Theodotus "the banker," who with others was able to supply a heretical bishop with a monthly salary of 150 denarii.[10] Among the professions forbidden to more orthodox Christians banking was not included.[11]

[6] This rigorist prefect (*homo severus, SHA Pertinax,* 4, 3) was admired by the rigorist Tertullian (*Ad nat.* 1, 16, 13-19).

[7] See G. LaPiana in *HTR* 18 (1925), 201-77; Hippolytus, *Ref.* 9, 12, 14.

[8] Hippolytus, *Ref.* 9, 11, 1. According to Acts 4:13, however, the apostles Peter and John were regarded as "illiterate and untrained," as were the Old Testament prophets according to Theophilus (*Ad Autol.* 2, 35).

[9] Hippolytus, *Dan. comm.* 3, 16; cf. Gal. 6:3, 2:6, and 2 Cor. 10:10.

[10] Eusebius, *H. E.* 5, 28, 8-12.

[11] Hippolytus, *Apost. Trad.* 16.

The early career of Callistus thus illuminates not only his own history but also that of the Roman church in his time. Both Victor and Zephyrinus were obviously concerned more with administrative prob!ems than with the theological scholarship of a man like Hippolytus, and the church as a whole shared their attitude. Under Callistus' influence, Zephyrinus regarded both Sabellius, who nearly identified the Son with the Father, and Hippolytus, who upheld a traditional Logos doctrine, as extremists. Zephyrinus' own creedal statements—as quoted by Hippolytus—were not remarkably acute, but they were not his chief concern.

After Zephyrinus' death in 217 it was Callistus, now about sixty years old, who was elected bishop of Rome, and he immediately excommunicated Sabellius, presumably contenting himself with no more than a warning to Hippolytus. He was concerned with the unity and the continuation of the church. Hippolytus, like other rigorists, found his policy intolerable.[12] First, Callistus declared that no sin was unforgivable and that he had the apostolic right to forgive all. Second, he admitted into the clergy men who had been married twice or even three times, and permitted clerics to marry. As authority he quoted Romans 14:4—"Who are you to pass judgment on the servant of another? It is before his own master that he stands or falls"—and described the church as containing both wheat and weeds (Matt. 13:29–30). Like Noah's ark, it was full of animals both clean and unclean. Third, he permitted women of high rank to live in *contubernium* with men either slave or free. Fourth, he permitted a second baptism, presumably for sinners being reconciled to the church. Three of these policy decisions obviously had to do only with the internal life of the Christian community. It was no concern of the state whether or not Christians were baptized twice, had all their sins forgiven, or employed married clergy. The relations between slaves and aristocratic women presented more difficulty.

Roman law, approvingly cited by Tertullian,[13] explicitly forbade marriage between slaves and free persons. In A.D. 52 a decree of the senate held that if a free woman even cohabited with a slave the owner could claim her and her subsequent offspring as his slaves.[14] As for members of senatorial families, a Lex Iulia of 18 B.C. forbade them to marry freedmen, actors, and children of actors. Under Marcus Aurelius a decree of the senate forbade the marriage of a senator's daughter or niece with a freedman. Septimius Severus forbade the marriage of a slaveholder and her freedman.[15] Obviously all this legislation was made necessary by the breaking down of class lines, though we should not make too much of the marriages between members of the imperial family

---

[12] Hippolytus, *Ref.* 9, 12, 20-25.
[13] *Ad uxorem* 2, 8; see A. Beck, *Römisches Recht bei Tertullian und Cyprian* (Halle, 1930), 95.
[14] M. Kaser, *Das römische Privatrecht*, I (Munich, 1955), 272.
[15] *Dig.* 23, 2, 62, 1; R. Leonhard in *RE* IV, 835-38.

and men of equestrian rank.[16] The gulf between royalty and the equestrians was by no means as great as between the upper classes and freedmen or slaves.

Callistus did not propose to violate the law. He simply recognized the existence of *contubernium* and insisted that there could be only one partner. His decision was undoubtedly influenced by Caracalla's decree of 212 or 214 by which Roman citizenship was conferred on most free persons within the empire. Perhaps his own slave origin played a part.[17]

For rigorists like Hippolytus and Tertullian, now a Montanist, Callistus' position was completely unacceptable. Hippolytus broke with the church and called it "the school of Callistus"; Tertullian denounced Callistus in his bitter treatise entitled *De pudicitia*. It would appear that Hippolytus set himself up as a rival bishop of Rome and occupied himself with his *Paschal Calendar* which gives the true astronomical full moons for the years 217–223. Since these years mark the episcopate of Callistus, one may suspect that he found some fault with Callistus' date for Easter. In any event, the calendar is engraved on the statue of Hippolytus which devoted admirers erected. After Callistus' death in 222 Hippolytus prepared his *Refutation of All Heresies,* a learned treatise in ten books in which most of the heresies are ingeniously derived from Greek philosophical doctrines. The peak of heresy is of course reached with the account of Callistus' career.

It has been suggested that Hippolytus' "outlook towards the State and the governing classes" may gradually have mellowed, since he dedicated his treatise *On the resurrection* to Julia Mamaea, mother of the emperor Alexander Severus.[18] Conceivably his attitude toward the Catholic bishop of Rome also changed. If the wording of a late account can be trusted—that "the bishop Pontianus and the presbyter Hippolytus were banished and deported to Sardinia" in 235—it may be that he had been reconciled to the church.[19]

Callistus was succeeded by Urban (222–230), Urban by Pontianus (230–235). Of Urban nothing is known, and of Pontianus only that at the request of Demetrius of Alexandria he convoked a synod to join in the condemnation of Origen. According to Jerome,[20] only the churches of Palestine, Arabia, Phoenicia, and Achaea took Origen's side. We do not know whether the criticism was based on his theology or on the presumed irregularity of his ordination, though Jerome explicitly says there were no theological grounds.

After the deportation of Pontianus, Anteros became bishop but held office only for a few weeks in 235. His successor Fabian was a layman, according to Eusebius elected and consecrated after a dove had settled on his head.[21] With

---

[16] As does S. Mazzarino, *The End of the Ancient World* (New York, 1966), 129-32.
[17] For a good sociological study of Callistus cf. H. Gülzow in *ZNW* 58 (1967), 102-21.
[18] Frend, *Martyrdom,* 377.
[19] Cf. L. Duchesne, *Etude sur le Liber Pontificalis* (Paris, 1877), 129.
[20] *Ep.* 33, 4 (*PL* 22, 447).
[21] Eusebius, *H. E.* 6, 29.

this scene Instinsky compares the popular enthusiasm accompanying the funeral of Pertinax, early in the reign of Septimius Severus.[22] The descent of the dove, however, as Eusebius himself observes, resembles what took place at the baptism of Jesus according to the gospels. The motif is primarily Christian. Fabian's administrative ability was admired not only by Cyprian of Carthage but also by the Roman clergy whom he ruled.[23] He joined Donatus of Carthage in condemning a heretical bishop, and to him, as to many others, Origen addressed defenses of his own orthodoxy.[24] To judge from the situation obtaining a little later, it was he who divided the districts of Rome among seven deacons and appointed seven subdeacons to assist them. On January 20, 250, he fell victim to the persecution under Decius.

The third-century bishops of Rome after Fabian are known chiefly from their correspondence with the churches of Carthage, Alexandria, and Antioch. From a letter of Cornelius we learn something of the size of the Roman community in 251. It is stated that under the jurisdiction of the Roman bishop were 46 presbyters, 7 deacons, 7 subdeacons, 42 acolytes, 52 exorcists, readers and doorkeepers, and more than 1,500 widows and persons in distress. All these were "supported by the grace and benevolence of the Master" or, in other words, from the common funds of the church.[25] Presumably as at contemporary Carthage[26] the clergy received monthly salaries. The church had evidently developed beyond the point at which Montanist evangelists could be criticized for receiving salaries. Its expansion had made necessary full-time work under supervision.

It is a question how much money was required for the support of the Roman church and its local benevolence. Harnack guessed at between half a million and a million sesterces a year,[27] but since both gold and silver coins were steadily deteriorating it is hard to guess what was hapening to the alloyed sestertius.[28] Presumably most if not all of the funds came from the monthly donations provided by some 30,000 to 50,000 Christians in the city.

The episcopate of Cornelius, like that of Callistus, was marked by division within the church. He had been elected by the majority, but he had to contend with a rival, Novatian, who like Hippolytus represented the rigorists, this time in regard to those who had lapsed during the Decian persecution. After consecration as Cornelius' rival, Novatian sent letters to Cyprian of Carthage, Dionysius of Alexandria, and Fabius of Antioch. Cyprian immediately denounced him;[29] Dionysius urged him to withdraw from his posi-

---

[22] H. U. Instinsky, *Bischofsstuhl und Kaiserthron* (Munich, 1955); cf. Dio 75, 4, 3-5.
[23] Cyprian, *Ep.* 9, 1; 30, 5.
[24] *Ibid.*, 59, 10; Eusebius, *H. E.* 6, 36, 4; cf. Jerome, *Ep.* 84, 10 (*PL* 22, 751).
[25] Eusebius, *H. E.* 6, 43, 11.
[26] Cyprian, *Ep.* 34, 6; earlier monthly collections: Tertullian, *Apol.* 39, 5.
[27] Harnack, *Mission*, p. 157.
[28] M. Grant, *Roman Imperial Money* (London, 1954), pp. 241-45.
[29] *Ep.* 50.

tion;[30] and since Fabius of Antioch was wavering Dionysius also wrote to him.[31] In addressing Fabius, Cornelius himself gave the statistics mentioned above and also described the consecration of Novatian as extremely irregular. Apparently he sent to a distant region of Italy for three "rustic and very simple" bishops; at Rome his followers got them drunk and they consecrated Novatian, though one of them later confessed his sin to the church.[32] Later in the year a synod of clergy including sixty bishops was convened at Rome and Novatian was excommunicated.

In two years' time, however, Cornelius himself was banished from Rome by the emperor Gallus, and his successor Lucius, bishop for eight months, is known only from a letter of Cyprian hailing his return from exile and another referring to him and Cornelius as martyrs—presumably confessors.[33] During the almost equally brief episcopate of Stephen (254–257) significant difficulties arose between Rome and the eastern churches. At first Cyprian was concerned when Stephen apparently supported an ex-bishop who, having obtained a certificate of sacrifice during the Decian persecution, had resigned but was now trying to be reinstated.[34] Next he advised Stephen to excommunicate Marcian, the Novatianist bishop of Arles.[35] Serious divisions arose in regard to those who had been baptized by heretics. Stephen, presumably supported not only by Italy but also by Gaul, advocated admitting them to communion after the imposition of hands. This view was opposed by most churches in Asia and Africa, while Dionysius of Alexandria advocated baptizing only the adherents of the more extreme heresies.[36] By the end of 256 the situation deteriorated, and Stephen proceeded to excommunicate the churches of Asia Minor and Africa, referring to Cyprian as "a false Christ and a false apostle and a traitor."[37] Dionysius of Alexandria urged him to respect the peace and unity of the eastern churches and later wrote his successors to the same effect.[38]

Stephen died in 257, and his successor Xystus (Sixtus) II was bishop of Rome for only a year; he restored the peace of the church during that time. In August 258 he entered the cemetery of Praetextatus in violation of a new imperial decree and was immediately put to death. Because of the severity of the persecution, no successor to him was elected until July 20, 260, when news of the emperor's death apparently reached Rome. During the years between 258 and 313 the deaths of the martyr apostles Peter and Paul were

[30] Eusebius, *H. E.* 6, 45.
[31] *H. E.* 6, 44.
[32] *H. E.* 6, 43, 8-12.
[33] *Ep.* 61; 68, 5.
[34] *Ep.* 67.
[35] *Ep.* 68, 2.
[36] Basil of Caesarea (*PG* 32, 664); cf. C. L. Feltoe, *The Letters and other Remains of Dionysius of Alexandria* (Cambridge, 1904), 41 n. 1, 48-49.
[37] Cyprian (Firmilian), *Ep.* 75, 25.
[38] Eusebius, *H. E.* 7, 5-9.

commemorated in the catacombs of San Sebastiano on the Via Appia, and it may possibly be that their relics were momentarily placed there during the persecution.[39] A graffito in these catacombs suggests that they were publicly restored to the church within a month after Dionysius' accession.

Dionysius, already a presbyter at Rome under Stephen, was a wise administrator and in his time the power and prestige of Rome steadily advanced. After receiving complaints from Egypt or Libya he investigated the orthodoxy of Dionysius of Alexandria and apparently dropped the question after Dionysius answered the charges against him. In 268 the Antiochene synod which condemned Paul of Samosata addressed its encyclical letter first to Dionysius of Rome, second to Maximus of Alexandria.[40]

His successor Felix (269–274) joined the other bishops in condemning Paul, and his position was reinforced in 272 when the emperor Aurelian recovered Antioch from Zenobia of Palmyra and expelled Paul, assigning the church property in the city to whatever candidate was recognized by the bishops in Rome and Italy[41]—of whom the bishop of Rome was the chief.

Eutychianus (274–283) is no more than a name; Eusebius thought he was bishop for less than a year.[42] Nothing at all is known of Gaius, perhaps because Eusebius decided not "to hand down to memory their [the bishops'] dissensions and unnatural conduct toward one another before the persecution,"[43] perhaps because nothing significant occurred during his episcopate. Gainus died in the spring of 296; his successor was Marcellinus, "whom the persecution overtook."[44] The evidence for the life and death of Marcellinus is remarkably confusing. Later Donatists alleged that he had somehow compromised with the authorities during the persecution, and it is at least clear that he died a natural death, probably on January 15, 304. Thereafter, although persecution at Rome ended in 305, there was no episcopal election until April 310. The church seems to have been under the charge of presbyters during the interval. The newly elected bishop Eusebius held office very briefly and was banished to Sicily, where he died probably on August 17, 310. Nearly a year later Miltiades became bishop, and it was he whom the emperor Maxentius soon authorized to recover the confiscated properties of the Roman church.[45]

[39] Cf. J. Toynbee and J. W. Perkins, *The Shrine of St. Peter and the Vatican Excavations* (New York, 1957), 167-82.
[40] Eusebius, *H. E.* 7, 30, 2.
[41] *Ibid.*, 7, 30, 19.
[42] *Ibid.*, 7, 32.
[43] Eusebius, *H. E.* 8, 2, 2.
[44] *Ibid.*, 7, 32, 1.
[45] Cf. E. H. Röttges in *Zeitschrift für katholische Theologie* 78 (1956), 385-420.

CHAPTER XIV
THE CHURCH IN AFRICA

Practically nothing is known of the church in Roman Africa during the second century; the first literary notices about it occur in the treatises of Tertullian of Carthage, and he did not write before the last decade of the century. One would suppose that Christianity reached Carthage at an early date, however, in view of the importance of the city. Herodian, writing in the third century, says that it was surpassed only by Rome and contended with Alexandria for second place in the empire.[1] The churches of Africa first came to the attention of the state in 180, when according to Tertullian the proconsul Vigellius Saturninus "first drew the sword upon us,"[2] and put to death twelve Christians at Carthage.

Tertullian himself was certainly a Roman of Carthage, though he came to be among those whom Ramsay MacMullen calls "enemies of the Roman order." Trained both in Latin and in Greek, he was brought up as a pagan student of rhetoric and of law. Two centuries later, Jerome said that Tertullian's father had been a proconsular centurion, but he was probably drawing

[1] Herodian 7, 6, 1.
[2] *Ad Scapulam* 3, 4.

an inference from a faulty text of the *Apology*.[3] The thirty-two treatises now extant were composed over a period of about twenty-five years after 197 or so. They reflect his initial concern with apologetics directed to the pagan world and his increasing emphasis on moral and theological issues within the church —which he left for the rigorous sect of the Montanists.

Naturally, the earliest works of Tertullian reveal no controversies within the church to which he had become a convert. His purpose was to show that Christianity was unjustly treated as a disloyal movement when Christians were imprisoned or threatened with imprisonment under such circumstances as the vendettas accompanying the rise of Septimius Severus to supreme authority.[4] The little treatise *De testimonio animae* was to indicate how natural conversion to Christianity was. During the next fourteen years, however, Tertullian entered into vigorous conflict not only with various heretical groups apparently flourishing at Carthage but also with the many "moderates" within the church there. The first and most important of the antiheretical writings was *De praescriptione haereticorum,* in which he argued that a preliminary decision or "stipulation" in favor of the church, the possessor of the scriptures, meant that heretics could not use them in support of their views. Heresy is unchristian, for it is based on Greek philosophy.[5] Tertullian did not let this point stand in the way of his own use of philosophy, however.

At an early date Tertullian was strongly influenced by the martyrdom of Vibia Perpetua and others in 203. According to the acts of her martyrdom, a vision of paradise revealed to the martyrs that the Carthaginian bishop Optatus and a presbyter, who cast themselves at their feet and asked for forgiveness. Angels told the bishop to correct his people and put an end to the dissension among them.[6] The constancy of the martyrs and their superiority to the clergy were themes which became important to him. He intended to reform the church of Carthage, not only by debate but by producing treatises.

In an early work *De spectaculis* he insisted that Christians could not attend games or theatrical performances, and indignantly rejected the argument that like the sun, God observes spectacles and is not contaminated;[7] evidently Christians at Carthage were accustomed to attend such shows. His treatise *De oratione* contrasts the Lord's Prayer with the *vacua observatio* of various rites.[8] In the book *De baptismo* he ostensibly attacks the heretical rejection

---

[3] *De vir. illustr.* 53; Tertullian, *Apol.* 9, 2 (reading *patriae nostrae,* not *patris nostri*).

[4] Later he noted that the emperor favored Christians (*Ad Scap.* 4, 5-6).

[5] *De praescr. haer.* 7, 9: *Quid ergo Athenis et Hierosolymis?* The rabbis too were aware of the difference between Jerusalemites and Athenians, but they took it less seriously; see the stories collected in *Midrash Rabbah* on Lam. 1:1, 4-14 (*Midrash Rabbah: Lamentations,* tr. A. Cohen, London, 1939, 74-80).

[6] *Mart. Perpet.* 13 (p. 41 Knopf-Krüger).

[7] *De spect.* 20, 1.

[8] *De orat.* 15, 1.

of baptism, but he is equally concerned with denouncing heretical baptisms, as well as the claim that it is faith, not baptism, that matters.[9] He also attacks the rather novel practice of baptizing infants.[10] Similarly in his book *De paenitentia* he insists that rigorous penance, not a simple affirmation, is necessary for forgiveness.[11] Evidently there were Carthaginian Christians who disagreed.

Several of his writings were concerned with questions raised by women. No feminist, Tertullian denounced women who wore expensive clothing or ornaments of gold or silver, or even pearls.[12] Some of them claimed that chastity was a physical matter, not one of adornment. Others claimed that they dressed conventionally so that "the Name" would not be slandered. Still others said that they did not need approval by men (like Tertullian?); God knew their character.[13] He was not convinced. In writing ostensibly to his wife he attacked the custom of remarrying after the death of one's spouse, ridiculing the desire of men for offspring and the claim of women that they wanted intercourse.[14] Worse than second marriage was marriage to a pagan husband. Such a man might let his Christian wife be a Christian, but he intended to take her dowry away. In some cases a "matron" might remarry simply to enjoy a large house. This was wrong.[15]

In a little book written about 209 Tertullian claimed that unlike most people he was wearing the old-fashioned Punic cloak, not the Roman toga; but this venture into local patriotism does not seem to have lasted long.[16]

About the same time he completed the first three books of his five-volume treatise *Adversus Marcionem*. This was the third version of the work, presumably begun about 200. He had been dissatisfied with the style of the first version, and had lost the second when, not yet given to the copyists, it was stolen by a Christian who became an apostate.[17] The first three books argue that (I) monotheism, not dualism, is tenable on philosophical and scriptural grounds, (II) the "good God" of Marcion is the Creator, and (III) Christ is the Savior predicted by the prophets and sent by the Creator. Somewhat later, as he came closer to Montanism, he added two more books to prove his case from Marcion's own Gospel and Apostle.

His disaffection from the Catholic Church of Carthage was now becoming more intense. As he wrote a book *De resurrectione mortuorum* he could cite an oracle of the Montanist prophetess Prisca;[18] as he wrote an *Exhortation to*

[9] *De bapt.* 1, 2; 15, 1-2; 13, 1.
[10] *Ibid.*, 18, 4.
[11] *De paen.* 5, 10.
[12] *De cult. fem.* 1, 5-6.
[13] *Ibid.*, 2, 1, 2; 2, 11, 3.
[14] *Ad uxorem* 1, 5, 1; 1, 6, 1.
[15] *Ibid.*, 2, 5, 1-3; 2, 8, 2.
[16] *De pallio.*
[17] *Adv. Marc.* 1, 1, 1-2; cf. 2, 1, 1.
[18] *De res.* 11, 2.

chastity he could speak of her as "holy."[19] Irritated by the Catholic argument that only clerics were forbidden to remarry, he replied that under certain circumstances the laity were priests and could offer the eucharist and baptize.[20]

The death of Septimius Severus in 211 brought the threat of renewed persecution, and Tertullian welcomed it. He vehemently praised the action of a soldier who refused a military crown. Others thought the soldier was rash and eager to make trouble for himself and other Christians. (Among the critics, it appears, was the bishop of Carthage.) They asked such questions as "Where are we forbidden to wear crowns?" and "Why rely on unwritten tradition?" Their claim, quite alien to Tertullian's mind, was that "what is not prohibited is permitted."[21]

Around the same time he produced a diatribe *De idololatria*. First he attacked those who claimed they needed employment or that continuing in their work was recommended by Paul; they thought they could make idols if they did not worship them.[22] Astrologers apparently regarded their work as quite different from idolatry. Tertullian attacked them and, as well, teachers of literature, in spite of their insistence on their need to make a living.[23] Christians concerned with idols claimed, like women of fashion, that they were keeping "the name" from slander by conforming.[24] Tertullian agreed with neither group. He found scandalous the provision of lamps and laurels in festal seasons, along with a mention of "render to Caesar."[25] On the other hand, he was still willing to admit the propriety of traditional Roman family ceremonies, or the necessary semireligious activities of slaves and officials.[26] Military service raised greater problems, as did anything connected with taking an oath.[27]

Up to this point, in spite of his increasing rigor, Tertullian had not really broken with the principle he had set forth in the *Apology* of 197: Christians are no different from anyone else.[28] In 212, however, persecution began in Mauretania and he addressed a defense of the Christians to a Roman administrator once more. In the course of it he had occasion to review the Roman policy as to Christians in Africa. Vigellius Saturninus had been the first persecutor, but four later proconsuls had released Christians brought before them.[29] These precedents, along with the example of the former emperor

[19] *Exh. cast.* 10, 5.
[20] *Ibid.*, 7, 3.
[21] *De cor.* 1, 4-6; 2, 4; 3, 1.
[22] *De idolol.* 6, 2.
[23] *Ibid.*, 9-10; 12, 2.
[24] *Ibid.*, 14, 1.
[25] *Ibid.*, 15, 1-3.
[26] *Ibid.*, 16-17.
[27] *Ibid.*, 19-23.
[28] *Apol.* 42, 1-3.
[29] *Ad. Scap.* 3, 4; 4, 3. The last proconsul mentioned, C. Valerius Pudens, was apparently in office just before Scapula; cf. B. E. Thomasson, *Die Statthalter der römischen Provinzen Nordafrikas* (Lund, 1960), II, 110-11.

Septimius Severus, suggested that a *modus vivendi* was possible. But Tertullian was in no mood for any compromise. His pamphlet ended with a threat.

The persecution he envisaged actually did take place, and in the face of it many African clerics favored fleeing from one city to another. Tertullian himself had once thought it might be better to flee than to deny one's faith.[30] Now he insisted on standing fast, and on not paying money for "redemption."[31] In his treatise on the subject he began by mentioning the Paraclete of the Montanists, and along the way he cited the authority of a Montanist oracle.[32] In this renewed persecution he had decided to take his stand with those who shared his rigorist views.

A doctrinal treatise around the same time spoke explicitly of Montanus and the prophetesses Prisca and Maximilla. It was an attack not only on an Asian theologian named Praxeas but also on the policies of the bishops of Rome, leaders of the Catholics whom Tertullian was beginning to call "psychics," men possessed of mere soul, not spirit.[33] Presumably he finished his books against Marcion about now, for in the fourth book the same usage of "psychic" appears.[34] He also finished his semiphilosophical treatise *De anima,* in which at one point he relied on the vision of a (Montanist) "sister" in church, at another on the revelations of the Paraclete.[35] From this point onward he wrote none but Montanist treatises. He insisted that virgins had to wear veils in all public places, appealing to Christ's truth (and the example of Arabian women) against custom. An angel had given similar instructions to a Montanist sister.[36] In his treatise *De monogamia* he fiercely denounced the "psychics" who still permitted remarriage. In the book *De ieiuniis* he attacked the Catholic laxity which viewed the Montanist "stations" and "dry meals" as pointless novelties introduced in imitation of oriental religions.[37] And in the *De pudicitia* he attacked a Catholic bishop who claimed to forgive such sins as adultery and fornication. Tertullian appealed to the justice of God against Catholic emphasis on his mercy, and denied that martyrs could forgive sins.[38]

To rely on Tertullian for a picture of the church life of Carthage—though we are forced to do so in the absence of much other evidence—is to be given a drastically distorted picture of church life there. Tertullian was alienated from any society in which he found himself. He claimed to have rejected Graeco-Roman culture when he turned to the church, though he did not do

---

[30] *Ad uxorem* I, 3, 4.
[31] *De fuga* 5-6; II, I; 12, I.
[32] *Ibid.,* I, I; 9, 4.
[33] *Adv. Prax.* I, 5-6.
[34] *Adv. Marc.* 4, 22, 5.
[35] *De anima* 9, 4; 58, 8.
[36] *De virg. vel.* I, I; 2, 2-3; 17, 2.
[37] *De ieiun.* 2, 4; 9-10.
[38] *De pudic.* I, 6; 2, I; 22, I.

so.[39] As a Christian he viewed nearly all his fellows as compromisers, unwilling to accept the full rigor of the gospel as he understood it. Though he was married he longed for celibacy. Though he was not a martyr he exalted martyrdom. He detested heresy and schism but became a militant Montanist. His love of paradox, evident throughout his writings, was thus reflected in his life.

He tells a good deal about the liturgical life of Carthaginian Christians, but only a passing allusion reveals that they were settled enough to possess a cemetery.[40] From his writings we should never guess that in his time, apparently about 220, the bishop Agrippinus convoked a synod of some seventy bishops from Africa and Numidia to deal with the problem of heretical baptism.[41] Several inferences may be drawn from this meeting. First, the influence of Tertullian may still have been strong even among the "psychics." In his treatise De ieiuniis, written shortly before 220, he praises the synods characeristic of the church in Greece.[42] Before this point, it appears, no synods had met in Africa. In addition, the synod's decision to rebaptize ex-heretics was in agreement with his views. Finally, the fact that the synod had to be convened suggests that diversity was still present among the African bishops, and that the problem was important because so many heretics were moving toward Catholicism.

It is easy enough to criticize Tertullian for his lack of balance and even common sense. Without men like him, however, the Christian movement might well have been assimilated to Graeco-Roman culture and might have become no more than one more religion in the real melting pot of third-century syncretism.

Of Agrippinus' immediate successors at Carthage we know nothing, but by the time when Fabian was bishop of Rome (236–250) his colleague at Carthage was named Donatus. The two bishops exchanged letters concerning a heretic who had been condemned by a synod of ninety bishops at Carthage.[43] On Donatus' death in 248 he was succeeded by a wealthy ex-lawyer named Thascius Caecilius Cyprianus. Though Cyprian had been a Christian for only two years, he had shown his devotion to the church by selling some of his estates before baptism and giving the proceeds to the poor; after baptism he also sold some gardens for the same purpose, though friends bought them back for him. Soon a deacon, then a presbyter, he was elected bishop by the Christian people of Carthage and confirmed in his position by the neighboring bishops, over the opposition organized by five presbyters of the city.[44] During the short time before the Decian persecution he occupied himself with main-

---

[39] For detailed proof cf. J. H. Waszink, Tertullian de Anima (Amsterdam, 1947).
[40] Ad Scap. 3, 1.
[41] Cyprian, Ep. 71, 4; 73, 3; cf. C. J. Hefele and H. Leclerq, Histoire des conciles I (Paris, 1907), 155-56.
[42] De ieiun. 13, 6.
[43] Ep. 59, 10.
[44] Ep. 43, 1.

taining discipline within the church; he forbade an actor to practice or teach dramatics and he denounced the common custom of "spiritual marriages."[45] When the persecution began he withdrew from the city in order to maintain his administrative work and to avoid endangering others. This step aroused much criticism, although as he pointed out his property was confiscated.[46] After the martyrdom of Fabian at Rome some Roman confessors attacked Cyprian in a letter sent to Carthage; he replied by questioning its authenticity.[47] In many further letters he tried to maintain discipline and to prevent premature reconciliation. Copies of thirteen of these were sent to the Roman clergy.[48]

The basic problem had to do with the treatment of the numerous Christians who had offered sacrifice or had bought certificates of sacrifice. At Carthage the most prominent Christians, including the "confessors," favored immediate restoration for the lapsed. At Rome, however, under the leadership of the presbyter Novatian, the tendency was to exclude them from the church. After Easter in 251 Cyprian returned to Carthage in order to hold a synod dealing with the urgent question. Before it, however, were laid documents from Rome announcing the election of Cornelius as Fabian's successor and others protesting his election and announcing the election of Novatian as a rival bishop. Since a schism in the great church of Rome was bound to have disastrous consequences elsewhere, Cyprian took great pains to ascertain the validity of Cornelius' election and to set forth his doctrine of the unity of the Catholic Church, sending his treatise on the subject to Rome.

In this treatise he argued that the church's unity was based on the promise of Jesus to Peter in Matthew 16:18–19.[49] At this point, however, the manuscripts diverge. In one version there is a quotation from John 21:17, Jesus' command to Peter to feed his sheep, followed by insistence upon the sole primacy of Peter and the one church (of Rome) and the one *cathedra Petri,* on which the church was established. In the other, the quotation is from John 20:21–23, addressed to all the apostles; the argument is that they participated equally in honor and power. The primacy of Peter is not mentioned elsewhere in the treatise, and since the sixteenth century the words *primatus Petro datur* have been viewed as interpolations. More recent study of the manuscripts and of Cyprian's life suggests that this is not the case. At the time he wrote the treatise he was willing to use expressions such as *locus Petri*[50] and *cathedra Petri,* and to speak of Rome as the *ecclesia principalis unde unitas sacerdotalis exorta est.*[51] It is highly probable that Cyprian

---

[45] *Epp.* 2; 4.
[46] *Ep.* 66, 4.
[47] *Epp.* 8-9.
[48] *Ep.* 20, 2.
[49] *De unitate* 4.
[50] *Ep.* 55, 8.
[51] *Ep.* 59, 14 (cf. Tertullian, *De praescr.* 36, 2-3).

first exalted Petrine primacy but, in the course of later struggles with Stephen, bishop of Rome, altered his own text.[52]

In the spring of 252 a persecution seemed to be impending under the new emperor Gallus, and a council of forty-two bishops met at Carthage on May 15. Their letter now readmitted all the *lapsi* who had continued to be penitent, though they had to obtain readmission from their bishop.[53]

Later in the same year the frontiers of Numidia were opened up by the Berbers; as Archbishop Benson put it, "their front line reached from Thubunae on the salt-marsh to the terebinth forests of Tucca, and they deported large numbers of the Christians of no less than eight sees."[54] Cyprian replied to a letter from the eight Numidian bishops by sending 100,000 sesterces as a grant-in-aid, asking for prayers for the donors and for the African bishops and presbyters.[55]

In 253 a synod of sixty-seven bishops met at Carthage to adjudicate the cases of a lapsed presbyter and a bishop. In the case of the presbyter they censured him for not consulting with the laity; the lapsed bishop was not readmitted because of his unworthy character.[56]

At the end of 254 another synod was held, this time in regard to the lapsed Spanish bishops Basilides and Martialis. They had been restored by Stephen of Rome and the churches appealed to Cyprian against this decision. The synod was attended by only thirty-seven bishops, eighteen of whom had not been present at the synod of 252. This relatively small group took a stand against Stephen, claiming that he was ignorant of the situation and had contradicted the ruling made by the "pacific and just" Cornelius.[57]

Meanwhile the plague to which Cyprian had devoted a brief treatise (*De mortalitate*) had struck at Carthage and elsewhere, and another synod in 255 was attended by only thirty-one bishops, who agreed against Stephen that all heretics had to be baptized, or rebaptized. "No one can be baptized outside the church."[58] This decision was communicated to eighteen Numidian bishops, already in agreement, and to Quintus, a bishop in Mauretania.[59]

In the spring of 256 bishops both African and Numidian to the number of seventy-one met at Carthage and reaffirmed their position against Stephen, sending him not only this decision but also copies of their previous letters to the Numidians and to Quintus.[60] Soon afterwards the Mauretanian bishop Iubaianus sent Cyprian a document in which the validity of Marcionite

[52] M. Bévenot, *St. Cyprian's De unitate chap. 4 in the Light of the Manuscripts* (London, 1938).
[53] *Ep.* 57.
[54] *DCB* I 747.
[55] *Ep.* 62.
[56] *Epp.* 64-65.
[57] *Ep.* 67, 5-6.
[58] *Ep.* 70, 1.
[59] *Ep.* 72, 1; *Epp.* 70-71.
[60] *Ep.* 73, 1; *Epp.* 70-72.

baptism was recognized on the ground that it was in the name of Jesus Christ.[61] The bishop of Carthage replied by sending Iubaianus a dossier of documents. When Iubaianus avowed himself convinced, Cyprian convoked a synod of no fewer than eighty-seven bishops from Africa, Numidia, and Mauretania; presbyters, deacons, and many of the people attended the meeting on September 1, 256. All the bishops spoke, in order of seniority, and all agreed. Some echoed what Cyprian had already written; others used language derived from Tertullian and now used against Rome.[62] Nemesianus, a Numidian bishop, described heretics in terms which Stephen was to use, or was using, of Cyprian himself.[63]

In so far as we can judge from the information we have, this synod demonstrated the firm control which Cyprian exercised in Africa. Of the eighty-seven bishops present, forty-two had not attended the synods of 252, 254, and 255. There was a solid core, however, of those who had been present at all three (fifteen bishops), and though few Numidians were present Cyprian could rely upon the support of the overwhelming majority. Indeed, everyone who spoke agreed with him.

The outbreak of persecution in 257 brought the controversy to an end for the moment, though the problems involved were to reappear in the Donatist struggle. Under the first edict of persecution, the proconsul of Africa simply banished Cyprian from Carthage (just as Dionysius was banished from Alexandria). Eleven months later a new proconsul allowed him to return to his home. After learning of the martyrdom of Xystus of Rome (August 6, 258) he was aware that his own end could not be far off. On September 13 he was arrested. The investigation was very brief. Cyprian stated that he was the *papa* of the Christians and refused to offer sacrifice in accordance with the imperial edict. His sentence included mention of sacrilege, nefarious conspiracy, and enmity to Roman gods and rites, it ended with condemnation to death by the sword. Accompanied by a crowd of Christian laymen and clergy, he was beheaded the next day.[64]

Though Cyprian's theological ideas as expressed in his writings are not unimportant, his primary significance for the history of Christianity lies in his moderation and his administrative skill. It was men like him and the bishops of Rome and Alexandria who made it possible for the churches to survive the persecutions of Decius and Valerian, and to reconstitute themselves without either laxity or rigor. His views on the lapsed, largely shared by the Roman church, kept the church from becoming a sect, though his insistence upon rebaptism was not to prove adequate. His deacon Pontius soon wrote "the

[61] *Ep.* 73, 4.
[62] Custom vs. truth: Tertullian, *De virg. vel.* 1, 1; Firmilian [Cypr.], *Ep.* 75, 19; *Sent.* 28; 30; 77.
[63] *Sent.* 5, p. 438 Hartel; cf. *Ep.* 75, 25, p. 827.
[64] The *Acta proconsularia* (5) state that he gave orders for his executioner to be presented with a gift of 25 aurei, a considerable sum even in Valerian's reign.

first Christian biography" in praise of him, and in it the expression "grades of honor," used of the Christian ministry, shows that the church was being viewed like the state as involving a *cursus honorum*.[65]

Cyprian's Romanization of the church of North Africa is evident not only from the biography but also from the conduct of church affairs in his time. Indeed his early enthusiasm for the primacy of the Roman see provides clear evidence of his attitude. In addition, there is the fact to which Batiffol drew attention: the deliberative procedure of the synods in Africa, Numidia, and Mauretania (obviously convening in relation to the Roman provinces from which the bishops came) was almost certainly based on the procedure of the Roman senate.[66] The members of the synods were bishops alone, although other clerics and the *plebs* were allowed to be present. The chief magistrate (Cyprian) provided a *relatio* or statement of the subject to be discussed; then the bishops were called upon, one by one, to express their judgments on it. The last to speak would ordinarily present the *sententia* which reflected the common opinion of the members, and the individual decisions (*placita*) would be sent out in *libellus* along with a joint letter which all would sign. This fact explains the form of the *sententiae episcoporum* which resulted from the synod held at Carthage on September 1, 256.[67] No doubt, at Batiffol insisted, Cyprian was not solely responsible for this use of the senatorial model, but it seems likely that he promoted it. It must be admitted that the African bishops may not have had the Roman senate alone in view, for provincial and municipal assemblies often followed the senatorial pattern. It was the Roman senate, however, which was the ultimate model for African synodal procedure.

The growth of the North African church is clearly indicated by the constantly increasing numbers of bishops who attended synods, as well as by the still extant Christian literature from the area. Probably in the middle of the third century a certain Commodian produced two Latin poems, the "Instructions against the gods of the pagans, on behalf of Christian teaching" and the "apologetic poem against Jews and gentiles." Commodian's inadequacies as a poet are exceeded only by his doctrinal peculiarities: he believed both that the Father had been crucified and that the kingdom of God was about to come on earth. Like the early apologists, he claimed that he had been converted from paganism by reading the scriptures. Half a century later, a teacher of rhetoric at Sicca Veneria, southwest of Carthage, was converted to Christianity and in the early days of Diocletian's persecution wrote seven books *Against the pagans*. Unlike Commodian, Arnobius seems to have known very

---

[65] *Vita Cypriana* 3, 3; cf. A. Harnack, *Das Leben Cyprians von Pontius: die erste christliche Biographie* (*TU* 39, 3, Leipzig, 1913).

[66] P. Batiffol in *Bulletin d'ancienne littérature et d'archéologie chrétiennes* 3 (1913), 3-19.

[67] *CSEL* 3, part 2, 433-61.

little about the Bible; he writes with the enthusiasm of a recent convert but is better equipped to denounce idolatry than to set forth positive Christian themes. According to Jerome,[68] the rhetorician Lactantius had been his pupil, but proof of this statement is lacking: Lactantius did not mention Arnobius and there are striking differences between the two authors.

In addition, inscriptions clearly prove that Christianity was constantly expanding in Africa, as does the rise of the Donatist schism there in the fourth century.[69]

[68] *De vir. illustr.* 80.
[69] See W. H. C. Frend, *Martyrdom*, 454-55.

CHAPTER XV
SCHOOL AND CHURCH
AT ALEXANDRIA

The beginnings of Christianity at Alexandria are exceedingly obscure. The only teachers whose names we know are those of the Gnostic Basilides, from the reign of Hadrian, and his son Isidore. Justin tells about a young Christian at Alexandria who petitioned the prefect of Egypt for permission to be castrated; he was trying to prove that the Christian "mystery" did not consist of promiscuous sexual intercourse, but the prefect denied his request.[1] This does not sound like orthodox second-century Christianity, and Walter Bauer was almost certainly right when he claimed that at Alexandria early Christianity was essentially Gnostic.[2]

Eusebius, on the other hand, believed that much could be said about Christian origins at Alexandria. In his view "it was a primitive custom that a school of sacred studies should exist" there.[3] What he had in mind was the Jewish sect of the Therapeutae, about whom he read in Philo's treatise *On the con-*

---

[1] Justin, *Apol.* 1, 29.
[2] W. Bauer, *Rechtgläubigkeit und Ketzerei im ältesten Christentum* (Tübingen, 1934), 49-64; cf. C. H. Roberts in *Journal of Egyptian Archaeology* 40 (1954), 92-96.
[3] Eusebius, *H. E.* 5, 10, 1; cf. 2, 17, 10-12.

templative life; he thought that Philo was describing Christians rather than Jews. Indeed in Eusebius' opinion Philo conversed with the apostle Peter when he visited Rome during the reign of Claudius.[4] This notion is not likely to be correct, since it reflects Eusebius' idea that Christianity, always the same, was philosophical when it began. It remains true, however, that at an early date it was thought that Peter's "interpreter" Mark brought the Christian mission to Alexandria.[5] More important, the ideas of Philo were more influential among early Christians than is often supposed,[6] and if the Epistle to the Hebrews and the Epistle of Barnabas are Alexandrian in origin the earliest Christians there were almost certainly Hellenistic Jews.

I·PANTAENUS

Though in the second century most Alexandrian Christians were Gnostics, the more orthodox Christians were able to present lists of the bishops who represented their views from a relatively early (but not determinable) date, and they could trace the beginnings of a fairly orthodox school at Alexandria to a certain Pantaenus, who flourished in the latter half of the second century. According to Eusebius, this man was once a Stoic but became a Christian missionary; he visited India before settling at Alexandria, where he taught Clement and Alexander, bishop of Jerusalem.[7] What Clement ascribes to earlier presbyters may go back to him, but only two fragments of his teaching certainly exist. One suggests that he knew something about the Hebrew language;[8] the other contains an almost Neoplatonic discussion of the way in which God possesses knowledge.[9] It is possible that Clement's acquaintance with the writings of Philo was due to Pantaenus, but we cannot be sure. Origen refers to Pantaenus with admiration but never speaks of Clement.

II·CLEMENT

The work of Clement of Alexandria was much more significant for most later writers than was that of Pantaenus. In all likelihood Clement was a convert to Christianity from paganism. His name, Titus Flavius Clemens, suggests

---

[4] *Ibid.,* 2, 17, 1.
[5] *Ibid.,* 2, 16, 1; from Clement of Alexandria, cf. M. Smith in *The New York Times,* Dec. 30, 1960.
[6] Cf. H. Chadwick, *St. Paul and Philo of Alexandria* (Manchester, 1966).
[7] Eusebius, *H. E.* 5, 10, 2-3; 6, 14, 9.
[8] Clement, *Ecl. proph.* 56, 2.
[9] Maximus Confessor, *PG* 91, 1085 B.

that he was probably descended from a freedman of the consul in 95 who bore the same name and may have been a relative of the Clement who wrote 1 Clement about the same time. After his conversion he studied "the true tradition of the blessed doctrine of the holy apostles" with teachers who came from all over the Roman world. In Greece he studied with an Ionian Christian; in Sicily or south Italy, with teachers from Coele Syria and Egypt; in "the east," with one born in Syria and in Palestine, with a Hebrew Christian.[10] His favorite teacher was evidently Pantaenus, and he went to Alexandria to study with him and eventually, perhaps about 190, to succeed him as head of a private Christian school. Presumably it was at Alexandria that he became a presbyter of the Christian church.[11] His influence was limited, however to those who shared his view that there was an authentic and secret Christian doctrine, inaugurated when "the Lord delivered the Gnosis to James the Just and John and Peter" and they "delivered it to the other apostles, the other apostles to the Seventy [Luke 10:1], of whom one was Barnabas."[12] In the *Stromata* it is made clear that the inner group of apostles also included Paul.[13] Perhaps Clement's idea of secret Gnosis came to him from the Epistle of Barnabas,[14] but a recently discovered letter presumably written by him tells of secrets known only to those who have been initiated in the "greater mysteries" (as at Eleusis) of the Alexandrian church.[15] Clement's idea of Christian teaching was, therefore, not very different from that he ascribes to the followers of Basilides, whose teaching was said to come from Glaucias, an "interpreter" of the apostle Peter, or those of Valentinus, who had been instructed by Theodas, a companion of Paul.[16] The content, not the form, of Clement's Gnosis was different from theirs. In some respects the content was just as individualistic as that offered by various Gnostic teachers. Clement's *Hypotyposes* or "outlines" are lost but were read in the ninth century by Photius.[17] Apparently he taught that matter was eternal, that there was a world of Platonic ideas, that souls transmigrated, and that there were "many worlds before Adam." His Logos doctrine allowed for the primal existence of two Logoi, one the Son, the other the "paternal Logos"; what became incarnate was neither one but "a certain power" of the Son.[18] In the *Stromata* Clement clearly indicated that his secret doctrine included teaching "about the Uncreated and his powers"[19]— presumably as reflected in the *Hypotyposes*. In addition, this book described

[10] *Str.* 1, 11, 2.
[11] *Paed.* 1, 37, 3 (*esmen*).
[12] Eusebius, *H. E.* 2, 1, 4.
[13] *Str.* 6, 68, 2.
[14] R. P. C. Hanson, *Origen's Doctrine of Tradition* (London, 1954), 53-72.
[15] *The New York Times*, Dec. 30, 1960.
[16] *Str.* 7, 106, 4.
[17] *Myriobibl.* Cod. 109=O. Stählin, *Clemens Alexandrinus* III, p. 202.
[18] Cf. R. P. Casey in *JTS* 25 (1923-24), 43-56.
[19] *Str.* 5, 80, 3.

Eve's origin from Adam "in shameful fashion"—presumably along Gnostic lines—and stated that the angels had intercourse with women and begat offspring. Photius found all this shocking, but it represents what Christian speculation could be at Alexandria late in the second century.

It is likely that while still at Alexandria Clement produced at least the first two volumes of his trilogy on the Christian life. The first, the *Protrepticus*, bore the same title as did works by contemporary philosophers who were trying to convert outsiders to philosophy. Clement aimed at the conversion of Greeks from their religion and philosophy to the "new song," the Christian revelation. The second was the *Paedagogus* or "instructor," three books "intended to provide catechumens and young Christians with instruction in Christian morality and etiquette."[20] It begins with a description of the true pedagogue or tutor, the Word of God, and continues with instructions about food and drink, household furnishings, entertainments, sleep, sexual relations, and the right and wrong use of jewelry, and a criticism of extravagance and luxury as contrasted with frugality and the proper use of physical exercise. Such counsel, we may suppose, was welcomed by the Christian bourgeoisie of Alexandria, who might well have recognized the quotations from the Stoic Musonius Rufus which Clement supplied without acknowledgment.

Before leaving Alexandria Clement certainly wrote the first few books of his major work, the *Stromata* or "patchwork"—again a title fairly common in his time. The seven books seem to follow a general outline although there are innumerable digressions from it; Clement claims that his meaning will become clear only to the attentive reader.[21] The first two books consist primarily of discussions of wisdom and philosophy among Greeks and Christians; they lead onward to the third book, where we find questions about marriage and sexuality and also about Gnostic errors. The fourth book provides something of an interlude between the earlier and the later sections. It deals with the Christian martyr, whom Clement admires but does not regard as following the only, or indeed the highest, path toward Christian perfection. Perhaps this book was written after he had left Alexandria during the persecution. The fifth and sixth books are developed in the fashion of the first two. Beginning with a discussion of the relation of faith to seeking, Clement deals with the nature of symbolism before turning to the mystery of God. After a brief discussion of Greek plagarism, he explains that God is the source of all and thus finally comes to the ideal Christian Gnostic. It is this kind of Gnostic whose studies he has been guiding throughout his work. In the seventh book polemic against Greek superstition and Christian heresy is intertwined with

[20] H. Chadwick, *Early Christian Thought and the Classical Tradition* (Oxford, 1966), 31.
[21] Cf. A. Méhat, *Étude sur les "Stromates" de Clément d'Alexandrie* (Paris, 1966), especially 276-79.

consideration of the nature of the Son of God and, once more, the ascent of the Christian Gnostic. This marks the climax of the book, and for all practical purposes its end. Clement planned to "proceed with his argument from a fresh starting-point,"[22] and it may be that the present eighth book, part of a treatise on logic, contains notes he intended to use as he began again. Other treatises of his certainly contain little more than notes: one is the "extracts from Theodotus and the so-called oriental doctrine in the times of Valentinus"; the other is the "selections from the prophets." Perhaps Clement planned to make use of all these materials in a new venture.[23]

In addition he wrote more practical treatises, such as his lost books on the paschal question, his treatise on the Christian value of wealth, and his sermon addressed to the newly baptized.[24]

Around 211 Alexander, later bishop of Jerusalem, was in prison probably in Cappadocia and sent a letter to the church of Antioch by the hand of "the blessed presbyter Clement," well known to his correspondents.[25] It is thus fairly clear that from Alexandria Clement had migrated first to Antioch, then farther north. By the time he wrote a letter to Origen, at a much later date,[26] "the holy Clement," his master and helper, was dead.[27]

The significance of Clement lies in his bold attempts to synthesize Christianity with the life and thought of the Graeco-Roman world. His ideas mark a break not only with the old apocalyptic eschatology but with the Gnostic heresies of his time. It was his claim that Christianity contained everything of value in older systems but offered a new revelation of God.

Both Pantaenus and Clement were private teachers of a Christian school at Alexandria, presumably with episcopal authorization but without episcopal authority, even though both were greatly admired by Alexander of Jerusalem. (It is worth noting that in their times there were "orthodox" Christians at Alexandria and that their community possessed a leader or bishop.[28]) A new direction in teaching was provided in 203, after Clement had left Alexandria, when the bishop Demetrius made a young man named Origen head of an episcopal school for catechumens.[29]

[22] *Str.* 7, 111, 4.
[23] On the outline of his principal works cf. W. Wagner in *Church History* 37 (1968), 251-60; cf. Méhat, *op. cit.*, 434.
[24] O. Stählin, *op. cit.*, 221-23.
[25] Eusebius, *H. E.* 6, 11, 6.
[26] Cf. P. Nautin, *Lettres et écrivains chrétiens des iie et iiie siècles* (Paris, 1961), 105-41.
[27] Eusebius, *H. E.* 6, 14, 9.
[28] Cf. W. Bauer, *Rechtgläubigkeit und Ketzerei im ältesten Christentum* (Tübingen, 1934), 57.
[29] Eusebius, *H. E.* 6, 3, 8.

III·ORIGEN

Almost all our information about Origen's early life comes from a biographical account in the sixth book of Eusebius' *Church History*. It may be that this account was based on two sources, one more legendary than the other,[30] but it is more probable that it is derived from a narrative provided by Origen himself, along with additions provided by Eusebius.[31]

Origen was born about 185 and was given a good Greek education by his devoutly Christian father Leonides, a man of some property at Alexandria. The father insisted that his son learn much of the Greek Bible by heart, though he was perturbed when the boy insisted upon seeking for allegorical interpretations—the natural result of his literary studies. In 202, when Origen was sixteen, his father was arrested and imprisoned as a Christian. His mother prevented him from joining Leonides in prison by exhortations and finally by hiding his clothes, but he wrote a letter urging his father "not to change your mind on our account." Leonides was executed, his property confiscated; Origen was left as the sole support of his mother and his six younger brothers. Fortunately a "very rich" woman of Alexandria aided him so that he could prepare himself for teaching Greek literature. In the following year, since all the catechists had left Alexandria, Demetrius put him in charge of the church's teaching.

Persecution at Alexandria continued, but though six of Origen's pupils were put to death he himself was not even arrested. Perhaps this immunity was due to the number of his pupils, perhaps to their rank. Now concentrating his attention upon "the divine scriptures," he sold his classical library for a small annuity and occupied himself with teaching and with severe self-discipline.[32] Around this time he may have taken literally the gospel saying about making oneself a eunuch "for the sake of the kingdom of heaven" (Matt. 19:12);[33] Eusebius says that he also wished to prevent slander aroused by his instruction of women, but the preventative seems unduly drastic.

While Zephyrinus was still bishop of Rome (to 217), Origen paid a visit in order "to see the most ancient church of the Romans"[34] and, according to Jerome, heard Hippolytus preach there.[35] Soon afterward—did Origen share Hippolytus' lack of enthusiasm for the Roman bishop?—Demetrius recalled

[30] M. Hornschuh in *ZKG* 71 (1960), 1-25, 193-214.

[31] Nautin, *op cit.* 133 n. 1.

[32] Eusebius (*H. E.* 6, 9, 3) gives the figure of 4 obols a day for the annuity and A. C. Johnson (in T. Frank, ed., *An Economic Survey of Ancient Rome* II, Baltimore, 1936, 302) takes it literally; it was proverbial, however.

[33] Cf. W. Bauer in *Neutestamentliche Studien G. Heinrici* (Leipzig, 1914), 235-44.

[34] Eusebius, *H. E.* 6, 14, 10.

[35] *De vir. illustr.* 61.

him to Alexandria. Around the same time the Alexandrian school was re-organized, presumably by the bishop. Origen's pupil Heraclas, later head of the entire school and after Demetrius bishop of Alexandria, took charge of the introductory course while Origen taught only advanced students. Origen's work was supported and encouraged by a rich Alexandrian named Ambrose, once a Valentinian Gnostic, who provided him with seven stenographers, seven copyists, and girls skilled in penmanship.[36] Under the auspices of Ambrose Origen wrote his *Commentary on John* and his much later treatise *Against Celsus*. He also dedicated his treatise *On Prayer* and the *Exhortation to Martyrdom* to his patron.

Probably around 214 the Roman legate of Arabia (possibly Furnius Iulianus, consul designate in that year[37]) sent on officer to Alexandria with letters addressed to both Demetrius and to the prefect of Egypt, L. Baebius Aurelius Iuncinus,[38] asking the latter to send Origen to him for an interview.[39] This request was highly important. The legate implicitly recognized the authority of Demetrius, under the prefect of Egypt, over the movements of his subordinate Origen. In addition, it opened the way for Origen's later dealings with Arabian churches vexed by heresy—and perhaps divisions within Christian communities brought about the legate's request.[40]

After a brief journey to Bostra in Arabia, Origen returned to Alexandria only to leave the city again in 215 at the time of Caracalla's visit there. This time he went to Caesarea in Palestine and by episcopal invitation preached in churches there and at Jerusalem. Since he had not been ordained presbyter, Demetrius soon sent Alexandrian deacons with a letter recalling him.[41]

Within a few years the publication of some of Origen's earlier and bolder theological treatises, now largely lost, undoubtedly augmented Demetrius' suspicions of his independent attitude. When the theological treatise *On first principles* appeared, perhaps about 225, the difficulties were not diminished. In the preface Origen stated that his philosophical theology was intended as filling in the gaps left by the teaching of the apostles, though it obviously went further toward a form of Platonist Christianity. The commentary on Genesis on which he was working treated almost everything in the opening chapters as allegory. By 230 the first five books of a commentary on John cannot have allayed Demetrius' questionings.

Around 230 Christian leaders at Athens requested Origen to visit them for a doctrinal discussion, and he left Alexandria again. It is not clear whether or not Demetrius gave his approval. In any event, upon reaching Caesarea

[36] Eusebius, *H. E.* 6, 23, 2.
[37] On legates of Arabia cf. H.-G. Pflaum in *Syria* 34 (1957), 136-44 (138-39).
[38] O. W. Reinmuth in *RE* XXII 2374.
[39] Eusebius, *H. E.* 6, 19, 15.
[40] On Origen and Arabia cf. G. Kretschmar in *Zeitschrift für Theologie und Kirche* 50 (1953-54), 258-79.
[41] Eusebius, *H. E.* 6, 19, 16-19.

he was ordained presbyter by his friends the bishops of Jerusalem and Caesarea. From Caesarea he proceeded to Athens and for some time was occupied with discussions of philosophy and heresy. When he returned to Alexandria in 231 Demetrius convoked a synod of bishops and presbyters and on their advice issued a decree banishing him from the city and forbidding him to teach there. Origen immediately left for Caesarea and settled there to continue his work, though at first without his staff of stenographers. Not unnaturally Demetrius was irritated by Origen's reception in Palestine, and he proceeded to assemble a few Egyptian bishops who agreed with him that Origen should be deposed from the presbyterate.[42] The Alexandrian letter of deposition and excommunication was accepted by synods at Rome and elsewhere, although it was ignored by the churches of Achaea, Phoenicia, Palestine, and Arabia, where his allies were in control.[43]

Writing to some friends at Alexandria, Origen denounced Demetrius and the other clerics who had "vainly" excommunicated him. He compared himself with the Old Testament prophets, for they too had criticized the shepherds, elders, priests, and princes of the people.[44] Soon afterward he resumed his work on the Gospel of John. God, he wrote, had brought him out of the land of Egypt, saving him as he had saved the children of Israel. After his departure, "the enemy redoubled his violence through his new writings truly alien to the gospel, and raised against us all the winds of wickedness in Egypt." Now, however, God had quenched the fiery darts of the enemy—evidently with the support of the Palestinian bishops.[45] In 232 when Julia Mamaea, mother of the emperor Alexander Severus, was at Antioch she sent a military escort to bring Origen to her for theological discussion[46] and thus created a precedent for his letters, written more than a decade later, to the emperor Philip the Arabian and his wife Severa.[47]

For about five years Origen occupied himself with the creation of a new school and church library at Caesarea. He continued his teaching of theology under the auspices of the bishops of Caesarea and Jerusalem and visited Cappadocia at the invitation of his pupil Firmilian, perhaps in 235 or 236, later taking part in conferences at Bostra in Arabia. It is not certain that he ever went back to Athens. The Origen who deeply impressed the Neoplatonic philosopher Plotinus may have been another man, and it is difficult to determine when or where such an encounter can have occurred.[48] Somewhat later,

---

[42] Photius, *Myriobibl.* Cod. 118 (*PG* 103, 398B), based on Origen's apologist Pamphilus.

[43] Jerome, *Ep.* 33, 4 (*PL* 22, 447).

[44] Jerome, *Apol. adv. libros Rufini* 2, 18 (*PL* 23, 461 AB).

[45] *Ioh. comm.* 6, 2; for Origen's self-portrait as an ideal wise man in this passage cf. E. Corsini, *Commento al Vangelo di Giovanni di Origene* (Torino, 1968), 289, n. 2.

[46] Eusebius, *H. E.* 6, 21, 3-4.

[47] *Ibid.*, 6, 36, 3; Hippolytus too addressed a treatise to a certain Severina.

[48] Porphyry, *Vit. Plotini* 14.

it would appear, he tried to win the favor of Fabian of Rome (235–250) by apologizing for some of his writings. He claimed that his patron Ambrose had published documents intended only for private reading.[49] This attempt to shift the blame may have produced the result, noted by Jerome, that in his will Ambrose left nothing to Origen.[50]

It is significant that though two of his sometime pupils became bishops at Alexandria Origen never returned to the city. The antagonisms aroused before and after his departure were deep and lasting.

Origen's teaching at Caesarea is described by his pupil Gregory Thaumaturgus, who studied for five years with him there, until either 238 or 243. This pupil, later a bishop in Pontus, had been on his way to study Roman law at Beirut when he encountered Origen and was persuaded to give up a military or legal career[51] in favor of philosophy. (He had already studied rhetoric for some time.) Under Origen he was introduced to dialectic, to physics with its subdivisions of geometry and arithmetic, and to ethics, where the four cardinal virtues served as an outline. Now ready for philosophical theology, he first turned to reading the ancient philosophers and poets, except for the atheists who denied the existence of God or of providence.[52] The culmination of the course lay in the exegesis of scripture. The enigmas and riddles of the Old Testament were made clear in Origen's Spirit-directed interpretation.[53] As Hal Koch showed, the basic outline of the course was derived from Middle Platonic sources.[54]

Origen was of course a preacher as well as a teacher. At Alexandria special church assemblies had been held on Wednesdays and Fridays so that the scriptures could be read and he could expound their meaning.[55] At Caesarea he preached in church on Sundays and at other times. It was only when he reached the age of sixty, however, that he was willing for stenographers to take down the content of his sermons; those still in existence therefore come from the period after 246.[56]

During the years before the Decian persecution Origen worked tirelessly. Eusebius tells us how he brought to completion such works, begun at Alexandria, as the commentaries on Genesis and John.[57] He also finished a commentary on Ezekiel at Athens and began one on the Song of Songs, completing it upon returning to Caesarea.[58] Equally important was his study of the Old

---

[49] Jerome, *Ep.* 84, 10 (*PL* 22, 751).
[50] Jerome, *De vir. illustr.* 66.
[51] P. Koetschau, *Des Gregorios Thaumaturgos Dankrede an Origenes* (Leipzig, 1894), p. 15, 23.
[52] *Ibid.*, p. 29, 5-20. These were Skeptics and Epicureans.
[53] *Ibid.*, p. 33, 25; p. 34, 6 and 13.
[54] *Pronoia und Paideusis* (Berlin, 1932), 243-53.
[55] Socrates, *H. E.* 5, 22.
[56] Eusebius, *H. E.* 6, 36, 1.
[57] Eusebius, *H. E.* 6, 24.
[58] *Ibid.*, 6, 32, 2.

Testament text. It was apparently begun at an early date, for one of the versions he used "was found at Jericho in a jar in the time of Antoninus the son of Severus"—i.e., Caracalla.[59] His researches, analogous to those of Alexandrian critics who worked on the texts of Homer and other poets, led to the production of two editions. The first was called the *Hexapla* because it contained six versions: a Hebrew text, a transliteration of the Hebrew into Greek, and four Greek translations, those of Aquila, Symmachus, "the Seventy" (i.e., the Septuagint), and Theodotion. The Septuagint, read in the churches, was the most important. Like the Alexandrian critics, Origen used critical signs to indicate the presence of variants. Thus the obelisk (†) marked clauses not found in the Hebrew, while an asterisk (*) pointed to clauses he himself had inserted from other versions. For some Old Testament books he added other materials; thus in the Psalms he used a total of seven Greek versions, including the one found at Jericho. The second textual work was the *Tetrapla,* which contained only the four Greek translations.

Origen was intensely devoted to the Christian revelation and incessantly endeavored to penetrate its inner meaning.[60] His textual and exegetical studies were the consequence of this devotion, also reflected in his teaching and his consultations on theological topics. He possessed a remarkable memory, especially for biblical texts, and a clear and penetrating intellect. Both memory and intellect can be seen at work in such a document as the report of a conference between him and certain bishops "on the Father, the Son, and the soul," of which a transcript exists on papyrus.[61] His life, in spite of his conflicts and travels, was highly disciplined. Sometimes he fasted; sometimes he "measured out the time for sleep." For many years he wore no shoes and took only enough food to sustain existence.[62] In the controversy over the forgiveness of capital sins he sided with Hippolytus and Tertullian against the more lenient bishops.[63]

During the persecution of Decius he suffered in prison at the hands of a judge who was trying to make him recant. A letter from Dionysius of Alexandria "on martyrdom" doubtless offered encouragement,[64] but after his imprisonment Origen seems to have produced no further writings for the church. It is possible that he turned to philosophy in his last years. According to the Neoplatonist Porphyry, he had been, like Plotinus, a hearer of Ammonius

---

[59] *Ibid.,* 6, 16, 3.

[60] For his devotion to work cf. the fragmentary letter "about Ambrose" (Lommatzsch XVII, 5). "There is no opportunity for us to have supper or afterwards to walk about and refresh our bodies. . . . Grammatical discussions extend far into the evening. I say nothing about the time from dawn to the ninth or at times the tenth hour, for all who wish to work devote this period to the study and reading of the divine oracles."

[61] J. Scherer, *Entretien d'Origène avec Héraclide et les évêques ses collègues sur le Père, le Fils, et l'âme* (Cairo, 1949).

[62] Eusebius, *H. E.* 6, 3, 9-12.

[63] Cf. *De orat.* 28, 10.

[64] Eusebius, *H. E.* 6, 46, 2.

Saccas and had agreed with his fellow pupils not to publish what had been taught. In two treatises, however. Origen revealed the doctrine. One was a work *On demons;* the other, *That the king* [God] *is the only creator,* appeared under Gallienus, hence after 253. Porphyry may be exaggerating the extent of Origen's debt to Ammonius, but the treatises he mentions may have been his last works.[65] He died at the age of sixty-nine, apparently in 255, and was buried at Tyre, where his memory was venerated by Christians.[66]

Origen was not, of course, the only Christian intellectual of his time, even though Alexandria was certainly the most important center for Christian studies. Indeed, Origen's devotion to theology marks his work as significantly different from that of two important contemporaries. One of them was Julius Africanus, who was born about 160 in Aelia Capitolina and was later at the court of the Christian king Abgar IX of Edessa (179–216). There he met a slightly older Christian leader, Bardesanes, whom we shall presently discuss. He also visited Armenia and Phrygia, perhaps from Edessa. About 215, after Heraclas had taken charge of the introductory studies in the Christian school at Alexandria, Africanus went there, attracted by the reputation of this teacher, not that of Origen.[67] He learned to admire the work of Clement, who he says had taught under Commodus, and he prepared a chronological study from the creation onward, in the manner of Clement's own work in the first book of the *Stromata*. This *Chronicle* at first ended with the year 217 but apparently was later extended to 221, the third year of Elagabalus. Meanwhile he had moved to Emmaus-Nicopolis in Palestine, and in 224 he was sent by the city as an emissary to the emperor Alexander Severus to obtain funds for rebuilding. While at Rome he designed a library "in the Pantheon near the baths of Alexander" for the emperor and undertook researches in this library for his twenty-four books of "magic girdles," dedicated to Alexander Severus himself.[68] This miscellany dealt with problems of Homeric criticism, with magic, and with military strategy and tactics.[69] After the emperor's death, Africanus was back in Palestine, where he attended a discussion in which Origen appealed to the authority of the story of Susanna. He thereupon addressed a letter to Origen in which he insisted that the story was fictitious and not a part of the book of Daniel. Origen replied, but not altogether convincingly. Perhaps around the same time, Africanus also tried to explain the discrepant genealogies of Jesus in the gospels.[70] It is evident that he was a polymath, not a theologian; he is more important for his witness to the Christian or semi-Christian culture of his time than for his contributions to the ongoing life of the church.

[65] Cf. F. H. Kettler in *RGG*[3] IV 1694-95.
[66] Jerome, *De vir. illustr.* 54.
[67] Eusebius, *H. E.* 6, 31, 2.
[68] P. Oxy. III 412; cf. W. Bauer, *Rechtgläubigkeit und Ketzerei im ältesten Christentum* (Tübingen, 1934), 162-67.
[69] Cf. J. Vieillefond, *Jules Africain, Fragments des Cestes* (Paris, 1932).
[70] Cf. W. Reichardt in *TU* 34, 3 (1909).

The other Christian layman who requires mention at this point was Bardesanes (Bar Daisan) of Edessa, who probably lived from 154 to 222. Africanus himself witnessed his skill in archery at the court of Abgar.[71] and he was later famous for his *Book of the Laws of the Countries,* a refutation of the claims of astrology. Drijvers comments enthusiastically: "Out of the sources, an erudite man comes to meet us, interested in astrology, philosophy, ethnology and history, a composer of religious hymns, a discriminating teacher, a courtier who did not despise the luxury of his day, in short, an aristocrat in every sense of the word."[72] Indeed, as he points out, it is hard to tell whether or not Bardesanes was a Christian in the ordinary sense. Eusebius thought he was a powerful defender of the faith but, as a convert from Valentinian Gnosticism, not completely orthodox.[73] It is by no means clear, however, that at Edessa Christian teaching was identical with what it was elsewhere.

IV·ALEXANDRIA AFTER ORIGEN

After Origen left Alexandria, his sometime pupil Heraclas, in charge of introductory studies for nearly twenty years and presumably "dean" during Origen's journeys, finally became head of the school. Within a year or two he succeeded Demetrius as bishop of Alexandria. Heraclas was not simply a disciple of Origen but had studied philosophy for five years on his own; unlike Origen, he was a presbyter of the church of Alexandria; and Africanus came to the school to hear him, not his colleague.[74] Presumably like Africanus he was more concerned with literature and history than with philosophical theology, and he evidently joined Demetrius in condemning Origen. All that is known of his career as bishop is that he held that those Christians who joined heretical groups and later returned to the church were to make public confession of their errors but were not to be rebaptized.[75]

During the episcopate of Heraclas another of Origen's pupils, Dionysius, was head of the school. His treatise *On nature,* an attempt to refute Epicurean atomism and theology, probably comes from this period.[76] When Heraclas died, in 247, Dionysius became bishop. It may be that his treatise *On promises* reflects the early years of his episcopate. The treatise contains a report on a conference of village presbyters and teachers in the Arsinoite

[71] Vieillefond, *op. cit.,* 48-49.

[72] H. J. W. Drijvers, *Bardaisan of Edessa* (Assen, Holland, 1966), 218-19.

[73] Cf. W. Bauer, *Rechtgläubigkeit und Ketzerei im ältesten Christentum* (Tübingen, 1934), 6-48.

[74] Eusebius, *H. E.* 6, 3, 2; 6, 19, 13-14; 6, 29, 4; 6, 31, 2; cf. Hugo Koch in *ZNW* 25 (1926), 278-82.

[75] *Ibid.,* 7, 7, 4; cf. C. L. Feltoe, *The Letters and Other Remains of Dionysius of Alexandria* (Cambridge, 1904), 53-54.

[76] Eusebius, *P. E.* 14, 23-27; Feltoe, *op. cit.,* 127-64.

nome, where schisms and apostasies of whole churches had taken place because of controversies over apocalyptic eschatology. Dionysius dealt with the book of Revelation, over which controversy had raged, in what seems to have been the manner of Heraclas. To the literalists he insisted that the book had a nonliteral meaning, but he agreed with them that it lay beyond his comprehension. He then proceeded to use literary critical techniques to show that it was not written by the apostle who wrote the Gospel and the First Epistle of John and therefore should not be quite so highly regarded as had been the case.[77] As bishop of Alexandria, Dionysius was also immediately confronted by the persecutions between 248 and 250 and by the problems of discipline arising out of them. A paschal letter probably of 250 was sent to Alexandria from Dionysius' retreat in Libya.[78] On his return to the city he wrote to various bishops in Egypt and even to some in Laodicea and Armenia; he also sent a letter on martyrdom to Origen.[79] His theme for the bishops was "repentance," that is, the condition under which Christians who had fallen away during the persecution were to be readmitted to communion.

Dionysius may already have been in touch with the church of Rome if, as Nautin suggested, his letter *diakonikē* "through Hippolytus"[80] already gave a report of his own election to Fabian of Rome. Possibly his letters on peace and on repentance were addressed to Cornelius when he became bishop in 251. He also wrote to the dissident Novatianist confessors at Rome and to Novatian himself, urging him to withdraw his claim to the episcopate. By the autumn of 251 he wrote Fabius of Antioch to explain that though the church of Alexandria had suffered greatly during the persecution, its martyrs had been willing to take back those who had lapsed.[81] After Demetrianus succeeded Fabius at Antioch and a synod there condemned Novatianism, Dionysius sent a report on the matter to Cornelius, perhaps in 253.[82]

During the next few years Dionysius was occupied with the question of the rebaptism of Novatianists and others returning to the church; fragments of six letters have been preserved, addressed to Stephen and Xystus, bishops of Rome, and to Dionysius, not yet bishop.[83] In these he insisted that rebaptism was contrary to tradition and to eastern practice. Apparently during this period he also wrote to Theotecnus of Caesarea in Palestine and praised the virtues of Origen, now dead.[84]

In the persecution of 257–258 Dionysius was banished from Alexandria

---

[77] *H. E.* 7, 24-25; Feltoe, *op. cit.*, 106-26.
[78] *Ibid.*, 7, 11, 20-25; Feltoe, *op. cit.*, 64-69.
[79] *Ibid.*, 6, 46, 1-2; Feltoe, *op. cit.*, 60-62.
[80] *Ibid.*, 6, 46, 5; P. Nautin, *Lettres et écrivains chrétiens des iie et iiie siècles* (Paris, 1961), 160-61.
[81] Nautin, *op. cit.*, 161-65.
[82] *H. E.* 6, 46, 3-4.
[83] *H. E.* 7, 5-9.
[84] Stephanus Gobarus in Photius, *Bibl. Cod.* 232 (*PG* 103, 1105A).

and his absence from the city aroused the ire of an Egyptian bishop named Germanus, who apparently also criticized his conduct during the reign of Decius. Dionysius replied by recounting his sufferings in both persecutions and explaining the circumstances under which he was absent from Alexandria. In the second persecution he had been able to perform his episcopal functions even while absent from the city. At the time he wrote he was still being harassed by Mussius Aemilianus, prefect of Egypt certainly as late as the autumn of 259, possibly until the summer of 262.[85]

The persecution by Valerian lasted for forty-two months, Dionysius wrote, and thus fulfilled the prediction in Revelation 13:5. (Evidently he was not always averse to apocalyptic prophecies!) Valerian had once favored Christianity but had been lead astray by "the teacher and *archisynagōgos*" of the Egyptian magicians (presumably the high priest of Egypt, as had been the case a decade earlier).[86] Now, however, Gallienus had obtained the throne and had restored the property belonging to the church. In a series of festal letters Dionysius described the civil wars and pestilence that accompanied the beginning of his reign.[87]

The troubles within the church after this persecution were more doctrinal than disciplinary. As early as 257 Dionysius had written to Xystus of Rome about a supposedly new heresy which had arisen in Libya.[88] This was the view, often ascribed to a certain Sabellius, that the Father was essentially identical with the Son. He also wrote letters to several bishops in Libya in order to denounce this view.[89] By the time the persecution ended, the new bishop of Rome, Dionysius, was ready to intervene. It was fairly obvious, though the Roman Dionysius did not say so, that in attacking Sabellius the Alexandrian Dionysius had followed lines already laid down in the teaching of Origen. A synod held at Rome, acting on accusations against the bishop of Alexandria, condemned him for separating the Father from the Son, for denying the eternity of the Son, for naming either person apart from the other, for failing to use the term *homoousios,* and for speaking of the Son as created by the Father and using misleading analogies.[90] Dionysius replied by denying the first three charges, by pointing out that *homoousios* was not a term to be found in the Bible, and by complaining that his critics had seized upon some of his analogies and neglected others.[91] For the time the controversy was allowed to die down.

In 264, as the first of several synods was about to meet at Antioch to

[85] *H. E.* 6, 40; 7, 11; Feltoe, *op. cit.,* 23-36. For Aemilianus cf. *H. E.* 7, 11, 18; O. W. Reinmuth in *RE* XXII 2376.
[86] *Ibid.,* 7, 10, 2-4.
[87] *Ibid.,* 7, 10, 2-6; 7, 21-23; Feltoe, *op. cit.,* 69-89.
[88] *Ibid.,* 7, 6.
[89] *Ibid.,* 7, 26, 1.
[90] Feltoe, *op. cit.,* 165-70.
[91] *Ibid.,* 170-76.

discuss the case of Paul of Samosata, Dionysius was invited to attend. Because of his age and feebleness he declined, though he sent his judgment of the situation in a letter to the church of Antioch. That year he died.[92]

During Dionysius' episcopate the school at Alexandria seems to have been under the direction of a devoted Origenist named Theognostus, from whom we have only fragments, along with a summary by Photius, of the seven books of *Outlines* containing the main points of his teaching.[93] His Christological ideas were much like those of Dionysius, and it may be that the *Outlines* were published when Dionysius came under attack.

His successor Pierius also represented the Origenist tradition and headed the school at least for a time. Only fragments of his theological and exegetical treatises survive; a lost work on Mary as *theotokos* ("God-bearer") was based on a term common later but apparently present in some of Origen's writings.[94] According to Eusebius, he served as a presbyter at Alexandria under the bishop Theonas while Achillas, another presbyter, was head of the school,[95] but Eusebius seems to know little about Alexandria in this period. We shall later discuss Pierius' life during the persecution.

Alexandrian church life did not revolve exclusively around the school, and though Eusebius knows only that Dionysius' successor Maximus was bishop for eighteen years (264–282), Theonas for nineteen (282–300/1), a papyrus letter gives more information. The letter was sent from Rome to Arsinoe in Egypt and deals with the writer's need to raise cash to meet some notes already sent to a certain Primitinus in Rome. Though the writer has tried to delay payment, Primitinus is insisting on spot cash at Alexandria, and the writer's correspondents at Arsinoe have agreed to raise it. He now asks them to buy linen clothing at Arsinoe, sell it at Alexandria, and deliver the proceeds either to Primitinus or to Maximus the bishop, obtaining a receipt. In addition, they are to sell both bread and linen and turn these proceeds over to Theonas for credit to the writer's account. This should be done at once because Primitinus is at Alexandria awaiting payment. The letter seems to end with references to previous dealings not only with Primitinus but also with the bishop and other rulers (local bishops?) associated with him.[96]

It is thus clear that the bishop of Alexandria was not only the spiritual leader of Egyptian Christians but also at times their depository in temporal

[92]Eusebius, *H. E.* 7, 27, 2; 7, 28, 3. It is hard to imagine what he would have made of the condemnation of Paul for using the term *homoousios*.

[93] A. Harnack in *TU* 24, 3 (1903); L. B. Radford, *Three Teachers of Alexandria* (Cambridge, 1908), 1-43.

[94] Socrates, *H. E.* 7, 32; cf. Origen, *Luc. hom.* 6 and 7 (pp. 44 and 50 Rauer); *Sel. in Deut.* (X, 378 Lommatzsch).

[95] Eusebius, *H. E.* 7, 32, 20.

[96] Wilcken, *Chrest.* 126; A. Deissmann, *Light from the Ancient East* (rev. ed., London, 1927), 205-13; cf. W. L. Westermann in *Journal of Economic and Business History* 3 (1930-31), 30-54.

affairs. The theologians might allegorize the apocryphal saying of Jesus, "Be approved money-changers,"[97] but it had a literal meaning too. Certainly Maximus was "approved." He had been a trusted agent of Dionysius during the Decian persecution and had accompanied him into exile in 257.[98] It may be that the Theonas mentioned in the letter was Maximus' successor. A letter purportedly written by him strongly recommends business honesty and the keeping of detailed accounts; unfortunately Harnack proved that it is a seventeenth-century forgery.[99] Even without the letter, however, one would expect that Theonas continued his predecessor's activities.[100]

There is no reason to suppose that finance constituted the principal concern of the Alexandrian bishops. The papyrus letter addresses the correspondents at Arsinoe as "brothers," hence Christians, and the use of the term "papa" for Maximus also indicates that the writer was within the church. Presumably his efforts were undertaken for the Christian communities and he was not the kind of bishop, mentioned by Cyprian, who "hunted the markets for mercantile profits" and "multiplied gains with accumulated usuries."[101] Maximus was no fourth-century George of Alexandria, accused of robbing heirs of bequests and of controlling monopolies in such diverse fields as nitre, papyrus, reeds, salt, and funerals.[102]

In 300 or 301 Peter, a severe critic of Origenist theology, became bishop of Alexandria. His episcopate was not marked so much by theological controversy, however, as by problems created by the persecution which broke out in 303. Following the precedent set by Dionysius, Peter withdrew from the city. In his absence, Meletius bishop of Lycopolis took over many of his episcopal functions, even ordaining presbyters and deacons in various towns and villages.[103]

We know little about the course of the persecution at Alexandria or elsewhere in Egypt. Eusebius mentions as a leading persecutor the prefect Clodius Culcianus, in office at least between February 28, 303, and May 29, 306.[104] He was the judge who informed the prisoner Phileas, bishop of Thmuis, that Pierius had somehow submitted to the order to offer sacrifice and thus, presumably by his example, had "saved many."[105] It must have been in consequence of defections like this that at Easter in 306 Peter issued his

---

[97] Clement, Str. 1, 177, 2; Origen, Luc. hom. 1; Ioh. comm. 19, 2; Matt. comm. 17, 31; Dionysius in Eusebius, H. E. 7, 7, 3.
[98] Eusebius, H. E. 7, 11, 3, 24.
[99] TU 24, 3 (1903), 93-117.
[100] Theonas also wrote against the Manichees.
[101] De lapsis 6.
[102] Epiphanius, Haer. 76, 1, 4-7.
[103] Cf. F. H. Kettler in ZNW 35 (1936), 155-93; RGG³ IV 845-46.
[104] H. E. 9, 11, 4; O. W. Reinmuth in RE XXII 2377; P. Oxy. 71 (Mitteis, Chrest. 62); P. Oxy. 1104.
[105] V. Martin, Papyrus Bodmer XX: Apologie de Phileas (Geneva, 1964), 26.

famous letter in defense of Christians who had lapsed or fled but were penitent. This letter resulted in a final break between Peter and Meletius.

As for Pierius, later legend treated him as a martyr, but more reliable testimony indicates that he went to Rome, never to return.[106] How a great church at Alexandria came to be associated with his memory remains unknown.[107] Presumably he returned to the church, for he wrote a biography, now lost, of Pamphilus of Caesarea, a martyr in 310.

Probably by April 8, 307, the famous Sossianus Hierocles, formerly *praeses* of Bithynia and a resolute opponent of Christianity, became prefect of Egypt, remaining in office for about a year.[108] Under him the martyr Aedesius was put to death.[109] In March 307 Satrius Arrianus was *praeses* of the Thebaid,[110] and he is known from the Coptic Synaxarion to have been an active persecutor.[111] Eusebius, who later visited the region, insists on the number of martyrs and confessors there.[112] Perhaps the "letter of Psenosiris" is related to the activities of this praeses; it tells of a Christian woman who had been sent to the great oasis by a "governor" and had died there. Her corpse had been brought to the presbyter Psenosiris by a group of gravediggers among whom were some Christians.[113]

In 308 persecution was renewed by Maximin Daia. Meletius was arrested and sent to the copper mines at Phaeno, where he joined a group of confessors who called themselves "the church of the martyrs." Upon his release from the mines he proceeded to ordain again, at Eleutheropolis, Gaza, and even Jerusalem.[114] Though Peter himself was beheaded at Alexandria in November 311, the Meletian schism did not come to an end. Fourteen years later there were thirty-four Meletian bishops, five presbyters, and three deacons.[115]

Alexander of Alexandria, bishop from 312 to 326, had to deal with the internal conflicts left by the persecution and raised by new theological issues. Administratively, even with the help of Athanasius, his secretary at Nicaea in 325, he was unable to solve these problems. He was able, however, to persuade a presbyter named Colluthus, said to have illegally ordained another named Ischyras, to submit to his authority and to be the first subscriber to

---

[106] Jerome, *De vir. illustr.* 76; cf. L. B. Radford, *Three Teachers of Alexandria* (Cambridge, 1908), 44-46.
[107] Cf. H. Delehaye in *Analecta Bollandiana* 40 (1922), 34-35.
[108] Cf. C. Vandersleyen in *Journal of Juristic Papyrology* 13 (1961), 109-22.
[109] Eusebius, *M. P.* 5, 3 (longer Greek version, p. 919 Schwartz).
[110] Mitteis, *Chrest.* 63.
[111] Cf. H. Delehaye in *Analecta Bollandiana* 40 (1922), 91-110.
[112] *H.E.* 8, 6, 10; 8, 9, 1-5; *M. P.* 9, 1.
[113] Wilcken, *Chrest.* 127; Deissmann, *op. cit.,* 213-15; W. Schubart, *Griechische Papyri* (Bielefeld, 1927), I, 75; II, 73-74.
[114] Epiphanius, *Haer.* 68, 3, 6-8; on Meletian ordinations, W. Telfer in *HTR* 48 (1955), 227-37.
[115] Athanasius, *Apol.* sec. 71, 6 (pp. 149-51 Opitz).

his condemnation of Arius.[116] One schism, at least, was headed off. In an attempt to unite the Alexandrian community he built a church in memory of Theonas, bishop before the time of troubles.[117]

We shall consider later events at Alexandria in relation to the reign of Constantine.

[116] Athanasius, *De decret.* 35, 21 (p. 34 Opitz).
[117] Athanasius, *Apol. ad Const.* 15 (*PG* 25, 613 A-B).

CHAPTER XVI
THE CHURCH AT ANTIOCH
AND ELSEWHERE

I·ANTIOCH

The early history of Christianity at Antioch is much more obscure than that of the churches in other great cities, chiefly because in early times it was relatively free from controversy. The name "Christian" was first used there (Acts 11:26), and Paul contended with Peter there over the question of eating in mixed groups of Jews and gentiles. For the latter half of the first century we possess no information about Antiochene Christianity, though from the letters of the gentile bishop Ignatius we can infer that many of the community's basic ideas were Jewish.[1] Perhaps about 115 Ignatius was arrested and sent overland to Rome with an escort of Roman soldiers. His letters reflect his concern for the unity and security of the church at Antioch, apparently reestablished when his successor was chosen. In part his concern was probably due to the presence of Gnostic teachers like Saturninus on the

---

[1] *After the New Testament* (Philadelphia, 1967), 37-54.

edge of the church. A period of about sixty-five years' silence after Ignatius may perhaps reflect a struggle with Gnosticism; but the solid, rather phlegmatic Christianity of Theophilus, bishop about 180, is based on Jewish-Christian precedents and is not notable for its concern with heresy, except occasionally in regard to the doctrines of Marcion. Theophilus' successor Serapion took a different tack, denouncing Montanism and writing against a Christian who in time of persecution was converted to Judaism. Probably because of his theological outlook Serapion was unable to find anything wrong with the docetists' *Gospel of Peter* until its errors were pointed out to him.[2]

The next few bishops are little more than names. Asclepiades (203–218) was "distinguished for his confessions in the persecution" and was mentioned in a letter of congratulations by Alexander of Jerusalem.[3] Philetus (218–229) and Zebennus (229–238) are virtually unknown; the next bishop, Babylas, was a confessor and died in prison in 250 or 251.[4] Fabius not unnaturally inclined toward Novatianist rigor; he received extended letters from Cornelius of Rome and Dionysius of Alexandria, urging moderation upon him.[5] Fabius' episcopate seems to have lasted only a year; his successor Demetrian (252) convoked a synod at Antioch which joined Rome and other churches in rejecting the views of Novatian. Demetrian's active episcopate ended in 256 when Antioch was captured by the Persians and he was deported to Persia with other prominent citizens.[6] His son Domnus may not have accompanied him; he was appointed bishop by a synod at Antioch in 268.

Apparently Demetrian died in Persia, and it was not until 261 that Paul of Samosata—possibly but not certainly a native Syrian—became bishop of Antioch. It is not clear whether Paul's career was originally governmental or ecclesiastical. His opponents criticized him for having acquired great wealth even though he had been born poor and therefore could not have inherited it. He had neither a profession nor a business; instead, the Christian religion was his trade. Indeed, they explicitly stated that he accepted bribes in the course of his functions as *procurator ducenarius*,[7] in charge of tax collections at Antioch. As procurator, he possessed a bodyguard, a tribunal with a throne, and a private council chamber. His pride of office was also expressed in the church, where, we are told, he had women sing psalms addressed to himself and encouraged applause during his own sermons and praise of himself in those of others. In addition, he kept two unmarried virgins "in the flower of youth and beauty" with him. Although it had to be admitted

---

[2] Eusebius, *H. E.* 5, 19; 6, 12.
[3] *Ibid.*, 6, 11, 4-6.
[4] *Ibid.*, 6, 39, 4.
[5] *Ibid.*, 6, 41-44.
[6] See G. Downey, *A History of Antioch in Syria* (Princeton, 1961), 309.
[7] A *ducenarius* was so styled because of his salary of 200,000 sesterces.

that his behavior with them was unquestionable, their presence led to sus-picions.[8]

Paul's difficulties were partly due to his high office and to the way in which he exercised it. They were also due to the complicated political situation at Antioch in his time. Paul had probably become bishop when Odenath of Palmyra recovered Antioch from the Persians; certainly Athanasius speaks of Zenobia, queen of Palmyra, as Paul's patroness.[9] It may be significant that the first moves made against him took place in 264, shortly after Roman coins began to be struck at the mint in Antioch, and that one of his leading op-ponents was head of a school of Greek rhetoric.[10]

Athanasius also said that Zenobia was an adherent of Judaism, and in part Paul's theology may reflect her interests. He sharply differentiated the man Jesus Christ (the "anointed") from the divine Logos and refused to allow psalms addressed to "our Lord Jesus Christ" to be sung in church.

The Logos was greater than Christ, for Christ became great through Wisdom [cf. Luke 2:40, 52]. Logos is from above, Jesus Christ is a man from here. Mary did not bear the Logos, for Mary was not before the ages. Mary bore a man like us but in every respect greater. . . .[11]

These quotations come from stenographic notes taken for Paul's opponent Malchion.[12] In addition, Paul seems to have been willing to speak of the Logos as *homoousios* with the Father; this notion too was condemned at the final synod of 268.

An earlier synod in 264 achieved no results, presumably because of Paul's political influence. The later synod of 268 excommunicated him and appointed Domnus, son of Demetrian, as bishop. It proved impossible to remove him, however, until 272 when Aurelian took Antioch and later captured Zenobia. The emperor expelled Paul from the city and assigned the church building to "those to whom the bishops of the doctrine in Italy and in the city of the Romans would send letters."[13] It is fairly clear that the emperor intended to restore Roman rule at Antioch in the church as well as in the civil adminis-tration. Paul's Palmyrene affiliations thus led directly to the increase of the power of the bishop of Rome. It may be that Aurelian's decision was based on the fact that Domnus had died in 271 or early in 272.[14] Nothing is known of Domnus' successors Timaeus (to 280) and Cyril (280–303?); the latter

[8] Eusebius, *H. E.* 7, 30. For a collection of sources see H. de Riedmatten, *Les actes du procès de Paul de Samosate* (*Paradosis,* VI, Fribourg, 1952).
[9] *Hist. Arian.* 71 (p. 221 Opitz).
[10] Downey, *op. cit.,* 263-64.
[11] De Riedmatten, *op. cit.,* 136; cf. 153.
[12] Eusebius, *H. E.* 7, 29, 2.
[13] Eusebius, *H. E.* 7, 30, 19.
[14] Cf. Downey, *op cit.,* 316.

may have died at the marble quarries in Pannonia as a victim of Diocletian.[15] Tyrannus, bishop until 312, was not apparently a martyr.

The most significant personage in the church of Antioch during this period was the presbyter and teacher Lucian, probably the Lucian mentioned by Alexander of Alexandria as not in communion with the church during the episcopates of the three bishops after Paul.[16] From Lucian we possess part of a letter addressed to the Antiochene Christians in general—not to the bishop—and announcing the martyrdom of Anthimus at Nicomedia in 303.[17] He himself became a martyr at Nicomedia, not at Antioch, although there were certainly martyrs in his native city.[18]

After the persecution, the church enjoyed the patronage of Constantine but continued to suffer from internal struggles.[19] In this regard it was not, of course, unique.

II·THE EXTENT OF CHRISTIANITY AT THE END OF THE THIRD CENTURY

We have now said something about the great cities of the Mediterranean world in which Christianity flourished during the third century. Its geographical extent, however, was even wider by 300, as we learn primarily from the numbers and names of the bishops who attended synods. The existence of Christian sees in Britain is known from the fact that bishops of London, York, and Colchester (?) attended the synod of Arles in 314.[20] At Arles there were representatives of sixteen churches in Gaul (though most of them were from the south), including twelve bishops. The synod of Elvira (= Illiberis = Grenada) in Spain, held in 300 or 309, was attended by nineteen bishops and fourteen presbyters, representatives of thirty-three churches mostly in southern Spain.[21] The number of bishops attending synods at Carthage increased from seventy about 220 to ninety in about 256; they came from Africa, Numidia, and Mauretania. A Roman synod in 251 was attended by sixty Italian bishops.[22] The westward expansion of Christianity was thus a significant event in the third century, though it did not move beyond the imperial frontiers.

[15] *Ibid.*, 329.
[16] *PG* 82, 900C; on this problem cf. G. Bardy, *Recherches sur S. Lucien d'Antioche et son école* (Paris, 1936), 47-59; Downey, *op. cit.*, 337-41.
[17] Philostorgius, *H. E.* (ed. J. Bidez, Leipzig, 1913), p. 203.
[18] Eusebius, *H. E.* 8, 13, 2; 8, 12, 2-5; *M. P.* 2, 1-5.
[19] Cf. Downey, *op. cit.*, 342-55.
[20] C. H. Turner, *Ecclesiae Occidentalis Monumenta Iuris Antiquissima* (Oxford, 1909-1939), I, 408; cf. I. A. Richmond in *Archaeological Journal* 103 (1946), 64.
[21] C. J. Hefele and H. Leclerq, *Histoire des conciles* I (Paris, 1907), 212-64.
[22] Eusebius, *H. E.* 6, 43, 2.

To the east, the client king Abgar IX (179–216) was converted to Christianity and made it the state religion, and during the third century the movement reached Adiabene and Elam; but "at the end of the third century the Christian church composed of these eastern Syrians was still only sketchily organized around the twin 'royal towns' of Seleucia-Ctesiphon between Babylon and Baghdad."[23]

A sketch of the extent of Christianity in the eastern Mediterranean is provided by a letter in which Dionysius of Alexandria tells Stephen of Rome about the unity prevailing among the churches there. He mentions Antioch, Caesarea, Aelia (= Jerusalem), Tyre, Laodicea, Tarsus "and all the churches of Cilicia," Caesarea "and all Cappadocia," and in addition, "the Syrias as a whole," Arabia, Mesopotamia, Pontus, and Bithynia.[24]

The Christian movement was not only spreading geographically but also steadily moving upward in Graeco-Roman society. Some leaders ranked high in education or in administrative skill.

The Antiochene presbyter Dorotheus, for example, was well educated in Greek but learned Hebrew—an unusual case—so that he could read the Old Testament. The emperor Diocletian placed him in charge of the purple dye works at Tyre because he had been a eunuch from birth; at any rate, such is the explanation given by Eusebius. Another scholar, Anatolius, "reached the pinnacle" of Greek learning and founded a Peripatetic school at Alexandria. During a revolt there he persuaded many rebels to escape to the Roman camp, and afterward both he and another proimperial Christian named Eusebius moved to Syria. There Eusebius became bishop of Laodicea and was succeeded by Anatolius, who was at first the coadjutor of Theotecnus of Caesarea in Palestine. The bishop of Laodicea after Anatolius was also devoted to philosophy but, as Eusebius says, did not show himself to be "a true philosopher" in the face of persecution. After he had concealed his faith during the persecution under Diocletian, "God himself" proclaimed as bishop a physician named Theodotus who restored the character of the church.[25]

All these examples illustrate the close correlation of third-century Christianity with the philosophical and governmental world of the time. Those who lived in the world did not necessarily treat their Christian allegiance lightly. Among the martyrs under Galerius were Philoromus, a judge at Alexandria, and Phileas, bishop of Thmuis and a philosopher. Their judges urged them to recant and retain their positions in society. They refused and were beheaded.[26]

The Christian movement toward penetration of Roman society and its

[23] H. I. Marrou in J. Daniélou and H. I. Marrou, *The Christian Centuries: The First Six Hundred Years* (New York, 1964), 224-25.
[24] Eusebius, *H. E.* 7, 5.
[25] Eusebius, *H. E.* 7, 32.
[26] *Ibid.*, 8, 9, 6-8.

inescapable concomitant, the secularization of the church, encountered opposition on the part of various Christians. Among them were the major theologians of the early third century: Tertullian, Hippolytus, and Origen. Bishops too often spoke out against what they regarded as lax discipline among the Christian *militia*. In order for the church to survive and grow it had to attract and keep its members, and in crises like that over Novatian in 251 the leaders could be depended on to oppose excessively rigid discipline. They had no desire for the church to become an insignificant sect even if it were to consist of none but the saints.

The world which the Christians were penetrating was itself in danger of collapsing, and in this period wealthy provincials often abandoned urban life because of the pressure of taxes and other civic responsibilities. Such men might turn to Christianity in the hope of finding a different world but would be disillusioned by Christian secularity. Thus groups arose within and on the edge of the church in which an appeal was made to the example of the apostles. Such a group, calling itself "apostolic," did arise in Asia Minor and taught the renunciation of marriage and private property; they were also known as Apotactites ("renouncers"). The Apotactites, along with the Novatianists and the Encratites ("continent"), were still flourishing in Phrygia in the fourth century;[27] imperial decrees denounced them all between 381 and 383.[28]

More important for the future was the case of the wealthy Christian orphan Antonius, who decided at the age of eighteen, in about 270, to practice the gospel precepts of perfection. Giving away his inheritance, leaving his sister and his home, he lived first in a tomb, later on a mountain near the Nile. For months at a time his diet was bread and water. Crowds came out to see and hear him, and many built cells nearby in order to practice asceticism under his guidance. Early in the fourth century he organized the monastic life of his fellow hermits and then withdrew to a mountain by the Red Sea. He emerged only to preach against Arianism at Alexandria.[29] Athanasius, who regarded him as a hero of the faith, wrote his life.[30] It is probably significant both theologically and sociologically that Eusebius, devoted to the Christian empire, never mentioned him. Antonius was hostile toward Eusebius' Christology; in addition, his withdrawal from the world meant withdrawal from the life of the empire in which, Eusebius believed, Christians should participate. According to Rufinus, however, the emperor Constantine was deeply impressed by Antonius and wrote to him "as to one of the prophets," requesting his prayers on behalf of himself and his children.[31]

---

[27] *MAMA* I 172-175 (cf. p. xv; W. M. Calder in *Anatolian Studies* (Manchester, 1923), 59-91.

[28] *Cod. Theod.* 16, 5, 7; 9; 11.

[29] Theodoret, *H. E.* 4, 27; Athanasius, *Vita Antonii* 69.

[30] Cf. R. Reitzenstein, *Des Athanasius Werk über das Leben des Antonius* (Heidelberg, 1914).

[31] *H. E.* 10, 8.

It is doubtless significant that Antonius probably could not read or write, though he dictated letters in Coptic which·interpreters translated into Greek.[32] The monastic movement which he began, however, had antecedents among pagans and Jews alike and was not as such in conflict with either church or state.

[32] Cf. G. Bardy, *La question des langues dans l'église ancienne* I (Paris, 1948), 45-46.

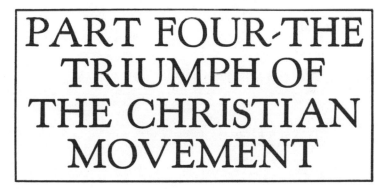

PART FOUR-THE TRIUMPH OF THE CHRISTIAN MOVEMENT

In spite of political and social disturbances, the Christian churches generally enjoyed forty years of peace after Gallienus issued his decree in 260. To be sure, the emperor Aurelian dedicated a temple to the sun god Sol Invictus on the Campus Agrippae in Rome in 274 and endeavored to have this god universally worshiped. An inscription pointing to Sol's special protection of the emperor dates from 275,[1] but no persecution accompanied this religious move. The atmosphere of syncretism in the late third century was such that, generally speaking, Christian peculiarities went unnoticed. Perhaps more significantly, Aurelian himself did favors for the church and doubtless expected some return. In addition, the empire from 260 until well into the reign of Diocletian was actually too weak to be able to indulge in persecution.

[1] *ILS* 580.

CHAPTER XVII
DIOCLETIAN AND
THE PERSECUTION

I. THE EMPEROR DIOCLETIAN

On November 20, 284, the military anarchy under which the empire had suffered for many years was brought to an end; a soldier from Dalmatia with the Greek name Diocles seized the throne, and as the Roman Diocletian he was to reign for two decades.[1] Naturally it took some time for the unrest to die down, and as one revolt followed another Diocletian broadened the scope of imperial rule; in the spring of 285 he appointed another Dalmatian soldier, Maximian, as Caesar, and sent him to Gaul to subdue the Bagaudae, peasants organized against Roman rule and taxation. According to a late martyrological tradition, probably unreliable, after Maximian had crossed the Alps he had to execute a "legion" of Christians from Egypt who refused

---

[1] A. H. M. Jones, *The Later Roman Empire* (Norman, Okla., 1964), I, 38. For the date cf. T. C. Skeat, *Papyri from Panopolis* (Dublin, 1964), 82: Papyrus 2, lines 162-63. On Diocletian generally cf. W. Ensslin in *CAH* XII 383-408 and *RE* VII A 2419-95; W. Seston, *Dioclétien et la tétrarchie* I (Paris, 1946), with the review by N. H. Baynes in *JRS* 38 (1948), 109-13.

to offer sacrifice to the gods.² More significant politically, the chief of the Baguadae was issuing coins on which he himself was called both Caesar and Augustus, and perhaps Maximian was raised to the rank of Augustus in 286 after he had put the Bagaudae down.³

Further revolts in Gaul and Britain as well as in the east tested the strength of the two emperors, and an inscription from Egypt in 288 shows that they had already put themselves under the protection of Jupiter and Hercules, with a view toward victory.⁴ After a serious revolt broke out in Egypt in 292, Diocletian decided to expand the administration still further. On March 1, 293, two more soldiers were given power, both as Caesars to the supreme Augusti. Along with these appointments came a reorganized administration. The provinces were too large for efficient control, and as Lactantius says, the emperor "chopped them into slices."⁵ At the same time the provinces were combined in larger groupings known as "dioceses," each under the control of a deputy of the praetorian prefects. This deputy was called a *vicarius,* a title which like "diocese" later occurs among Christians.⁶ At the top of the administration were the Augusti Diocletian and Maximian, whose governments were ruled from Nicomedia in Bithynia and from Milan. Diocletian's Caesar Galerius ruled part of the east from Sirmium; Maximian's Caesar Constantius Chlorus ruled Gaul and Britain (after 297) from Trier. This tetrarchy was bound together by alliances, for each Caesar married the daughter of his Augustus. The emperors stood under the protection of Jupiter and Hercules, and Diocletian called himself *Jovius,* Maximian *Herculius.*⁷ They thus did not identify themselves with these gods, and an inscription referring to them as "generated gods and parents of gods" was using merely traditional language— or so it would appear.⁸

II·RELIGION AND PERSECUTION

Problems of religion and social ethics were woven together in the cases of those Christians who became "military martyrs." On March 12, 295, a young man named Maximilian refused induction into the army at Theveste in

---

² D. van Berchem, *Le martyre de la légion thébaine* (Basel, 1956); negative conclusions not refuted by L. Dupraz, *Les passions de S. Maurice d'Agaune* (Fribourg, 1961).

³ Cf. R. MacMullen, *op. cit.,* 211-13.

⁴ *ILS* 617.

⁵ *De mort. persec.* 7, 4.

⁶ On vicarius cf. W. Ensslin in *RE* XXII 2418 and VIII A 2023-44.

⁷ N. H. Baynes (*JRS* 34, 1944, 136) notes that the Christian apologist Lactantius especially ridicules Jupiter and Hercules.

⁸ *ILS* 629; cf. W. Ensslin in *Sitzungsberichte der Bayerischen Akad. der Wiss., Philos-hist. Abt.,* 1943, no. 6, 44 and 29; also N. H. Baynes in *JRS* 38 (1948), 111.

Numidia. Though the proconsul of Africa reminded him that other Christians were soldiers, he remained obdurate and was executed.[9] On July 21, 298, the centurion Marcellus publicly renounced his military oath; three months later he was put to death by the vicar of the Spanish provinces.[10] These martyrs may have been unwilling to recognize the emperors as Jovii and Herculii,[11] but this point is not made in the martyr acts themselves.[12]

Under the tetrarchy there was much concern for the revival of Roman religion. An edict on marriage (May 1, 295) clearly shows that legislation and religion were closely associated. "The Roman empire has attained its present greatness by the favor of all deities only because it has protected all its laws with wise religious observance and concern for morality."[13] The immortal gods guard Rome because she deserves their protection. On March 31, 297, an edict against the Manichees was based on religious and political considerations. Refugees and missionaries from Persia were active in Africa, arousing violent disturbances. They could be expected to infect the whole empire with their Persian immorality. The emperors therefore denounced the Manichees in the name of the immortal gods and the ancient religion. "It is highly criminal to discuss doctrines once and for all laid down and settled by our forefathers." The obstinacy (*pertinacia*) of the Manichees therefore deserved punishment.

The penalties provided were much like those appointed for Christians in the time of Valerian. Leaders of the sect were to be burned alive; the Manichaean scriptures were also to be destroyed. Followers were subject to the death penalty and to the confiscation of property. Romans of the upper classes who joined the sect or espoused Persian doctrines were to have their property confiscated, while they themselves would be sent to mines at Phaeno in Arabia or on the island of Proconnesus in the Sea of Marmara.[14]

Diocletian's rescript stated that Manichaean doctrine was like a poison infecting the empire, and the same point is made by Eusebius in his account of Mani. This echo and others suggest that he knew the rescript. He does not mention it, however, for it would detract from his picture of the church as the only victim of persecution.[15] Certainly Christian leaders loyally welcomed the imperial pronouncement. A bishop of Alexandria, probably Theonas (282–300), denounced the Manichees as insane in a letter still preserved on papyrus, while about 300 the Neoplatonist Christian Alexander, from Lycopolis in Egypt, attacked their doctrine and their Persian origin.[16]

---

[9] *Acta Maximiliani* (pp. 86-87 Knopf-Krüger).
[10] *Acta Marcelli* (pp. 87-89).
[11] W. Seston in *Mélanges Goguel* (Neuchatel, 1950), 239-46.
[12] Study by John Helgeland.
[13] *Coll. Mos. Rom. leg.* 6, 4.
[14] *Coll. Mos. Rom. leg.* 15, 3.
[15] Eusebius, *H. E.* 7, 31.
[16] A. Adam, *Texte zum Manichäismus* (Berlin, 1954), 52-56.

An incident between 298 and 301, however, suggested that trouble might arise. Omens were being taken in the presence of both Diocletian and Galerius when Christian courtiers made the sign of the cross to avert demons; the omens were not a success. Diocletian thereupon ordered that everyone in the palace offer sacrifice to the gods or be beaten. Military commanders were also told that soldiers were to sacrifice or be discharged from the army.[17]

Around this time the synod of Elvira in Spain insisted that a Christian who sacrificed to idols would be permanently excommunicated; landowners who received products offered to idols would be subject to excommunication for five years; idols were not to be located in Christian houses except on account of non-Christian slaves.[18] This kind of exception, due to social pressure, was also made in the cases of flamens (priests of the imperial cult) and certain other priests and magistrates. Flamens were to be excommunicated if they presided over gladiatorial combats or immoral shows; if they had not offered sacrifice they could be restored to communion after penance or, if they were catechumens, could be baptized after a three-year period. If as priests they had merely worn crowns they could be restored after two years. As duumvirs for a one-year term they should stay away from the church. Any Christian present at sacrifices in a local Capitolium would have to do penance for ten years. On the other hand, anyone killed because he tried to smash an idol was not to be regarded as a martyr; there was no precedent for his action either in the gospel or among the apostles.[19] All in all, the decisions of Elvira upheld the basic Christian position but did so in a rather conciliatory fashion.

The situation of the empire was deteriorating, however, and anti-Christian sentiment was growing at the same time. Colossal government expenditures, both military and civil, led to increased taxation and devalued currency. Indeed, to preserve the purchasing power of money Diocletian issued orders to burn the books of "the ancient Egyptians" with prescriptions for transmuting base metals into gold and silver. Even alchemy, it was supposed, was a threat to the Roman currency.[20] The Christian apologist Lactantius thus described the crisis:

The number of persons receiving funds was so much greater than that of the taxpayers that enormous assessments were levied. Consequently, the tenant farmers were exhausted, fields were abandoned, and cultivated areas were transformed into wilderness.

Diocletian (not unnaturally) "would never permit the treasury to be diminished," and his "various iniquities produced enormously high prices."[21]

---

[17] Lactantius, *De mort. persec.* 10; Eusebius, *H. E.* 8, 4, 3; cf. N. H. Baynes in *CAH* XII 663-64.

[18] Elvira, Can. 1 (pp. 221-22 Hefele-Leclerq); 40-41 (pp. 244-45).

[19] Elvira, Can. 2-4 (pp. 222-24); 55-56 (pp. 251-53); 59-60 (pp. 254-55).

[20] W. Seston, *Dioclétien et la tétrarchie* I (Paris, 1946), 155-56.

[21] *De mort. persec.* 7, 3-12.

Lactantius does not mention the activities of speculators who on news of impending devaluation immediately exchanged money for "all kinds of goods at whatever price" had to be paid.[22] Another apologist, Arnobius, noted the charge that because of Christianity "poverty of agricultural produce and scarcity of grain have a more relentless grip." In reply he pointed to the period of three hundred years since the beginning of Christianity. "Has there been no time at all when things have been cheap and abundant?" Indeed, in the past there had been "many periods of low prices and abundance of commodities" when low prices had caused "an amazing paralysis of business undertakings."[23]

In 301 Diocletian took steps to curb the runaway price spiral, issuing an edict to fix maximum prices and, in many instances, wages as well. In his preamble he referred to the insatiable avarice of speculators and profiteers and prescribed the death penalty for violation of the regulations. He spoke of the past favor shown Rome by the immortal gods and insisted upon the religious attitude with which the common good was to be pursued.[24] Lactantius, as could be expected, saw nothing good in this edict but spoke only of the blood spilled because of such "trivial matters." Because of fear, no goods appeared on the market and prices soared. "In the end, after many people had lost their lives, it became absolutely necessary to repeal the law."[25] To some extent Lactantius' attitude was justified. No action had been taken to mitigate the underlying causes of the price inflation. His bitterly hostile attitude toward Diocletian, however, did not lead him to an understanding of the economic problem.

During the winter of 302–303 a series of conferences between Diocletian and Galerius took place at Nicomedia. Galerius, supported by several civil and military advisers, argued that Christianity had to be repressed. Among the advisers the chief was Sossianus Hierocles, *praeses* of Bithynia and author of two books against the Christians; Lactantius calls him the *auctor et consiliarus* of the persecution,[26] Diocletian preferred to forbid the practice of Christianity simply among court officials and in the army, but after the oracle of Apollo at Miletus supported Galerius' position he yielded; he still refused to allow bloodshed.[27]

The festival of the Terminalia on February 23, 303, was set for the termination of Christianity, and at dawn imperial officers broke into the church near the palace in Nicomedia. The scriptures were burned and the building was first looted, then demolished by praetorian guards. The next day the so-called

[22] P. Ryl. 607 (N. Lewis and M. Reinhold, *Roman Civilization* II, New York, 1955, 463).

[23] *Adv. gent.* I, 3; I, 13-14.

[24] Preamble, *ILS* 642.

[25] *De mort. persec.* 7, 6-7.

[26] *Ibid.*, 16, 4; he had been *praeses* of Arabia after 293 (*CIL* III 1661; *L'année épigraphique* 1932, 79) and would continue active persecution as prefect of Egypt in 307 (C. Vandersleyen in *Journal of Juristic Papyrology* 13, 1961, 109-22).

[27] Frend, *Martyrdom*, 363.

first edict was published. Churches were to be destroyed, assemblies forbidden, scriptures burned. Christians of rank were to lose all privileges; imperial servants were to be reduced to slavery.[28]

Most of these provisions seem to have been based on the old edicts of Valerian. For the moment, however, there was no question of the death penalty, and sacrifice was not yet required. There were two innovations: the destruction of Christian buildings and, as in the case of Egyptians and Manichees, the burning of literature.

At Oxyrhynchus in Egypt as late as February 5, 304, a lector from the "former church" of the village of Chysis was making a declaration of the church's property and insisting that it had not possessed any gold, silver, money, clothing, beasts, slaves, lands, or property derived either from grants or from bequests. It had owned only a bronze gate, already on its way to Alexandria in accordance with the orders of the prefect of Egypt, Clodius Culcianus. This declaration, preserved in triplicate, ends with an oath by the Genius of the emperors—the two Augusti and the two Caesars.[29]

Two mysterious fires in the palace, variously ascribed to Christians, to agents of Galerius, and to lightning, along with revolts in Melitene and Syria, led to the promulgation of a second edict requiring the imprisonment of the higher clergy. "On all sides," says Eusebius, "prisons built long ago for murderers and grave-robbers were filled with bishops, presbyters and deacons, readers and exorcists, so that no space was left for condemned criminals."[30] Diocletian was aware of the situation and at Rome that summer he proclaimed an amnesty as part of the celebration of the twentieth year of his reign. For this celebration an arch was erected at Salonica, with images of Pluto, Hades, Proserpina or Hecate, Oceanus and Terra, Diocletian's protector Jupiter (but not Maximian's Hercules), the Dioscuri, and even Serapis and Isis.[31] Christians were left in prison until November, when a third edict offered them freedom if they would sacrifice to the gods. If they did not do so, they were liable to torture though not necessarily to the death penalty.[32] The crucial fourth edict, promulgated in the east in the spring of 304, renewed the demand made by Decius half a century earlier. "All the people in all the cities in a body" were to offer sacrifices and libations to the gods. The alternatives were death or hard labor in the mines—the same mines to which Manichees had been sent since 297—or enslavement in the government operated weaving mills.[33]

The edicts were differently enforced in the west and in the east. In Gaul

---

[28] Lactantius, *De mort. persec.* 11-13; Eusebius, *H. E.* 8, 2, 4.
[29] P. Oxy. 2673.
[30] *H. E.* 8, 6, 9.
[31] Seston, *op. cit.*, 250-57; for the date, 392.
[32] Eusebius, *H. E.* 8, 2, 5.
[33] Eusebius, *M. P.* 3, 1; *V. C.* 2, 34.

and Britain Constantius Chlorus demolished a few churches in 303, but there were no martyrs in his territories, and he must never have published the fourth edict.[34] In the territories under Maximian there were few martyrs, though an inscription, now lost, from Haidra in North Africa lists thirty-four Christians who suffered in "the persecution of Diocletian and Maximian."[35] No Christians are certainly known to have been executed in the west after December 304, and the chief problem there was caused by *traditores* who obeyed the first edict and handed over the Christian scriptures. In the east, on the other hand, all four edicts were enforced, and the sacrifices made by many Christians later presented difficulties.[36]

By the spring of 305 it seemed evident to Diocletian that neither he nor his fellow Augustus Maximian could solve the problems of the empire. On May 1 he announced his abdication at Nicomedia, claiming that he had already saved the world. Maximian retired at Milan; the two Caesars became Augusti, Galerius in the east and Constantius in the west. Galerius' nephew Maximin Daia became his Caesar, but Constantine, the son of Constantius, was passed over in favor of an Illyrian soldier named Severus.

The new order, accompanied by a lull in the persecution, seems to have suggested to Peter of Alexandria that it was time for a declaration of amnesty in the church. Issued shortly before Easter in 306, Peter's letter insisted on the possibility of restoration for almost anyone who repented of his lapses. No penalties at all were assigned to those who had first denied and then confessed, to those who had bribed the authorities, or to those who abandoned their property and fled. Those who had lapsed under torture and had been penitent for three years were now to fast for forty days. Six months of penance were provided for Christians who had pretended to offer sacrifice or for Christian slaves sent to sacrifice by their masters (the masters were assigned three years of penance). One year was provided for those who had lapsed in prison without torture, three years for those who had simply concealed themselves. Confessors in prison had written him about those who had been forced to consume sacrifices with bridles or chains holding their mouths open, or had had their hands burned at the sacrificial fire. Such men were to be regarded as confessors of the church. Peter was also convinced that voluntary martyrs were not true martyrs at all. Clerics who volunteered and then lapsed were to be deposed, though not excommunicated.[37]

Before Easter, however, Maximin Daia issued a new edict requiring universal sacrifice at temples. Heralds summoned sacrificers to the temples, while army

[34] Lactantius, *De mort. persec.* 15, 6; Eusebius, *H. E.* 8, 13, 13.

[35] *ILT* 470; cf. H. Delehaye in *Analecta Bollandiana* 54 (1936), 312-14; N. et Y. Duval in *Mélanges Piganiol* (Paris, 1966), II, 1153-89.

[36] G. E. M. de Ste. Croix in *HTR* 47 (1954), 75-113.

[37] M. J. Routh, *Reliquiae Sacrae* (ed. 2, Oxford, 1846), IV, 23-45; cf. G. Fritz in *DTC* XII 1802-4.

officers checked census lists of individuals; but Eusebius mentions only three martyrs in Palestine during the whole year.[38]

The administrative problems of the empire prevented full attention from being paid to the Christian problem. Constantine had fled to Britain in order to be with his ailing father Constantius, who died at York on July 25, 306; the legions hailed the son as Augustus, and Galerius tried compromise by making Severus Augustus with Constantine as his Caesar. Maximian's son Maxentius soon joined a tax revolt against Severus in Italy and on October 26 assumed the title PRINCEPS INVICTUS. Constantine, eager for support, married Maxentius' sister Fausta in 307.

In November 308 Diocletian emerged from retirement to preside over an imperial conference at Carnuntum on the Danube. The only change now made was the appointment of Licinius, an old ally of Galerius, as Augustus of the west. Constantine was to be his Caesar. The claims of Maxentius were dismissed. Presumably at the close of the conference, "the most religious Augusti and Caesars" identified themselves as Jovii and Herculii and expressed their official gratitude to the Unconquered Sun, patron of the empire, by renovating the principal Mithraeum at Carnuntum.[39] Around the same time, Diocletian was having a colossal statue of the sun god erected at Sirmium, while Constantine, it was well known, was devoted to the same god.

Maximin Daia returned from the conference determined to eradicate Christianity in Libya, Egypt, Palestine, Syria, and Cilicia. He did not attack at once but waited until 309, then issuing a new edict providing for the rebuilding of pagan temples and for compulsory participation in public sacrifices. Every article for sale in the market was to be "defiled" (the Christian term) by libations and sacrificed blood.[40] This edict met no popular response, although between November 309 and March 311 twenty Christians were executed in Palestine—in addition to a Marcionite bishop whom Eusebius does not regard as a Christian.[41] This Marcionite was the only bishop from Palestine to be executed during the entire persecution, though Silvanus of Gaza died of old age or sickness after working in the mines at Phaeno.[42] The total number of martyrs in Palestine was approximately ninety-one.

All in all, as Grégoire, de Ste. Croix, and others have claimed, the number of martyrs even in the areas under Maximin's control was not large. In 308–309 precisely 97 Egyptian Christians were sent to the mines at Phaeno; a little later they were followed by 130 more, some to Phaeno, others to Cilicia.[43] After two years almost all of them were released.

---

[38] Eusebius, *M. P.* 4-6. Christians were compelled to sacrifice and, if enlisted, could not leave the army; cf. *MAMA* I 170.

[39] *ILS* 659; E. Swoboda, *Carnuntum* (ed. 4, Graz-Köln, 1964), 72.

[40] Eusebius, *M. P.* 9, 2.

[41] *Ibid.*, 9, 2—11, 31; 10, 3.

[42] *Ibid.*, 13, 4-5.

[43] *Ibid.*, 8, 1 and 13; G. E. M. de Ste. Croix in *HTR* 47 (1954), 102 n. 105.

During the crisis period at the end, Roman administrators sometimes came to suspect that Christians were engaged in a foreign conspiracy. Some Egyptians brought before the *praeses* Firmilian at Caesarea in 310 gave their names as Elijah, Jeremiah, Isaiah, Samuel, and Daniel; they claimed that they were natives of Jerusalem, a country which lay to the east.[44] In fact there was a Christian "dispersion"; in 324 Constantine stated that during the persecution under Diocletian Christians had fled from the Roman world and had been welcomed by "barbarians," doubtless including the Christians of Armenia.[45]

In the spring of 311 Galerius, now suffering from an illness that was to prove fatal, was at Nicomedia and brought to an end the persecution once begun there. He stated that the Christians, ordered to "return to the institutions of the ancients," had simply abandoned their own rites without participating in Roman religion. Imperial clemency now made toleration necessary. Christians were therefore "once more free to live as Christians," and they could reestablish their churches provided that nothing was done contrary to public order. For the moment, nothing was said of the right to make converts, to rebuild church edifices, and to recover church properties,[46] but it could be expected that permission would soon follow.

After Galerius' death his successor Maximin Daia, ruler in Asia Minor, Syria, and Egypt, reluctantly accepted the edict, and his praetorian prefect instructed the provincial governors to liberate Christian prisoners.[47] At the same time, however, he let it be known that he would welcome petitions against the Christians from the cities. Such a petition from the citizens of Nicomedia[48] resulted in the execution of Lucian of Antioch on January 7, 312. Petitions had doubtless caused the deaths of Peter of Alexandria and Silvanus of Emesa. Other petitions were made at Antioch, Tyre, and Arykanda in Lycia.[49] Maximin also endeavored to promote a revival of pagan religion by appointing priests of the gods in each city and high priests in each province. Forged *Acts of Pilate* were supplied for study in the schools.[50] By the end of 312, however, Maximin discerned the signs of the times and sent a letter to provincial governors urging toleration.[51] Shortly before his defeat by Licinius in April 313 he finally issued an edict to this effect.[52]

The signs he discerned included the failure of a brief campaign in Armenia, where he had tried to impose pagan worship on the Christians, and a disastrous famine due to the failure of crops. According to Eusebius, the price of one

[44] Eusebius, *M. P.* 11, 8-12.
[45] Eusebius, *V. C.* 2, 53.
[46] Lactantius, *De mort. persec.* 34; N. H. Baynes in *CAH* XII 347.
[47] Eusebius, *H. E.* 9, 1, 2-9.
[48] *Ibid.*, 9, 9ᵃ, 4.
[49] *Ibid.*, 9, 2; 9, 7, 3-14; *OGIS* 569 = *ILCV* 1.
[50] *Ibid.*, 9, 4, 2—5, 1.
[51] *Ibid.*, 9, 9ᵃ, 1-9.
[52] *Ibid.*, 9, 10, 7-11.

measure of wheat (fixed at 100 denarii in Diocletian's edict of 301) reached 2,500 denarii at this point.[53] Under the circumstances, Maximin was unable either to carry through an invasion of Europe or to withstand Licinius' counterattack. The political and social situation made it impossible for the persecution to go on.

[53] *Ibid.*, 9, 8, 4. On the "Attic" denarius cf. T. C. Skeat, *Papyri from Panopolis* (Dublin, 1964), xxxi. Wheat at 10,000 drachmae in 314: G. Mickwitz, *Geld und Wirtschaft im römischen Reich des vierten Jahrhunderts n. Chr. (Societas Scientiarum Fennica, Comment. human. Litt.* 4, 2, Helsingfors, 1932), 99-100.

CHAPTER XVIII
CONSTANTINE AND THE CHURCH

In 311, when Galerius issued his edict of toleration, the *de facto* ruler of Italy was Maxentius, son of Maximian; he too issued an edict of toleration and restored the properties of the Roman church to the bishop Miltiades.[1]

In the following year Constantine left Gaul and moved against him. After crossing the Alps with a fairly small army, he finally reached the outskirts of Rome, apparently having already seen a vision of the cross standing above the sun. On the cross were the words, "By this conquer." Christ appeared to him and told him to place this pattern on a military standard. Thus originated the *labarum,* a spear with the Chi Rho at the top and a crossbar from which hung a banner with busts of Constantine and his sons. The account of this vision, according to Eusebius, came from the emperor himself.[2] According to Lactantius, Constantine was outside Rome on the night of October 26 when he dreamed that he should draw the Chi Rho on his soldiers' shields in order to win victory[3] These accounts presumably refer to different events.

[1] Augustine, *Brevic. collat. cum Donat.* 34 (*PL* 43, 645).
[2] Eusebius, *V. C.* 1, 27-32.
[3] *De mort. persec.* 44, 5.

Within the capital city Maxentius was preparing for combat by offering sacrifices and consulting the Sibylline books, where he found the enigmatic prophecy that an enemy of the Romans would perish.[4] On October 27 he took up a position across the Tiber from Rome, with the Milvian bridge (supplemented by pontoons) behind him. In defeat he withdrew across the bridge and the pontoons collapsed; his body was found in the river the next day. The Romans enthusiastically hailed Constantine, who claimed to be restoring the Roman senate and people to their pristine glory and freedom.[5] He was now sole ruler in the west, while Licinius, now his ally, ruled eastern Europe. His victory had been due to the power of Christ. How was he to respond?

Early in 313 Constantine met Licinius at Milan, and they agreed upon the terms of a letter concerning the Christians which was issued at once by Constantine and in May or June by Licinius, after his victory over Maximin.[6] In addition, it would appear, the emperors agreed upon the form of a prayer to be used by Licinius' troops before encountering the enemy. Addressed to the *summus deus,* it commended the imperial cause to him and requested divine aid.[7] The letter concerning the Christians states that the emperors had conferred about "the advantage and security of the state" and had concluded that it would be served by granting freedom of religious choice not only to Christians but to all others as well. Under such circumstances the *summa divinitas,* now freely worshiped, might bestow his favor upon the empire and its rulers. They intended not to dishonor any religion, whatever it might be. In consequence, all confiscated churches in the possession of the treasury or of private persons were to be returned to Christians; no indemnity would be paid. Other church properties were also to be restored, and the treasury would indemnify those who had purchased church lands.

Three points deserve emphasis. First, the basic purpose of the letter was to ensure divine favor for the state by worship of the *summa divinitas.* Second, this favor was also to be elicited by the return of church properties. Third, it was assumed that there was one united body of Christians, distinguishable from adherents of other religious cults.

I·THE DONATIST PROBLEM

The last of these assumptions was abruptly shaken soon afterward when Constantine, now master of Africa, received word from the proconsul about divisions within the Christian church. In reply he instructed the proconsul

[4] Zosimus, 2, 16; Lactantius, *op. cit.,* 44, 8.

[5] Eusebius, *H. E.* 9, 9; *V. C.* 1, 38-40; cf. *ILS* 694.

[6] Lactantius, *De mort. persec.* 48, 2-12; Eusebius, *H. E.* 10, 2-14.

[7] Lactantius, *op. cit.,* 46, 6; cf. Eusebius, *V. C.* 4, 20; N. H. Baynes in *CAH* XII 688-89.

to restore the properties which belonged to "the Catholic church of the Christians." He also wrote directly to Caecilian, Catholic bishop of Carthage, providing him with a gift of 3,000 *folles* and the promise of more if necessary. Troublemakers at Carthage were to be brought before Roman judges. A month or two later he went further by directing the proconsul to exempt from civic responsibilities the clerics of "the Catholic church governed by Caecilian."[8]

The problems in Africa had arisen as early as 305, when the election of a bishop at Cirta had been troubled by charges that an elector, the senior bishop in Numidia, had been a *traditor,* i.e., had handed over the scriptures to the authorities. The accuser, according to a later Catholic critic, was himself a confessed murderer; the bishop finally elected took bribes for ordaining men to the presbyterate.[9] In 311 troubles broke out again. A deacon of Carthage denounced the emperor Maxentius as a tyrant, and the bishop Mensurius, ordered to surrender him, went to Rome himself but died there soon thereafter. His archdeacon Caecilian succeeded him. Unfortunately Caecilian had alienated a rich and pious woman named Lucilla by insisting that before receiving the communion she was not to kiss the bones of a martyr not recognized by the church. Lucilla provided lavish gifts (400 *folles*) for seventy Numidian bishops meeting at Carthage, and they denounced Caecilian as having been consecrated by *traditores.* The lector Majorinus, a member of Lucilla's household, was made rival bishop of Carthage.[10] It was this situation in which Constantine intervened.

From Caecilian's opponents came a petition asking that the case be heard in Gaul where, thanks to the emperor's father, there had been no persecution.[11] Constantine responded by ordering Caecilian to appear at Rome with twenty other bishops, evenly divided between friends and foes, and to present his case before Miltiades of Rome and three bishops from Gaul.[12] The court, soon expanded by the addition of fourteen Italian bishops, heard testimony for three days and on October 2, 313, excommunicated Donatus of Casae Nigrae, the leader of Caecilian's opponents, and recognized Caecilian as bishop. The Donatists (whose name was derived either from this Donatus or from the next schismatic bishop of Carthage) did not accept the decision and asked the emperor for a new trial—thus appealing to the state against the church.

The synod which assembled at Arles in August 314 marked a new stage in the life of the church. Whereas the synod at Rome in 313 had been attended only by bishops from Italy, Africa, and Gaul, and had dealt only with charges brought against Caecilian by the Donatists, the synod of Arles had a much

---

[8] Eusebius, *H. E.* 10, 5, 16—7 ,2. On the *follis,* worth about 12,500 debased denarii, cf. A. H. M. Jones in *JRS* 49 (1959), 34-38.

[9] Optatus 1, 13; on these problems cf. W. H. C. Frend, *The Donatist Church* (Oxford, 1952).

[10] *Ibid.,* 1, 19.

[11] *Ibid.,* 1, 22.

[12] Eusebius, *H. E.* 10, 5, 16-18.

broader representation and its decisions were far more wide-ranging. Letters are still in existence from the emperor to Alafius, vicar of Africa, concerning the transportation of bishops to the synod, and to Chrestus, bishop of Syracuse in Sicily, who apparently acted as president in the absence of Silvester of Rome.[13] No Donatist representatives were present, but the synod was attended by representatives of forty-four churches in Britain, Gaul, Spain, Sardinia, Sicily, Italy, and Dalmatia, as well as from Mauretania, Numidia, and Africa. Most of the churches were represented by bishops, some (including Rome) by presbyters and/or deacons. A few exorcists and lectors were also present.[14] The twenty-two canons promulgated by the synod began with the question of paschal uniformity and went on to moral problems, especially those arising in consequence of the recent persecution. The questions raised by the Donatists were discussed: evidence against so-called "traditors" could be taken only from public records, while false accusations were to result in permanent excommunication. The Donatists themselves were explicitly condemned.[15]

The Donatists immediately replied at Carthage by bringing charges against Felix, bishop of Aptunga, who had consecrated Caecilian. They presented documentary proof that he had been a "traditor" and requested an investigation of his conduct. In February 315 a trial before the proconsul of Africa ended with the demonstration that the documents were forgeries. During the year the schismatic bishop of Carthage died and was succeeded by the more famous Donatus, a man of great vigor who in 316 resisted an imperial edict expropriating Donatist churches. Bloodshed was halted in 317 by an imperial letter, and in North Africa Donatism continued to flourish. A synod held about 330 was attended by no fewer than 270 Donatist bishops.[16]

Donatism was significant not only because of its insistence upon the attitudes and actions of those who held office in the churches but also because of its complex relationship to the state. Donatus himself asked, "What has the emperor to do with the church?"[17] His own party, however, had once appealed to the state against a hostile Catholic community. The problem had arisen out of the recognition of the church by the emperor. Once Constantine recognized the church he had to decide what kind of church it was. Recognition led to intervention. He was the first emperor to use the power of the state against schism, and he did so without success.

On May 5, 321, Constantine issued a rescript to the vicar of Africa and

[13] C. H. Turner, *Ecclesiae Occidentalis Monumenta Iuris Antiquissima* (Oxford, 1909-1939), I, 2, 376-79: *CSEL* 26, 204; Eusebius, *H. E.* 10, 5, 21-24.

[14] *Ibid.*, 396-414.

[15] *Ibid.*, 381-95; on the synod cf. also C. J. Hefele and H. Leclerq, *Histoire des conciles* I (Paris, 1907), 275-98.

[16] Augustine, *Ep.* 93, 43; cf. Frend, *op. cit.*, 167.

[17] For the form of this question, significant in Christian controversies, cf. 2 Cor. 6:14-16 and Tertullian, *De praescr. haer.* 7, 9. Donatus' question: Optatus 3, 3.

informed him that no further persecution of the Donatists would take place,[18] and around the same time he wrote to the bishops and laity of Africa, expressing his regret that the measures he had taken to promote peace and unity had not been successful. God himself would bring Donatism to an end; meanwhile the church people of Africa had to endure their trials with patience.[19]

The emperor's concern for unity was doubtless related to the steps he was taking against Licinius. In 320 the consuls were himself and his son Constantine II; in 321 they were his sons Crispus and Constantine, both described as Caesars. Licinius, pointedly ignored, proceeded to unify his own realm on a pagan foundation. He had been willing if not eager to tolerate Christian diversity; thus in 318–319 a "synagogue of the Marcionites . . . of the Lord and Savior Jesus Christ" was built near Damascus.[20] Now, however, he forbade the meetings of synods and, indeed, of Christians within the cities; he also insisted that men and women were not to worship together. As Eusebius suggests, he viewed Christians as supporters of Constantine.[21]

Battles between July and September 324 left Constantine master of the Roman world. (The year is established by a papyrus rent receipt which shows that Licinius was still emperor on September 3, 324 but not on July 24, 325.[22]) For the moment he spared Licinius' life at the request of his own sister Constantia, wife of the defeated ruler, and he issued a letter to all the people of the eastern provinces. He desired peace, concord, and tranquillity, to be ensured by equal privileges for pagans and Christians alike. Christianity alone was true, but he prayed to God that pagans might also enjoy God's blessing.[23] It is fairly clear that he had learned the folly of enforced unity from his experiences with the Donatists.

II·THE ARIAN PROBLEM

Constantine apparently did not realize what difficulties he had acquired along with the realm of Licinius, and he was on his way from Nicomedia to the Holy Land when news of the troubles at Alexandria reached him.[24] He then sent his ecclesiastical adviser Ossius of Cordova to the city with a letter to the bishop Alexander and the presbyter Arius, locked in combat. It would

---

[18] H. von Soden, *Urkunden zur Entstehungsgeschichte des Donatismus* (Bonn, 1913), no. 30.

[19] Optatus, App. ix (*CSEL* 26, 212-13).

[20] *OGIS* 608.

[21] *H. E.* 10, 8, 10; *V. C.* 1, 51 and 53.

[22] S. Eitrem and L. Amundsen, *Papyri Osloenses* II (Oslo, 1931), no. 44.

[23] Eusebius, *V. C.* 2, 56.

[24] Eusebius, *V. C.* 2, 72.

appear that the definitive break between them had occurred only about July 323.[25]

Arius was a highly independent Christian who had been ordained deacon by Peter but twice excommunicated for defending Meletius. Advanced to the presbyterate by Peter's successor Achillas, he almost became bishop himself after Achillas died in 312. A decade later he denounced the bishop Alexander for Sabellianism and insisted that only God the Father could be called eternal and uncreated. Alexander, assisted by his young and energetic arch-deacon Athanasius, demanded that Arius renounce such teaching and then summoned a synod of a hundred bishops from Egypt and Libya. The synod met in 323 and excommunicated Arius, who then sought support first in Palestine, then at Nicomedia. In this city he won the support of the bishop Eusebius, a distant relative (at a later date) of the emperor Julian and perhaps of Constantine himself.[26] Relative or not, as bishop of the eastern capital Eusebius was one of the few eastern bishops known to the emperor, and Constantine's letter to Alexander and Arius doubtless owed something to him as well as to Ossius.

In the letter the emperor reiterated his desire for peace as the basic need of church and empire alike. The points at issue should never have been raised in public; both contestants were to recognize their ultimate unity while agreeing to differ on such minor questions.[27] Ossius was unable to obtain agreement to the letter, and on his way back to Nicomedia he visited Antioch, where the Arian question had created difficulties. He convened a synod of bishops from the surrounding regions; almost all agreed to condemn the Arian position. Only three of them, including Eusebius of Caesarea, dissented and were ex-communicated. They were given permission, however, to attend a general council which Constantine now—probably in February 325—proposed to convene at Ancyra.[28] In March Alexander of Alexandria with some suffragans visited Nicomedia in order to appeal to the emperor.[29] Soon thereafter the emperor transferred the proposed council to Nicaea because of its favorable climate and general accessibility.[30] It would be not only the first council he had summoned but, indeed, the first general council of the Christian church.

On May 20 more than 250 bishops assembled at Nicaea. Only five of them were from the west; because of old age Silvester of Rome could not attend, but he was represented by two presbyters. The president of the council was Ossius of Cordova; apart from him, the most prominent bishops were

[25] W. Telfer in *JTS* 47 (1946), 129-42.
[26] Ammianus Marcellinus, 22, 9, 4.
[27] Eusebius, *V. C.* 2, 64 = H. G. Opitz, *Urkunden zur Geschichte des arianischen Streites* (Berlin, 1934-1935), no. 17.
[28] Opitz, *op. cit.*, no. 18.
[29] Philostorgius, *H. E.* 1, 7.
[30] Opitz, *op. cit.*, no. 20.

Alexander of Alexandria, Eustathius of Antioch, and Macarius of Jerusalem.[31] The emperor had made every effort to make the council representative; indeed, he had even invited the Novatianist bishop Acesius, later of Constantinople.[32] He himself opened the proceedings by delivering a brief official address in Latin, expressing his hope that military victory over tyrants would now be followed by peace in the church of God.[33] The sessions of the council took less than a month to complete. The three bishops excommunicated by the synod of Antioch were reinstated, and Eusebius of Caesarea presented to the council his church's traditional statement of the faith. This was generally accepted by the council members, and indeed was used as the foundation for the original "Nicene creed" itself. The emperor himself, it would appear, was responsible for making one addition: the word *homoousios*, used to indicate that the Son was "consubstantial" with the Father. Presumably the term resulted from a compromise among eastern bishops and was intended to prevent Eusebius' creed from being interpreted in Arian fashion. Constantine himself explained that it implied no corporeal substance or any division or separation of the Son from the Father, for the immaterial, spiritual, and incorporeal nature could not suffer any corporeal change. It was to be taken in a divine and mysterious sense, without analysis. "After our most wise and pious emperor made this philosophical statement," says Eusebius, the bishops accepted his amendment;[34] they also removed any mention of the Logos from the creed and added anathemas against such Arian views as "there was a time when he was not" or "before he was begotten he was not." The council also decided to accept the date for Easter in favor at Rome and Alexandria (unfortunately in 326 the two dates were different![35]), tried to resolve the controversy over Melitius at Alexandria,[36] and issued twenty canons.[37] Most of them had to do with the organization of the ministry. The bishops of Alexandria were to rule over Christians in Egypt, Libya, and the Pentapolis; they were metropolitans like the bishops of Rome and Antioch (6). The bishop of Aelia (Jerusalem) had a primacy of honor not specifically differentiated from that of the metropolitan at Caesarea (7). Bishops were not to be chosen from recent converts (2); they were to be approved by all provincial bishops (4). No clerics were to be castrated (1; the case of Origen) or to live with "spiritual sisters" (3; the case of Paul of Samosata). The ordinations of presbyters could be invalidated on moral grounds (9). Pre-

---

[31] Socrates, *H. E.* I, 13; Gelasius, *H. E.* 2, 28, 1-7 (a slightly different sequence).
[32] *Ibid.*, I, 10. A total about 250: Eusebius, *V. C.* 3, 8; for the typical figure 318 cf. M. Aubineau in *RHE* 61 (1966), 5-43; H. Chadwick, *ibid.*, 808-11.
[33] Eusebius, *V. C.* 3, 12.
[34] Socrates, *H. E.* I, 8.
[35] C. J. Hefele and H. Leclerq, *Histoire des conciles* I (Paris, 1907), 469.
[36] *Ibid.*, 488-503.
[37] *Ibid.*, 528-620; cf. H. Chadwick in *HTR* 53 (1960), 171-95.

sumably with regard for the turmoil of Licinius' reign, the council decided that clerics were not to be transferred from one area to another (15–16); they were not to take interest on loans (17); deacons were to be subordinate to presbyters (18). Provisions for the reinstatement of all those who had lapsed under persecution by Licinius were carefully worked out (10–14), as in the case of Novatianists (8) and followers of Paul of Samosata (19) returning to the church. The procedure for excommunication was regularized (5), and finally it was held that Christians shou'd not kneel at services on Sundays or the days between Easter and Pentecost (20).

On June 19 the creed and canons were signed by almost all the bishops, and the emperor asked them to hear him once more. He spoke of peace and unity and the need for mutual forbearance, and he asked them for their prayers.[38] On July 25 he celebrated the twentieth anniversary of his reign with a banquet for the bishops. To Eusebius of Caesarea the festivities were like a dream. They seemed to present an image of the kingdom of Christ, now almost already present.[39] It is likely that not only the emperor but many of his bishops believed that peace had finally come to the church. Neither Eusebius of Nicomedia nor Theognius of Nicaea was present, however, for both had refused to agree to the condemnation of Arius. Two Egyptian bishops who had supported him had been exiled from Egypt, and he himself had been banished too.

The Council of Nicaea thus provided an ambiguous precedent for the east similar to the one given in the west by the emperor's intervention in the Donatist controversy. There the problem of schism had reached no solution when imperial decrees were employed.[40] Here the question of heresy was not settled even when the emperor worked as a Christian with Christian bishops and gave guidance in their council, then endeavoring to enforce the decisions by the power of the state. In both instances the unity of the church, long precariously maintained under the threat of impending persecution, was nearly shattered once this external pressure was removed. In the west the problem of discipline, acute for nearly a century, came to the fore; in the east the unfinished business of speculative theology created violent controversy.

Soon after the council Constantine addressed a letter to the church of Nicomedia to explain his banishment of their bishop. Much is a rehearsal of political grievances. Eusebius had shared Licinius' cruelty (the execution of Licinius was thus justified) and had killed other bishops. He had brought presbyters and deacons to spy on Constantine before Licinius' defeat. At Nicaea he had sent messengers to win the emperor's favor for Arius and had

---

[38] Eusebius, *V. C.* 3, 21.

[39] *Ibid.*, 3, 15.

[40] It may or may not be merely coincidental that in March 321 and June 325 the emperor provided special concessions for veterans; on these cf. R. Thouvenot in *Mélanges Piganiol* II (Paris, 1966), 843-48.

thus perverted his judgment. Finally he had received ex-Christians from Alexandria after the council.[41] This letter does Constantine small credit. Eusebius had actually been Licinius' ambassador and had not killed any bishops; the emperor himself was certainly responsible for his own decisions. To be sure, he held that "what has commended itself to the judgment of three hundred bishops cannot be other than the judgment of God,"[42] but this belief was no excuse for slander.

In 327 Arius was recalled by a second council at Nicaea, and a petition from the Bithynian bishops led to their restoration.[43] Athanasius, bishop of Alexandria from 328, claimed that the restored Eusebius persuaded the emperor to threaten him with deposition if he did not admit Arius to communion at Alexandria.[44]

Within a few years, perhaps in 330, troubles broke out at Antioch, where the bishop Eustathius denounced Eusebius of Caesarea as an Arian. Eusebius counterattacked by calling Eustathius a Sabellian. A synod at Antioch then deposed Eustathius and the emperor banished him, partly because he was said to have insulted the queen mother on her visit to the east several years earlier.[45]

Affairs at Alexandria continued to be equally chaotic. The Meletians falsely accused Athanasius of imposing an unauthorized tax on linen tunics, and he was summoned to Nicomedia. There he was also accused of having had a presbyter break the chalice used by Ischyras, and of having conspired against the emperor. Both charges were dismissed and Athanasius returned home after Easter in 332. Soon afterwards, however, the charge about the chalice was revived and it was added that Athanasius had murdered the Meletian bishop Arsenius. Athanasius was summoned to court again but was able to trace Arsenius to a monastery in Tyre, thus refuting his accusers.[46]

In 333 Constantine made up his mind again and decided to offer a final solution to the Arian problem. The books of Arius, like those of the anti-Christian philosopher Porphyry, were to be burned; the discovery of such writings if concealed was to result in the application of the death penalty.[47] In the same year he sent a letter of denunciation to Arius and his followers, pointing out that Arius' presence in Libya had been predicted in the Sibylline Oracles, three thousand years previously, and—more practically—ordering them to return to the church or suffer a tenfold increase in their poll taxes.[48]

These actions solved nothing, and further charges brought against

[41] Gelasius, H. E. 3, App. 1; Theodoret, H. E. 1, 20.
[42] Socrates, H. E. 1, 9.
[43] Ibid., 1, 14; Sozomen, H. E. 2, 16; Gelasius, H. E. 3, 13.
[44] Athanasius, Apol. c. Ar. 59.
[45] Athanasius, Hist. Ar. 4; Socrates, H. E. 1, 23-24.
[46] Socrates, H. E. 1, 28.
[47] Ibid., 1, 9, 30; cf. Cod. Theod. 16, 5, 66.
[48] Opitz, op. cit., no. 34; cf. p. 74 n.: Cod. Theod. 16, 5, 1 (of 326) provides for the subjection of heretics and schismatics diversis muneribus.

Athanasius led the emperor to convene a synod at Caesarea under the presidency of Eusebius. Bishops, presbyters, and others were summoned by imperial letters; a document from the Meletian monastery at Hathor shows how the monks chose their representative. The synod met on March 19, 334, to discuss "the purgation of the holy Christian body,"[49] but Athanasius refused to attend because he regarded the president as prejudiced.[50]

The next year Constantine convened another synod, this time at Tyre, and summoned Athanasius once more. Before leaving Alexandria the bishop conducted a purge of the Meletians there, arresting and exiling bishops and having some of them scourged. In spite of this activity he was undecided about attending. The Meletians noted that emissaries came for him; he had his baggage put aboard ship, then taken off again.[51] Finally he went. At Tyre he was once more accused of using violence and perjury to gain his ends, charges in part confirmed by the Meletian document. The synod decided against him and he was taken in custody by imperial officers. He was able, however, to reach Constantinople and appeal to the emperor himself. In response Constantine ordered the synod to meet again in the capital city. There in 336 Athanasius confronted his enemies again.

This time he was accused of threatening to place an embargo on the grain sent from Egypt to supply Constantinople. This charge was extremely grave. Constantine himself had inaugurated a dole of bread in the capital city only four years earlier.[52] The Neoplatonist Sopater had recently been beheaded on the ground that he had used magic to stop the supply of grain.[53] Constantine, weary of divisions within church and empire, seized the opportunity to banish Athanasius to Trier, little realizing that the bishop would now exercise his influence there as well.

By this time the emperor was concerned with arrangements for the continuance of his house. In 335 he had divided the empire among his heirs. Constantine II received Britain, Spain, and Gaul; Constantius was given Asia, Syria, and Egypt; Constans obtained Italy and Africa. Two nephews were also assigned territories: Dalmatius as Caesar received Illyricum, while Hannibalianus—in view of an impending Persian campaign—was made king of Armenia and Pontus. (Neither nephew survived a massacre soon after the emperor's death.)

[49] H. I. Bell, *Jews and Christians in Egypt* (London, 1924), 45-53, especially 49, lines 6-7.
[50] Sozomen, *H. E.* 2, 25; Theodoret, *H. E.* 1, 28.
[51] Bell, *op. cit.*, 53-71.
[52] Socrates, *H. E.* 1, 34-35; A. H. M. Jones, *The Later Roman Empire* (Norman, Okla., 1964), 696.
[53] Eunapius, *Vit. soph.* p. 462 Boissonade.

III-CONSTANTINE'S POLICY

Constantine was unable to solve the complex theological and administrative problems of the Christian church. It is hard to believe that his failure was due to any lack of theological acumen.[54] More important was the actual state of division within the church and, to some extent, the lack of understanding of its history on the part of emperor and bishops alike. If Constantine read the *Church History* of Eusebius it gave him little help. His program of tolerance and persuasion within the church was frustrated by "true believers" of various kinds, though it is worth noting that all but two of the bishops at Nicaea were willing to agree, at least verbally.[55]

The emperor's letters to Alexander and Arius and to the churches on the Easter question show that he viewed his position in the church as like that of a bishop.[56] On various occasions he further developed this theme. "You are bishops of those inside the church," he said, "while I have been appointed by God as bishop of those outside."[57] By "those outside" he seems to have meant not only non-Christians but all the people of the empire, over whom God had placed him.[58] He was responsible for Christians and non-Christians alike. Indeed, at one point he addressed a letter to the Persian king Sapor, urging him to protect Christians within his dominions. "Love them as befits your love of man."[59] As emperor, however, he retained the old title of *pontifex maximus*,[60] and as late as 326 he was willing to provide the Eleusinian *dadouchos* with transportation to sacred sites in Egypt.[61] A rescript issued as late as 333 shows that he accepted religious traditions in honor of his family. The citizens of Hispellum in Umbria had asked permission to honor the Flavian house by erecting a temple, providing a priest, and holding theatrical games and gladiatorial combats. Constantine approved their proposal, but he stipulated that "the temple dedicated to our name should not be defiled by the falsehoods of any contagious superstitions."[62] The last two words show how times had changed; two centuries earlier Pliny had applied them to Christianity.

Early in his reign the emperor was careful not to disturb traditional religious practices. Though he used the Chi Rho on official medallions, it did not appear

[54] On this cf. Dörries, *op. cit.*, 286-412.
[55] N. H. Baynes in *Proceedings of the British Academy* 15 (1929), 359.
[56] Eusebius *V. C.* 2, 69, 72; 3, 17.
[57] *Ibid.*, 4, 24.
[58] J. Straub in *TU* 63 (1957), 678-95; *V. C.* 2, 21-24.
[59] *V. C.* 4, 13.
[60] *ILS* 695-97; 8941-42.
[61] *OGIS* 721; date: J. Baillet in *Comptes rendus de l'Acad. des Inscriptions*, 1922, 282-96.
[62] *ILS* 705.

on his coinage before the defeat of Licinius, and his triumphal arch of 315 refers to the *divinitas* as his guide, nothing more specific.[63] A rescript of 321 stated that when public buildings were struck by lightning the *haruspices* were to be consulted for the meaning of the portent. Only private divination, regarded as dangerous by the emperor's predecessors, was forbidden.[64] On the other hand, apparently in 331 he took the step of confiscating some temple endowments, though he did not act against the Vestal virgins or other old Roman cults.[65] For his new imperial city he compelled Delphi to contribute its tripod, Helicon its statues of the Muses; but this was the act of an art collector, not a religious enthusiast. According to Eusebius, three important temples were finally destroyed: a healing shrine of Asclepius in Cilicia and two temples of Aphrodite, associated with ritual prostitution, in Syria.[66] It is most unlikely that he explicitly forbade all pagan sacrifices and other rites, unless perhaps he did so at the very end of his reign.[67]

Constantine was a Christian, however, and he was eager to provide Christian buildings equal in magnificence to the old temples. At Rome he built no fewer than seven churches, as well as others in Italy at Ostia, Albinum, Capua, and Naples.[68] He built churches at Cirta in Africa, at Trier in Gaul, at Antioch in Syria, and at Nicomedia in Asia.[69] He adorned his new capital city with two great churches dedicated to Peace and to the Holy Apostles.[70] Lavish endowments were also provided for many of these churches.[71]

His edifices in Palestine were part of his "Holy Land plan." In 324 he had been on his way there from Nicomedia when he received news of the conflicts at Alexandria and had to return. In order to unify the churches he built great churches on the holy places such as the Church of the Holy Sepulchre near Jerusalem and another at Mamre, where God had appeared to Abraham. His mother Helena built a church on the Mount of Olives to commemorate the Ascension and another at Bethlehem in honor of the Nativity.[72] Presumably he intended to round out this program with a final dramatic celebration when he himself would be baptized in the Jordan river; but this was not to be.[73]

[63] *ILS* 694 = *ILCV* 2.
[64] *Cod. Theod.* 16, 10, 1.
[65] A. H. M. Jones, *The Later Roman Empire* (Norman, Okla., 1964), 92.
[66] Eusebius, *V. C.* 3, 54-58.
[67] *Ibid.,* 2, 44-46; cf. 2, 60.
[68] *Liber Pontificalis* 34.
[69] Optatus, App. 10; Socrates, *H. E.* 3, 50.
[70] *Ibid.,* 1, 16.
[71] Jones, *op. cit.,* 90.
[72] Eusebius, *V. C.* 3, 25-43; 51-54. Constantine and his mother were not, of course, the only builders of churches; M. Julius Eugenius, bishop of Laodicea in Lycaonia, describes his own work in *MAMA* I 170.
[73] W. Telfer in *TU* 63 (1957), 696-700.

IV·THE DEATH OF CONSTANTINE

At Easter in 337 the emperor dedicated the Church of the Holy Apostles in Constantinople,[74] but soon thereafter he was overcome by a fatal ailment. He visited the baths at Helenopolis in vain, and then proceeded to confess his sins in the Church of the Martyrs. At Ancyrona near Nicomedia, he prepared his will, leaving the empire to his three sons, and in the presence of a group of local bishops he was baptized by the bishop with whom he had fought so often, Eusebius of Nicomedia. To this prelate was entrusted the will, with instructions to deliver it to Constantius, Caesar of the east. Wearing the white robe of a neophyte, Constantine died on Pentecost, May 22.[75]

Official mourning began at once. Soldiers placed his coffin, adorned with purple and a diadem, on a golden couch and solemnly bore it to the imperial palace in Constantinople. There generals and other officers made obeisance to the dead emperor and swore allegiance to his sons. Upon Constantius' arrival the coffin was carried to the Church of the Holy Apostles and placed among the sarcophagi dedicated to the Twelve. In the presence of a vast throng the bishops conducted an elaborate funeral with a requiem eucharist.[76]

The dead emperor was not mourned by Christians alone. A comet announced his death to the Roman world, just as one had appeared when Augustus gave games in honor of the deified Julius Caesar. Eutropius explicitly speaks of the consecration of Constantine: *inter divos meruit referri,* "he was deservedly enrolled among the divine emperors."[77] Eusebius does not mention it and denies that Constantine's immortality is like that of the phoenix, consumed by the flames of a pyre; the coins to which he refers, however, clearly portrayed the consecrated emperor.[78] Inscriptions from the emperor's own time gave his father the title *divus.*[79] Now inscriptions under his sons spoke of him as *divus Constantinus.*[80] His body rested, however, not in any Flavian mausoleum or with any of the great pagan emperors before him but, by his own choice, among the memorials of the twelve apostles.[81]

The story of the Christian revolutionary movement may well end at this

---

[74] For the reliability of Eusebius' account cf. J. Vogt in *Hermes* 81 (1953), 111-17.

[75] Eusebius, *V. C.* 4, 61-64; cf. H. Kraft in *TU* 63 (1957), 642-48.

[76] *V. C.* 4, 71; cf. H. Dörries, *Das Selbstzeugnis Kaiser Konstantins* (Göttingen, 1954), 413-24.

[77] Eutropius 10, 8, 2; cf. Suetonius, *Julius* 88, and K. Scott in *Classical Philology* 36 (1941), 257-72.

[78] *V. C.* 4, 72-73; cf. H. Cohen, *Description historique des monnaies frappées sous l'empire romain* VII (Paris, 1888), 318 (Constantine, nos. 760-61).

[79] E.g., *ILS* 697 of the year 328.

[80] E.g., *ILS* 707 and 2942.

[81] For a full discussion cf. P. Franchi de' Cavalieri in *École française de Rome: Mélanges d'archéologie et d'histoire* 36 (1916-1917), 205-61.

point, for the relation of Christianity to the society in which it was now established is another matter. The acceptance for which Christians had long been seeking had been achieved. Clement of Alexandria had believed that the iron-bronze state of the Greeks was inferior to the silver of the Jews and the gold of the Christians.[82] Now the golden age had dawned.

If we try to answer the question as to how Christianity reached this point, and how it changed as it did so, we may suggest that it could have won either by violence or by nonviolence. If it had attempted to use violence it would have contradicted its own nature in so far as it was based on the expectation of divine, not human, intervention and aid. In addition, the practical example provided by the failure of the Jewish revolts discouraged the use of arms, as did the Christian theological analysis of this failure. The nonviolent approach was obviously in harmony with the teaching of Jesus and the apostles. Practically speaking, however, it could be expected to succeed only when Greeks and Romans were convinced that Christianity was not only politically valuable but also philosophically and culturally meaningful. Such a conviction could arise in part from the observable virtue of Christians. It could also arise from the futility of continued persecution and from the power of Christian proclamation and argument. In this regard Christians necessarily laid emphasis on points of contact between their own views and those of their neighbors. A certain measure of adjustment or even compromise was inevitable. At the same time, by insisting upon the absoluteness of the Christian revelation, as understood within the church, and upon the existence of salvation only within the church, Christians were able to maintain the cohesiveness without which the movement would not have survived.

The nature of this exclusiveness and cohesiveness was not entirely religious. Indeed, we should not expect it to have been so either in ancient times or in more recent circumstances. Is anything purely religious? The good will of the Roman emperor, however, created formidable problems as he tried to solve others, and his legislation was to compound the difficulties of the church in later times as well as in his own era.

We have already mentioned the fact that in 326 he informed the vicar of the diocese of the Orient that clerical privileges were to benefit only Catholic clergy. "It is our will, moreover, that heretics and schismatics shall not only be alien from these privileges but also shall be bound and subjected to various public services."[83] In other words, an effort to harass non-Catholic clerics was to be made. Beyond this lies an imperial letter of uncertain date in which Constantine proceeeded to treat heretics just as his predecessors had

---

[82] Clement, *Str.* 5, 98, 1-4 (Plato, *Rep.* 5, 497 e). The question was politically important, for Commodus persuaded the senate to name his reign "the golden age" (Dio 72, 15, 6; cf. *SHA Comm.* 14, 3); Dio later noted the "golden kingdom" of Marcus Aurelius and the rusty iron of Commodus (71, 36, 4).

[83] *Cod. Theod.* 16, 5, 1.

treated Christians, and as Diocletian had dealt with Manichees. He spoke of the poison, the pollution, and the disease produced by Novatianists, Valentinians (Gnostics), Marcionites, Paulianists (followers of Paul of Samosata), and Cataphrygians (Montanists), and forbade their assemblies. All public meetinghouses were to be surrendered to the Catholic Church, while private houses used for meetings were to be confiscated by the state.[84] The unity of the Christian movement was to be maintained by the power of the empire.

This cohesiveness and exclusiveness, in turn, complicated the controversies within the church, especially in the early fourth century. As we have already suggested, the uncompromising claims of Novatianists and Donatists proved to be irreconcilable with Catholic inclusiveness, even when the inclusive view was supported by the power of the state. What we may call the revolutionary rigor of the sects was not now maintained by most Christians, but it could not be suppressed. Similarly the rather archaic theological ideas of Arius, once they had been made popular at Alexandria and elsewhere, could not be put down by authority either ecclesiastical or imperial. Because of the absoluteness with which philosophical and theological ideas were maintained by almost all Christians, there was practically no room for compromise or, indeed, for conversation.

The church had finally achieved a large measure of political, social, and even cultural freedom. It had combined accommodation at some points with intransigence at many others. Whether or not it was really ready for freedom remained to be determined, but in any event the movement had succeeded. The question to which we must finally turn involves the continuity of the movement with its origins. To what extent was the church of the fourth century continuous with its earlier modes of existence?

[84] Eusebius, *V. C.* 3, 64-65. This letter presumably preceded an edict of 326 according to which Novatianists were allowed to keep their buildings (*Cod. Theod.* 16, 5, 2); cf. Dorries, *op. cit.*, 82-84. Lactantius (*Div. inst.* 4, 30, 10) gives an identical list, except that he has "Anthropiani" (cf. Cyprian, *Ep.* 73, 4) for "Paulianists."

PART FIVE·THE CONTINUITY OF CHRISTIANITY

In order to try to assess or assay the "gold" of the Christian movement to which Clement of Alexandria referred, it is necessary to look for the principal elements of continuity within it. It is obvious that continuity was provided simply by the existence of the communities as such and of their leaders. The idea and the actuality of succession from the apostles played a highly significant role within the Christian church. Beyond this factor, however, there was also continuity expressed in Christian ways of life and moral teaching, in creedal formulations in which the main points of the common, traditional faith were expressed, and above all in the common acts of worship which bound communities together and remained relatively unchanged from the first century to the fourth.

The word "relatively" is very important. In view of the historical events which have already been discussed, it is not to be expected that anything resembling immutability will be found in Christian morals, creeds, and liturgies. On the other hand, there was at least a relative stability in these aspects of Christian life and thought which can be overlooked if one considers only the more exciting changes and transitions in the internal and external history of the Christian revolution.

CHAPTER XIX
CHRISTIAN WAYS OF LIFE

The fact that the mission of Jesus, like that of Paul, was based on expectation of the imminent coming of the reign of God meant that the proclamation involved a way of life based on absolute devotion and obedience to God. The intensity of the message and of the response to it could be maintained as long as there were few followers of Jesus or the apostles, and as long as the expectation remained vivid. Such was doubtless the situation at Jerusalem in the first few years after the death of Jesus. When Luke describes the early Christians as sharing their possessions and as being one heart and one soul (Acts 4:32), he may well not be exaggerating. Presumably he tells the story of Ananias and Sapphira, who did not fully share their property but lied about it, because he is mindful of problems in the church of his own time. The discipline and the sharing of the early church at Jerusalem recalls that of the sectarian community at Qumran. Both in Mark and in the common source of Matthew and Luke there is a strong emphasis on absolute devotion—to God, to Jesus, to the gospel, and to the movement in which the gospel was being proclaimed.

I·THE NEW TESTAMENT

In the letters of Paul and in the gospel writings as such this emphasis is modified in the direction of practicability. No one can read 1 Corinthians without seeing that Paul is having to adjust his absolutes to the situation of the community; similarly both Matthew and Luke (as well as Mark) have reinterpreted the teaching of Jesus in various ways for the use of the church. Such a tendency is also found in the *Didache,* notably in the counsel that "if you can bear the whole yoke of the Lord, you will be perfect; but if you cannot, do what you can" (6, 2). The book of Acts shows that the apostles and presbyters of Jerusalem resisted the demand of Pharisaic Jewish Christians to have gentiles circumcised and instead issued a decree requiring only abstinence from foods sacrificed to idols, from "blood," from the flesh of strangled animals, and from "fornication" (Acts 15:29). This decree contains nothing that would have seemed novel to the Jewish Christians of Jerusalem, for whom the code of Leviticus 17–19—including the commandment, "You shall love your neighbor as yourself" (Lev. 19:18)—was regarded as binding. Apparently something like these chapters in Leviticus also underlies the ethical instructions which Paul provided during his mission to Thessalonica (1 Thess. 4:2–12; cf. 5:23).

It was at Corinth that the difficulty of dealing with gentile converts, not acquainted with the Jewish law, came to the fore. The problems confronted by Paul in 1 Corinthians clearly reflect a disorder that is in part based on the absence of clear norms for behavior. Paul points out that "not even among the gentiles" does a man live with his father's wife, i.e., his stepmother (1 Cor. 5:1), in violation of Leviticus 18:8. Christians are taking legal cases before pagan judges, whereas they should be judged within the community (6:1–8). They seem to lack any clear guidance in regard to marriage and separation (c. 7). Some of them claim that since idols have no real existence they can eat foods sacrificed to them (cc. 8, 10). Some women are refusing to wear veils at worship (11:10–16). At the Lord's Supper, "each one goes ahead with his own meal, and one is hungry while another is drunk" (11:21). There is rivalry among those who claim to possess spiritual gifts; some are very proud of their ability to "speak in tongues" (cc. 12, 14). And some Corinthian Christians even deny the resurrection of the dead (15:12).

In his response to this situation, Paul does not lay down a code of morals. He agrees with the Corinthians that in principle "all things are lawful" (6:12; 10:23), for "the sting of death is sin, and the power of sin is the law" (15:56). Like them, he is free and is not under the law (9:1, 20), but he is under "Christ's law" (9:21),[1] and he must therefore exercise his freedom

[1] Cf. C. H. Dodd in *Studia Paulina J. de Zwaan* (Haarlem, 1953), 96-110.

in responsibility for his neighbor. The letters to the Corinthians, especially the first, show how Paul tried to work out the implications of such responsibility for the guidance of his converts.

At some points he relied on Old Testament precedents, for example in dealing with the case of the man living with his stepmother. In other instances he referred to eschatological sanctions or to his own Spirit-guided judgment. In speaking of marriage and divorce he referred to a commandment of Jesus on this subject and differentiated it from the inferences he himself drew.[2] Similarly in arguing that Christian missionaries were entitled to support by the communities he offered parallels from apostolic precedent and from the cases of soldiers, vinedressers, and shepherds. He provided an allegorical interpretation of "the law of Moses" and a comparison with the work of Jewish priests. Only at the end of his discussion did he refer to the fact that "the Lord commanded that those who proclaim the gospel should live off the gospel."[3] This is to say that for his converts, at any rate, the teaching of Jesus was not the sole ethical authority; and he did not regard ethical teaching as the essence of the gospel. It is fairly likely that the Corinthians did not possess a document containing the ethical teaching of Jesus. Conceivably none was in existence at the time when Paul wrote his letters to them.

In Mark, the earliest of the synoptic gospels, and in the Gospel of John there is little explicit ethical or moral teaching. Indeed, Mark gives the impression that Jesus was concerned chiefly with divorce and remarriage (10:1–12), property and its renunciation (10:17–31), the payment of the Roman poll tax (12:13–17), and the question of the greatest commandment in the Old Testament law (12:28–34). The first three of these discussions seem to have an original setting in the mission of Jesus himself. The question of divorce and remarriage would inevitably arise after John the Baptist had condemned the divorce and remarriage of Herod Antipas (6:17–19). The second was related to the renunciation of property for the sake of future rewards in the kingdom of God. The third was a problem which had been important since the revolt of Judas of Galilee when the Roman census was first taken in A.D. 6. The "greatest commandment" was not so directly related to the historical setting, but we know that other Jewish teachers were concerned with such questions. They looked for a commandment which would serve as a key to the whole law and to the constantly developing oral tradition. It is therefore not surprising to find that Jesus, who severely criticized the oral tradition, should have provided his hearers with the double commandment based on the *Shema,* employed in synagogue worship ("Hear, O Israel . . ."), and on the holiness code of Leviticus (19:18, love of neighbor). In the Gospel

[2] I Cor. 7:10-13, 25.
[3] I Cor. 9:3-14; cf. H. von Campenhausen, "Die Begründung kirchlicher Entscheidungen beim Apostel Paulus," *Sitzungsberichte der Heidelberger Akademie der Wissenschaften,* 1957, no. 2.

and the First Epistle of John the latter of these injunctions comes to the fore. "I give you a new commandment, to love one another" (John 13:34). Indeed, in 1 John the point is made that one who claims to love God but hates his brother is a liar, for no one can love the invisible God unless he loves his visible brother (4:20).

In the traditional materials common to Matthew and Luke the implications of such love of neighbor are more extensively worked out so that love of enemies and persecutors is included.[4] Indeed Matthew explicitly criticizes an interpretation of love of neighbor as involving hatred of an enemy, a notion apparently related to views held among the sectarians of Qumran and, inevitably, among Jewish revolutionists.[5] Retaliation against enemies is specifically excluded.[6]

The primacy of this kind of love is expressed not only in materials derived from the early oral tradition but also in the letters of the apostle Paul. In 1 Corinthians 13:4–7 the apostle describes love as essentially not self-centered; then he goes on to claim that it will outlast any temporary gifts of the Spirit. It is a quality of life which will be characteristic of the future reign of God. Because of the absolute significance of love, he can write to the Galatians (5:13–14): "Through love be servants of one another, for the whole law is summed up in one sentence: You shall love your neighbor as yourself." The same point is made more fully in Romans (13:8–10).

Owe no one anything, except to love one another; for he who loves his neighbor has fulfilled the law. The commandments, You shall not commit adultery, you shall not kill, you shall not steal, you shall not covet—and any other commandment—are summed up in this sentence: You shall love your neighbor as yourself. Love does no wrong to a neighbor; therefore love is the fulfilling of the law.

Though the commandment of love lies at the foundation of Paul's moral teaching, he inevitably made use of materials derived from contemporary ethical doctrines, especially those found in Hellenistic Judaism. He could list categories of persons who would not "inherit the kingdom of God" (1 Cor. 6:9–10); he could follow and modify Hellenistic Jewish lists of virtues and vices (e.g., Gal. 5:19–23; Rom. 1:29–31); he could come close to the Hellenistic Jewish conception of a moral law of nature (Rom. 1:26–27; 2:14–15).[7] In Philippians 4:8 he could urge his readers to consider "whatever is true, whatever is honorable, whatever is just, whatever is pure, whatever is lovely, whatever is highly regarded—if there is an excellence and if

---

[4] Matt. 5:43-48 (cf. 7:12); Luke 6:27-28, 32-36.

[5] Cf. K. Schubert in K. Stendahl, ed., *The Scrolls and the New Testament* (New York, 1957), 118-28.

[6] Matt. 5:38-42; Luke 6:29-30.

[7] On lists cf. A. Vögtle, *Die Tugend- und Lasterkataloge im Neuen Testament* (Münster, 1936); on the law of nature, W. R. Schoedel, *The Appeal to Nature in Graeco-Roman and Early Christian Thought* (Chicago dissertation, 1963).

there is any praise." He assumes that excellence and praise do exist, and the qualities he lists are characteristic of Greek popular philosophy. Whether or not he wrote Colossians, this letter contains a list of the duties and responsibilities of members of a household (wives-husbands, children-fathers, slaves-masters) toward one another. Such lists, fairly common among Stoic ethicists of the time, were presumably mediated to Christians through Hellenistic Judaism and were later in widespread use.[8] It is in the Pastoral Epistles that we find the most extensive New Testament presentation of practical moral counsel, for example in the lists of qualifications for officers of the Christian communities and in the advice offered to Christians in general. The roots of this teaching lie in Judaism, especially the Judaism of the Graeco-Roman world.[9]

The Epistle of James, though sometimes regarded as antithetical to the Pauline epistles, contains a similar mixture of materials derived from primitive Christian Judaism and from the Hellenistic diatribe as utilized among Hellenistic Jews. Conceivably it reflects traditional moral teaching in the Jerusalem church even before the fall of the city in 70. In it the eschatological note has been muted, as it must have been muted if James remained active in the city until the year 62.[10]

II·EARLY JEWISH CHRISTIANITY

It would appear that emphasis was laid on moral codes especially in Jewish Christian circles. The prime example is provided by the manual entitled "The Lord's teaching through the twelve apostles, to the gentiles"—the *Didache*. This late first-century document begins with four chapters on "the way of life," laying especial emphasis on love of God and neighbor, especially as set forth in an interpretation of the Decalogue, from which rather elaborate inferences are drawn. The tone of the advice closely resembles what we find in the Hebrew wisdom literature, especially Ecclesiasticus. The "way of death" is depicted as the opposite of the way of life, and the little catechism ends on a Jewish-Christian note. "Concerning food, bear what you can, but keep strictly away from what is offered to idols, for this is the worship of dead gods" (6, 2–3). Toward the end of the work the Christian emphasis on reconciliation appears (14, 2; 15, 3). The importance of the "two ways" can be seen from the fact that the same ideas recur in the more radically Hellenistic-Jewish Epistle of Barnabas (cc. 18–20). In addition, Barnabas contains a

[8] For Philippians, J. N. Sevenster, *Paul and Seneca* (Leiden, 1961), 154-56; on duties, M. Dibelius and H. Greeven, *An die Kolosser* (Tübingen, 1953), 48-50.

[9] Cf. B. S. Easton, *The Pastoral Epistles* (New York, 1947); C. Spicq, *Les épîtres pastorales* (Paris, 1947).

[10] Cf. J. H. Ropes, *The Epistle of St. James* (New York, 1916).

good deal of moral teaching explicitly derived from the Old Testament prophets, along with some admonitions based on Greek stories about animal life (c. 10).

Other documents lay emphasis on special themes because of their circumstances. 1 Clement is specifically concerned with disorder and makes much use of Hellenistic themes related to cosmic order. 2 Clement, as its author says (15, 1) is chiefly "on self-control." Though in his work there are few traces of Greek ideas, the theme itself reminds us of the Hellenistic synagogue.

The *Shepherd* of Hermas, compiled at Rome early in the second century, marks a movement toward more systematic ethical teaching, though the results are not altogether successful. Hermas likes to speak of groups of seven or twelve virtues; thus he once refers to faith at the beginning and love at the end, providing continence, simplicity, innocence, reverence, and knowledge between the two.[11] He provides twelve commandments perhaps in imitation of the Twelve Tables of Roman law, but they are entirely based on commonplaces of contemporary Judaism.[12] They begin with faith in the one creator-God and recommend faith, fear, and continence; others favor simplicity, truth, purity, patience, faith-fear-continence (again!), fear of the Lord and continence (again!); then we find condemnation of "double-mindedness," grief, the teaching of false prophets, and evil desire. What Hermas provides is something like the *Manual of Discipline* found among the Dead Sea Scrolls.[13]

Though the ethical themes of the *Shepherd* generally remain within the limits of Jewish teaching, the personification of various virtues suggests that the author may have known such a Hellenistic school book as the *Pinax* of Cebes, where the same teaching method is used for moral instruction.

In most early Christian writings there is an emphasis on almsgiving exactly as in the Judaism of the time. Such is the case in the *Didache,* Barnabas, Polycarp, and 2 Clement. It is also expressed by Ignatius, who criticizes his opponents on the ground that "for love they have no regard, none for the widow, none for the orphan, none for the distressed, none for men imprisoned or released, none for the hungry or thirsty."[14] Indeed charity came to occupy a prominent role in the life of the communities. According to Justin, "we who formerly loved money and property more than anything else now place what we have in the common fund and share with everyone in need."[15] The nature of the common fund should not be misunderstood. It was not intended to supply the needs of non-Christians and, indeed, could not have done so in view of the small numbers of the Christians themselves. In addition, the sharing to which Justin refers was not compulsory. When he

[11] *Vis.* 3, 8, 3-7; cf. *Mand.* 8, 9; *Sim.* 9, 15, 2.
[12] Cf. M. Dibelius, *Der Hirt des Hermas* (Tübingen, 1923).
[13] J.-P. Audet in *Revue biblique* 60 (1953), 41-82.
[14] *Smyrn.* 6, 2. The Gnostic *Gospel of Thomas,* on the other hand, claims that almsgiving does harm to the giver's spirit (Saying 14).
[15] *Apol.* 1, 14, 2.

describes the offering of such gifts at the eucharist he goes out of his way to state that they were entirely voluntary.[16]

The uses of these offerings shed considerable light on Christian concerns. According to Justin, the "president" of the congregation employed them for the care of orphans and widows, for the sick and others in need, for those in prison, and for foreign visitors. In general, the presiding officer was the *kēdemōn* of all who were in need, equivalent to the Latin *curator* of an association. Tertullian makes the situation even clearer.[17] The community possesses a common treasury to which monthly contributions are made. From the treasury funds are drawn for the support and burial of the poor and for the support of poor orphans, aged household slaves, shipwrecked persons, and any persons who are in the mines, on islands, or in prisons because of their Christian confession. According to these descriptions, the Christian churches thus clearly resembled other voluntary associations or *collegia* established as corporations under Roman law, with the right to hold corporate property for the specific purposes in view. It is significant that such *collegia* were granted the right "both to have and to free slaves[18] and to acquire legacies under a testament."[19] Some *collegia* existed in order to provide social gatherings, others to provide burial for their members; monthly collections made by a burial league at Lanuvium in 136 are mentioned in an inscription.[20] This is not to say that Christians regarded themselves, or were regarded by the state, as members of a *collegium*; it is only to say that their charitable activities resembled the activities of other groups in the empire.[21]

III·GNOSTIC WAYS OF LIFE

Among the various Gnostic sects of the second century there was militant rejection of the Old Testament law and of the generally accepted tenets of Graeco-Roman morality. In place of conventional moral teaching, the Gnostics insisted either on an extreme asceticism, involving the rejection of sexual intercourse and abstinence from meat and wine, or on compulsive "immoralism." Both kinds of schools agreed that the world was evil and could not have been made by a good god. They disagreed concerning the actions appropriate to this situation.

[16] *Ibid.*, 1, 67, 6. Among second-century Christians only the Gnostic Epiphanes seems to have advocated communism (see below).
[17] *Apol.* 39, 5-6.
[18] Compare Ignatius on slaves and the common fund, p. 269.
[19] A. Berger, *Encyclopedic Dictionary of Roman Law* (*TAPS* 43, 2, 1953), 395.
[20] *ILS* 7212.
[21] If they were regarded as *collegia* at all they must have been regarded as illegal; cf. D. Daube in *JRS* 33 (1943), 91-92.

The "immoralist" schools often believed that their souls were imprisoned in bodies on earth and would continue to transmigrate until they had experienced every conceivable activity. Some put it more explicitly: they had to perform every sin.[22] In this regard they were not unlike the popular Cynic teachers of the time, although Cynics did not usually feel obligated to practice everything they preached.

Not all of them neglected philosophical discussion, and from Epiphanes we have fragments of a treatise *On Righteousness* in which he advocated absolute communism. He appealed to nature as his norm. There is equality in the heavens as shown by the stars; sunlight is given to all equally; crops were meant to be shared by all. Starting from these examples, Epiphanes went on to claim that land, money, and women should be held in common.[23] Clement of Alexandria had no difficulty in showing that the idea of the community of women came from Plato, not from Christian doctrine, but he did not provide a reasoned reply to the whole argument—unless he did so indirectly in his defense of wealth (see below).

IV-ANTI-GNOSTIC ETHICS

In opposition to the teaching of Gnostics, Christian leaders at the end of the second century laid strong emphasis on traditional Jewish-Christian morality and upon the permanent validity of most of the Old Testament law. Such an emphasis, as we have already seen, was expressed in such Jewish-Christian documents as the *Didache* and the *Shepherd* of Hermas, which remained influential in the major churches. But it was now reinforced by anti-Gnostic writers like Theophilus and Irenaeus.

Indeed it is clear that among the Christians of this period the "apostolic decree" of Acts 15:29 was widely regarded as still binding. At Lyons a martyr asked her persecutors, "How could they eat their children when they may not even eat the blood of irrational animals?" Other texts of the same time and later show that Christians observed this regulation.[24] It must be admitted, however, that not all of them did so, and around this time the mention of "blood" in the apostolic decree was coming to be viewed as a reference to murder. It looks as if both Theophilus and Irenaeus so interpreted it.[25]

The moral teaching of Christianity at Antioch toward the end of the second century is clearly set forth in Theophilus' three books *To Autolycus*. The first

[22] Irenaeus, *Adv. haer.* I, 25, 4; I, 31, 2.

[23] Epiphanes in Clement, *Str.* 3, 6-9; cf. R. M. Grant, *Gnosticism: An Anthology* (London, 1961), 39-40.

[24] Eusebius, *H. E.* 5, 1, 26; cf. A. A. T. Ehrhardt, *The Framework of the New Testament Stories* (Manchester, 1964), pp. 276-90.

[25] Theophilus, *Ad Autolycum* 2, 34; Irenaeus, *Adv. haer.* 3, 12, 14.

book argues that God is visible only to those who live in accordance with Paul's precepts and "cleanse themselves from every defilement" (1, 2). The second book points to the divine and holy law and the prophets as expressions of God's will (2, 34–35). And an extensive section of the third book (3, 9–15) deals with the content of the law—especially the Decalogue—and shows that in regard to repentance, justice, chastity, and love of others it agrees with prophets and gospels. Theophilus insists that among Christians "self-control is present, continence is practised, monogamy is preserved, purity is guarded, injustice is thrust out, sin is uprooted, justice is exercised, the law is lived . . ." (3, 15). For him the observance of law is evidently essential to the Christian life. Indeed, he seems to be bringing Pauline ideas into a more Jewish-Christian context when he writes that "as by disobeying, man procured death for himself, so by obeying the will of God, whoever wishes can acquire eternal life for himself" (cf. Rom. 5:19). Immediately afterward he says that "God gave us a law and holy commandments [cf. Rom. 7:12]; everyone who does them can be saved" (2, 27).

Theophilus' emphasis on the Old Testament law is quite remarkable, for we find nothing similar in the letters of his predecessor Ignatius. It must reflect the continuing influence of Jewish Christianity, and of Judaism, in the church at Antioch. Indeed, the Decalogue is so important to him that he has to rewrite it, leaving out the commandments no longer regarded as binding upon Christians (3, 9).[26]

According to Irenaeus too, Christian morality is solidly based on the observance of the Old Testament law, though two changes have taken place. First, men can now freely obey it because they are no longer slaves to it; second, what counts in it is not the particular ritual commandments, often criticized within the Old Testament itself, but the universal commandments, "natural" and permanently valid, set forth especially in the Decalogue. The Decalogue itself, however, is to be modified because it was not known to the patriarchs (predecessors of Christians) and because the ultimate law is the law of love.

Specifically, Irenaeus does not have much to say about details of the Christian way of life. It is significant, however, that like some Stoic teachers he regards the possession of private property as based on sinful actions. "All of us," he says, "have either small or great possessions, derived from 'the mammon of iniquity'" (Luke 16:9; 4, 30, 1). The possessions came to us, first, from avarice before our conversion, or second, from the injustice of parents, relatives, or friends, not to mention, third, our own efforts as Christians. But he goes on to argue that the Christian is justified when he uses his property for the Lord's service; he does not advocate giving up "the necessities of our life." It is in this context that he speaks of the world as enjoying peace because of the Roman state, and refers to Christians in the imperial

[26] See my article in *HTR* 40 (1947) 1-17.

palace. From Irenaeus' letter to Florinus[27] we know that the latter Christian, many years earlier, was "faring brilliantly in the imperial palace" and was also "in the company of Polycarp." Neither in Asia nor in Gaul were Christians hostile to the Roman state or to society as such.[28]

V·SYSTEMATIZATION

The need for relatively systematic ethical teaching, already reflected in the Jewish-Christian manuals of which we have spoken, was met to some extent by the apologists of the second century, whose writings were probably based on current church teaching. Justin, for example, arranged gospel sayings under such headings as "self-control," "universal love," "being blameless, universally helpful, and without anger," and "paying taxes."[29] Theophilus went further by combining texts from the prophets and the gospel under the headings of "repentance," "justice," and "chastity."[30]

The next step was taken when Christian maxims were combined with other maxims of Pythagorean and Stoic origin. This we find, late in the second century, in the so-called *Sentences of Sextus,* which explain how to achieve moral and spiritual perfection by the cultivation of the soul. The Christian begins with faith and ends with likeness to God. He practices a rigorous asceticism, especially in relation to sex.[31]

A further fusion took place at Alexandria when Clement, with lavish and often unacknowledged borrowing from the Jewish philosopher Philo, not only produced detailed instructions in Christian morality but also accepted the Platonic-Stoic idea that there were four cardinal virtues. Like his predecessors he did not rigidly adhere to a fixed list, though he usually named forethought, self-control, justice, and courage. At one point he followed Philo by including piety (*eusebeia*) among them.[32] What was happening in Clement's discussion was that Christianity was being viewed not as a sect but as a community living and working in the world.

Clement's treatise entitled *Who is the Rich Man who is being Saved?* deserves special consideration as an example of Hellenization in the ethical sphere. He begins by denouncing speeches which praise the rich—presumably because he is aware that his own work might be classified among them.

---

[27] *H.E.* 5, 20, 5.
[28] This point, however, cannot be used to show that the social status of Christians was high; the persons involved may have been no more than members of "Caesar's household" as in Phil. 4:22. See G. W. Clarke in *HTR* 59 (1966), 95-97.
[29] Justin, *Apol.* I, 15-17.
[30] Theophilus, *Ad Autol.* 3, 10-14.
[31] Cf. H. Chadwick, *The Sentences of Sextus* (Cambridge, 1959).
[32] Clement, *Str.* 2, 121, 4.

Actually rich Christians should be treated neither with "insolent rudeness" nor with a fawning attitude. Instead, they should be shown that through obedience to the commandments they can inherit the kingdom of heaven. He then proceeds to quote the difficult text of Mark 10:17–31, explaining that the words must not be taken literally. The Savior was not commanding his hearer to "fling away his property"; he was telling him to banish concern about money from his soul. Men who have rid themselves of property are often deeply concerned with it; one who possesses sufficient funds does not suffer distress about property and can share with others. Wealth must be used as an instrument of righteousness. What counts is the inner attitude of the soul.

Clement's view of the origin of wealth is quite different from that of Irenaeus. "What wrong does a man do if by careful thought and frugality he has gathered sufficient property before his conversion, or—with still less blame—from the very first has been placed by God, the distributor of fortune, in a househo'd of such men, in a family surrounded by riches and powerful in wealth?"[33] Wealth in moderation is a positive good. On the other hand, possessions are by nature unrighteous if they are held only for personal advantage and not for the common good. The rich man, therefore, can express his love of God and of neighbor by sharing with Christians in need. The form of Clement's treatise is almost purely Greek. His practical conclusions about almsgiving are those of Jewish Christians before his day. What he has done is to express traditional Jewish and Christian ideas in the context of Graeco-Roman society, specifically at Alexandria.

In his early years Tertullian, like the author of the *Epistle to Diognetus,* insisted that Christians were just like everyone else. "We are not Brahmins or Indian gymnosophists, dwellers in the forests or exiles from ordinary life. . . . We sail with you and serve in the army and till the ground and engage in trade as you do; we engage in public crafts and services for your profit."[34] When Bardaisan noted the moral superiority of Christians to others he did not compare them with Greeks and Romans, but with the barbarian tribes whose peculiarities had long been criticized by Greek and Roman writers.[35]

The differences had to do with Christian obedience to the will of God and the belief that Christians though in the world were not fully at home in it. "Be ready," says Hermas, "so that whenever the master of this city wishes to expel you for resisting his law you may depart from his city and go to your own."[36] At this point, as in some New Testament passages, there was anticipated the doctrine which was to be more fully worked out in Augustine's *City of God.* The problem faced by Christians had to do with reconciling their

[33] *Quis dives salv.* 26.
[34] Tertullian, *Apol.* 42, 1.3; *Ep. ad Diognet.* 5.
[35] W. Cureton, *Spicilegium Syriacum* (London, 1855), 32-33; cf. L. W. Barnard in *VC* 22 (1968), 172.
[36] *Sim.* 1, 6; cf. Phil. 3:20; Heb. 11:13-16; 13:14; 1 Pet. 2:11; also Philo, *De Conf. ling.* 77-78; Clement, *Paed.* 3, 8, 1.

allegiance to Caesar with their allegiance to God. It was a problem of the conflict of laws.

By the time Hippolytus of Rome wrote his *Apostolic Tradition,* about 215, it was fairly clear that some vocations were suitable for Christians while others were not. One of the forbidden vocations was acceptable if no other trade was available; this was "teaching children worldly knowledge." In addition, sculptors and painters could become catechumens if they did not make idols. Other occupations, however, were absolutely rejected. The ban applied to panderers, actors and producers of shows, charioteers and other participants in games, gladiators and trainers, officials concerned with gladiatorial shows, huntsmen and others concerned with wild-beast shows, priests and guardians of idols, soldiers involved in combat or in taking the military oath, military commanders and civil magistrates, prostitutes of both sexes, enchanters, astrologers, diviners, users of charms, and makers of amulets. In addition, Christians whether baptized or not could not volunteer for military service; to do so was to despise God.[37]

There seems to be no particular order in the list Hippolytus provides, but it is obvious that some occupations are excluded because they had to do with idolatry and magic, others with killing and bloodshed, and still others with sexual immorality. In this attempt to regulate vocations the church was obviously entering into the affairs of the world and taking a particular stand in relation to Graeco-Roman society. The list does not reflect an ethic of withdrawal but a strong stand against what were regarded as abuses in the society.

VI·SOCIAL ETHICS

The evidence we have thus far cited might suggest that early Christianity, at least in the Roman world, was essentially a middle-class movement. Certainly the evidence on slavery points toward this conclusion, and a few further quotations may give it support. The Latin apologist Minucius Felix explicitly says that "we do not come from the lowest levels of society," and Origen argues for a spiritual interpretation of one of the beatitudes by stating that "not even a stupid person would praise the poor indiscriminately; the majority of them have very bad characters."[38] Only at a time long after the recognition of Christianity by the state could Jerome claim that Christians originated *de vili plebicula,* and his claim was not strictly true.[39]

Christians were not, however, concerned with the social structure as such.

---

[37] *Apost. Trad.* 15, 10-22.
[38] Minucius Felix, *Oct.* 31, 6; Origen, *Contra Celsum* 6, 16.
[39] *Comm. in Ep. ad Gal.* III (*PL* 26, 428A); for aristocratic converts cf. P. R. L. Brown in *JRS* 51 (1961), 1-11.

They were concerned with conversion and moral transformation. According to the Gospel of Luke, Jesus himself said, "I came to call not the righteous but sinners to repentance,"[40] and Paul pointed out that the Corinthian Christians had once been sinners but were now transformed.[41] Justin claimed that men who had indulged in sexual immorality or magic or the pursuit of possessions, or had hated one another, now lived in response to Jesus' call.[42] Celsus denounced Christians for appealing to sinners, women, and children. Origen accepted the accusation and replied that sinners were called for transformation by God; women and children were called out of pagan society to a life of virtue.[43] It is this transformation with which Christians were primarily concerned, not with social status.

VII-LATIN MORALISTS

The most important Christian moralists of the third century wrote not in Greek but in Latin, and both of them taught at Carthage in Roman Africa. The earlier of them was Tertullian, whose works are generally marked by defensive hostility first toward the world and later toward the worldliness of the church. "I am most wretched," he wrote in discussing patience, "always sick with the fever of impatience." This sentence, as J. M. Fuller pointed out, sums up much of his thought.[44] In addition, he betrays a curiously perverse love of paradox, often for its own sake. This trait was not merely literary but was reflected in his own life. Married, he inveighed against women and sex; vehemently orthodox, he became a Montanist; a fierce advocate of martyrdom, he was no martyr.

We have already mentioned his little tract on patience. His other moral writings fall into two classes. First, there are five treatises on problems related to pagan society. They contain denunciations of circuses and all theatrical spectacles, as well as of Christians involved in making idols, in astrology, in teaching pagan literature, and in observing pagan festivals. Christian soldiers must not wear the customary laurel crowns. Christians under persecution cannot leave their homes or offer bribes. God wills and commands martyrdom. He desires the death of men. ("What you call perversity I call reasonable," Tertullian declares. "What you call cruelty I call kindness.") Second, there are five treatises which deal with women. Christian women must avoid ornamenting themselves in any way; they must expiate the sin of Eve, who was

[40] Luke 5:32 (cf. Mark 2:17; Matt. 9:13).
[41] I Cor. 6:9-11.
[42] Justin, *Apol.* I, 14, 2-3; 15, 7; 16, 4.
[43] Origen, *Contra Celsum* 3, 44-81; cf. A. Mehat, *Étude sur les "Stromates" de Clément d'Alexandrie* (Paris, 1966), 388.
[44] *DCB* IV 864; cf. B. Nisters, *Tertullian, seine Persönlichkeit und sein Schicksal* (Münster, 1950).

the "door of the devil." They must wear veils both outside the church and inside it. Second marriages are absolutely forbidden. Finally, only God can forgive the deadly sins of adultery and fornication; the church cannot do so. One further treatise, on fasting, insists on Montanist asceticism.

Christian writers generally denounced theatrical performances as representations of immorality, but Tertullian provided two examples of the bad effect of plays. One woman, he says, came home from the theater possessed by a demon. Finally expelled by exorcism, the unclean spirit was rebuked for having entered into a Christian believer. "But I did so quite rightly," he replied, "for I found her in my territory." Another heard a tragic actor's recitation, and later in a dream she was shown a linen sheet and the actor's name was pronounced. Five days later she was no longer alive.[45] No other early Christian writer attacked Graeco-Roman culture as vividly as Tertullian did. Small wonder he became a Montanist.

The other important Latin moralist of the third century was Cyprian, bishop of Carthage. According to Jerome, he greatly admired the writings of Tertullian and used to ask his secretary to hand him the writings of "the master."[46] Conceivably the practice was Jerome's not Cyprian's, for the bishop never mentioned Tertullian's name in his writings.[47] It is undeniable that he used his predecessor's books, but his own statements on the same or similar themes were invariably more sober and temperate. Cyprian wrote not one but two treatises on patience (De bono patientiae, De zelo et livore), as well as a moderating work De habitu virginum.[48] These offer many points of contact with Tertullian, as does the treatise De dominica oratione; but Tertullian could never have written De opere et eleemosyniis or a letter in which liberal almsgiving is commended because good works "cover" sins after baptism as baptism itself provides forgiveness for previous sins.[49] Tertullian called Seneca saepe noster; Cyprian tacitly borrowed many expressions and ideas from him[50] —and at the same time denounced Novatian for accepting the Stoic doctrine that all sins were equal and that a serious man was not easily turned from his course.[51]

During the persecution under Diocletian the apologist-rhetorician Lactantius was occupied with his Divinae institutiones, which he regarded as comparable to institutiones civilis iuris.[52] The first four books contain criticisms of polytheism and philosophy and a defense of "true wisdom and religion." At the

[45] De spect. 26.
[46] De vir. illustr. 53.
[47] C. Mohrmann in VC 5 (1951), 111-12.
[48] Cyprian habitually used the terms temperare and moderari; cf. Hugo Koch, Cyprianische Untersuchungen (Bonn, 1926), 275-77.
[49] Ep. 55, 22.
[50] Koch, op. cit., 286-313.
[51] Ibid., 272-75.
[52] Div. inst. I, I, 12.

beginning of the fifth book, "on justice." Lactantius mentions two anti-Christian writers whom he is refuting[53] and then turns to justice as the supreme virtue, originating in religion and expressed in equity.[54] He also touches upon patience,[55] but reserves his discussion of other virtues for the sixth book. In this book he insists that justice involves union with God (*religio*) and with man (*misericordia* and *humanitas*).[56] Philosophical ethics, he claims, is inadequate; what matters is what has been revealed by God.[57] The emotions of anger, desire, and libido are God-given but can be misused;[58] man can be led astray by the pleasures of the senses.[59] In the seventh book Lactantius explains that at the end of six thousand years the Roman empire will collapse and the saints will live in a "holy city . . . in the middle of the earth."[60] After a thousand years the final transformation will occur.[61]

Lactantius presents a fascinating mixture of quotations from oracles and philosophical argument, in this regard resembling the Neoplatonists of his time. His apocalyptic eschatology was fortified by what he found in the *Sibylline Oracles,* and after Constantine's conversion he had to insert praise of this just and Christian ruler at several points in his treatise.[62] One might say that he reversed the New Testament movement of thought; his praise of the emperor recalls Romans 13, while his earlier statement was more like the Revelation of John.

In spite of Lactantius' assiduous use of Cicero for his ethical discussions, and of Minucius Felix, Tertullian, and Cyprian for ideas related to Christianity,[63] his book is not fully integrated. He criticizes Tertullian for his lack of rhetorical ability and his obscurity, but his own work, while clear and readable, presents a juxtaposition rather than a synthesis of Christian and classical themes. It is important, however, as an indication of the direction in which some Christians were moving in the early fourth century.

What has happened is that the unsystematic insights of the New Testament have been roughly correlated with classical ideals and in large measure have been deprived of their eschatological sanctions. To be sure, Lactantius tried to maintain the primitive view, but his ethical discussions depend far more on Cicero than on apocalyptic eschatology. His adulation of Constantine may have led to his appointment as tutor to the young prince Crispus;[64] it is hard

---

[53] *Ibid.,* 5, 2-4 (cf. 5, 11, 15 for Hierocles, *praeses* of Bithynia).
[54] *Ibid.,* 5, 14, 7.
[55] *Ibid.,* 5, 22, 1-4.
[56] *Ibid.,* 6, 10, 2.
[57] *Ibid.,* 6, 18, 1-4.
[58] *Ibid.,* 6, 19.
[59] *Ibid.,* 6, 20-24.
[60] *Ibid.,* 7, 24, 6.
[61] *Ibid.,* 7, 26, 5-7.
[62] *Ibid.,* 1, 1, 13-16; 7, 27, 2.
[63] *Ibid.,* 5, 1, 22-28.
[64] Jerome, *De vir. illustr.* 80.

to imagine how he could have combined ethics and eschatology for his pupil. More adequate solutions lay in the future.

We may now sum up the general early Christian attitudes toward some major questions of social ethics, dealing first with property, next with slavery, then with sexual matters, and finally with war.

VII-ATTITUDES TOWARD PROPERTY

It is clear that at Jerusalem a kind of religious communism was once practiced, presumably in imitation of the Jewish sectarian community at Qumran.[65] A more common attitude seems to be expressed by Paul, who had to collect funds to support the Jerusalem church. As far as we can tell, there was no compulsory sharing in the Pauline churches, though charity was of course commended. The moral statements in the Pastoral Epistles reflect similar views, and only Irenaeus among the early fathers suggested that the ownership of property was due to avarice. To be sure, almost all criticize love of money for its own sake and insist upon the positive duty of almsgiving; but no one seems to have suggested that Jesus' advice to a rich young man, to give away what he possessed, was to be applied generally.[66] Clement, as we have seen, insists on the importance of inner attitudes; Lactantius states that "the ownership of property contains the material of both vices and virtues, but communism [communitas] contains nothing but license for vice."[67] The right to own private property was taken for granted—though it must be admitted that before Constantine's time Christians did not often encounter large accumulations of wealth.[68]

At one particular point, it is sometimes claimed, the Christians' ideas in regard to property went beyond those of their contemporaries. This point is the taking of interest on loans. Up to the early fourth century, however, Christian writers hardly ever discussed the subject. Admittedly the details of Jesus' parables do not necessarily convey his own view, but in the parable of the talents or pounds a slave is told that he should have deposited a sum with bankers so that it would earn interest.[69] Lending money for the sake of a return is not commended by Jesus, while lending it without hope of recovering it is praised; but these are counsels having to do with love of enemies, not

---

[65] Cf. F. M. Cross, Jr., *The Ancient Library of Qumran* (Garden City, N.Y., 1961), 84-85.
[66] Cf. H. von Campenhausen, *Tradition and Life in the Church* (Philadelphia, 1968), 90-101.
[67] *Div. inst.* 3, 22, 7. God wills equality, without which there is no justice; but what counts is spiritual equality (5, 14, 15—15, 7).
[68] For an unusual example of Gnostic communism see p. 260 above.
[69] Matt. 25:27; Luke 19:23; cf. G. Le Bras in *DTC* XV 2323.

with commercial transactions.[70] It is true that in the Old Testament law the taking of interest from a "brother" was forbidden;[71] but it is not certain that this commandment underlies the saying of Jesus.

In early patristic literature there are three references to the taking of interest. The first occurs when Clement of Alexandria insists that it is not to be taken from a brother; he is tacitly quoting lengthy extracts from the writings of Philo.[72] The second is to be found at a point where Tertullian, arguing against Marcion, claims that the lending of money at interest is condemned both by Jesus and by the prophet Ezekiel.[73] The third is in a passage in Cyprian's treatise *De lapsis* in which he is criticizing the avarice of the clergy.[74] These references do not provide convincing proof that the taking of interest was forbidden. On the other hand, the question certainly came to the fore early in the fourth century. At the synod of Elvira both clerics and laymen were forbidden to take interest,[75] while at Nicaea clerics were forbidden to do so or to take a share of farm produce in payment.[76]

IX·ATTITUDES TOWARD SLAVERY

In regard to slavery too no basic questions were raised. It might be that in writing to Philemon on behalf of the runaway slave Onesimus the apostle Paul was suggesting that he be emancipated,[77] but in 1 Corinthians 7:20 Paul definitely urged slaves to make Christian use of their condition, not to seek for freedom. Slaves and freemen alike were to remain in the state in which they were called; they had mutual responsibilities, but the emphasis was laid on the slaves' obedience.[78] Ignatius of Antioch had to urge Polycarp not to look down on slaves, while reminding him that they were not to be "puffed up" or try to obtain emancipation at the expense of the church.[79] Clement of Rome wrote not of emancipation but of self-sale: many Christians, he said, had fed others with the price they obtained for themselves.[80]

As the eschatological impetus began to wane, ex-slaves came to the fore in some Christian communities, notably at Rome, as was the case in the

[70] Luke 6:34-35.
[71] Exod. 22:25; Lev. 25:36; Deut. 23:19.
[72] Clement, *Str.* 2, 84, 4; Philo, *De virt.* 82.
[73] Tertullian, *Adv. Marc.* 4, 17, 1; Ezek. 18:8.
[74] Cyprian, *De lapsis* 6.
[75] Elvira, Can. 20 (pp. 232-33 Hefele and Leclerq); cf. Arles, Can. 12 (p. 288; clerics).
[76] Nicaea, Can. 17 (pp. 604-10); cf. *Cod. Theod.* 2, 33, 1.
[77] Cf. J. Knox, *Philemon Among the Letters of Paul* (Chicago, 1935).
[78] Col. 3:22-25; Eph. 6:5-8; 1 Pet. 2:18-20; 1 Tim. 6:1-2; Tit. 2:9-10; *Did.* 4:10-11.
[79] Ignatius, *Polyc.* 4, 3.
[80] 1 Clem. 55, 2; cf. R. Taubenschlag, *The Law of Greco-Roman Egypt in the Light of the Papyri* (New York, 1944), 55-56.

empire generally. The prophet Hermas and the bishop Callistus had once been slaves; Hippolytus looked down on the bishop.[81] According to Athenagoras, Christians owned slaves, "some more, some fewer," and none brought accusations against their masters.[82] On the other hand, at Lyons about 177 some slaves did make such accusations,[83] and Tertullian called the slaves of Christians their enemies "from their very nature."[84]

The emancipation of slaves is recommended in later church orders,[85] but only in regard to those enslaved in times of persecution. The idea that slavery is immoral because all men are equal before God is expressed only in the Gnostic *Acts of Thomas*.[86]

X-ATTITUDES TOWARD SEXUAL MATTERS

As regards marriage and the family, it is obvious that the guidelines set forth in the New Testament are primarily expressed from the huband's standpoint. The Matthaean statements about divorce are concerned with the husband first and with the wife and her adultery only second (Matt. 5:31–32; 19:3–9), even though in Mark 10:11–12 divorce and remarriage are forbidden for both husband and wife. In 1 Corinthians 7:2–16 (cf. 32–34) Paul expresses an ethic of mutual obligation, but from a later passage (1 Cor. 11:3–12) it is clear that he envisages the husband as set in charge of the wife (cf. 14:34–35). Other New Testament passages make it plain that the wife is to obey her husband; it is he who loves her.[87]

The same attitude is expressed by Ignatius. Christian women are to "love the Lord and be content with their husbands in flesh and spirit," while their husbands are "to love their wives as the Lord loved the church." Ignatius is the first Christian writer to require that marriages take place "with the consent of the bishop" so that they may be related to the Lord and not to lust.[88]

Following Jewish precedent, several New Testament writers militantly condemn both adultery (with a married person) and fornication (with an unmarried person), as well as homosexual acts of any sort.[89] Sexual intercourse as such is not condemned, however, and indeed the apostle Paul can speak

[81] *Ref.* 9, 12, 1.
[82] *Leg.* 35, 1.
[83] Eusebius, *H. E.* 5, 1, 14.
[84] *Apol.* 7, 3.
[85] *Const. Apost.* 4, 9, 2.
[86] *Acta Thomae* 82-83 (pp. 198-99 Bonnet). Cf. the canon of Elvira noted below, p. 277.
[87] Col. 3:18; Eph. 5:22; 1 Pet. 3:1.
[88] *Polyc.* 5, 1-2.
[89] E.g., 1 Cor. 5:1-13, 6:9-20; Matt. 15:19=Mark 7:22; Rom. 1:26-27.

of it as a necessary function of marriage,[90] even though he regards his own unmarried state as more desirable.[91]

An ascetic sexual ideal is encouraged by several writers in the early second century. In 2 Clement, for example, there is a quotation from apocryphal tradition: when the Lord was asked when his kingdom would come, he replied, "When the two become one, and the outside as the inside, and the male with the female neither male nor female." This is taken to mean that "when a brother sees a sister he should have no thought of her as female, nor she of him as male" (2 Clem. 12). According to Ignatius, "if anyone is able to remain in continence in honor of the flesh of the Lord, he is to do so without boasting." Boasting or publicity will bring about his destruction, though the bishop may be informed.[92]

In the Syrian church, it would appear, only unmarried Christians could be baptized,[93] and during the second century there were evidently bishops farther to the west who advocated compulsory continence. One of them was Pinytus of Cnossus in Crete, who was asked by Dionysius of Corinth not to lay such a burden on his people. Pinytus in turn criticized Dionysius for not giving more "solid food" to the Corinthians.[94] It would appear that the rigorist position was not influential, however, outside Syria. The fact that it was advocated by many ascetic-minded Gnostics was not in its favor.

On the other hand, an ascetic view was encouraged by conflict with licentious Gnostics, by opposition to popular slanders about Christian promiscuity, and by the penalty of *stupratio* sometimes imposed upon Christian women by Roman judges.[95]

In the *Didache* (2, 2) we find a list of sexual sins—based on the Decalogue —extended to include acts of pederasty and abortion, as well as the killing of a new born infant. The same condemnation was provided in Barnabas (19, 4–5). In general, the early Christian view was based on the axiom stated by Justin: "we either marry for the purpose of bringing up children or we abstain from marriage and are completely continent."[96] The idea that the sole purpose of marriage was the procreation of offspring, while not to be found in the New Testament (cf. 1 Cor. 7:2–9), was a commonplace in contemporary philosophy[97] and was reiterated by such writers as Athenagoras and Clement of Alexandria. "A man who marries for the sake of begetting children must

[90] 1 Cor. 7:3-5.
[91] 1 Cor. 7:7-8.
[92] Ignatius, *Polyc.* 5, 2.
[93] A. Vööbus, *Celibacy a Requirement for Admission to Baptism in the Early Syrian Church* (Stockholm, 1951).
[94] Eusebius, *H. E.* 4, 23, 7-8.
[95] Cf. F. Augar in *TU* 28, 4 (1905). For Gnostic sex mysticism cf. S. Benko in *VC* 21 (1967), 103-19.
[96] Justin, *Apol.* 1, 29, 1; see J. T. Noonan, Jr., *Contraception* (Cambridge, Mass., 1965), 9-106.
[97] R. Harder, *Ocellus Lucanus* (Berlin, 1926), p. 122.

practise continence so that it is not desire he feels for his wife, whom he ought to love [*agapan*], and that he may beget children with a chaste and controlled will," for the Christian ideal is "not to experience desire at all."[98] Origen's ascetic viewpoint is very clear. "God has allowed us to marry wives, because not everybody is capable of the superior condition which is to be absolutely pure."[99]

It is conceivable that Christian influence is reflected in some imperial rescripts of the third century. For instance, Alexander Severus maintained the tax on prostitutes, criticized by both Justin and Tertullian, but diverted it from the *sacrum aerarium* to the support of public spectacles.[100] The emperor Philip, whether a Christian or not, forbade male prostitution, also condemned by Christian writers.[101]

What had come to be the common Christian emphasis on virginity was also expressed in the *Symposium* of a certain Methodius, perhaps a bishop, who produced many treatises in the last third of the third century. The *Symposium* consists of eleven discourses, mostly in praise of virginity (marriage and procreation are permissible but inferior), and ends with a marriage hymn addressed to the bridegroom Christ. The title suggests that Methodius is imitating the *Symposium* of Plato, and Platonic echoes occur throughout. There are numerous digressions indicating the author's need to come to terms with the culture in which he lives; these are on such matters as astrology, numerology, the symbolism of trees, and physiological matters. Methodius occasionally mentions martyrdom, but the struggle for virginity seems to have replaced it. The earlier eschatological expectations are mentioned, but the end will not come until the seventh millennium.

It is probably significant that just as in the case of the hermit Antonius, Eusebius of Caesarea says nothing about Methodius. He actually quotes an extract from one of his books but ascribes it to an otherwise unknown Maximus.[102] Presumably the grounds for this silence were theological. Methodius had attacked Origen, one of Eusebius' heroes, and therefore deserved being ignored.[103] In addition, his ideas seemed to have little to offer in the new age of church life now dawning under Constantine's rule.

---

[98] Athenagoras, *Leg.* 32-34; Clement, *Str.* 3, 57-58. See also *Sexti Sententiae* 231-32; Soranus, *Gynaec.* 1, 30-32 (pp. 20-22 Ilberg).

[99] Origen, *C. Cels.* 8, 55.

[100] *SHA Severus Alexander* 24, 3-4; cf. Justin, *Apol.* 1, 27, 2; Tertullian, *De fuga* 13, 3.

[101] *SHA Severus Alexander* 24, 4; Aurelius Victor, *De Caesaribus* 28, 6; cf. Quintilian, *Inst. orat.* 4, 2, 69.

[102] *P. E.* 7, 22.

[103] J. Sirinelli, *Les vues historiques d'Eusèbe de Césarée* (Dakar, 1961), 457.

XI·ATTITUDES TOWARD WAR

The only point, though it was a crucial one, at which Christian teaching sharply diverged from that of most Greek and Roman moralists was in relation to war and military service. Jesus' pronouncements about nonresistance left an indelible impression on the minds of the early Christians.[104] Early Christian theologians condemned murder and cited war as a prime instance.[105] Manuals of church discipline refused to allow for the possibility of military service and insisted that upon conversion a soldier had to leave the army.

It must be admitted, however, that those who most vehemently denounced war were leaders of minority groups within the church—Tatian, Tertullian as Montanist, Hippolytus, and Origen. Before becoming a Montanist, Tertullian explicitly stated that Christians served in the army.[106] The facts of Christian life confirm his statement. As early as the latter years of the second century there were Christian soldiers in the legions, and it is likely that their numbers steadily increased in spite of the problems presented by Roman religion in the army. By 314 the synod of Arles, convened at the emperor's command, decreed that Christians resigning from the army in peacetime were to be excommunicated.[107] Within half a century Athanasius of Alexandria, himself not averse to violence, held that it was lawful and even praiseworthy to kill enemies in time of war.[108]

Because of the general outlook of theologians before the reign of Constantine, the question of a just war was not directly faced. The anti-Christian writer Celsus evidently asked for Christian support in a just war, involving the defense of civilization against "the most lawless and savage barbarians."[109] In reply Origen claimed that Christians did fight on behalf of the emperors who reigned justly; by their prayers they strove on behalf of "those who fight in a just cause."[110] The principle of a just war is thus accepted, but Christians are said to share in it only by nonviolent means. The prohibition of killing was absolute.

Because of this absolute, early Christian theologians did not deal with the question of just means of warfare. Josephus, for example, insisted that Jews

---

[104] Cf. C. J. Cadoux, *The Early Christian Attitude to War* (London, 1919); R. H. Bainton in *HTR* 39 (1946), 189-212.

[105] H. Gollwitzer in *RGG³* IV 67: Justin, *Dial.* 110, 3; Tatian, *Or.* 19; Cyprian, *Ad Donat.* 6.

[106] *Apol.* 42, 3: *militamus.*

[107] *Canon* 3, p. 385 Turner.

[108] *Ep. ad Amunem, PG* 26, 1173 B.

[109] Origen, *C. Cels.* 8, 68.

[110] *Ibid.*, 8, 73.

at war did not practice incendiarism, the cutting of cultivated trees, the pillaging of corpses, or the abuse of prisoners.[111] Christian writers were not concerned with the means because the end was forbidden. Clement of Alexandria once mentions the prohibition of "cutting the land," but he is simply reproducing a passage from Philo.[112] The Christian layman Julius Africanus not only recommended a compound that would ignite spontaneously but advocated the destruction of trees and fields;[113] he must have been writing as a military theorist rather than as a churchman.

In seeking for parallels to the early Christian attitude, S. J. Case long ago found remarkably few apart from poetic statements about a golden age.[114] Some Epicureans were opposed to war as to all public life.[115] The Stoic Chrysippus seems to have stated that wars were brought on by the gods because of overpopulation;[116] it is hard to view this as an antimilitarist statement. Seneca denounced war,[117] but one cannot be sure that he would have done so on principle.

XII·CHRISTIAN DISCIPLINE

From a very early time Christian leaders exercised disciplinary functions over members of the community. The story of Ananias and Sapphira shows the apostle Peter pronouncing a divine judgment upon those who made a false accounting of their property to the Jerusalem church (Acts 5:1–11); he also condemns the Samaritan Simon Magus for attempting to practice simony (8:14–24). At Corinth the apostle Paul ordered the church to expel an offender who "had his father's wife" and, indeed, to "deliver him to Satan for the destruction of his flesh" (I Cor. 5:1–5). The precedent he followed was apparently found in the rabbinic formula of "extirpation," although there are parallels in practices at Qumran.[118] Similarly a fragment of church law in Matthew 18:15–17 states that a Christian who sins against his brother is first to be rebuked privately, then in the presence of one or two others, and finally before the whole community. If he refuses to hear the church, he is

---

[111] C. Ap. 2, 212: cf. Deut. 20:19-20.

[112] Str. 2, 95, 1; Philo, De virt. 150.

[113] J. Vieillefond, Jules Africain: Fragments des Cestes (Paris, 1932), 56-57; cf. p. 12, lines 39-40.

[114] American Journal of Theology 19 (1915), 179-99.

[115] H. Usener, Epicurea (Leipzig, 1887), fr. 560*; Lucretius, De rer. nat. I, 29-43.

[116] SVF II 1177.

[117] Nat. quaest. 5, 18, 5-10.

[118] Cf. S. E. Johnson in K. Stendahl, ed., The Scrolls and the New Testament (New York, 1956), 139.

to be treated as a gentile and a tax collector; in other words, he has become an outsider. Just so, Paul told the Corinthians not even to eat with a so-called Christian who was a conspicuous sinner.[119]

Problems of order naturally arose in the common assemblies, and Paul insisted that sickness and even death had come upon church members who ate and drank "unworthily" at the Lord's supper (1 Cor. 11:30). The unworthiness was probably related to division within the community. According to Matthew 5:23–24, reconciliation with one's brother had to precede the offering of a gift at the altar (in Jerusalem), and in the *Didache* (14, 2) a saying like this was applied to the eucharist. The "two ways" section of Barnabas ends with the mention of reconciliation, confession of sins, and not going to prayer with an evil conscience (19, 12).

The confession of sins is associated with healing in James 5:14–16, where the Christian is instructed to call upon the presbyters of the church in case of sickness; they will pray over the sick man and anoint him with oil, and the Lord will raise him up. If he has committed a sin, it will be forgiven. Mutual confession, followed by prayer, will bring healing. Similarly the *Didache* (4, 14) insists on confession "in church."

The forgiveness of sins (ultimately, of course, in God's hands) is assigned to Peter and to the other disciples in the Gospel of Matthew, where the words "binding" and "loosing" apparently come from rabbinic language about forbidding and permitting. Whatever the original meaning may have been, in the Gospel of John a similar saying is definitely related to sin and forgiveness: the risen Jesus says to the disciples, "Receive the Holy Spirit; the sins of any that you forgive, they are forgiven them; those of any that you retain, they are retained."[120] Thus Paul not only ordered the Corinthians to expel an offender but asked them to take one (the same?) back (2 Cor. 2:5–11).

Some sins were considered not to be forgivable. In the synoptic tradition it was stated that "blasphemy against the Holy Spirit" could not be forgiven, while the author of Hebrews held that apostasy after baptism was unforgivable.[121] According to 1 John 5:16, there is a "mortal sin" for which prayer is of no avail. Such sins, then, were not to be forgiven in consequence of the repentance, prayer, fasting, and almsgiving which, in Jewish-Christian circles, would normally suffice.[122]

Among the Montanists of the mid-second century there was a reaction against the emphasis on universal forgiveness. Montanus himself advocated more rigorous regulations and stated, "The church is able to forgive sins, but I will not do so lest others sin." By the time of Tertullian, however, the

[119] Paul also envisaged the creation of church courts to deal with disputes among Christians (1 Cor. 6:1-11), following Jewish precedent.
[120] Matt. 16:19; 18:18; John 20:22-23.
[121] Mark 3:29 and parallels; Heb. 6:4-6.
[122] 2 Clem. 16, 4.

churches at least in Rome and North Africa had developed a regular mode of penance, involving public confession, prayer, and reception back into the community. Difficulties arose because confessors and martyrs claimed the right to forgive all sins including those regarded as mortal: apostasy, murder, and adultery. When Tertullian became a Montanist he insisted that only "the church of the Spirit" could forgive such sins, and like Hippolytus of Rome he was deeply offended by the claims of bishops like Callistus to do so. In general the church rejected his position. Bishops with the whole community could and did exercise forgiveness and impose penance, though mortal sins could be forgiven only once.

In the east, especially under Alexandrian influence, a somewhat different view of penance prevailed. There it was regarded as a process not so much disciplinary as educational. The church, like the world itself, was viewed as a school for learning and practicing God's ways, and teachers thus were assigned a special role as spiritual directors. Presumably questions of this sort were involved in Origen's quarrel with Demetrius of Alexandria. Certainly he came to reject the bishop's disciplinary actions, but it must be remembered that he had a high regard for the authority of Fabian of Rome.[123]

Christian morality, discipline, and organization were closely interrelated, and the canons enacted by the synods of the early fourth century give a clear picture of the way in which discipline was administered. For the gravest sins the penalty was permanent excommunication; in other cases excommunication could be imposed for periods from one year (playing at dice for money[124]) to ten years (after returning to the Catholic Church from apostasy or heresy[125]). Fully a quarter of the eighty-one canons of Elvira have to do with marriage and sexual problems; it is worth noting that one canon refers to the *copia puellarum* or, actually, "oversupply" of Christian girls as tending to result in mixed marriages.[126] No fewer than six canons, including the first four to be promulgated, are concerned with the *flamines,* provincial or municipal priests who in the provinces were in charge of the imperial cult. Christians could hold this office provided that they did not offer sacrifices. If they held the municipal office of *duumvir* they were merely to stay away from the church during the one-year term.[127] On the other hand, Christians were absolutely forbidden to be charioteers or pantomimists, and the decision of Elvira was reiterated at Arles.[128]

Among the regulations having to do with clerics may be mentioned the provision made at Elvira for them to engage in business within Spain, though

---

123 On the whole question cf. P. Meinhold in *RGG*[3] I 1544-54.
124 Elvira, Can. 79 (C. J. Hefele and H. Leclerq, *Histoire des conciles* I, Paris, 1907, 263).
125 Elvira, Can. 46 (p. 248), 22 (p. 233).
126 Elvira, Can. 15 (pp. 230-31).
127 Elvira, Can. 1-4 (pp. 221-24), 55-56 (pp. 251-53).
128 Elvira, Can. 62 (p. 256); Arles, Can. 4-5 (p. 283).

usury (taking interest on loans) was forbidden.[129] In addition, the synod of Elvira insisted that all clerics were to abstain from sexual intercourse with their wives or be deposed.[130] The synod of Ancyra permitted deacons to marry only if at ordination they had stated their intention to do so.[131] The ascetic rigor of Elvira was advocated at Nicaea a generation later, probably by Ossius of Cordova, a member of both councils. It was proposed that clerics should not have sexual intercourse with their wives, but opposition to this western innovation was led by Paphnutius, a bishop from the Thebaid in Egypt who had lost an eye in the persecution and was renowned for his lifelong asceticism. He insisted that marriage was an honorable state and pointed to the practical dangers in marital asceticism for the clerics and their wives alike. In his view, accepted by the council, clerics should not marry after ordination.[132] All that the council did reject was the practice of allowing clerics to live with "spiritual sisters."[133] This practice, notorious in the case of Paul of Samosata, had been condemned at Antioch in Paul's time and by the synods of Elvira and Ancyra.[134]

All such regulations can be viewed as attempts to regularize the discipline of the church and to maintain the strength of the institution in the new age now dawning. Several canons explicitly indicate the social situation of Christians. At Elvira, for example, it was decided that if a Christian mistress were to beat a slave girl to death she should be excommunicated for seven years if the killing was intentional, for five if it was by accident.[135] Freedmen were not to be ordained during the lifetime of their patrons.[136] As we have already noted, at Arles it was stated that desertion from the army in peacetime was to result in excommunication.[137] This canon supplemented the death penalty provided by the army itself for desertion in time of war. The denunciations of bestiality promulgated by the synod of Ancyra may point toward the unsettled social and political situation in the east.[138]

It has often been claimed that Christianity exercised a beneficent effect upon the general level of its adherents' morality. To prove this hypothesis is very difficult, once one passes beyond the period of eschatological fervor or the claims of the second-century apologists. On the other hand, one would expect because of the nature of the movement that the kind of change upon

[129] Elvira, Can. 19-20 (pp. 232-33); cf. Arles, Can. 12 (p. 288); Nicaea, Can. 17 (pp. 604-10).
[130] Elvira, Can. 33 (pp. 238-39).
[131] Ancyra, Can. 10 (pp. 312-13).
[132] Socrates, H. E. 1, 11; Sozomen, H. E. 1, 23; Gelasius, H. E. 2, 32; Hefele and Leclerq, op. cit., 620-24; cf. Const. apost. 6, 17, 1.
[133] Nicaea, Can. 3 (pp. 536-39); cf. H. Achelis, Virgines subintroductae (Leipzig, 1902).
[134] Elvira, Can. 27 (p. 236); Ancyra, Can. 19 (pp. 321-22).
[135] Elvira, Can. 5 (pp. 224-25); cf. Ancyra, Can. 22-23 (pp. 324-25).
[136] Elvira, Can. 80 (p. 263).
[137] Arles, Can. 3 (pp. 282-83).
[138] Ancyra, Can. 16-17 (pp. 317-20).

which Christian writers insist would often have been a reality. When F. Joxe argues on the basis of papyrus letters that no change occurred in regard to "family feeling,"[139] one must remember that the base is rather small and, more important, that in the early period Christianity was not concerned so much with family feeling as with individual choice and salvation.

[139] F. Joxe in *Acta Antiqua Academiae Scientiarum Hungaricae* 7 (1959), 411-20.

CHAPTER XX
CREEDAL FORMULATIONS
AND ESCHATOLOGY

From the first two centuries of the church's life we possess hardly any formulas that can definitely be called creeds. The formulas and formulations that are preserved are usually related to the Christian's profession of faith before baptism. This rite of entrance into the community was originally "in the name of the Lord Jesus" and involved the declaration that "Jesus is Lord." It is possible that from such a declaration there then developed two-part formulations containing mention of God the Father and the Lord Jesus Christ. An example is provided by Paul's affirmation in 1 Corinthians 8:6. "For us there is

> one God the Father,
>> from whom are all things and
>> for whom we exist, and
> one Lord Jesus Christ,
>> through whom are all things and
>> through whom we exist."

To the two-part declarations there would finally be added a third member, resulting in baptism "in the name of the Father and the Son and the Holy

Spirit" (Matt. 28:19).[1] To be sure, it is not certain that the development actually went in just this direction. It may be that three-part declarations were prior to those in two parts. It is likely, however, that there was a movement from the more simple toward the more complex—and that it accompanied a movement from life within Judaism to life in the gentile world.

One of the earliest formulations we know occurs in a Gnostic setting. The baptismal formula used there clearly suggests the prior existence of a more "orthodox" statement, as we can easily see by paraphrasing it. The baptism is "in the name of the unknown Father of all [Father], in Truth the Mother of all [Spirit], in the one who descended into Jesus [Christ], in unity [church], redemption [forgiveness of sins], and the communion of the powers [resurrection or communion of saints]."[2] Something like the later baptismal creed therefore existed around the middle of the second century.

What underlies the Gnostic formulation corresponds with the testimony provided by Justin in the middle of the second century. At baptism, it is clear, the candidate was expected to make a profession of faith "that what we teach and say is true." What was taught and said was obviously related to baptism "in the name of God, the Father and master of all, and our Savior Jesus Christ and the Holy Spirit."[3] At other points in the *Apology* and *Dialogue* Justin summarizes the Christian proclamation about Jesus, who is usually described as born of the Virgin, crucified, dead, and as having arisen and ascended into heaven.[4] As Kelly observes, this proclamation, though it seems to echo the liturgy, is not related, thus far, to the baptismal profession of faith; he asks if it was not perhaps used in exorcism or at the eucharist.[5] For our purposes it is significant that out of eight such summaries in Justin's writings only two speak of Jesus' future coming again.[6] This is to say that only two lay emphasis on a futurist eschatology.

From this point we may turn to the definitely baptismal interrogations provided in the *Apostolic Tradition* of Hippolytus.[7]

Do you believe in God the Father Almighty?

Do you believe in Christ Jesus, the Son of God, who was born of the Holy Spirit and the Virgin Mary, who was crucified in the days of Pontius Pilate, and died, and arose the third day living from the dead and ascended into the heavens, and sat at the right hand of the Father, and will come to judge the living and the dead?

Do you believe in the Holy Spirit in the Holy Church, and the resurrection of the flesh?

[1] Cf. *Did.* 7, 1-3.
[2] Irenaeus, *Adv. haer.* I, 21, 3.
[3] *Apol.* I, 61, 3.
[4] E.g., *Apol.* I, 46, 5; other passages in J. N. D. Kelly, *Early Christian Creeds* (London, 1950), 73-74.
[5] *Ibid.,* 75.
[6] *Dial.* 126, 1; 132, 1.
[7] *Apost. Trad.* 21, 12-18.

It is easy enough to see how from such creedal formulas and baptismal interrogations the later creeds developed, largely by a process of addition and assimilation. The creeds are highly conservative documents and have resisted change through the years. It is worth noting, however, that what the apologetic leader Justin reports has very little emphasis on the future coming of Christ as judge and no mention of the future reign of God. Indeed, in his *Apology* he explicitly states that the kingdom is "with God" and that it is no "human kingdom" at all.[8] As for Hippolytus, he treats the future coming of Jesus as judge as part of the specifically Christological section of the creed and does not relate it to the future resurrection of the flesh, somehow an appendix to the third clause. By themselves these bits of evidence would not show that Christian expectations for the future were being modified. Taken in the context of the whole situation they seem relatively significant.

What has happened to Hippolytus' time is that the threefold interrogation and answer has been integrated with the traditional "apostolic preaching" about Jesus[9] as a summary of the essential content of the Christian faith. This combination was characteristic of western Christianity and is reflected in the earliest extant form of the "old Roman symbol." In the east, on the other hand, there was more emphasis on the functions of God and Christ in creation, less on the life of the incarnate Lord, on the life of the church, and on eschatology.

The oldest extant formulations of western and eastern creeds are provided by Rufinus[10] and by Eusebius of Caesarea.[11]

The differences between these two formulations clearly reflect the history of Christianity in west and east. In the west there had been struggles with heretics who denied the reality of Christ's life and of the work of redemption he had affected; hence the emphasis on his birth, his suffering, and his burial, as well as on the church, the forgiveness of sins, and the resurrection of the flesh. This is not to say that these matters were neglected in the east. It is simply to say that whereas the west was especially concerned with the work of redemption, the east under the influence of Alexandrian theologians was especially concerned with trinitarian doctrines and with the role of the Father and the Son in the work of creation. To put the point with some exaggeration, the west told the story of Jesus and redemption, while the east speculated about the cosmic meaning of Christ. One might even go further and suggest that in general the west was therefore concerned primarily with schism, while the problem of the east was that of heresy. The basic conflicts during Constantine's reign point in the same direction. For the west troubles arose over Donatism; in the east they arose over Arianism.

---

[8] *Apol.* I, II.
[9] Cf. C. H. Dodd, *The Apostolic Preaching and Its Developments* (Chicago, 1937).
[10] Rufinus in *PL* 21, 335-86; cf. J. N. D. Kelly, *Rufinus* (Westiminster, Md., 1955).
[11] Athanasius, *De decretis Nicaenae synodi* 33, 4 (p. 29, 11-17 Opitz).

West	East
I believe in God	We believe in one God
the Father Almighty,	the Father Almighty,
	Maker of all things visible and in-
	visible,
and in Christ Jesus	and in one Lord Jesus Christ,
	the Logos of God, God of God, Light of
	Light, Life of Life,
his only Son our Lord,	the only Son,
	Firstborn of all creation, begotten of
	the Father before all the ages,
	through whom everything came to be;
who was born of the Holy Spirit	who for our salvation was incarnate
and the Virgin Mary,	and lived among men,
who was crucified under Pontius	and suffered
Pilate and was buried;	
on the third day he arose from	and arose on the third day
the dead and ascended into heaven;	and ascended to
he sits at the right hand of	
the Father, whence he	the Father,
will come	and will come again in glory
to judge the living and the dead;	to judge the living and the dead.
and in the Holy Spirit,	And we believe in one Holy Spirit.
the Holy Church,	
the forgiveness of sins,	
the resurrection of this flesh.	

The only eschatological note expressed in the creeds is thus to be found in the expectation of the return of Christ to judge the living and the dead, and in the western reference to the resurrection of the flesh.[12] The eastern creed looks back to creation and meditates upon the origin and the work of the divine Logos. The western creed tells of Christ's birth, death, resurrection, and ascension in the past, and of the present situation in which he sits at the Father's right hand and the Holy Spirit is at work in the church for the forgiveness of sins. Obviously there are links between these statements and the faith of the apostolic church; but the differences are equally marked. The whole setting of the Christian movement had been transformed, and the development of its theologies had accompanied the political and social modifications of which we have spoken in earlier chapters. As the movement went out into the Graeco-Roman world, its tenets were inevitably expressed in modes of thought at first Jewish (both Palestinian and Hellenistic, in so far

[12] Cf. J. Daniélou, *Théologie du judéo-christianisme* (Tournai, 1958); *Message évangélique et culture hellénistique* (Tournai, 1961).

as a distinction can be drawn), then Greek and, finally, Roman.[13] The use of these modes was accompanied by a lessening of the eschatological emphasis, whether lessening was the cause or the effect of the new situation.[14] As H. Kraft has pointed out, from the second century through the fourth three approaches to eschatology were taken. First, it could actually be maintained as an essential element of the "history of salvation"; the principal witnesses are Irenaeus, who tended to sympathize with Montanism, and Tertullian, who became a Montanist. Second, it could be kept in isolation from a theology not influenced by it; Kraft cites Lactantius as his prime example, but one must suppose that many Christians experienced similar difficulties. Third, the primitive Christian eschatology was "spiritualized away" in two different, but compatible, directions. On the one hand, the temporal categories of eschatology were replaced by the categories of what one might call "spiritual space." Though eschatology is not completely absent from Gnostic teachings, especially in the case of Basilides,[15] Gnosticism in general had no place for the reign of God on an earth he did not create. Under the influence of Middle Platonism, both Clement and Origen of Alexandria completely reinterpreted earlier eschatological doctrines.[16] On the other hand, for a court theologian like Eusebius of Caesarea (himself an admirer of Origen) the golden age had really been initiated by the reign of the Christian emperor Constantine. The victory of the church was clearly a close approximation to the coming of God's reign. We have already seen that in some measure the ideas of Eusebius were anticipated in the second century by apologists like Melito of Sardis, while the notion of a Christian golden age was set forth by Clement.

We shall not attempt to say anything further about the development of Christian theology, for the field belongs to its own cultivators. For our present purposes it is enough to observe that just as in the case of ethical teaching the Christian movement was not static or bound exclusively to its origins. It was a movement of change and adaptation from the beginning to the reign of Constantine.

[13] Cf. M. Werner, *Die Entstehung des christlichen Dogmas* (Bern, 1941); *The Formation of Christian Dogma* (New York, 1957).

[14] *RGG* II[3] 673-80; cf. also H. Conzelmann, *ibid.*, 655-72.

[15] Cf. G. Quispel in *Eranos-Jahrbücher* 16 (1948), 89-139.

[16] For Origen's reinterpretation of sayings of Jesus cf. my book *The Earliest Lives of Jesus* (London and New York, 1961), 107-10.

CHAPTER XXI
CHRISTIAN WORSHIP

In looking for elements of close continuity within the life and history of early Christianity, we have now found that moral teaching and creedal-theological matters do not reflect any static or immutable areas of practice or thought. All alike were influenced by the ongoing movement of Christians out of first-century Jewish eschatology and into the world of Graeco-Roman culture. Conceivably, however, it may be supposed that in Christian worship there was something unchanging and that "in church" the Christian generations remained much the same.

Certainly Christian worship was central to the life of the communities. This point is only implicit in much of the New Testament, but it becomes clear if one considers the contexts of the various documents and their parts. The "passion narrative," for example, was almost certainly developed in relation to the Christian cultus.[1] The letters of Paul were written to be read at common worship. The hymns of the book of Revelation, supposedly sung in heaven, were presumably not altogether different from hymns sung on earth. What is

[1] This point was long ago made by G. Bertram, *Die Leidensgeschichte Jesu und der Christuskult* (Göttingen, 1922).

implicit in the New Testament becomes explicit by the time of the *Didache,* probably in the latter half of the first century. There we find catechetical instruction, regulations about baptism, fasting, prayer, and eucharist, arrangements for the ministry, and finally a description of the signs to be expected before the coming of the Lord.

The importance of common worship is clearly expressed in the writings of the Apostolic Fathers. Thus the Didachist argues that by meeting together Christians will seek for the good of their souls and attain perfection. The Epistle of Barnabas contrasts meetings for the common good with an isolated style of life which might be suitable for men already righteous but not for Christians.[2] Ignatius, bishop of Antioch, is especially concerned with common worship, in which grace is present[3] and prayer is effective. Frequent meetings are for giving thanks and glory to God; they express the harmony of faith and destroy the divisive powers of Satan. Only the proud, whom God resists, remain separate.[4]

In 2 Clement emphasis is laid on the relation of worship to other aspects of life. Christians are not to "seem to believe" while the presbyters are instructing them; instead, when they have returned home they are to remember the Lord's commandments. They should meet more frequently in order to "make progress in the Lord's commandments."[5]

It is obvious, then, that common life and worship were closely related. The most important common rites were baptism and the eucharist.

I·BAPTISM

The origins of Christian baptism, as is to be expected, are to be found within the context of eschatology. All the evangelists clearly indicate that the rite was practiced by John the Baptist, an eschatological prophet who took his stand near the Jordan river about the year 27[6] and proclaimed the necessity of being baptized there "for the remission of sins."[7] The last judgment was at hand; only baptism could protect the repentant and forgiven sinner from the eschatological fire. John's baptism has been compared with the later Jewish practice of baptizing proselytes and with the washings characteristic of the sectarians at Qumran,[8] but the specifically eschatological note seems to

---

[2] *Did.* 16, 2; Barn. 4, 10.
[3] *Eph.* 20, 2; cf. the prayer in the *Didache.*
[4] *Eph.* 5, 2-3; 13, 10.
[5] 2 Clem. 17, 3.
[6] Luke 3:1-2.
[7] Mark 1:4; Luke 3:3 (cf. Matt. 3:6).
[8] On proselyte baptism cf. J. Jeremias in *TZ* 5 (1949) 418-28; the washings at Qumran were repeated, not administered once.

differentiate it from either. To be sure, in describing John's baptism the historian Josephus eliminates the eschatological emphasis and says it was a bath for men who were already virtuous;[9] but Josephus was eager to reduce the importance of apocalyptic eschatology among first-century Palestinian Jews. According to both Matthew and Luke, John spoke of the impending wrath of God. "The axe already lies at the root of the trees; every tree that does not produce good fruit is cut down and cast into the fire."[10]

Jesus himself was baptized by John, and according to the Fourth Gospel several of John's disciples followed him as their master. During Jesus' ministry he himself apparently did not baptize any of his followers. A statement to the effect that he did so occurs only in the Gospel of John, and the evangelist immediately adds (4:2) that "Jesus himself did not baptize; his disciples did so." On the other hand, baptism was evidently a rite of the early community at Jerusalem. The apostle Peter is represented as calling upon "men of Israel" to repent and be baptized "in the name of Jesus Christ" for the remission of their sins.[11] It is also significant that at the end of the Gospel of Matthew the risen Lord is depicted as commanding his disciples to baptize "in the name of the Father and the Son and the Holy Spirit."[12] While Christian baptism thus developed, after the death of Jesus, out of the baptism of John, there were Christians who knew only traditions about Jesus and practiced "John's baptism." In the book of Acts they are described as being introduced by Paul to baptism "in the name of Jesus."[13]

The apostle Paul, indeed, seems to have played an important part in the development of Christian thought on baptism. In his view, "by one Spirit we were all baptized into one body, whether Jews or Greeks, slaves or free men, and we were all made to drink of one Spirit" (1 Cor. 12:13). In his view the rite did not produce magical effects, even though by washing the Christians were consecrated and justified.[14] Though at the Exodus the Israelites were prefiguratively baptized, they suffered drastic punishments when they later sinned. Baptism had to produce results in the Christian's life. Those baptized into Christ Jesus died and were buried with him so that they could rise and live in "newness of life."[15]

But Paul's idea that the Spirit was conveyed at baptism was not at first shared by all Christians. The early stories in Acts do depict the gift of the Spirit as accompanying baptism; they also depict Christian baptism without the Spirit and the gift of the Spirit as preceding baptism.[16]

---

[9] *Ant.* 18, 117.
[10] Matt. 3:7-10; Luke 3:7-9.
[11] Acts 2:37-42.
[12] Matt. 28:19-21.
[13] Acts 18:24—19:6.
[14] 1 Cor. 6:11 (cf. 1:30).
[15] 1 Cor. 10:5-10; Rom. 6:3-11.
[16] Acts 8:38-39; 8:15-19; 10:44-48.

Paul's idea of baptism as equivalent to dying with Christ or being buried with him (Col. 2:12) may have antecedents in the sayings of Jesus, where "baptism" seems to be used metaphorically of death (Mark 10:38; Luke 12:50). Commentators have sometimes compared the baptismal fragment in Ephesians 5:14—"Awake, O sleeper, and arise from the dead, and Christ will shine upon you"—with a formula employed in one of the mystery religions. According to the fourth-century Christian writer Firmicus Maternus, the image of a god was placed on a bed and mourned for as though dead; later a light was brought in and the priest said, "Rejoice, initiates of the god who has been saved; for to us there will be salvation from our sufferings."[17] Because of this parallel and others, it has been supposed that Paul borrowed his conception of dying and rising with Christ from the mysteries. Such a theory is highly improbable, since whether as Jew or as Christian Paul had no contact with or respect for pagan religions. We must probably conclude that his interpretation arose on inner-Christian grounds and was related to his conception of imitating Christ and being united with him. Paul himself had died with Christ, he believed, at the time of his conversion (Gal. 2:19–20). This, it would apear, was his baptism, and he interpreted the baptism of others in its light (cf. Rom. 6:3–4).

Similarly in 1 Peter we find that baptism provides the context for much of the letter. Christians have been "reborn not of a perishable seed but of an imperishable one, through the word of the living and enduring God" (1:23). In a later sentence (2:1–2) the author speaks of his readers as having "put off" all kinds of wickedness and "like newborn infants" desiring the nourishment of "spiritual milk."[18] They have now become a holy priesthood and can therefore offer "spiritual sacrifices acceptable to God through Jesus Christ." After an extended discussion of the Christian way of life, consequent upon baptism (2:11 3:17), the author compares Christ's preaching to "the spirits in prison" with God's saving action in the time of Noah— "through water" (3:19–20). What now corresponds to this action is baptism itself, and baptism is not "the removing of dirt from the body" (i.e., just a bath) but "the petition of a good conscience to God through the resurrection of Jesus Christ." The following mention of Christ's exaltation and ascension (3:21–22) suggests that his death and resurrection were being acknowledged at baptism.

The most significant feature of this discussion lies in his treatment of baptism as rebirth. Paul, as we have seen, preferred the figure of death and resurrection, or even new creation (cf. 2 Cor. 5:17; Gal. 6:15). He thus emphasized the radicalness of the baptismal transformation somewhat more strongly than do the authors who use the figure of birth and rebirth; but rebirth too is an image of novelty. We find it ascribed to Paul in the Epistle to

[17] *De errore profanarum religionum* 22, I.
[18] Cf. I Cor. 3:2; Heb. 5:12.

Titus (3:5–7, "a washing of regeneration") and to Jesus himself in John 3:3–8. Whether resurrection or rebirth is mentioned, Christians are insisting that in becoming members of the community they are not what they were.[19]

The significance of baptism may seem to be minimized in the anonymous Epistle to the Hebrews (of uncertain date), for its author speaks of proceeding toward perfection while leaving behind more elementary matters such as "repentance from dead works, faith in God, teaching about 'baptisms,' the laying on of hands, the resurrection of the dead, and eternal condemnation" (6:1–2). Nevertheless it is clear that all these matters are related to Christian conversion and initiation, and that though they may be elementary they are also indispensable. Indeed the author immediately proceeds to state that those who have once been "illuminated" and have "tasted the heavenly gift and have been made sharers in the Holy Spirit and have tasted the word of God and the powers of the age to come" cannot "become new for repentance" if they have fallen away from the faith (6:4–6). It is sometimes thought that when he mentions "baptisms" in the plural he has in mind not Christian baptism but something like the ritual baths employed at Qumran and elsewhere. This idea is improbable because of the context of Christian ideology. He is actually insisting on the meaning of the rite; what matters is illumination and participation in the Holy Spirit and the gifts of God. The language about "tasting" clearly recalls Paul's words about drinking the Spirit at baptism (I Cor. 12:13).

"Illumination" is sometimes viewed as a term derived from contemporary mystery religions, but it was not a term denoting initiation.[20] The idea is reflected in the baptismal fragment in Ephesians 5:14, mentioned above. If we seek for an explanation of it beyond the ordinary Hellenistic reference to intellectual illumination, we may suggest that it comes from meditation on the first creation story, where God says, "Let there be light" (Gen. 1:3). Light was characteristic of the new creation as well (cf. 2 Cor. 4:4–6).

Another passage in Hebrews clearly shows that the importance of baptism was not being minimized. Here (10:22–25) we find mention of faith, of purifying our hearts of an evil conscience and washing our body with pure water; then comes an appeal to maintain the confession of hope, to recognize one another with love, and not to give up the Christian assembly. This combination of baptismal elements suggests that in speaking of "purifying" and "washing" the author has baptism in mind. He makes more of purifying the heart than of washing the body, but this emphasis is shared by all New Testament writers.[21]

Early Christian baptism was always by immersion, at least in New Testa-

---

[19] See also Jas. 1:18.
[20] A. D. Nock, *Early Gentile Christianity and Its Hellenistic Background* (New York, 1964), 136.
[21] Cf. I Cor. 6:11, Eph. 5:26, Tit. 3:5, John 3:8.

ment times, and ordinarily this was the later practice. At first it involved the acknowledgement of Jesus as Lord, later the acknowledgment of Father, Son, and Holy Spirit.[22] Obviously some catechetical instruction was needed before the rite was administered, and such instruction probably underlies some of the epistles.[23] With the passage of time it was combined with the laying on of hands, as in Acts 8:17–18, and with the use of chrism, perhaps reflected in 1 John 2:20. These usages, derived from contemporary Judaism, did not essentially modify the meaning of the rite but emphasized its initiatory aspects.

II·EUCHARIST

Like baptism, the early Christian eucharist took shape within an eschatological context. According to the synoptic evangelists, there were three "moments" of liturgical action at the last supper of Jesus with his disciples. These were the blessing, breaking, and distribution of bread, identified with the body of Jesus; the blessing and distribution of wine, identified with the covenant-ratifying blood of Jesus; and the oath which Jesus took not to drink wine again until the coming of God's reign.[24] The eschatological emphasis is most strongly made in the Gospel of Luke, in which Jesus swears first not to eat the paschal meal until it is "fulfilled" in the kingdom of God and then, as in the other gospels, that he will not drink of "the fruit of the vine" until the kingdom of God has come.[25] In Luke, as in the *Didache*, the order bread-wine is reversed,[26] but in both traditions eschatology is highly significant. Paul's account of the last supper makes a similar point. "Whenever you eat this bread and drink the cup, you proclaim the Lord's death, until he comes" (1 Cor. 11:26).

At a very early time, however, there seem to have been eucharistic meals not so closely related to the death of Jesus. In the Gospel of John, at least in its present form, eating the flesh of Jesus and drinking his blood is connected not with the last supper but with the miraculous feeding of the five thousand in Galilee.[27] An early passage in the book of Acts refers to the Christian "breaking of bread," which in Luke 24:35 has been described as the setting for an appearance of the risen Jesus to two disciples.[28] For this reason, among others,

---

[22] 1 Cor. 12:3; Rom. 10:9; Phil. 2:11; Acts 2:38, 8:16, 10:48. On the transition cf. O. Cullmann, *The Earliest Christian Confessions* (London, 1949).

[23] Cf. P. Carrington, *The Primitive Christian Catechism* (Cambridge, 1940); E. G. Selwyn, *I Peter* (London, 1946).

[24] Mark 14:22-25; Matt. 26:26-29; cf. J. Jeremias, *The Eucharistic Words of Jesus* (transl. N. Perrin, New York, 1966).

[25] Luke 22:15-20.

[26] The textual problems of Luke 22:19-20 do not affect this point.

[27] John 6:51-58.

[28] Acts 2:42, 46.

it has been argued that the origin of the eucharist lies not in the story of the last supper but in fellowship meals of Jesus with his disciples, continued after his death.[29]

In either case the early Christian eucharist was a real meal. The gospels make it clear that the miraculous feedings took place for the benefit of men who were hungry; the setting of the last supper was an evening meal. Paul explains to the Corinthians that they are not gathering to eat "the Lord's supper" because each one takes his own supper; one goes hungry while another gets drunk (1 Cor. 11:20–21). To be sure, he says that they have houses where they can eat and drink and not put to shame those who do not have food (11:22). He seems to offer an individualistic solution to the problem. But it is practically certain that the abuse he was trying to correct grew out of the more primitive practice of sharing at meals. It is reflected in the common "breaking of bread" in the church of Jerusalem.

Whether eucharistic origins are to be found in the feeding of the five thousand or in the last supper, however, the eschatological reference remains, for the feeding is almost certainly to be viewed as an anticipation of the "messianic banquet," or even as the preparation of a revolutionary movement in the desert.[30] It may well be significant that according to John the feeding was followed by Jesus' recognition that he might be made a king.[31]

By Paul's time, though this kind of emphasis was still fairly prominent other aspects were coming to the fore. For him the eucharist was a sacrament of unity. The cup blessed by Christians was participation or sharing in the blood of Christ; the broken bread was participation in the body of Christ. "For we, though many, are one loaf, one body; for we all share in the one loaf."[32] The relationship of identity among Christians was based on their eucharistic sharing. Such an idea must have been based on the words of Jesus, quoted by Paul, to the effect that the bread was his body.[33]

In this regard it is highly significant that the *Didache,* our earliest witness to what seems to be the eucharistic liturgy of Jewish Christians, contains no reference to the death of Jesus. The prayers of the *Didache* are closely related to contemporary Jewish prayers, even though the language has been reinterpreted for Christian use.[34] Over the cup, there is a thanksgiving for the Vine of David (presumably the Messiah and his congregation), known through Jesus. Similarly over the bread, there is a thanksgiving for the life

---

[29] H. Lietzmann, *Messe und Herrenmahl* (Bonn, 1926); in English, *Mass and Lord's Supper* (Leiden, 1953 ff.).
[30] Cf. H. W. Montefiore in *New Testament Studies* 8 (1961-62), 135-41.
[31] John 6:15; cf. Brandon, *Jesus and the Zealots* (New York, 1967), 353.
[32] 1 Cor. 10:16-17 (note the sequence cup-bread).
[33] 1 Cor. 11:24.
[34] Cf. M. Dibelius in *ZNW* 37 (1938), 32-41; E. Peterson in *Ephemerides Liturgicae* 58 (1944), 3-13. On benedictions like those in the *Didache* cf. E. Bickermann in *Revue biblique* 69 (1962), 524-32.

and knowledge made known through Jesus, and a petition for the gathering together of the church into God's kingdom. At the end there is a thanksgiving for the gift of God's Name and for the knowledge, faith, and immortality made known through Jesus. A specifically eucharistic thanksgiving is concerned with the universal gifts of creation, food, and drink and with the gifts of spiritual food and drink, and eternal life, to Christians through Jesus. A prayer of petition asks for the deliverance and perfection of the church and for its gathering together into God's kingdom. Finally there are some very brief formulas, perhaps to be recited antiphonally. "Let grace come and let this world pass away. Hosanna to the God of David. If anyone is holy, let him come; if he is not, let him repent. *Marana tha* [our Lord, come]. Amen."

Each of the main sections of the prayers is followed by a brief doxology not unlike the one with which the Didachist ends the Lord's Prayer (*Did.* 8). It is clear that the communities in and for which he wrote were accustomed to the use of carefully constructed, even "stylized" prayers, although he does state that prophets may say eucharistic prayers as they wish. There was a tradition of prayer in relation to which individual freedom was exercised.[35]

It should be added that for the Didachist the eucharist is definitely a sacrifice, to be offered in accordance with the prophecy of Malachi 1:11 ("in every time and place offer me a pure sacrifice"). It is presumably to be offered by the bishops and deacons who "minister the ministry of the prophets and teachers" (15, 1).

Around the time of the *Didache* was also find allusions to eucharistic worship in the Roman letter known as 1 Clement. There it is stated that the bishops, equivalent to presbyters, "offer the gifts" (44, 4)—gifts analogous to the sacrifices of the Jerusalem temple (41, 2). It is likely that a prayer at the end of 1 Clement, with its mention of God's "beloved servant Jesus Christ, through whom he called us . . . to knowledge of the glory of his name" (59, 2), is related to eucharistic worship. As a leader of the Roman community Clement undoubtedly offered the eucharistic prayer and probably echoed it in his letter. From what he says we should infer that for him as for the Didachist the eucharist was a sacrifice of praise and thanksgiving offered to God for his gifts through Jesus.

There is a considerable difference, however, between the prayers of the *Didache* and those of 1 Clement. According to the *Didache*, Christians give thanks for God's gifts primarily to themselves and pray for the deliverance, perfection, and gathering of the church into God's kingdom. "Let grace come and let this world pass away." The end is near. Clement prays for the church as set within "the eternal framework of the world." He prays for universal concord and peace and for "health, peace, concord, and security" for the rulers

---

[35] For the whole problem of the eucharistic prayers in the *Didache* and their possible relation to the *agape* see J.-P. Audet, *La Didachè: instructions des apôtres* (Paris, 1958), 372-433, especially 406 f.

to whom God has given authority. Though he does not deny that God's kingdom will soon come, all his emphasis is placed upon the peace and harmony of God's world. He is no apocalyptic eschatologist but a Roman Christian deeply influenced by Hellenistic Judaism.

III·SACRAMENTS IN THE EARLY SECOND CENTURY

In the writings which reflect Jewish Christianity, more or less Hellenized, at the beginning of the second century there are few references to eucharist, many to baptism. 1 Clement implies the existence of baptism; in the letter there is a quotation from Isaiah 1:16–20 which begins with the words, "Wash yourselves and become pure," and there is a reference to God's call of Christains from darkness to light, from ignorance to knowledge.[36] Although the two passages are obviously unrelated, Clement must have baptism in mind. In the Epistle of Barnabas baptism possesses cardinal importance. As christains from darkness to light, from ignorance to knowledge.[36] Although the they set their hope on the Name, are created anew, and by placing their hope in Jesus, in the Spirit, they bear fruit in their hearts. The rite is comparable to circumcision, but unlike circumcision it is unique; furthermore, circumcision has now been abolished. Baptism is the "seal" of the new convenant, and it relates the newborn Christian to the eschatological hope of the community. All the explicitly baptismal passages in Barnabas make this clear.[37]

The *Shepherd* of Hermas reflects the same picture. At baptism "we went down into water and received remission of our previous sins." "Before a man bears the Name of the Son of God, he is dead; but when he receives the seal he puts off mortality and receives life. The seal, then, is the water; they go down to the water dead and come up alive."[38]

Hermas had had to face the problem posed by the doctrine of Hebrews 6:4–6 (known at Rome in the time of 1 Clement) that, as he expresses it, "there is no second repentance beyond the one when we went down into the water and received remission of our previous sins."[39] This problem already occurs in the *Visions* (2, 2, 4–5): a day has been set after which Christians can no longer repent; and in *Mandate* 4, 3, 6 one occasion of repentance is mentioned.

It would appear that Christians, especially in circles close to Judaism, confronted something of a crisis over postbaptismal sins and repentance toward

[36] 1 Clem. 8; 59:2.
[37] Barn. 11:11, 16:8; 4:8. Cf. A. Benoit, *Le baptême chrétien au second siècle* (Paris, 1953), 34-58.
[38] *Mand.* 4, 3, 1; *Sim.* 9, 16, 3-4.
[39] *Mand.* 4, 3, 1.

the beginning of the second century. An oriental prophet named Elchasai, who saw signs of the end in Trajan's Dacian victories, announced that angels would participate in the wars after three years of Trajan's reign. Under the inspiration of two chief angels—one, male, called the Son of God; the other, female, the Holy Spirit—Elchasai announced "a new remission of sins in the third year of Trajan's reign" and with it a new baptism. Men who desired to obtain this remission were to be baptized again, "in the name of the great and most high God and in the name of his Son, the great king."[40]

The eschatological meaning of Elchasai's mission is obvious not only from his teaching but also from an Aramaic formula he used: "I bear witness for you on the day of the great judgment." We thus see that the problem with which he was concerned was much the same as that faced by Hermas. He solved it by a second baptism; Hermas simply spoke of a day of repentance for the baptized. At a later date, with less eschatological emphasis, a different solution would be proposed: distinctions among sins and the concomitant penitential system.

Not all Christians were so much concerned with the problem. In 2 Clement, though there is a vigorous emphasis on the coming of the day of judgment, repentance is actually characteristic of the Christian's whole life and is to be expressed in good works.[41] Entrance into God's kingdom depends on "keeping our baptism pure and undefiled" (6:9), on "keeping the seal" (7:6). The seal is kept undefiled by observing the Lord's commandments and thus obtaining eternal life (8:4–6).[42] Baptism is thus the seal of God's action, confirming Christians for the last judgment. Clement's emphasis on the need for continuing repentance shows that it did not work automatically.

It has sometimes been thought that the idea of the seal came from Gnosticism or from the mystery religions. Certainly Mithraists were branded on their foreheads or tattooed on the hands.[43] The fact seems less relevant than the analogy Christians drew with circumcision or Paul's mention of "sealing" in relation to the gift of the Spirit.[44] The "seal" probably originated in Jewish Christianity.

Ignatius of Antioch shows how baptism was viewed in the more gentile communities. He probably has the seal in mind when he speaks of the "stamp" of God impressed on believers so that they may bear it in love through Jesus Christ.[45] In general his ideas are more like Paul's than those we have just encountered. Baptism is the rite of entrance into the military

---

[40] Hippolytus, *Ref.* 9, 16, 4; 9, 13, 4; 9, 15, 1.

[41] 2 Clem. 8:1-3, 9:8, 13:1, 16:1.

[42] Cf. Hermas, *Sim.* 5, 6-7.

[43] Tertullian, *De praescr. haer.* 40, 4; cf. M. J. Vermaseren, *Mithras the Secret God* (New York, 1963), 131; F. Cumont in *HTR* 26 (1933), 151-60.

[44] A. Benoit, *op. cit.*, 151-60.

[45] *Magn.* 5, 2.

service of God: with faith, love, and endurance it constitutes the armament of the Christian.[46] It also continues the work of Jesus, who was "baptized by John so that all righteousness might be fulfilled by him"[47] and also "so that by the Passion he might purify the water."[48] The latter explanation of Jesus' baptism must mean that, as for Paul, baptism is analogous to the death of Jesus. Paul is the one with whom Ephesian Christians are "fellow-initiates."[49]

The baptismal rite obviously involved the use of water,[50] possibly also the use of chrism: "the Lord received ointment on his head so that he might breathe imperishability upon the church."[51] Ignatius mentions the ointment before he speaks of baptism, and he may be reflecting the chrism-baptism sequence found in later Syrian writers.[52] Baptism, in his view, could not be administered apart from the bishop of a local community.[53]

The eucharist was practically even more important than baptism, for it was constantly repeated and ensured the continuing unity of the church. It was a common meal in which bread was broken and a cup of wine was drunk.[54] But it was much more than a common meal, for the bread was "the bread of God, which is the flesh of Jesus Christ," and the cup was "for union with his blood."[55] Ignatius' ideas are clearly Johannine, as is his description of the bread as "the drug of immortality, the antidote so that we should not die but live forever in Jesus Christ."[56] It is sometimes claimed that the notion of a "drug of immortality" comes from the mystery religions,[57] but there is no evidence to show that such religions used the expression, and he himself employed a similar metaphor elsewhere.[58] The eucharistic action was the action of the whole community in unity. Ignatius urged Christians to "come together in grace" and to break one bread.[59] There could be only one eucharist, just as there was one flesh, one cup, one sanctuary, and one bishop in a community.[60] Ignatius' opponents abstained from the eucharist and from common prayer simply because they did not recognize the eucharist as the flesh of Jesus.[61] Only within the one sanctuary was the bread of God to be

[46] Polyc. 6, 2.
[47] Smyrn. I, I (Matt. 3:15).
[48] Eph. 18, 2.
[49] Eph. 12, 2.
[50] Eph. 18, 2.
[51] Eph. 17, I.
[52] Cf. T. W. Manson in JTS 48 (1947), 59-61.
[53] Smyrn. 8, 2.
[54] Eph. 20, 2; Philad. 4.
[55] Rom. 7, 3; Philad. 4.
[56] Eph. 20, 2.
[57] E.g., R. Reitzenstein, Die hellenistischen Mysterienreligionen (ed. 3, Leipzig, 1927), 83 and 399-400.
[58] Trall. 6, 2; II, I; cf. Seneca, Dial. I, 3, 12.
[59] Eph. 20, 2.
[60] Philad. 4.
[61] Smyrn. 7, I.

found, for the prayer of the bishop and the whole church brought God's response to it—the presence of Jesus among them.[62] For this reason the only "valid" eucharist was the one celebrated by the bishop or by someone whom he appointed.[63]

It is hard to tell whether or not Ignatius had noneucharistic assemblies in mind. In writing to the Magnesians he did not mention the eucharist but spoke of a meeting involving "one prayer, one supplication."[64] To the Smyrnaeans he mentioned the eucharist and then said that one must not baptize or "hold an *agapē* apart from the bishop.[65] Were *agapē* and eucharist the same?

The problem of the *agapē* meal, to which we earlier alluded, is given some illumination by what Pliny reported concerning his investigation of Christians in Bithynia and Pontus. Unfortunately we do not know just how representative these Christians were. They told him that they met "on a fixed day" (presumably Sunday) before dawn in order to sing hymns and apparently to receive catechetical instruction. "After this they were accustomed to depart and then meet again for a meal." Was the first meeting rather like a synagogue service? Was the meal a eucharist, or an *agapē,* or both? It has been argued that it must have been an *agapē* because the Christians said they had stopped convening for it after Pliny forbade the existence of sodalities.[66] They must, it is supposed, have continued to meet for the eucharist. But it should be observed that those who gave the testimony were not practicing Christians; they themselves claimed to be ex-Christians, and we do not know what others were doing. Less is known about the *agapē* than we should like to know.

IV-SACRAMENTS IN THE LATER SECOND CENTURY

The evidence from the early second century has to do chiefly with the meaning of baptism and eucharist; the actual rites, except in the *Didache,* are taken for granted. It is from the period after 150 that we have evidence to give a somewhat clearer picture of what actually went on in the Christian assemblies, in relation both to what was said and to what was done. We begin with Polycarp of Smyrna, proceed to Justin of Rome and Theophilus of Antioch, and go through anti-Christian authors to later Christian writers.

Statements about Polycarp, made by Irenaeus,[67] show us that in the middle

[62] *Eph.* 5, 2; cf. Matt. 18:19-20.
[63] *Smyrn.* 8, 1.
[64] *Magn.* 7, 1.
[65] *Smyrn.* 8, 1-2.
[66] Pliny, *Ep.* 10, 96, 6-7; cf. E. G. Hardy, *C. Plinii Caecilii Secundi Epistulae ad Traianum Imperatorem cum eiusdem Responsis* (London, 1889). 214.
[67] Eusebius, *H. E.* 5, 24.

of the second century eucharistic worship occupied a central position, though considerable variety of usage existed even in a single community. Irenaeus pointed out that earlier bishops of Rome could and did send the eucharistic elements to those Roman Christians who celebrated Easter on a day different from the one observed by the majority. Indeed, when Polycarp visited Anicetus the Roman bishop invited him to celebrate the eucharist.

In addition, resemblances to other eucharistic prayers, such as those in the *Didache,* suggest that we can find echoes of such prayers in the prayer Polycarp uttered before his martyrdom.[68]

Lord God Almighty, Father of the beloved and blessed *pais* Jesus Christ, through whom we received knowledge concerning thee: God of angels and powers and the whole creation, and of the people of the righteous who live in thy presence: we praise thee, bless thee, glorify thee for all things, through the eternal and heavenly High Priest, thy beloved *pais,* through whom to thee, with him and the Holy Spirit, be glory both now and for the ages to come. Amen.

The word *pais,* which means "servant" or "child" or even "son," occurs in the prayers of the *Didache,* where was also find explicit ascription of glory to God through Jesus Christ, thanksgiving for revelation and creation, and intercession for the church. To be sure, nothing is said in the *Didache* about Christ as high priest; but this theme, already present in I Clement, is a feature of Polycarp's own thought as reflected in his letter to the Philippians, and undoubtedly expresses what he taught and prayed at Smyrna.[69]

The writings of the apologist Justin, produced at Rome around the same time, show that the same themes were expressed in eucharists there. On various occasions, undoubtedly including eucharistic worship, Christians offer prayers and hymns of thanksgiving "for our creation and all the means of health, the various kinds of creatures and the changes of the seasons"; they make petitions "for our living again in imperishability on account of our faith in him" (God).[70] The eucharistic prayer, accompanying the offering of the bread as a memorial of Christ's suffering,[71] is directed to God "not only for his having created the world and everything in it for the sake of mankind but also for his having freed us from the wickedness in which we were born and for having destroyed the principalities and powers through him who became passible in accordance with his will."[72] The eucharistic thanksgiving therefore begins with God's work in creation and providential care and goes on to his gift of redemption through Christ's sacrifice.

[68] *Mart. Polyc.* 14.
[69] Articles by various authors in *JTS,* vols. 21, 23, and 24, make this point.
[70] *Apol.* I, 13, 2.
[71] Cf. Lucian, *De Syria dea* 6: feasts in memory of Adonis' passion (C. K. Barrett, *The First Epistle to the Corinthians,* New York, 1968, 267).
[72] *Dial.* 41, 1.

The first aspect of the thanksgiving, much more fully developed in later liturgies such as the one found in the fourth-century *Apostolic Constitutions*,[73] also seems to underlie the description of the wonders of creation given by Theophilus, bishop of Antioch a generation after Justin.[74] As Bousset and Goodenough pointed out, such eucharistic prayers are thoroughly Jewish in origin and intent.[75] What has been added by Christians is thanksgiving for redemption; but this too is probably Jewish in origin, being based on thanksgivings for God's work of redemption in delivering Israel from Egypt and bringing her into the promised land under Joshua (in Greek, Jesus).

The eucharist, in Justin's time as earlier, is only for those who have been baptized. He explains that before baptism there is catechetical instruction, followed by prayer and fasting. Then comes the baptism itself, in water and in the name of "the Father . . . and our Savior Jesus Christ and the Holy Spirit." This, he says, is "the way in which, made new through Christ, we offer ourselves to God." He adds that it is called "illumination" because "those who learn these things are illuminated in their understanding."[76] We may suspect that this is in part an intellectualizing explanation of an older term, in view of Justin's apologetic purpose.

After the baptism came a service of worship which can be called "antecommunion." The baptized person was now brought into the common assembly for common prayers on behalf of the universal church "that we may be judged worthy, through our works, to be proved good citizens [of the Christian society] and guardians of the commandments, and be saved with eternal salvation." These prayers ended with the "holy kiss" or "kiss of peace" mentioned in the New Testament.[77]

Justin describes both the baptismal eucharist and the ordinary Sunday eucharist, but they were evidently much the same. On Sundays what preceded the eucharistic rite proper was a reading from the gospels or the prophetic books (of the Old Testament), then a moral homily on the text, delivered by the "president," presumably the bishop. After the homily ended the congregation arose and offered prayers in common. At this point, as after baptismal common prayers, the eucharist proper began.

Bread and a cup of wine mixed with water were brought to the presiding officer, who took them and began the eucharistic prayer—perhaps with a formula recently isolated in Justin's *Dialogue*.[78]

[73] *Const. Apost.* 7, 34-35.
[74] *Ad Autol.* 1, 6-7; cf. my note in *ATR* 30 (1948), 91-94.
[75] W. Bousset in *Nachrichten . . . Göttingen, phil.-hist. Klasse*, 1915, 435-85; E. R. Goodenough, *By Light Light* (New Haven, 1935), 306-58.
[76] *Apol.* 1, 61, 1 and 10-12.
[77] 1 Thess. 5:26; 1 Cor. 16:20; 2 Cor. 13:12; Rom. 16:16; 1 Pet. 5:14. Cf. K. Hofmann, *Philema Hagion* (Gütersloh, 1938).
[78] *Dial.* 29, 1; cf. D. Gill in *HTR* 59 (1966), 98-100.

Let us glorify God with the gentiles who have assembled,
  for he has been our overseer;
let us glorify him
    through the King of Glory,
    through the Lord of the Powers [Ps. 23:10 LXX],
  for he has shown favor to the gentiles
  and gladly receives [our] sacrifices.

Praise and glory were directed to "the Father of all" through the name of the Son and the Holy Spirit; then came "an extended thanksgiving"[79] for God's gifts and for Christian's having been judged worthy to receive them. Thanksgiving must have led into *anamnesis*, for the eucharistic food was consecrated "through the word of prayer which comes from him" (Jesus)—the words of institution at the last supper. The people then signified their assent to the prayers by uttering the Hebrew word "Amen" (= "so be it").

The consecrated elements, no longer "ordinary food or ordinary drink" but the flesh and blood of Jesus, were then distributed to those present by the deacons, who also took them to those who were absent. Finally, there was an offering, deposited with the presiding officer, for the benefit of orphans, widows, the sick, prisoners, and itinerant Christians.[80]

The eucharistic prayers of Polycarp and Justin, as well as the one perhaps echoed by Theophilus, clearly show that Christian intentions had changed since the time of the Didache. The thanksgiving is primarily for God's work in creation, only secondarily for redemption. The lack of emphasis on redemption may be due to gaps in our information. If so, it remains striking that redemption too is largely a matter of a past event. When Justin quotes the words of Jesus at the last supper he presents them thus: "Do this in remembrance of me; this is my body; this is my blood."[81] The eschatological note expressed in Jesus' oaths has completely vanished. It is therefore not surprising that Justin was disturbed by the similarity between the eucharist and the mysteries of Mithras, in which bread and a cup of water were set before initiates with the use of "certain formulas."[82] Presumably he would have found even more difficult the likelihood that both in Christianity and in Mithraism the meals were now regarded as preparatory for the eternal life of the participants.[83]

Under these circumstances we find for the first time something of an explanation as to how the bread and the wine become the body and blood of Jesus, Justin employs a rather complicated analogical method for this pur-

---

[79] The evidence already cited shows how extensive the thanksgiving was; cf. also the lengthy invocation mentioned in regard to Marcosians by Irenaeus, *Adv. haer.* I, 13, 2.
[80] For these eucharists cf. Justin, *Apol.* I, 65-67.
[81] *Apol.* I, 66, 3.
[82] *Ibid.*, I, 66, 4. Justin was the only early Greek apologist to mention Mithras (cf. *Dial.* 70, 1; 78, 6), presumably because the religion was flourishing at Rome in his time (cf. M. J. Vermaseren, *De Mithrasdienst in Rome*, Nijmegen, 1951).
[83] Cf. M. J. Vermaseren, *Mithras the Secret God* (New York, 1963), 98-103.

pose. The transformation resembles first the process by which "through the Logos of God" Jesus himself assumed flesh and blood in the incarnation and, second, the process of digestion by which human blood and flesh are nourished.[84] However Justin may have intended his explanation to be understood, it is significant that he thought it ought to be provided.

The picture of a baptismal eucharist provided by Justin is indirectly confirmed by some of the slanders against Christians current in the second century. Minucius Felix, following a pagan source perhaps to be identified with the rhetorician Fronto, says that

an infant, concealed in bread to deceive the unwary, is placed before the one who performs the rites. That infant disguised by the bread is killed, with hidden and unseen wounds, by the novice summoned to strike seemingly harmless blows. Horrible to relate, they thirstily lick up his blood; they eagerly distribute portions of him.[85]

Obviously this is a garbled description of the eucharist. The infant is Jesus, called *pais* in eucharistic prayers; he is "concealed" in the eucharistic bread. He is not killed by the novice, for he has already died and risen, but the Christians do drink his blood and distribute portions of his body.

From Irenaeus, toward the end of the second century, we learn that though the bread and wine come to be "heavenly" when sanctified by invoking God, they remain earthly also, just as the bodies of Christians by receiving the eucharist are no longer perishable because they have obtained the hope of resurrection.[86] Irenaeus' language recalls what Ignatius had said about the "drug of immortality," though it is more carefully qualified. In passing he says that the eucharistic doxology included the words "to the ages of the ages" and that the Valentinians read their "aeons" into this expression;[87] it is actually characteristic of Jewish prayers. (Tertullian quotes a slightly different formula, "to the ages from the age";[88] this too is Jewish in origin.)

At Carthage a few years later Tertullian listed the additions made to the baptismal rite since apostolic times. These included a renunciation of the devil, a triple immersion with responses "somewhat more extensive than what the Lord decreed in the gospel," the reception of the baptized person by his sponsors, the tasting of milk and honey (symbols of entrance into the land of promise), and abstinence from bathing during the week after baptism.[89] It is obvious that most of these additions are based on the practice of adult baptism, and in his treatise *De baptismo,* written about 200, he denounced the baptism of infants as a recent innovation.

---

[84] *Apol.* 1, 66, 2; cf. F. H. Colson in *JTS* 23 (1921-22), 166-68.
[85] *Oct.* 9, 5.
[86] *Adv. haer.* 4, 18, 5.
[87] *Ibid.,* 1, 3, 1.
[88] *De spectac.* 25, 5. Compare the formulas in the Mishnah, *Berakoth* 9, 5.
[89] *De cor.* 3, 2-3.

According to Tertullian, the eucharistic feast was held only before dawn and the elements were to be received only from the hands of the presiding officers.[90] He does not fully describe it in his writings, but what he tells of a service of prayer closely resembles the eucharist as depicted by Justin.[91] This service began with prayers for the world and its administrators and for the delay of the end; then came readings from the scriptures and exhortations by "approved presbyters," men who also administered the charitable funds of the church on behalf of the poor, orphans, and others.

He also described the mysterious *dilectio* or *agapē,* a kind of church supper. This kind of meal may have been known to Ignatius, and certainly it flourished at the end of the second century and the beginning of the third. It was preceded by prayer and followed by the washing of hands and the introduction of bright lights. Afterward each worshiper sang praise to God either from the scriptures or of his own composition.[92] Clement of Alexandria scorned it as "a little supper smelling of fat and gravy."[93] When Tertullian became a Montanist he claimed that it led to sexual license.[94] It held its own during the third century, however; Hippolytus describes it;[95] and it was outlawed only later. Conceivably it was a survival from the earliest days of Christianity, when the eucharist was a real meal at which food was shared with the poor.[96]

By the end of the second century and the beginning of the third, the nature of the eucharist had been somewhat modified. We recall that Paul had laid emphasis on the eucharistic proclamation of the Lord's death "until he comes," while in the *Didache* there were prayers for the coming of grace, for the passing away of this world, and for the return of the Lord. The Gnostic liturgy of the Marcosians illustrates a change in the direction of "realized eschatology." The Marcosians prayed for the coming of grace in their eucharists and found it fully present when women prophesied at worship.[97] This is to say that the eucharist was not so much an anticipation of the kingdom as an actualization of it. So too among more orthodox Christians the eschatological note was muted. At baptism one tasted milk and honey as symbols of an entrance into the land of promise already made. The prayers mentioned by Tertullian contain intercessions for the existing world and petitions not for the end but for its delay. In explaining the petition "Thy kingdom come" in the Lord's Prayer both Tertullian and Origen modified its meaning. Tertullian insisted both on the future coming of the kingdom and on its realization within and among

---

[90] *Ibid.,* 3, 3.
[91] *Apol.* 39, 2-6.
[92] *Ibid.,* 39, 14-19.
[93] *Paed.* 2, 4, 3.
[94] *De ieiun.* 17, 3.
[95] *Apost. trad.* 26.
[96] Cf. J. Leipoldt in *RGG*[3] I 169-70.
[97] Irenaeus, *Adv. haer.* I, 13, 2-3.

Christians.[98] Origen went further and said that the kingdom was within the Christian, who prayed for it to rise up and bear fruit and be perfected. Following Stoic sources, he defined the kingdom of God as "the happy state of the mind and the ordered condition of wise reasonings"[99]—a notion which recalls that held by Paul's opponents at Corinth.

Indeed, at Alexandria both baptism and eucharist underwent remarkable changes—if we can rely on the authenticity of a fragment from Clement discovered by Morton Smith. This fragment, from a highly esoteric letter, refers to some Alexandrian Christians as having been initiated into "the greater mysteries" and having passed through seven veils.[100] If the fragment is trustworthy, it is evident that Alexandrian Christianity had borrowed extensively not only from literature about the mysteries but from actual cultic practices. Presumably both Clement and Origen reacted against this tendency when they wrote on the eucharist and treated it as both spiritual and ethical in significance. In neither case, however, was there any attempt to restore its eschatological meaning.

V·THIRD·CENTURY DEVELOPMENTS

From the early third century we possess a liturgical manual in the *Apostolic Tradition* composed by Hippolytus of Rome for the guidance of his bishop. It begins with the bishop's consecration and the eucharist and continues with discussions of other forms of ministry: presbyters, deacons, confessors, widows, readers, virgins, subdeacons, and healers. The second half of the document deals with the reception and baptism of catechumens, the *agapē* and the widows' meal, and miscellaneous notes on worship. Not everything Hippolytus says is descriptive of Roman tradition; the appeal to apostolic precedent usually implies reform of some sort. What he says of baptism and eucharist, however, may be regarded as generally reliable.

In his view baptism is to be preceded and followed by anointing; it consists of a triple immersion with a threefold confession of faith. The eucharist begins with the offering of bread and wine and a series of versicles and responses. Then comes the prayer of thanksgiving for the action of the Word of God in creation, incarnation, passion, and at the last supper.[101] Along with the thanksgiving there is an *epiclesis* or invocation of the Holy Spirit, perhaps replacing an earlier invocation of the Word.[102] Hippolytus defends the bishop

[98] Tertullian, *De orat.* 5.
[99] Origen, *De orat.* 25, 1.
[100] Preliminary notice in *The New York Times*, Dec. 30, 1960.
[101] Cf. G. Dix, *The Shape of the Liturgy* (London, 1945), 48.
[102] Cf. L. Bouyer, *Eucharist* (Notre Dame, 1968), 168-84.

who uses a fixed form of the thanksgiving, and evidently, as R. P. C. Hanson has shown, extemporaneous prayer (along with a relatively fixed outline) had been customary.[103]

From Alexandrian Christian writers we learn little about the sacraments. Clement barely mentions them, though he did write an address to the newly baptized and in his *Protrepticus* compared Christian initiation with the Eleusinian mysteries.[104] Origen reveals that the eucharistic prayer followed a sermon, for at the end of his 39th homily on Luke he said, "Therefore let us arise and pray to God that we may be worthy to offer him the gifts, so that he may restore them to us and may bestow heavenly gifts for earthly ones, in Christ Jesus." He paraphrased the prayer in his apologetic treatise *Contra Celsum*.[105]

We give thanks to the Creator of all and eat the loaves set forth with thanksgiving and prayer over what has been given, loaves which because of the prayer have become a holy body and make holy those who use it with a sound offering. . . . We give him back the first-fruits; we send up the prayers to him, and we have a great high priest who has passed through the heavens, Jesus the Son of God (Heb. 4:14).

Origen also insists upon the moral consequences of the eucharist. The food which is "consecrated through the word of God and supplication" (1 Tim. 4:5) does not automatically consecrate the recipient. As such, the consecrated food is merely material, goes into the belly and is cast away in the drain (Matt. 15:17). The prayer is what counts, making it helpful to vision with the mind and to moral conduct.[106]

We thus see that for Origen, and to some extent for Clement, the spiritual meaning of the eucharist is what matters, not the rite as such. This is not to say that either of them neglected the rite. It is only to say that in accordance with their Platonizing theological outlook they looked for reality behind and beyond the sacraments, not in the water or the bread and wine.

We have already mentioned the most important liturgical innovation of this period: the novel practice of infant baptism. This custom, explicitly recommended by Hippolytus and in Origen's later writings called "apostolic," cannot be found in Christian literature before Tertullian, though it may have arisen in some localities toward the end of the second century. It reflects the extent to which the church was beginning to consist of families hereditarily Christian, and it was accompanied by a new emphasis on the doctrine of original sin.[107]

103 *VC* 15 (1961), 173-76.
104 *Protr.* 120, I.
105 *Contra Celsum* 8, 33-34.
106 *Matt. comm.* 11, 14.
107 Cf. J. Jeremias, *Die Kindertaufe in der ersten vier Jahrhunderten* (Göttingen, 1958); K. Aland, *Did the Early Church Baptize Infants?* (Philadelphia, 1963).

In the mid-third century one very significant development is to be noted in regard to the eucharist. Early Christians had often spoken of it as a sacrifice, but without exception they had identified the sacrifice with the offering of bread, wine, and prayers to God. Both Justin and Hippolytus lay emphasis on the memorial of the Passion, but they do not treat the eucharist as the representation of Christ's sacrifice. A letter of Cyprian written in 253, however, supports the use of wine in the eucharist by the argument that the priest is imitating what Christ did in offering himself as a sacrifice; indeed, "the passion of the Lord is the sacrifice which we offer."[108] It might seem natural that since, at least from Paul's time, the bread and the wine had been practically identified with the body and blood of Christ (1 Cor. 10:16–17), the sacrifice would also have been identified with Christ's sacrifice. But there is no evidence to show that such a step had been taken, and though the idea may have existed before Cyprian's time it surely owed something to his emphasis on the related sacrifices of the martyrs. Indeed, in a letter from African bishops to Cornelius of Rome written in 252 Cyprian had stated that "we priests who daily celebrate the sacrifices of God prepare sacrifices and victims for God"— the martyrs.[109]

Along with this concern for martyrdom and sacrifice went an emphasis on the solidarity of the living with the dead. Such an emphasis is already reflected in Paul's discussions of the resurrection of the dead with the living,[110] and in the practice at least at Corinth of baptism on behalf of the dead.[111] Late in the second century Polycarp's bones were carefully preserved at Smyrna and the "birthday of his martyrdom" was celebrated there.[112] Such customs seem to have arisen out of Jewish precedents; Judas Maccabaeus offered prayers and sacrifices for the dead.[113] The epitaph of the Phrygian bishop Abercius contains a request for the prayers of Christians.

By the early third century eucharistic offerings were made for the dead, both for martyrs and for other Christians,[114] and it was customary to pray for the repose of their souls, for their "refreshment" (refrigerium), and for their sharing in "the first resurrection." Such eucharists were conducted in cemeteries on the anniversaries of deaths.[115]

A problem in relation to all such rites was soon drawn to the attention of Christian apostles and apologists. This was the question of the relation of Christian rites to those found in other religions. The apostle Paul had already found it necessary to tell the Corinthians that they could not "drink the cup

[108] Ep. 63, 14 and 17.
[109] Ep. 57, 3.
[110] 1 Thess. 4:13-18; 1 Cor. 15:51.
[111] 1 Cor. 15:29; M. Rissi, Die Taufe für den Toten (Zurich-Stuttgart, 1962).
[112] Mart. Polyc. 18, 2-3.
[113] 2 Macc. 12:39-45.
[114] Didasc. apost. 6, 22; Tertullian, De corona 3, 3.
[115] Tertullian, De monog. 10, 4; Exh. cast. 11, 1; cf. J. H. Srawley, The Early History of the Liturgy (ed. 2, Cambridge, 1947), 124.

of the Lord and the cup of demons" or "share in the table of the Lord and the table of demons" (1 Cor. 10:21). Justin explained that the use of bread and a cup of water in the mysteries of Mithras was due to demonic imitation of the eucharistic words of Jesus.[116] Tertullian mentioned the same point and also referred to the Mithraic use of something like the sign of the cross.[117] In his treatise *On baptism* he attacked the notion that the water itself was efficacious by pointing to the initiatory washings in the cults of Isis and Mithras and to the washings for "regeneration" and the forgiveness of perjury in other rites.[118]

This problem became acute as the early Jewish and eschatological emphasis waned, and the meaning of Christian rites was sometimes hard to differentiate from others. It was resolved, however, as the church became stronger and Christians could simply dismiss the resemblances. The final solution was provided by the proscription of paganism.

VI·PRIVATE ACTS OF WORSHIP

In the early church there were private acts of worship and devotion in addition to the sacraments and other community rites. Such acts are already encouraged in the *Didache*: the Lord's Prayer is to be said three times a day, while fasting is to be practised on Wednesdays and Fridays.[119] The injunction about prayer is repeated by later writers,[120] and Hippolytus provides reasons for praying six times a day. He refers prayers at the third, sixth, and ninth hours to episodes in Christ's crucifixion. Prayer at midnight is related to the cosmic worship which occurs then, as well as to the possible coming of the Lord. Prayer at cockcrow means "awaiting in hope the dawn of the eternal light at the resurrection of the dead." The themes are thus both historical and eschatological. Only a prayer at bedtime is given no explanation.[121] As for fasting, both Clement and Tertullian insist upon Wednesdays and Fridays.[122] Hermas does not mention a particular day but says that the money saved by fasting should be given to the poor.[123] It was among the Montanists that fasting was especially encouraged. Catholics severely criticized them for their extra fasts, for the prolongation of fasting in general, and for their biennial "xerophagies." They compared the Montanists with worshipers of Apis, Isis, and

---

[116] *Apol.* 1, 66, 4.
[117] *De praescr. haer.* 40, 4.
[118] *De bapt.* 5, 1; on the text cf A. D. Nock in *JTS* 28 (1926-27), 289-90.
[119] *Did.* 8, 1-3.
[120] Clement, *Str.* 7, 40, 3-4; Tertullian, *De orat.* 25, 1; *De ieiun.* 10, 3.
[121] Hippolytus, *Apost. Trad.* 36.
[122] Clement, *Str.* 7, 75, 2; Tertullian, *De ieiun.* 14, 2.
[123] *Sim.* 5, 3, 7.

the Great Mother, and claimed that fasting should be conducted voluntarily, not by command. Tertullian replied by insisting that the Montanist regulations were biblical and beneficial. The Catholics were less religious than pagans were.[124] The result of this controversy was inconclusive, for after Tertullian's time fasting became more prevalent in the church as a whole—not only in relation to Easter and baptism but at other times as well.

VII·THE SACRAL ASPECTS OF TIME

Brought up within Judaism, the earliest Christians were well aware of the existence of the Jewish calendar, although Jesus insisted that the Sabbath, for example, was made for man, not man for the Sabbath (Mark 2:27 and parallels; cf. 3:4). Though he himself related the last supper to the Passover, it is not clear that his disciples continued to observe the Jewish calendar. Paul speaks explicitly of Christ himself as "our Passover" (1 Cor. 5:7), and though he mentions Pentecost (16:7) he seems to refer to it only as a well known date.[125] The Galatian Christians must not observe "days and moons and seasons and years" (Gal. 4:10); the Colossians must not relate themselves to "a festival or a new moon or sabbaths" (Col. 3:16). Similarly in the Gospel of John the Jewish festivals are usually described as belonging to the Jews—alone.

Fairly early, it would appear, Christians observed a day different from the Sabbath, the first day of the week. We cannot be sure that Paul speaks of Sunday worship when he asks Corinthian Christians to set aside gifts on the first day (1 Cor. 16:2), but John's statement that he was in the Spirit on the Lord's Day (Rev. 1:10) clearly shows that at least by the end of the first century that day had a special Christian significance. One would naturally assume that the significance was derived from the tradition that the resurrection had taken place on Sunday. According to the *Didache* (14, 1) the eucharist is observed "each Lord's Day of the Lord." Ignatius (*Magn.* 9, 1) describes Christians as "no longer observing the Sabbath but living in accordance with the Lord's Day, on which our life sprang up through him and his death." And Barnabas (15, 8–9) contrasts the Sabbath with the eighth day, celebrated by Christians as marking the beginning of another world because on it Jesus arose and ascended into heaven. Justin lays similar emphasis on Sunday worship.[126]

The Constantinian veto of litigation and lawsuits on Sunday (*dies solis*), enacted in 321,[127] seems to reflect a fusion of Christian and pagan concerns.

[124] *De ieiun.* 2, 4; 16, 7-8.
[125] According to Acts 20:16, however, he wants to observe Pentecost at Jerusalem.
[126] *Did.* 14, 1; Ignatius, *Magn.* 9, 1; Barn. 15, 8-9; Justin, *Apol.* 1, 67, 3, 7.
[127] *Cod. Theod.* 2, 8, 1.

No doubt he had the Christian festival in mind,[128] but at least since Justin's time the day was known as "the day of the sun" among Christians.[129] (Ignatius may have been referring to the rising of the sun as well as to the resurrection of Christ.)

Generally speaking, Christians tended to pay attention to traditional pagan festivals as well as to their own holy day or days. Tertullian claimed that they should not observe the Saturnalia or the Kalends of January, but obviously Christians at Carthage were doing so.[130] The same problem arose among Jews, for in the Mishnah business transactions with gentiles were forbidden for three days before the Kalends (of January), the Saturnalia, and the anniversaries of emperors' accessions and births.[131]

Though among first-century Christians there is no clear trace of annual festivals such as Easter, it is likely that annual commemorations arose by the beginning of the second century. Certainly the Basilidian Gnostics in Egypt observed the day of Jesus' baptism as a festival,[132] and at a later date this festival seems to have developed into Epiphany. Presumably it was around the time of Basilides, early in the second century, that the Easter festival became popular. Irenaeus traced it back at Rome at least to the time of Xystus, perhaps about 120.[133] To be sure, Polycrates of Ephesus said that the 14th day (of the Jewish month Nisan) had been observed by two of the apostles and by Polycarp of Smyrna, but he was speaking primarily in regard to the Passover and, in any event, Polycarp's episcopate was little if any older than that of Xystus.

Presumably Easter had a double origin, reflected in later controversies. In all churches there was a fast before Easter, though it varied in length. At Rome the fast ended on the Sunday after the Jewish Passover, for Sunday was the day of the resurrection. In Asia the fast ended on the 14th of Nisan, the beginning of the Jewish Passover, and was immediately followed by the "salvific Passover" of Christians.

Some Christians viewed this diversity as harmless or even beneficial. According to Irenaeus, some fasted for one day, some for two, others for forty. "The diversity in fasting supports the harmony of the faith."[134] On the other hand, some traditions were universal and came from the apostles. One should not kneel on Sunday or on Pentecost, for the resurrection was being celebrated;[135] kneeling was a specific sign of penitence.[136]

[128] H. Dörries, *Das Selbstzeugnis Kaiser Konstantins* (Göttingen, 1954), 181-82.
[129] Justin, *Apol.* 1, 67, 3.
[130] *De idolol.* 14, 4 (cf. 14, 6).
[131] '*Aboda Zara* 1, 1; 1, 3 (cf. W. A. L. Elmslie, *The Mishna on Idolatry, Texts and Studies* VIII 2, Cambridge, 1911).
[132] Clement, *Str.* 1, 146, 1.
[133] Eusebius, *H. E.* 5, 24, 14.
[134] Eusebius, *H. E.* 5, 24, 13.
[135] Irenaeus, Frag. 7, pp. 478-79 Harvey.
[136] Tertullian, *De orat.* 23; Origen, *De orat.* 31, 2-3.

About 190 Victor of Rome evidently tried to strengthen the Christian communities by moving toward a measure of liturgical uniformity. In his view the Roman practice of observing Easter on a Sunday, the day of the Lord's resurrection, was to be maintained everywhere. He issued a call for synods to meet in various areas and report on the procedure being followed. The bishops in Palestine came from Jerusalem, Caesarea, Tyre, and Ptolemais; they vouched for their own usage and that of the Alexandrians. Palmas, the oldest bishop in Pontus, presided over the bishops there. The bishops in Osrhoëne to the east also sent a letter; Bacchylus of Corinth sent a personal note; Victor himself and Irenaeus in Gaul provided testimony. According to Eusebius, "great numbers of others" agreed with these bishops in adhering to the Roman custom.[137] It is odd, however, that he mentions no letters from Antioch and that he has to cite Jerusalem authority for Alexandrian usage. The picture of pro-Roman uniformity is not quite in focus.

Indeed as a loyal supporter of the Roman position Irenaeus had to write letters in defense of it. One letter went to the Roman presbyter Blastus, who held that "the Passover was not to be observed except in accordance with the law of Moses, on the 14th day of the month.[138] When he would not change his position he was deposed by Victor.[139] Another was sent to "an Alexandrian" and argued that Easter was to be observed on a Sunday.[140] Evidently there was opposition to Victor's proposal both at Rome and at Alexandria.

Victor's principal opponent was Polycrates of Ephesus, who insisted upon the antiquity and continuity of Asian usage. As Lohse has shown, the Asians kept a Christian Passover on the same day as the Jewish festival and dated Easter in relation to it.[141] Polycrates relied upon the precedents provided by the evangelist Philip (whom he calls one of the twelve apostles[142]), John the Lord's disciple, Polycarp of Smyrna (bishop and martyr), Thraseas of Eumenia (bishop and martyr), Sagaris (bishop and martyr), "the blessed Papirius" (probably of Smyrna) and Melito of Sardis. All these men, as well as seven of Polycrates' relatives who had been bishops, had celebrated the Christian paschal feast on the 14th of the month Nisan.[143]

Victor responded to Polycrates by excommunicating the Asian church and those who were in agreement with it. At the same time Irenaeus urged a more moderate policy on him, but we do not know what the upshot was. The customs of the Quartodecimans certainly lingered on through the third century, for they were condemned at the Council of Nicaea in 325. As late as the seventh century they were to be found in Britain.

[137] Eusebius, *H. E.* 5, 23 and 25.
[138] Pseudo-Tertullian, *Adv. omn. haer.* 8.
[139] Eusebius, *H. E.* 5, 15.
[140] Irenaeus, Syr. frag. 27 (Harvey).
[141] B. Lohse, *Das Passafest der Quartadecimaner* (Gütersloh, 1953).
[142] Presumably he relied on John 1:43, etc.
[143] Eusebius, *H. E.* 5, 24, 2-8.

We have already seen that second-century writers refer to Sunday, Passover (Easter), and Pentecost. In Origen's treatise *Contra Celsum* (8, 22) there is a specific notice that Christians observed four festivals. These were the Lord's Day (Sunday), the Preparation (Good Friday), the Passover (Easter), and Pentecost. Obviously the first was weekly while the other three were annual, related to the crucifixion (cf. John 19:31) and resurrection of Jesus and to the coming of the Holy Spirit upon the church (Acts 2:1).

The next festival to be developed was that of the Epiphany, or manifestation of Christ upon earth. There was no trustworthy tradition concerning the date of Christ's birth; Clement of Alexandria cites scholarly attempts to fix it on April 19, April 20, and May 20. Among the followers of the Gnostic teacher Basilides, however, there was a traditional festival commemorating Christ's baptism on either January 6 or January 10.[144] What they celebrated was the manifestation of heavenly light upon Jesus, son of Mary,[145] and it could have been called Epiphany. The date January 6 was presumably chosen because of pagan festivals celebrating the "birth" of the new year.[146] By the early fourth century the feast of Christ's Epiphany at his birth was being observed by Christians in the eastern half of the empire.

Since the early third century the "birthday of the sun" had been observed in Egypt on December 25, when the days began to lengthen after the winter solstice, and at Rome after Aurelian's erection of a temple to *Sol invictus* in 274 the same date was celebrated as the *natalis Invicti,* with thirty races in the circus.[147] By 336 Chistians at Rome began observing December 25 as Christ's birthday.[148] It is highly probable that this observance was due to the Constantinian concern for the relation between pagan and Christian celebrations. Constantine's legislation of 321 spoke of the *dies solis* though he himself was concerned with the Christian Sunday.[149] His mother Helena built a church upon the presumed site of Christ's birth at Bethlehem, and it is likely that her concern (and his) gave impetus to the creation of a new festival in the west— a festival which would replace that of the sun god. (Within half a century most churches in east and west alike observed both festivals.)

The continued observance of Easter and Pentecost thus in part commemorates the origin of Christianity as a movement within Judaism, as well as its separation from its origin at a fairly early date. For Paul it was Christ who was "our Passover" (1 Cor. 5:7); for the author of Acts the day of Pentecost was the day on which the Holy Spirit was given to the church (Acts 2:1–4). The festivals of Epiphany and Christmas commemorate the triumph of Christianity in the Roman empire. Both were related to the new

144 Clement, *Str.* I, 145-46.
145 Cf. Hippolytus, *Ref.* 7, 26, 8.
146 Cf. Epiphanius, *Haer.* 51, 22, 8-10.
147 *CIL* I (ed. 2), p. 338; cf. Marbach in *RE* III A 910.
148 B. Botte, *Les origines de la Noël et de l'Epiphanie* (Louvain, 1932), 32-37.
149 Cf. H. Dörries, *Das Selbstzeugnis Kaiser Konstantins* (Göttingen, 1954), 343-47.

year and the victory of the sun over the darkness of winter. Christ was the true sun, born or made manifest soon after the winter solstice.

What may be called the political significance of the Christmas festival is even more marked if we accept the suggestion of J. Lafaurie that the *dies imperii* of Constantine as Augustus was December 25, 307. It is highly probable that this day occurred at the end of December and also that Constantine's known devotion to *Sol invictus* before his conversion would have led him to set the day on the sun's birthday. After defeating Licinius Constantine no longer referred to *Sol* on his coinage, and perhaps at this point his *dies imperii* was put back to July 25, 306, the day he succeeded his father at York.[150] If these hypotheses prove tenable, it may be suggested that after the defeat of Licinius the way was opened for the celebration of Christ's birthday on December 25.

To these major festivals—Easter, Pentecost, Christmas, Epiphany—others were gradually added, especially to commemorate the "birthdays" of the martyrs, at first locally and later more generally. The local observance of such celebrations was closely related to the maintenance of the holy places where the martyrs were buried and to the general concern for the geographical reality of the tradition. Early Christians were often more conscious of the importance of places than their successors, either medieval or modern, have been. Their religion, though often otherworldly, had roots in space and time to which they paid more than lip service. Just as Jews went on pilgrimage to Jerusalem, so in the middle of the second century Melito of Sardis visited Palestine to find out about the authentic canon of the Old Testament.[151] More pointedly, about 212 a Cappadocian bishop named Alexander made a pilgrimage to Jerusalem to pray and to "see the places"; while there he was made bishop of the local church.[152] Origen too visited the holy land and made use of geographical knowledge in his exegesis.[153] The greatest impetus toward Christian travel came, however, after the Council of Nicaea in 325, when visits to the new and magnificent churches built by Constantine and others were encouraged. Constantine's mother Helena, at the age of nearly eighty, eagerly visited the holy land and had churches built at Bethlehem and on the Mount of Olives.[154] By 333 a pilgrim came from Bordeaux and was given something like a guided tour.[155]

Most of early Christian "archaeology" was the product of a later time,

[150] *Mélanges d'archéologie et d'histoire offerts à André Piganiol* II (Paris, 1966), 795-806. The foundation of the hypothesis lies in an inscription from Brigetio (*L'année épigraphique* 1937, 232) with Constantine as TR P VII IMP VI COS and Licinius as TR P IV IMP III COS, presumably late in December 311.

[151] Eusebius, *H. E.* 4, 26, 13-14.

[152] *Ibid.*, 6, 11, 2.

[153] Cf. *Ioh. comm.* 6, 40-41.

[154] Eusebius, *V. C.* 3, 42-47.

[155] Text in *CSEL* 39, 1-33; cf. H. Leclerq in *Dictionnaire d'archéologie chrétienne et de liturgie* XIV 65-176.

but as early as 336 Constantine was able to acquire the coats and cloaks of the evangelist Luke and the apostle Andrew. These he placed in the Church of the Apostles at Constantinople. His mother was later said to have discovered the crosses on which Christ and the two thieves had been crucified. The earliest account, already legendary, of her achievement occurs in the *Church History* of Rufinus, written about 400.[156]

Helena had made inquiries of the natives and was directed to a location where "ancient persecutors" had erected a shrine of Aphrodite. Encouraged by visions, she had the area excavated and found three crosses "in a confused order," along with the superscription made for Pilate in Greek, Latin, and Hebrew (John 19:20). In order to determine which one was the true cross, the bishop of Jerusalem proposed to take a grievously sick woman and place her on each one. After his prayer for divine guidance she was placed on the first two, with no result; the third, evidently the authentic "saving wood," restored her health. The queen mother built a church on the spot and kept part of the cross there in silver reliquaries. She sent the nails from the cross, and part of the cross itself, to her son Constantine.

This story illustrates not only the credulity of the age but also the way in which, supported by royal favor, Christians now looked backward to the cardinal events with which their religion had begun. The reign of God had never fully come, but they saw it partly realized in the life of the church under a Christian emperor. Rufinus, indeed, goes on to say that "the more Constantine subjected himself to God with piety and humility, the more God subdued everything to him."

Yet as we near the end of our story we must still beware of simple explanations of what happened. One might suppose that a fresh or increased emphasis upon the past was an indication that the Christian movement had grown up or had grown old and that it was no longer so much concerned with present and future. But reverence for tombs and other memorials of the great heroes of the Judaism out of which Christianity first arose was widespread in Palestine during the first century.[157] If the fourth century marks the end of the history of the early church, it must be noted that in this respect the end was like the beginning.

The tombs and memorials of which we speak are symbols of the fact that early Christianity from the first century to the fourth was not oriented exclusively toward present or future but also provided an interpretation of the past. It was Marcion, not Jesus or Paul or the leaders of the church, who insisted that the gospel was an absolutely new and unique phenomenon,

---

[156] *H. E.* 10, 7-8. Cyril of Jerusalem, however, had referred to the true cross as early as 346 (*Cat.* 4, 10; 10, 19; 13, 4).

[157] Cf. J. Jeremias, *Heiligengräber in Jesu Umwelt* (Göttingen, 1958); additions in *ZNW* 52 (1961), 95-101.

unrelated to anything in human experience.[158] Christian theologians and churchmen were connected by ties to their predecessors in the faith;[159] the Christian movement was thus both radical and conservative.

VIII·CONCLUSION

At the beginning, the Christian movement had been chiefly eschatological. One might also call it strictly religious. As Frend points out, the early Christian lived "under the guidance of the Spirit in the Last Times" and "felt no call to imitate his Jewish neighbour and rebel against the earthly dominance of Rome." His conviction that the one God would soon act and, indeed, was already acting led him to witness to this God and to reject idolatry, specifically the idolatry he believed was being encouraged by the Roman state.[160] As the life of Christians on earth continued their loyalty to God did not change. What changed was their understanding of the situations in which they found themselves, and of the historical life of their own movement. The Christianity which came to power under Constantine was ready to welcome the emperor's vision of a cross which brought him military victory.[161]

From the apostolic age onward, however, Christmas had been compelled to face the continuing reality of the world in which they lived. It may be that the apologists were excessively optimistic when they appealed to Roman justice and to what they viewed as the best elements of Graeco-Roman culture. It may also be that they were justified in doing so and that the final victory of Christianity was largely due to Roman acceptance of their claims. Indeed, as E. Bickerman suggests, "among the reasons for the triumph of Christianity, the impartial historian has in the first place to name the principles of fair play followed by the Roman Emperors in dealing with the Christians."[162] Persecutions failed in large measure because they seemed unjust not only to Christians but to the leaders of the Roman world, who finally recognized that for the preservation of the world justice was as important as order. It may be claimed that the church came to terms with the world. As it did so, however, the world finally came to terms with the church.

What had the Christian movement wanted? This seems fairly clear from the evidence we possess. It wanted the right to exist, and it wanted the con-

---

[158] The preface to his *Antitheses* (F. C. Burkitt in *JTS* 30, 1928-29, 279-80) is related to Pauline language but distorts Paul's views.

[159] Cf. J. J. Pelikan, *Development of Christian Doctrine: Some Historical Prolegomena* (New Haven, 1969), 45.

[160] *JRS* 50 (1960), 283.

[161] I owe this point to Mr. Fred Klawiter.

[162] *Rivista di filologia* 96 (1968), 315.

comitant rights of freedom of assembly and for propaganda. Toward this goal its apologists asked for justice for Christians who, they claimed, were like other "good citizens" of the empire.[163] During the first three centuries many Roman administrators recognized the validity of the Christian goal, and finally it was accepted by the emperor himself.

The basic problem was religious, as J. Vogt has insisted.[164] The Christian gospel involved the proclamation of the reality of the one true God and, consequently, the absolute rejection of the gods recognized by the Roman state. The Christians regarded worship of these gods, including deified emperors, as idolatry and absolutely refused to participate in it. In principle their eschatology was opposed to Roman views of the everlastingness (*aeternitas*) of the empire, but this eschatology was reinterpreted in various ways; it was not so important as was militant monotheism.[165] The social ethics of early Christians was not a significant point of conflict.

By implication, however, what the Christians insisted upon was the relativizing of the authority of the emperor and the empire. In their view, the state was supreme only when its actions were in conformity with the will of the one true God, known to the church through his self-revelation in Jesus Christ.

163 Cf. *The Apostolic Fathers, I. An Introduction* (New York, 1964), 188-89 (to be qualified by the present study).

164 J. Vogt, *Zur Religiosität der Christenverfolger im Römischen Reich* (*Sitzungsberichte der Heidelberger Akademie der Wissenschaften, Philo.-hist. Kl.*, 1962, no. 1).

165 Cf. E. Peterson, *Der Monotheismus als politisches Problem* (Leipzig, 1935); reprinted in *Theologische Traktate* (Munich, 1951).

ROMAN EMPERORS AND BISHOPS

14–37	Tiberius		
37–41	Caligula*	c. 40	Christians at Rome?
41–54	Claudius		
54–68	Nero*	c. 64	Peter and Paul martyrs*
		?67–?76	Linus
68–69	Galba*		
69	Otho*		
69	Vitellius*		
69–79	Vespasian	?76–?88	Anacletus
79–81	Titus		
81–96	Domitian*	?88–?97	Clement
96–98	Nerva	?97–?105	Evaristus

98–117	Trajan		?105–?115	Alexander
			?115–?125	Xystus I
117–138	Hadrian		?125–138	Telesphorus (martyr)*
138–161	Antoninus Pius		138–141	Hyginus
			141–155	Pius
			155–166	Anicetus
161–180	Marcus Aurelius		166–175	Soter
			175–189	Eleutherus
180–192	Commodus*		189–199	Victor
193	Pertinax*			
	Julianus*			
193–211	Septimius Severus		199–217	Zephyrinus
211–217	Caracalla*		217–222	Callistus (martyr?)*
217–218	Macrinus*			
218–222	Elagabalus*			
222–235	Alexander Severus		222–230	Urban
			230–235	Pontianus
235–238	Maximinus Thrax*		235–236	Anteros
			236–250	Fabian (martyr)*
238	Gordiani*			
	Pupienus*			
238–244	Gordian III*			
244–249	Philip Arabian*			
249–251	Decius*			
251–253	Decius' sons, etc.*		251–253	Cornelius
253–260	Valerian*		253–254	Lucius
			254–257	Stephen
			257–258	Xystus II (martyr)*
			259–268	Dionysius
260–268	Gallienus*		269–274	Felix
268–270	Claudius Gothicus		275–?283	Eutychianus
270–275	Aurelian*			
275–276	Tacitus*?			
	Florianus*			
276–282	Probus*			
282–283	Carus*			

WEST		EAST		BISHOP OF ROME	
283–285	Carinus*	283–284	Numerian*	?283–?296	Gaius
284–286	Diocletian	284–305	Diocletian		
286–305	Maximian			?296–304	Marcellinus
305–306	Constantius	305–311	Galerius	308–309	Marcellus
307–337	Constantine	308–324	Licinius*	309–310	Eusebius
after 324,	Constantine alone			311–314	Miltiades
				314–335	Silvester
				336	Marcus
				337–352	Julius

(*=killed)

ROMAN MONEY

The basic unit was the *denarius*, a silver coin which in first-century Palestine constituted a day's wage for a laborer (cf. Matt. 20:2). The gold *aureus* was equivalent to twenty-five *denarii;* four brass *sestertii* (sesterces) equaled a *denarius,* while four *asses* made one *sestertius,* four *quadrantes* one *as.* Generally speaking the *denarius* was viewed as equivalent to the Greek *drachma.* The evangelists Mark and Luke refer to a tiny unit called a *lepton,* according to Mark 12:42 equivalent to half a *quadrans.* Large sums were sometimes calculated in *minas* and *talents;* the value of these tended to vary; at one point the Syrian talent was worth 4,500 Attic *drachmae,* while apparently the Attic talent was 6,000 *drachmae.*

There is no adequate way to translate any of these units into modern equivalents, for both ancient and modern money have rather steadily depreciated, and the goods for which ancient funds were used had price patterns rather different from modern goods. For examples of prices, etc., one may consult T. Frank (ed.), *An Economic Survey of Ancient Rome* (reprint, Paterson, N.J., 1959); on money itself see L. C. West, *Gold and Silver Coin Standards in the Roman Empire* (New York, 1941).

SELECTED READING LIST

This list of books and articles is in no way exhaustive and does not include every item mentioned in the footnotes. It is simply intended to provide suggestions for further reading, chiefly in English, although some works in other languages than English are included. Whenever possible, the relevant articles in RAC, RE, and RGG³ should be consulted.

For the introductory chapters 1-3 the list is arranged systematically; for succeeding chapters it is arranged chronologically in order to give some sense of an ongoing discussion.

CHAPTER I - THE ROMAN EMPIRE

I - THE ROMAN WORLD

H. Volkmann, ed., *Res Gestae Divi Augusti*. Ed. 2, Berlin, 1964.
R. Syme, *The Roman Revolution*. Oxford, 1939.
M. I. Rostotzeff, *Social and Economic History of the Roman Empire*. Ed. 2, 2 vols., Oxford, 1957.

T. Frank, ed., *Economic Survey of the Roman Empire*. 5 vols., Baltimore, 1933-1940; reprint, Paterson, N. J., 1959.
N. Lewis and M. Reinhold, *Roman Civilization: Selected Readings*. 2 vols., New York, 1951-1955; reprinted 1966.
H. M. D. Parker, *The Roman Legions*. Oxford, 1928.
C. G. Starr, *The Imperial Roman Navy*. Ed. 2, Cambridge, 1960.
R. O. Fink, A. S. Hoey, and W. F. Snyder, "The Feriale Duranum," *Yale Classical Studies* 7 (1940), 1-222.
G. H. Stevenson, *Roman Provincial Administration*. Oxford, 1939.
D. Magie, *Roman Rule in Asia Minor*. 2 vols., Princeton, 1950.
B. E. Thomasson, *Die Statthalter der römischen Provinzen Nordafrikas von Augustus bis Diocletianus*. 2 vols., Lund, 1960; review by E. Birley in *JRS* 52 (1962), 219-27.
O. W. Reinmuth, "Praefectus Aegypti," *RE* XXII 2353-77; also Suppl. VIII 525-39; also "A Working List of the Prefects of Egypt," *Bulletin of the American Society of Papyrologists* 4 (1967), 75-128.
H. F. Jolowicz, *Historical Introduction to Roman Law*. Ed. 2, Cambridge, 1954.
A. H. M. Jones, *Studies in Roman Government and Law*. Oxford, 1960.
J. Crook, *Law and Life of Rome*. Ithaca, New York, 1967.
W. Liebenam, *Fasti Consulares Imperii Romani*. Bonn, 1910.
A. Degrassi, *I fasti consolari dell' impero romano*. Rome, 1952.

II - THE HELLENISTIC BACKGROUND

P. Wendland, *Die hellenistisch-römische Kultur in ihren Beziehungen zu Judentum und Christentum*. Ed. 2-3, Tübingen, 1912.
W. W. Tarn, *Hellenistic Civilisation*. Rev ed. with G. T. Griffith, London, 1952.
M. I. Rostovtzeff, *Social and Economic History of the Hellenistic World*. 3 vols., Oxford, 1941.
M. P. Nilsson, *Greek Piety*. Oxford, 1948.
F. H. Cramer, *Astrology in Roman Law and Politics*. Philadelphia, 1954.
A.-J. Festugière *L'idéal religieux des grecs et l'évangile*. Ed. 2, Paris, 1932.
F. Cumont, *Les religions orientales dans le paganisme romain*. Ed. 4, Paris, 1929.
A. D. Nock, *Conversion*. Oxford, 1933.
E. R. Dodds, *Pagan and Christian in an Age of Anxiety*. Cambridge, 1965.
F. Cumont, *Lux perpetua*. Paris, 1949.
H.-I. Marrou, *Histoire de l'éducation dans l'antiquité*. Ed. 2. Paris, 1950.

CHAPTER II - ROME AND THE JEWS

M. Simon and A. Benoit, *Le judaïsme et le christianisme antique*. Paris, 1968.
B. Reicke, *The New Testament Era*. Philadelphia, 1968.
J. Juster, *Les juifs dans l'empire romain*. 2 vols., Paris, 1914.
M. Mansoor, *The Dead Sea Scrolls*. Grand Rapids, 1964.
J. Hempel, "Qumran," *RE* XXIV 1334-96.
M. Hengel, *Die Zeloten*. Leiden/Cologne, 1961.
K. Wagenast, "Zeloten," *RE* IX A 2474-99.
H.-W. Kuhn, *Endererwartung und gegenwärtiges Heil. Untersuchungen zu den Gemeindeliedern von Qumran mit einem Anhang über Eschatologie und Gegenwart in der Verkündigung Jesu*. Göttingen, 1966.
S. Sandmel, *The First Christian Century in Judaism and Christianity*. New York, 1969.

CHAPTER III - CHRISTIAN ORIGINS

I - EARLY CHURCH HISTORY

L. Duchesne, *Histoire ancienne de l'église.* 3 vols., Paris, 1906-1910.
H. Lietzmann, *Geschichte der alten Kirche.* 4 vols., Berlin, 1932-1942.
P. Carrington, *The Early Christian Church.* 2 vols., Cambridge, 1957.
J. Daniélou and H. I. Marrou, *The Christian Centuries: the first Six Hundred Years.* New York, 1964.
J. G. Davies, *The Early Christian Church,* London, 1965.
W. H. C. Frend, *The Early Church.* Philadelphia, 1966.
H. Chadwick, *The Early Church.* Penguin Books, 1967.

II - THE HELLENISTIC BACKGROUND

F. J. F. Jackson and K. Lake, *The Beginnings of Christianity.* 5 vols., London, 1920-1933.
F. C. Grant, *The Economic Background of the Gospels.* Oxford, 1926.
H. J. Cadbury, *The Making of Luke-Acts.* New York, 1927.
J. Weiss, *The History of Primitive Christianity.* 2 vols., New York, 1937.
H. Conzelmann, *The Theology of St. Luke.* New York, 1960.
E. Haenchen, *Die Apostelgeschichte.* Göttingen, 1960.
A. N. Sherwin-White, *Roman Society and Roman Law in the New Testament.* Oxford, 1963.

III - THE MISSION OF JESUS

S. G. F. Brandon, *The Fall of Jerusalem and the Christian Church.* London, 1951.
W. R. Farmer, *Maccabees, Zealots, and Josephus.* New Work, 1957.
P. Winter, *On the Trial of Jesus.* Berlin, 1961.
N. Perrin, *The Kingdom of God in the Teaching of Jesus.* Philadelphia, 1963.
S. G. F. Brandon, *Jesus and the Zealots.* New York, 1967.
N. Perrin, *Rediscovering the Teaching of Jesus.* London, 1967.
S. G. F. Brandon, *The Trial of Jesus of Nazareth.* New York, 1968.

CHAPTER IV - CHRISTIAN ORGANIZATION

B. Reicke, *Diakonie, Festfreude und Zelos, in Verbindung mit der altchristliche Agapenfeier (Uppsala Universitets Årsskrift,* 1951, no. 5).
O. Cullmann, *Petrus: Jünger—Apostel—Märtyrer.* Zurich, 1952.
E. Dinkler, "Zur Probleme der Ethik bei Paulus: Rechtsnahme und Rechtsversicht (1 Kor. 6, 1-11)," *Zeitschrift für Theologie und Kirche* 49 (1952), 167-200.
H. von Campenhausen, *Kirchliches Amt und geistliche Vollmacht in den ersten drei Jahrhunderten.* Tübingen, 1953; English translation, *Ecclesiastical Authority and Spiritual Power in the Church of the First Three Centuries.* Stanford, 1969.
A. Ehrhardt, *The Apostolic Succession.* London, 1953.
H. von Campenhausen, "Die Begründung kirchlicher Entscheidungen beim Apostel Paulus" *(Sitzungsberichte der Heidelberger Akademie der Wissenschaften, Philos.-hist. Klasse,* 1957, no. 2).
D. Georgi, *Die Geschichte der Kollekte des Paulus für Jerusalem.* Hamburg, 1965.

CHAPTER V - SOME CHRISTIAN CONTROVERSIES

W. Bauer, *Rechtgläubigkeit und Ketzerei im ältesten Christentum*. Tübingen, 1934; new ed., 1965.
F. V. Filson, "The Significance of the Early House Churches." *JBL* 58 (1939), 105-12.
W. Nigg, *Das Buch der Ketzer*. Zurich, 1949.
H. J. Schoeps, *Theologie und Geschichte des Judenchristentums*. Tübingen, 1949.
W. Schmithals, *Die Gnosis in Korinth*. Göttingen, 1956.
D. Georgi, *Die Gegner des Paulus im 2. Korintherbrief*. Neukirchen, 1964.
M. Simon, et al., *Aspects du judéo-christianisme*. Paris, 1965.
A. H. M. Jones, *Were Ancient Heresies Disguised Social Movements?* Philadelphia, 1966.

CHAPTER VI - ROME AND THE CHRISTIANS

H. Delehaye, *Les passions des martyrs et les genres littéraires*. Brussels, 1921.
R. Knopf and G. Krüger, *Ausgewählte Märtyrerakten*. Ed. 3, Tübingen, 1929.
H. Grégoire, *Les persécutions dans l'empire romain*. Brussels, 1951; ed. 2, 1964.
E. Peterson, *Theologische Traktate*. Munich, 1951.
H. A. Musurillo, *The Acts of the Pagan Martyrs*. Oxford, 1954.
C. Saumagne, "La 'passion' de Thrasea," *Revue des études latines* 33 (1955), 241-57.
F. M. Cross, Jr., "La lettre de Simon ben Kosba," *Revue biblique* 63 (1956), 45-48.
R. Syme, *Tacitus*. Oxford, 1958.
G. E. M. de Ste. Croix, "Why were the Early Christians Persecuted?" *Past and Present* 26 (1963), 6-31.
A. N. Sherwin-White, *The Letters of Pliny*. Oxford, 1966.
P. R. Coleman-Norton, *Roman State and Christian Church*. A Collection of Legal Documents to A.D. 535. 3 vols., London, 1966.
W. H. C. Frend, *Martyrdom and Persecution in the Early Church*. Garden City, N. Y., 1967.
W. R. Schoedel, *Polycarp, Martyrdom of Polycarp, Fragments of Papias*. Camden, N. J., 1967.
T. D. Barnes, "A Note on Polycarp," *JTS* 18 (1967), 431-37.
T. D. Barnes, "Legislation Against the Christians," *JRS* 58 (1968), 32-50.
T. D. Barnes, "Pre-Decian Acta Martyrum," *JTS* 19 (1968), 509-31.
E. Bickerman, "Trajan, Hadrian, and the Christians," *Rivista di filologia* 96 (1968), 290-315.

CHAPTER VII - THE APOLOGETIC MOVEMENT

J. Geffcken, *Zwei griechische Apologeten*. Leipzig, 1907.
A. Puech, *Les apologistes grecs du iie siècle*. Paris, 1912.
E. R. Goodenough, *The Theology of Justin Martyr*. Jena, 1923.
A. D. Nock, *Conversion*. Oxford, 1933.
P. de Labriolle, *La réaction païenne*. Paris, 1934.
M. Pellegrino, *Gli apologeti greci del II secolo*. Rome, 1947.
H. Chadwick, *Origen: Contra Celsum*. Cambridge, 1953, 1965.
C. Andresen, *Logos und Nomos*. Berlin, 1955.
M. Elze, *Tatian und seine Theologie*. Göttingen, 1960.

E. R. Dodds, *Pagan and Christian in an Age of Anxiety.* Cambridge, 1965.
H. Chadwick, *Early Christian Thought and the Classical Tradition.* Oxford, 1966.
N. Hyldal, *Philosophie und Christentum: eine Interpretation der Einleitung zum Dialog Justins.* Copenhagen, 1966.
R. M. Grant, *After the New Testament.* Philadelphia, 1967.

CHAPTER VIII - THE GNOSTIC CRISIS

(see also Chapter V)

W. Bousset, *Hauptprobleme der Gnosis.* Göttingen, 1907.
E. de Faye, *Gnostiques et gnosticisme.* Paris, 1913.
W. H. C. Frend, "The Gnostic Sects and the Roman Empire," *JEH* 5 (1954), 25-37.
H. J. Schoeps, *Urgemeinde—Judenchristentum—Gnosis.* Tübingen, 1956.
H. Jonas, *The Gnostic Religion.* Boston, 1958.
R. M. Grant, *Gnosticism and Early Christianity.* New York, 1959; rev. ed., 1966.
G. G. Scholem, *Jewish Gnosticism, Merkabah Mysticism, and Talmudic Tradition.* New York, 1960.
C. Colpe, *Die religionsgeschichtliche Schule,* I. Göttingen, 1961.
B. Gaertner, *The Theology of the Gospel of Thomas.* New York, 1961.
R. M. Grant, ed., *Gnosticism: an Anthology.* New York 1961.
R. McL. Wilson, *The Gospel of Philip.* New York, 1962.
U. Bianchi, ed., *Le origini dello gnosticismo.* Leiden, 1967.
J. M. Robinson, "The Coptic Gnostic Library Today," *New Testament Studies* 12 (1967-1968), 356-401.

CHAPTER IX - THE MONTANIST CRISIS

P. de Labriolle, *Les sources de l' histoire du montanisme.* Paris, 1913.
P. de Labriolle, *La crise montaniste.* Paris, 1913.
W. Schepelern, *Der Montanismus und die phrygische Kulte.* Tübingen, 1929.
W. Kühnert, "Der antimontanistische Anonymus bei Eusebius," *TZ* 5 (1949), 436-46.
G. S. P. Freeman-Grenville, "The Date of the Outbreak of Montanism," *JEH* 5 (1954), 7-15
H. Kraft, "Die altchristliche Prophetie und die Entstehung des Montanismus," *TZ* 11 (1955), 249-71.
P. Nautin, *Lettres et écrivains chrétiens des iie et iiie sièles.* Paris, 1961.
K. Aland, "Montanismus," *RGG³ IV* 1117-18.

CHAPTER X - CHRISTIAN ORGANIZATION

(see Chapter 4)

CHAPTER XI - ROME AND THE CHRISTIANS

(see also Chapter 6)

J. de Guibert, "La date du martyre de SS. Carpos, Papylos, et Agathonicé," *Revue des questions historiques* 83 (1908), 5-23.
P. Franchi d' Cavalieri, "La persecuzione di Gallo in Roma," *Studi e Testi* 33 (1920), 181-210.

J. R. Knipfing, "The Libelli of the Decian Persecution," *HTR* 16 (1923), 345-90.
A. Alföldi, "Die Hauptereignisse der Jahre 253-261 n. Chr. im Orient im Spiegel der Münzprägung," *Berytus* 4 (1937), 41-68.
A. Allföldi, "Zur den Christenverfolgungen in der Mitte des 3. Jahrhunderts," *Klio* 31 (1938), 323-48.
J. Vogt, *Zur Religiosität der Christenverfolger im Römischen Reich* (*Sitzungsberichte der Heidelberger Akademie der Wissenschaften, Philos.-hist. Klasse*, 1962, no. 1).
K. H. Schwarte, "Das angebliche Christengesetz des Septimius Severus," *Historia* 12 (1963), 185-208.
G. W. Clarke, "Some Victims of the Persecution of Maximinus Thrax," *Historia* 15 (1966), 445-53.

CHAPTER XII - THE PROBLEM OF GROWTH

(see also Chapters 13-16)

D. Fishwick, "On the Origin of the Rotas-Sator Square," *HTR* 57 (1964), 39-53.
R. Krautheimer, *Early Christian and Byzantine Architecture*. Baltimore, 1965.
A. Grabar, *Christian Iconography: A Study of Its Origins*. Princeton, 1968.

CHAPTER XIII - THE CHURCH AT ROME

G. La Piana, "The Roman Church at the End of the Second Century," *HTR* 18 (1925), 201-77.
G. La Piana, "Foreign Groups in Rome during the First Centuries of the Empire," *HTR* 20 (1927), 183-403.
G. Dix, *The Apostolic Tradition of St. Hippolytus*. London, 1937.
R. Walzer, *Galen on Jews and Christians*. Oxford, 1949.
R. Marichal, "La date des graffiti de la basilique de Saint-Sebastien à Rome," *Revue des études anciennes* 5 (1953), 119-20.
H. U. Instinsky, *Bischofsstuhl und Kaiserthron*. Munich, 1955.
E. H. Röttges, "Marcellus-Marcellinus," *Zeitschrift für katholische Theologie* 78 (1956), 385-420.
J. Carcopino, *De Pythagore aux apôtres*. Paris, 1956.
H. Gülzow, "Kallist von Rom. Ein Beitrag zur Soziologie der römischen Gemeinde," *ZNW* 58 (1967), 102-21.
D. W. O'Connor, *Peter in Rome*. New York, 1969.

CHAPTER XIV - THE CHURCH IN AFRICA

E. W. Benson, *Cyprian: his life, his times, his work*. London, 1897.
P. Monceaux, *Histoire littéraire de l'Afrique chrétienne*. Vols. 1-2, Paris, 1901-1902.
P. Batiffol, "Le règlement des premiers conciles africains et le règlement du senat romain," *Bulletin d'ancienne littérature et d' archéologie chrétienne* 3 (1913), 3-19.
H. Koch, *Cyprianische Untersuchungen*. Bonn, 1926.
B. Nisters, *Tertullian: seine Persönlichkeit und sein Schicksal*. Münster, 1950.
C. Mohrmann, "Saint Jérôme et Saint Augustin sur Tertullien," *VC* 5 (1951), 111-12.
W. H. C. Frend, *The Donatist Church*. Oxford, 1952.

CHAPTER XV - SCHOOL AND CHURCH AT ALEXANDRIA

C. L. Feltoe, *The Letters and other Remains of Dionysius of Alexandria*. Cambridge, 1904.

L. B. Radford, *Three Teachers of Alexandria*. Cambridge, 1908.

C. Bigg, *The Christian Platonists of Alexandria*. Ed. 3, Cambridge, 1913.

H. Delehaye, "Les martyrs d' Egypte," *Analecta Bollandiana* 40 (1922), 5-154, 299-364.

H. Koch, "Zum Lebensgang des Origenes und des Heraklas," *ZNW* 25 (1926), 278-82.

A. Miura-Stange, *Celsus und Origenes (Beiheft ZNW* 4, 1926).

A. Deissmann, *Light from the Ancient East*. New ed., London, 1927 (205-13).

R. Cadiou, *La jeunesse d'Origène*. Paris, 1935.

J. Danielou, *Origène*. Paris, 1948.

J. Scherer, *Entretien d'Origène avec Héraclide*. Cairo, 1949.

H. Chadwick, *Origen: Contra Celsum*. Cambridge, 1953, 1965.

R. P. C. Hanson, *Origen's Doctrine of Tradition*. London, 1954.

M. Hornschuh, "Das Leben des Origenes und die Entstehung der alexandrinische Schule," *ZKG* 71 (1960), 1-25, 193-214.

P. Nautin, *Lettres et écrivains chrétiens des iie et iiie siècles*. Paris, 1961.

H. Crouzel, *Origène et la philosophie*. Paris, 1962.

A. Méhat, *Étude sur les "Stromates" de Clément d' Alexandrie*. Paris, 1966.

F. H. Kettler, *Der ursprüngliche Sinn der Dogmatik des Origenes (Beiheft ZNW* 31, 1966).

F. H. Kettler, "Origenes," *RGG³* IV 1692-1701.

CHAPTER XVI - THE CHURCH AT ANTIOCH AND ELSEWHERE.

G. Downey, *A History of Antioch in Syria*, Princeton, 1961.

C. H. Kraeling, "The Jewish Community at Antioch," *JBL* 51 (1932), 130-60.

R. M. Grant, *After the New Testament*, Philadelphia, 1967, 37-54; 57-69; 126-57.

H. de Reidmatten, *Le actes du procès de Paul de Samosate (Paradosis, VI)*. Fribourg, 1952.

G. Bardy, *Recherches sur saint Lucien d'Antioche et son école*. Paris, 1936.

M. Spanneut, *Recherches sur les écrits d'Eustathe d'Antioche*, Lille, 1948.

CHAPTER XVII - DIOCLETIAN AND THE PERSECUTION

M. Hyamson, *Mosaicarum et Romanarum Legum Collatio*. London, 1913.

N. H. Baynes, "The Great Persection," *CAH* XII (1939), 646-77.

W. Seston, *Dioclétien et la tétrarchie*, I. Paris, 1946; review by N. H. Baynes in *JRS* 38 (1948), 109-13.

W. Seston, "À propos de la 'Passio Marcelli centurionis,' " *Mélanges Goguel (Neuchâtel*, 1950), 239-46.

G. E. M. de Ste. Croix, "Aspects of the 'Great' Persecution," *HTR* 47 (1954), 75-113.

D. van Berchem, *Le martyre de la legion thébaine: Essai sur la formation d'une légende (Schweizerische Beiträge zur Altertumswissenschaft* 8) Basel, 1956.

L. Dupraz, *Les passions de S. Maurice d'Agaune*. Fribourg, 1961.

A. Momigliano, ed., *The Conflict Between Paganism and Christianity in the Fourth Century*. Oxford, 1963.

A. H. M. Jones, *The Later Roman Empire*. 2 vols., Norman, Okla., 1964.
R. MacMullen, *Enemies of the Roman Order*. Cambridge, Mass., 1966.

CHAPTER XVIII - CONSTANTINE AND THE CHURCH

P. Franchi di' Cavalieri, "I funerali ed il sepolcro di Costantino Magno," *École Française de Rome: Mélanges d'archéologie et d'histoire* 36 (1916-1917), 205-61.
J. Maillet, "Constantin et le dadouque d'Eleusis," *Comptes rendus de l'Académie des Inscriptions*, 1922, 282-96.
N. H. Baynes, "Constantine the Great and the Christian Church," *Proceedings of the British Academy* 15 (1929), 341-442.
A. Alföldi, "The Helmet of Constantine with the Christian Monogram," *JRS* 22 (1932), 9-23.
A. Piganiol, *L'empereur Constantin*. Paris, 1932.
N. H. Baynes, "Constantine," *CAH* XII (1939), 678-99.
W. Telfer, "When Did the Arian Controversy Begin?" *JTS* 47 (1946), 129-42; comments by N. H. Baynes, *ibid.*, 49 (1948), 165-68; reply by Telfer, *ibid.*, 50 (1949), 187-91.
G. H. Williams, "Christology and Church-State Relations in the Fourth Century," *Church History* 20 (1950), no. 3, 3-33; no. 4, 3-25.
C. Pharr, *The Theodosian Code*. Princeton, 1952.
J. Vogt, "Der Erbauer der Apostelkirche in Konstantinopel," *Hermes* 81 (1953), 111-17.
H. Dörries, *Das Selbstzeugnis Kaiser Konstantins (Abhandlungen der Akademie der Wissenschaften in Göttingen, Philol.-hist. Klasse, III 34)*. Göttingen, 1954.
A. H. M. Jones and T. C. Skeat, "Notes on the Genuineness of the Constantinian Documents in Eusebius' Life of Constantine," *JEH* 5 (1954), 196-200.
H. Kraft, *Kaiser Konstantins religiöse Entwicklung*. Tübingen, 1955.
K. Aland, "Die religiöse Haltung Kaiser Konstantins," *TU* 53 (1957), 549-600.
L. Voelkl, *Die Kirchenstiftungen des Kaisers Konstantins im Lichte des römischen Sakralrechts*. Cologne, 1964.
J. Lafaurie, "Dies imperii Constantini Augusti: 25 décembre 307," *Mélanges d'archéologie et d'histoire offerts à André Piganiol* II (Paris, 1966), 795-806.

CHAPTER XIX - CHRISTIAN WAYS OF LIFE

C. J. Cadoux, *The Early Church and the World*. Edinburgh, 1925.
M. S. Enslin, *The Ethics of Paul*. New York, 1930.
H. Koch, *Quellen zur Geschichte des Askese und Mönchtums in der alten Kirche*. Tübingen, 1933.
J. Stelzenberger, *Die Beziehungen der frühchristlicher Sittenlehre zur Ethik der Stoa*. Munich, 1933.
H. Greeven, *Das Hauptproblem der Sozialethik in der neueren Stoa und im Urchristentum*. Gütersloh, 1935.
A. Nygren, *Agape and Eros*. Revised ed., London, 1953.
D. S. Bailey, *Sexual Relation in Christian Thought*. New York, 1959.
H. Chadwick, *The Sentences of Sextus*. Cambridge, 1959.
J. Noonan, Jr., *Contraception: A History of Its Treatment by the Catholic Theologians and Canonists*. Cambridge, Mass., 1965.
G. Crescenti, *Obiettori di coscienza e martiri militari nei primi cinque secoli del cristianesimo*. Palermo, 1966.

CHAPTER XX - CREEDAL FORMULATIONS AND ESCHATOLOGY

J. N. D. Kelly, *Early Christian Creeds*. London, 1950.
J. Daniélou, *Théologie du judéo-christianisme*. Tournai, 1958.
H. A. Wolfson, *The Philosophy of the Church Fathers*, I. Cambridge, Mass., 1958.
J. Daniélou, *Message évangélique et culture hellénistique*. Tournai, 1961.
H. Chadwick, *Early Christian Thought and the Classical Tradition*. Oxford, 1966.
R. M. Grant, *The Early Christian Doctrine of God*. Charlottesville, Va., 1966.
E. Meijering, *Orthodoxy and Platonism in Alexandria: Synthesis or Antithesis*. Leiden, 1968.

CHAPTER XXI - CHRISTIAN WORSHIP

H. Lietzmann, *Messe und Herrenmahl*. Göttingen, 1926; English translation with additions, *Mass and Lord's Supper*, Leiden, 1953—.
J. H. Srawley, *The Early History of the Liturgy*. Ed. 2, Cambridge, 1947.
A. Benoit, *Le baptême chretien au second siècle*. Strasbourg, 1952.
J. Jeremias, *Die Kindertaufe in der ersten vier Jahrhunderten*. Göttingen, 1958.
J.-P. Audet, *La Didachè*. Paris, 1958.
K. Aland, *Did the Early Church Baptize Infants?* Philadelphia, 1963.

INDEX